Yen

MESMERISING MELBOURNE

Whether drawn by a major sporting event, a cultural occasion or simply a business trip, visitors will quickly succumb to the spell of this cosmopolitan city

"Melbourne has become accustomed, through sheer force of insistence on its individual merits, to regard itself as everything a modern city ought to be, and as most things that other cities are not. It prides itself on a great deal – on its music, its art, its culture, its architecture, its good looks, and its intelligence. In the matter of dress, it aspires to set the fashion for Australia."

Remarkably, this assessment of the Victorian capital was penned by English novelist Alfred Buchanan in 1907. Remarkably, because so much of his analysis still applies today, with maybe just a little less emphasis on the "sheer force of insistence". Melbourne knows very well that it has a great deal going for it, that it's a wonderful place to live – there are enough placings at the top of the world's "most liveable" cities lists to confirm this – and it doesn't need to do anything so vulgar as boast about it. Or not too much.

Physically, the city draws much of its character from the proud Victorian structures built on gold-rush prosperity, the ones that prompted the term "Marvellous Melbourne". Even so, the last 20 years have seen a refocusing. Development along the Yarra River and in the old Docklands has opened up new vistas and playgrounds. Modern apartment towers and conversions of old commercial buildings have reinvented the city centre as somewhere to live as well as work. Dingy old city laneways and back alleys have become the new destination for trendy bars and restaurants, adventurous shopping and edgy artwork. It's like an urban counter-culture built on word of mouth. As author John Birmingham puts it: "Melbourne is a grown-up city that has suddenly come to terms with how much cooler it is than everyone else – which is to say, way cooler."

It's not all urban thrills, however; parks and gardens abound, and the suburbs – integral to Melbourne's spirit – play far more than mere supporting roles. And then there are the beaches, some of the world's best dining and, further afield, the varied appeal of rural Victoria.

Read on for the full picture and you should begin to understand why 2007 Australian of the Year, Tim Flannery, can say: "For my money, the Melbourne of the 21st century is the truly Marvellous Melbourne." ❑

PRECEDING PAGES: the Melbourne skyline and yachts from Williamstown Marina; Centre Place, one of the city's laneways. **LEFT:** window cleaning above Fed Square.

MELBOURNE PEOPLE ARE...

...snobbish, conservative, smug, materialistic and judgemental – according to their arch-rivals in Sydney. Melburnians prefer to think of themselves as amiable, sophisticated, cosmopolitan, culturally diverse and creative – and, by and large, they're right

Enjoying and appreciating Melbourne is not about sensationalism, a fleeting moment of awe or ticking off another must-see. It involves a more subtle accumulation of the layered charms of a city that combines a solid grounding in history with sleek modernity, and strikes a balance between the pleasures of the body and the exertions of the mind.

This is a personable city where human interactions really matter. Brusqueness and indifference, often the tourist experience in a busy metropolis such as New York, Paris or even Melbourne's traditional rival, Sydney, is not the norm here. A certain *politesse* applies; pushing in or jumping the queue is not the civilised thing to do in Melbourne. Road manners are just that.

In the 1950s, the evangelist Billy Graham described Melbourne as "the most moral city in the world". He may have been mistaken.

Old rivalries

When the acerbic Sydney-born former Labor Prime Minister Paul Keating once claimed, "If you're not living in Sydney, you're camping out", Melburnians shrugged at what they see as their northern rivals' need to boast of their superiority. If they see Sydney people as brash and needing continual reassurance and acknowledgement, the view in the other direction has Melburnians as smug and far too slow to be overtly "matey". And not only smug but rather too concerned with matters of the mind and suspiciously more coy about the body.

These perceptions have a historic dimension. As recently as the 1960s, Melbourne was a bleak and sober place to visit, with limited nightlife and a snobby reputation. But Melburnians have long since thrown off the more strait-laced image of earlier eras to become a sophisticated, cosmopolitan bunch who treasure the vaunted liveability of their

LEFT: fairground frolics at the St Kilda Festival.
RIGHT: grounds for celebration. Melbourne is the place for some of the best coffee in the world.

medium-sized city and the plethora of opportunities it offers to enjoy a peaceful, relaxed and thoroughly social lifestyle.

The physical layout – from Robert Hoddle's 1837 central grid outwards – and human scale of the place support this general amiability. The current renewal in the inner city and surrounding districts is further lessening the already gentle divide between the central city area and the distinctive suburban locales. To really know Melbourne means not only exploring the Central Business District (CBD), with its labyrinth of lanes and alcoves, but also visiting the shopping and eating strips of, for example, Carlton, Fitzroy, St Kilda, Prahran, Collingwood and the newly developed Docklands precincts. One of Melbourne's strengths and real pleasures is its rich array of small independent shops and boutiques with their idiosyncratic atmospheres, selling locally designed clothes, jewellery and furniture. It is the opposite of the homogenised and franchised city.

Footie and food

Homogenisation, such as it is, comes in other areas. Some stereotypes of the city, while never universal in application, still stand up to scrutiny. Sport is huge in Melbourne, especially the footie (Australian Rules, naturally), but any sport, even top-level lawn bowls, will gather the crowds. And within those crowds, many will be knowledgeable, bordering on the obsessive, but others will be along for a good day out – something easily achieved where spectators cross generational and gender boundaries, and eschew the antagonistic elements of tribalism that elsewhere require the

A MODERN GREAT CITY

When Mark Twain visited Melbourne on a lecture tour in 1895, he was entranced by what he saw: "It is a stately city architecturally as well as in magnitude. It has an elaborate system of cable-car service; it has museums, and colleges, and schools, and public gardens, and electricity, and gas, and libraries, and theatres, and mining centres and wool centres, and centres of the arts and sciences, and boards of trade, and ships, and railroads, and a harbor, and social clubs, and journalistic clubs and racing clubs, and a squatter club sumptuously housed and appointed, and as many churches and banks as can make a living. In a word, it is equipped with everything that goes to make the modern great city."

strict segregation of opposing fans. Rivalry here usually stops at wisecracks.

The same love of occasion drives Melburnians to cultural events, especially festivals, to markets, especially the Queen Victoria, and to food, especially eating out. And they love conversation, particularly over coffee.

A rich brew

There is one common claim for Melbourne that the statistics put beyond doubt: it is one of the most ethnically and culturally diverse cities on earth, and at all levels of society. Take this snapshot: just after the Commonwealth Games, staged in Melbourne in 2006, the Victorian Premier was Steve Bracks, from a Lebanese background; the State Governor, renowned medical researcher Professor David De Kretser, was born in Sri Lanka; and John So, Melbourne's celebrated former Lord Mayor, hailed from Hong Kong.

> *Melburnians (like the British) love to talk about the weather. A sure-fire way to start a conversation is to say: "I'm new to Melbourne. Is the weather always as good (or bad) as this?"*

When Europeans first arrived in the Port Phillip district in the early 19th century, there were five local Aboriginal tribes – the Wurundjeri, Boonerwrung, Wathaurong, Taungerong and Jaara people – all part of the Kulin nation, and before the Victorian gold rushes of the 1850s, most of the 90,000 or so settlers in the area were from the United Kingdom. Gold sparked a population explosion, with a significant proportion of the avid wealth-seekers arriving from other parts of the world. There have been waves of immigration ever since, both assisted and self-funded. After the end of World War II, the ethnic mix shifted markedly from largely UK arrivals to Continental European, Asian, Middle Eastern and African immigrants.

Melbourne now has a population of about four million, with almost a third of these born

ABOVE LEFT: Australia hasn't always been wary of boat people. **ABOVE:** Robert Doyle, the Lord Mayor of Melbourne, with the Nervo Twins. **TOP RIGHT:** locals converse over a beer in a pub. **RIGHT:** looking over the city from the Eureka Tower's Skydeck 88.

overseas, about one in five in a non-English-speaking country and one in 10 in an Asian country. This means that more than a quarter

> *"Wominjeka Wurundjeri Balluk yearmenn koondee bik" is the traditional greeting used by the Wurundjeri people at welcome-to-country ceremonies.*

of the population speaks a language other than English at home. Mandarin, Italian, Greek and Vietnamese are the four most common of over 150 languages. Almost half of all Australian Greeks and Turks, over a third of Australia's Italians, Vietnamese and Indians and more than a quarter of the country's Chinese residents live in Melbourne.

The evidence of this is in the faces on the street and in the rich diversity of eating and cultural options throughout the city. There are pockets where particular groups cluster, especially where there has been a spike in immigration numbers of one nationality, but over the generations, each group seems to assimilate and become more widely dispersed. The universities thrive on this diversity and attract a large foreign student population, mostly drawn from China and Southeast Asia, to add to an already high percentage of Asian-Australian students.

Despite the pre-settlement density of the indigenous societies in the area, the city now contains a tiny proportion of Aboriginal citizens – less than half of one per cent of the total population. However, Joy Murphy-Wandin, an Aboriginal Elder and a cultural guardian of the Wurundjeri people, is a familiar figure at many formal Melbourne occasions, welcoming participants to the traditional lands and sharing eucalyptus leaves symbolically to enhance harmony, despite a bloody and shabby history between the original inhabitants and European settlers. A formal apology for the misdeeds of the past *(see page 42)* was delivered by Prime Minister Kevin Rudd after a Federal Labor Government was elected in 2007.

A young, secular population

For its first 50 years or so, Melbourne was predominantly male – pioneering pastoralists and, particularly, the gold rush saw to that. However, by 1870 there was a gender balance, and within another 10 years, a slim female majority. Social attitudes and opportunities were slower to change, although finding the legendary male "ocker" of Bazza McKenzie fame (a fictional character created by Barry Humphries) around Melbourne today is much harder than it was. He is probably working in Western Australia as part of the resources boom.

ABOVE LEFT: the Wallabies attract the more discerning fans. **ABOVE:** diners on Lygon Street in Carlton. **ABOVE RIGHT:** craftsman with didgeridoo. **ABOVE FAR RIGHT:** Moomba march merriment. **RIGHT:** Robert Menzies. **FAR RIGHT:** Bob Hawke.

The religious texture of the city has shifted, too. Old Melbourne was more Anglican, but these days almost a third of the population claims to be Catholic, outnumbering Anglicans more than two to one. However, one in five professes no religious belief or affiliation at all. Where Melbourne was once a hotbed of sectarian push and shove, exploding into a painful 1950s schism in the Australian Labor Party that was deeply connected to religious fealty, these days religion is a low-key aspect of the city's life, and a confident secularism rules. The current official median age of 36 confirms the casual visitor's impression of a young person's city.

An educated city

Melbourne also has a reputation as an intellectual, cultured metropolis, an antidote to

MELBOURNE MEN WHO LED THE COUNTRY

Twenty-six men have held the office of Australian Prime Minister since Federation in 1901, and many of them had strong Melbourne connections. A century before Melbourne staged the "friendly" Olympic Games in 1956, **Alfred "Affable Alfred" Deakin** was born in working-class Collingwood. This remarkable orator, scholar and forger of the nation, before and after Federation, was Prime Minister three times and left an indelible stamp on the political and social fabric of the country. Deakin died in much more salubrious South Yarra and is buried in the famous St Kilda cemetery.

Through most of the "Roaring Twenties", the urbane, elegant **Stanley Melbourne Bruce** led Australia as a member of the Nationalist Party. He was born in the posh suburb of Toorak and was the first Prime Minister – before John Howard – to lose his parliamentary seat while in the top job.

Australia's longest-serving Prime Minister and founder of the centre-right Liberal Party, **Robert Menzies** was born in rural Victoria but was a Melbourne man. He was Prime Minister twice: for a couple of years before and at the beginning of World War II, and then for 16 years through the 1950s and half the '60s, a period many look back on through a nostalgia-misted lens. His successor, **Harold Holt**, was born in Sydney but moved to Melbourne. He disappeared in late 1967 under mysterious circumstances off the southern Victorian coast while snorkelling in roiling seas.

Other Prime Ministers with Melbourne in their blood have included: **James Scullin**, a sober Labor man who carried the heavy burden of leadership during the Great Depression and was the first Prime Minister to appoint an Australian as Governor-General (another Melburnian, Isaac Isaacs); much-loved wartime Labor Prime Minister **John Curtin**, born in Melbourne's Brunswick; the most "larrikin" Prime Minister, former fighter-pilot **John Gorton**; and Melbourne-born **Gough Whitlam**, Australia's most reformist head of government, who was infamously dismissed by the Governor-General in 1975.

Bob Hawke lived in Melbourne as President of the Australian Council of Trade Unions during the 1970s; the man he defeated as Prime Minister in 1983, **Malcolm Fraser**, was also born in Toorak and still lives in Melbourne after many years as a grazier in rural Victoria.

The Australian Prime Minister has two official residences – The Lodge in Canberra, and Kirribilli House on the shores of Sydney Harbour near the Harbour Bridge. There is, as yet, no official residence for current Melbourne-based Prime Minister, Julia Gillard, to call home.

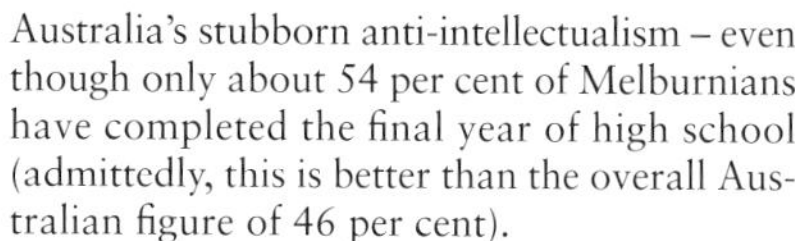

Australia's stubborn anti-intellectualism – even though only about 54 per cent of Melburnians have completed the final year of high school (admittedly, this is better than the overall Australian figure of 46 per cent).

Historically, there has been a strong tilt towards private-school education, and funding policies of federal governments have consolidated that trend. One in five students attends an independent private-school, and if you add those at Catholic schools, the ratio increases to more than two in five outside the state system. Even today, "What school did you go to?" is a very Melbourne enquiry – indicative of a persistent old-school-tie mentality, especially within the political and business fraternity. Funky, cosmopolitan, experimental Melbourne, while in the ascendancy, cohabits with an older, more conservative and judgemental city whose values hark back to an era of sharper divisions by social class, education and wealth, partly rooted in its original status as a non-convict colonial settlement.

For many visitors, however, it is the funky side that will make the deeper impression. Anyone spending time in the CBD or the inner suburbs cannot fail to pick up on the vibe created by the new bars, clubs and cafés. Dingy city laneways have been reinvigorated, and even Paul Keating has been swept along by the momentum, lamenting the state of Sydney's pubs compared with what he finds in the Victorian camp: "Melbourne has got a level of sophistication Sydney doesn't have. You don't get all this guffawing and noise."

Melbourne's intellectual status was nurtured early in the life of the settlement, with the University of Melbourne and the State Library

In the Pink

Sydney holds the reputation as Australia's pink capital, with its annual Gay and Lesbian Mardi Gras parade. Melbourne is, characteristically, less flamboyant about its lively gay scene. In the CBD, the laneways are again the key to discovering the best bars and venues – Flinders Lane and Little Collins Street are a good starting point. North of the city, Collingwood, Abbotsford and Northcote are renowned for a diverse party scene, and Brunswick Street in Fitzroy has its appeal. To the south, Commercial Road Prahran is the main gay strip, matched by St Kilda's bars and venues that proliferate around Acland and Fitzroy streets. The Midsumma Festival is the umbrella for a host of drama, musical, cabaret and even sporting events, which run over two weeks in January and February. It attracts over 100,000 people, takes place in over 70 venues across the city, and its big open-air party features drag acts and other entertainers.

opening within the first years. Inventiveness, especially in the medical-research field, has always been a strength, and today Melbourne is a centre for biotech research, computer games and animation, and home to Australia's Synchrotron, an expensive and sophisticated tool for scientific and industrial research.

Amongst many technological advances, two examples will serve. Graeme Clark's research on electrical stimulation of human auditory pathways at the University of Melbourne led to the development of a practical, multi-channel, cochlear implant, or "bionic ear". It can even be implanted in very young children before they develop language, and has transformed the prospects of thousands around the globe.

Another device that has indirectly saved many lives is the "black box" flight recorder conceived and first built by David Warren and his colleagues working at Melbourne's Aeronautical Research Laboratory.

ABOVE FAR LEFT: och aye the roo. Cultural mix on the Anzac Day parade. **ABOVE LEFT:** enjoying the beach on the Mornington Peninsula. **LEFT:** out and about at the Midsumma Festival. **ABOVE:** Saints preserve us. St Kilda fans look on the bright side.

Famous Melburnians

Melbourne has been the birthplace, launch pad or nurturing environment for many notable Australians who have earned national and international reputations in science and technology, arts and culture, politics, business and finance, sport and adventure, and just for being themselves.

In the early years of the city, when the white settlers had barely a toehold on the continent, the men who braved the unknown interior were regarded as heroes. So it was that much of Melbourne watched as a local police officer, Robert O'Hara Burke, and a surveyor, William John Wills, set off, on 20 August 1860, on their attempt to be the first to cross Australia from south to north. The expedition almost made it to the Gulf of Carpentaria in

> *Helen Porter Mitchell adopted the name Nellie Melba in deference to her native city, and went on to become the great operatic diva of her age. It is probably fortunate that she didn't hail from Bendigo.*

Australia's far north, but the pitiless landscape and their own miscalculations eventually saw the deaths of both men. Their success and failure is woven into Australian legend. After several moves, the Burke and Wills memorial statue now stands on the corner of Collins and Swanston streets in the city, while a memorial can be found in the Melbourne General Cemetery.

Myers and Murdochs

Another local legend grew out of an altogether different adventure. Simcha Baevski, later Sidney Baerski Myer, was born in what is now Belarus into a Jewish shopkeeping family. In 1899 he migrated to Melbourne, where, with his brother Elcan, he created the large and thriving Myer retail business, with its main emporium in central Melbourne. After his death in 1934, a charitable trust was set up, today known as the Myer Foundation, to sustain the philanthropic works of the man who arrived in Australia poor and without English. The Sidney Myer Music Bowl, one of the trust's first major contributions, is a Melbourne landmark *(see page 141)*.

Melbourne has also spawned a number of outstanding business entrepreneurs, including one whose progeny have affected the globalised media world. Keith Murdoch was a journalist and founder of a newspaper dynasty; his son Rupert is one of the world's most powerful media magnates. Keith's widow, the philanthropist and patron of the arts Dame Elizabeth Murdoch, still lives on the original Murdoch estate at Langwarrin,

LIVEABLE CITY

For some years now, Melbourne has featured at or near the top of *The Economist's* World's Most Liveable Cities table, usually vying with Vancouver in Canada. The survey considers crime levels, transport and communications infrastructure, education, culture, weather, stability and susceptibility to terrorism amongst its criteria. Locals are quietly chuffed about this, but, as with all statistics, the survey has to be treated with some caution. It's probably best not to mention the 2010 Mercer Quality of Living Survey that places Melbourne a lowly 18th. This is hardly a disaster in itself, but Sydney makes the list at 10th, and that clearly is.

near Frankston, on the Mornington Peninsula. One of her grandsons, Michael Kantor, was recently the artistic director of Melbourne's second main stage drama company, the highly rated Malthouse Theatre *(see page 132)*.

Shining Stars

From Dame Nellie Melba onwards, the city of Melbourne has been linked to a disproportionate number of artists and entertainers. Oscar-winners Geoffrey Rush and Cate Blanchett are both tied to the city: Rush was born in Queensland but lives in Melbourne; Blanchett was born and grew up in Melbourne but is based in Sydney.

Eric Bana, with a Croatian father and German mother, typifies the multicultural roots of so many Melburnians growing up in the working-class west, near Tullamarine airport. After an early career in comedy, Eric has had a turbocharged ride with films such as *Black Hawk Down*, *Troy*, *Munich*, the critically acclaimed *Romulus, My Father* and the self-produced documentary, *Love the Beast*.

Local girl Rachel Griffiths has starred in the major US television series *Six Feet Under* and *Brothers and Sisters*. What is almost forgotten now is her Lady Godiva-style topless protest outside the opening of Melbourne's Crown Casino in 1997.

Barry Humphries and his domineering "close associate" Dame Edna Everage are without a doubt Melbourne's most famous comedic and theatrical exports. Dame Edna

emerged from Humphries' ambivalent reaction to what he perceived as the stifling suburban ethos of 1950s and 1960s Melbourne, but this hasn't stopped the city from embracing him and his creation, culminating in the renaming of a city laneway in his, or rather her, honour.

> *"Dame Edna really is part of the DNA of Melbourne, if not the DNA of Australia, and what is DNA if you add the letter 'E'?" Barry Humphries explains the appeal of his most famous creation.*

Political cartoons have always flourished in the city, and occasionally break through to a wider global audience. Much loved but controversial, Michael Leunig combines "naïve" poetry and fragile whimsy with passionate savagery and accusation. His enduring character is Mr Curly, a *faux naïf* abroad in a ruthless world. A raft of others – Ron Tandberg, Peter Nicholson, John Spooner and the doyen of Australian cartoonists, Bruce Petty – are all to be found in newspapers still. ❑

FAR LEFT: Rupert Murdoch. **TOP LEFT:** Geoffrey Rush in *Exit the King* at the Malthouse Theatre. **ABOVE LEFT:** music scene veteran "Molly" Meldrum. **ABOVE:** Dame Edna Everage. **ABOVE RIGHT:** Eric Bana, who was born in Melbourne, in the film *Love the Beast*.

BAKER &
PROPRIETARY
SOLE
KODAK
SEARS
COLE'S
SPRING ST
18 SOUTH 18
MELBOURNE

THE MAKING OF MELBOURNE

In less than 200 years, a small settlement on the banks of a muddy river has grown into one of the world's great cities, but it has, at times, been a bumpy ride

Long before explorers from Europe or Asia came anywhere near the "Great South Land", it was home to an Aboriginal population, which was estimated at 300,000 at the time of Captain Cook's arrival in Botany Bay in 1770. Of these, at least 50,000 occupied the area now known as Victoria, in three main groups: the Kurnai of Gippsland, the Yotayota of the eastern Murray and the Kulin of the Central Divide. These groups were subdivided into about 34 distinct tribes, each with its own territory, customs, laws, language and beliefs.

They were hunter-gatherers, living in extended families of 50–100 members. The region was rich in plants and wildlife, while the sea provided further sustenance, as evidenced by the shell middens dotted along the coast.

The site where Melbourne was established had been a traditional meeting place for clans of the Kulin nation, a confederacy based on similar languages and customs.

The Aborigines exploited the land efficiently by "firestick farming" – using deliberate fires to regulate and maintain the plants and animals that provided their food. Their religious culture was based on an intimate relationship with the land and the elements.

LEFT: Collins Street in 1909, from the corner of Swanston Street. **ABOVE RIGHT:** the first city streets were established by the late 1830s.

The coming of the colonists

Sydney was the focal point of the British colony of New South Wales that grew haltingly from the arrival of the "First Fleet" in 1788, and initial expansion was in the direction of Moreton Bay (now Brisbane), Norfolk Island and Van Diemen's Land (Tasmania), all set up as penal colonies. It was some years later that the colonists' attention turned to the land of what is now Victoria, with results for the local Aboriginal people that were as catastrophic as they were predictable, even though official intentions were seemingly benign.

Their lands and hunting grounds were indiscriminately taken from them, they were ravaged by "European" diseases, and many were the victims of violent frontier conflicts. Aborigines were pressurised into living on stations, missions and reserves such as Coranderrk, near Healesville, in Melbourne's east. Through Melbourne's first decades, however, they continued to interact with the invaders, trading goods in town markets or providing much-needed labour for squatters. But their numbers were in serious decline, falling an estimated 90 per cent by the late 1850s.

European knowledge of the Melbourne area dates from 1803, when the *Cumberland* brought a naval survey party to explore Port Phillip Bay. Later that year, Lieutenant-Governor David Collins arrived in Port Phillip on the *Calcutta* and established a short-lived convict settlement at the site of present-day Sorrento. Intended to deal with the increasing numbers of convicts in Sydney, as well as deter French designs on the area, the Sorrento settlement soon failed due to the unsuitability of the site, poor soil and the lack of fresh water. Little trace was left after Collins moved to the Derwent River in Van Diemen's Land, though an escaped convict, William Buckley, famously survived by living with local Aborigines until he was found by an exploring party in 1835.

By the 1830s, pastoralists from Van Diemen's Land were looking to expand their enterprises into the south coast of New South Wales around Port Phillip Bay. The first was Edward Henty, who left with his family to settle on the mainland in what is now Portland (362km/225 miles west of modern Melbourne). Soon afterwards, a group of investors and pastoralists estab-

WELCOME TO MELBOURNE

Elders of the Wurundjeri people, traditional owners of the land where Melbourne now stands, are often invited on official occasions to conduct their *Tanderrum*, or welcome-to-country ceremony. As a traditional gesture of welcome, participants are offered a gum leaf and, in accepting this token, are given freedom of the bush and asked to protect and look after the land as indigenous people have done before them. As part of the indigenous community that has lived in the Melbourne region for at least 45,000 years, the Wurundjeri have a strong connection with the land.

lished the Port Phillip Association, and in 1835 John Batman was dispatched across Bass Strait as the company's forward scout. During Batman's reconnaissance he claimed to buy 600,000 acres (240,000 hectares) for the syndicate from representatives of the Kulin peoples, in exchange for a yearly tribute of blankets, knives, tomahawks, clothes, looking-glasses, scissors and flour. Whereas Batman viewed his treaty as a purchase of land, the Aborigines may have interpreted the exchange in terms of their own *Tanderrum* ritual *(see box, left)*, which gave access to but not ownership of their lands.

Who founded Melbourne?

Batman's rival as Melbourne's founder was John Pascoe Fawkner, a Launceston publican who financed a party to sail to the mainland in his schooner, the *Enterprize*. In August 1835 the *Enterprize* arrived at Port Phillip Bay and sailed up the Yarra River. Within a month, huts were being constructed, numerous gardens planted, and the new settlement was beginning to take shape. Fawkner himself arrived with his family in October, and set about becoming an influential figure in the infant town.

So who founded Melbourne? For present-day Melburnians the debate is somewhat academic, and both "founders" have at different periods of the city's history achieved mythic status. The claims of the Fawkner camp now seem more established, and the date when the *Enterprize* was moored at the site of the future city (30 August) is now celebrated by the city – albeit discreetly – as "Melbourne Day". Melbourne's foundation legends symbolise residual pride that the city did not bear the stain of convict heritage (unlike Sydney), and perhaps residual guilt at the appropriation of land from its original inhabitants.

> *John Fawkner opened the town's first hotel, launched its first newspaper, the* Melbourne Advertiser, *and later served as a member of the Legislative Council.*

The rage for Port Phillip

The legitimacy of Batman's "treaty" was questionable, and the New South Wales Governor, Sir Richard Bourke, soon proclaimed it null and void since it contradicted the notion of *terra nullius* (no man's land) by acknowledging that it was the local tribe's to sell in the first place. Realising that the "rage for Port Phillip" was unstoppable, he set about turning the situation to the advantage of the government and establishing an authorised settlement. Bourke recommended to Lord Glenelg, Secretary of State for the

ABOVE LEFT: the Aboriginal population of the area was decimated by European diseases.
ABOVE: John Batman's reconnaissance in 1835.
ABOVE RIGHT: John Pascoe Fawkner.

Colonies, measures for land survey, the formal disposal of crown land at Port Phillip, the appointment of a police magistrate and an officer of customs, and the provision of schools. Six months later, in April 1836, Glenelg wrote to Bourke sanctioning settlement under government control.

Melbourne's exact location had been determined by the existence and the characteristics of a modest river now known as the Yarra. Any commercial settlement in the early 19th century needed fresh water to drink and salt water on which to float its trading ships. The availability of fresh water above rocky falls at a site on the river 10km (6 miles) from its mouth had persuaded John Batman, in 1835, that "this will be the place for a village". After a preliminary survey by Robert Russell, Governor Bourke himself visited the site in March 1837, agreed with the spot chosen by the initial settlers and, with surveyor Robert Hoddle, "traced the general outline of a township" *(see panel, left)*. On 9 March, Bourke gave the name "Melbourne" to the new town, after the British Prime Minister of the day. Melbourne was officially gazetted on 29 March 1837. The settlement's first census, later the same year, registered the population as 145 men and 35 women.

The centre of town in the late 1830s was located at the junction of Collins and William streets, and churchgoers were required to go into the "bush" (the east end of Collins Street) to worship. Lonsdale Street was, at this time, the northern boundary. At the first land sale in June 1837, the most coveted blocks (at the junction of William Street with Flinders and

HODDLE'S GRID

Surveyor Hoddle's simple and expedient gridiron plan, aligned to the river, gave Melbourne a distinctive "New World" feel, in contrast to Sydney's more tortuous layout and narrower streets. The grid was simple to survey, easy and quick to lay out, facilitating the immediate sale of land, and was extendable at a future date in any direction while successfully maintaining the original sense of order and continuity. Hoddle only took a couple of hours to survey the square mile of Melbourne with chain and theodolite, finishing in time to have lunch with the Governor.

Collins streets) were situated near the wharf and the likely future business centre of the town. By 1840, streets running east to west were considered the principal thoroughfares, and the eastern end of Collins Street, with its residences and churches, was identified as the most fashionable part of the young town.

While property in Queen Street was deemed by land advertisements to be desirable and well known to every inhabitant, and parts of Lonsdale Street were conveniently located commanding airy views of the bay, allotments in Collins Street near the wharf, customs house and marketplace were at "the very centre of communications". From the 1840s, the grid was gradually filled in as the town spread into its eastern and northern portions. Immigrants were soon attracted to this burgeoning town, as it became the gateway to a developing pastoral hinterland.

After a depression in the early 1840s when the land market was glutted, conditions slowly improved. In the three years, from 1839–41, more than 1,100 immigrants arrived in the district from the United Kingdom, raising Melbourne's population to 4,500 in March 1841 and nearly 8,000 by the end of 1842, almost balancing the sexes and drastically reducing the proportion of ex-convicts. Housing such an influx placed an enormous burden on the district's resources. Superintendent Charles Joseph La Trobe had arrived as administrator of the settlement in 1839, but the infant town, effectively ruled as it was from Sydney, still experienced shortages of labour and finances, and the development of urban infrastructure was slow.

Before the settlement was officially named Melbourne, it was also known as Batmania, Bearbrass, Bearport, Bareheap and Bearbury. (The Aboriginal name for the area was Berren or Bararing.)

The Port Phillip Patriot and Melbourne Advertiser (24 August 1840) argued for the establishment of an independent Melbourne council, claiming it would manage affairs better than "a few irresponsible strangers, six hundred miles off, who could not say, to their own knowledge, whether we lived like opossums in trees, or underground like bandicoots". Melbourne's first Town Council was established in 1842 (the same year as Sydney's), and recovery in the pastoral industry through the decade consolidated Melbourne's firm economic base.

Separation and gold fever

Through the 1840s, Melbourne's wealth subsidised Sydney's needs as much as its own, and calls for greater independence in managing its own affairs gained momentum. In 1850, a separation act was passed, and the news that Victoria was to be created as an independent colony was greeted in Melbourne on 11 November 1850 with much celebration. The new state of Victoria was formally proclaimed on 1 July 1851.

Victoria now had political independence, but it was the discovery of gold almost immediately afterwards that was the catalyst for a new era of wealth and optimism. Although the major discoveries were

TOP LEFT: Collins Street in 1838. **ABOVE RIGHT:** an early emigrant ship from Europe. Average journey time was around three months, and the crowded, unsanitary conditions on board claimed many lives from dysentery and other diseases. **RIGHT:** off to the goldfields, 1855.

inland – at places such as Ballarat, Bendigo and Mount Alexander – Melbourne became the gateway for immigrants and capital. In a period of only four months in 1852, more than 600 ships arrived at Hobson's Bay, while the following year a total of 2,594 ships brought fortune-hunting immigrants to a city now straining to accommodate them. Around half the migrants were from the UK, just under one-tenth were Chinese, American, German or Irish, and the rest came from elsewhere in Australia.

Victoria's population trebled between 1851 and 1854, and the infrastructure of a city not yet 20 years in existence could barely cope with housing, feeding, clothing and employing its latest inhabitants. A temporary village known as Canvas Town sprang up on the south bank of the Yarra, containing about 5,000 inhabitants at its peak in the mid-1850s.

The gold rush brought Melbourne unprecedented wealth, which the city used to establish some of its cultural and civic institutions – the Public Library, the University of Melbourne and the first police force (all in 1853), the Melbourne Museum and *The Age* newspaper (1854), and the Theatre Royal (1855). In 1856 the first Parliament of Victoria was officially opened, and in the same year building workers at the University downed tools and marched through the city agitating for a reduced working day of eight hours. The eight-hour day soon became an important part of labour practice in the city.

> *Many Chinese diggers from the goldfields drifted back to Melbourne in the mid-1850s and established a thriving Chinatown in Little Bourke Street.*

Boom and bust

In 1885, visiting London journalist George Augustus Sala proclaimed the city "Marvellous Melbourne". The haphazard town of the 1850s had matured into the Queen City of the Southern Hemisphere. Negative connotations could, it seems, be removed with the stroke of a pen. In 1876, Romeo Lane, with its "disorderly" and "immoral" associations, was rebranded as Crossley Street, and Stephen Street was renamed Exhibition Street for the 1880 International Exhibition.

A land boom saw property speculation reach dizzying heights by the late 1880s.

ABOVE LEFT: the population trebled in the early gold-rush years. **ABOVE:** temporary accommodation at Canvas Town. **RIGHT:** Elizabeth Street/Collins Street in 1889.

Suburban growth advanced along the radial railway lines, the middle classes colonising the picturesque country to the east and south-east, with industry and working-class housing mainly concentrated in the flatter reaches to the north and west.

In 1888, the Victorian Parliament spent £250,000 on the Great Centennial Exhibition. Nothing was too much in such fanciful times. Among the alluring attractions of the exhibition were seals in an aquarium, paintings on loan from famous overseas galleries, and a trip up in the hydraulic lift to survey all of Melbourne from the great dome of the Exhibition Buildings – all followed by tea at one of the many dainty pavilions.

Melbourne saw itself as one of the proudest, most progressive cities in the world. The village had become a metropolis, and nothing seemed able to impede its progress. The network of roads, river craft and trains improved communications rapidly, and the electric telegraph, overseas cables, telephone, electric lights and rapid-printing presses spread the benevolent influences of British civilisation.

However, the irresponsible years of land boom had to be paid for and, in the 1890s, they

SWELLS AND SMELLS

Melbourne's opulent character found a counterpoint in its image as "Marvellous Smellbourne". Open sewers, decomposing animal carcasses in the city streets and overflowing cesspits produced a pervasive stench and a decidedly unhealthy atmosphere. The river was little better, as the *Port Phillip Gazette* reported in 1840: "The river Yarra, on the purity of whose waters the health of Melbourne depends, is made the receptacle for the dead bodies of all animals that die within a mile of its banks. To the deleterious effects of its brackish water is thus superadded the abominable and poisonous qualities communicated by putrescent carcasses. The compound thus formed is of a kind the most noxious which it is possible to conceive."

By the late 1880s, the city's unhealthy and unsanitary condition was the subject of a Royal Commission. Infant mortality was already at a higher level than in London, with dysentery and gastroenteritis the main culprits, while typhoid was also beginning to take hold.

The outcome of the Royal Commission was the establishment of the Melbourne and Metropolitan Board of Works in 1891, with a mandate to construct an underground sewerage system for the city. By 1897, the first dwellings were being connected to the network.

were repaid with interest in the most severe depression Australia has ever suffered. In 1888, there had already been a collapse of land prices and the beginnings of public unease in Melbourne. In 1892, there had been a run on the banks in Sydney, and the Melbourne business world looked on with great anxiety. The directors of the Australian Deposit and Mortgage Bank closed their doors, and the Colonial Investment Company failed. Thousands of small depositors in banks and land companies were ruined. In the whole of Australia, only 10 banks survived the depression, with those in Victoria being the worst hit.

Victorian Values

In addition to its enduring sobriquet of "Marvellous Melbourne", the boom-time years left the city a grand Victorian architectural legacy. This is best observed in some of Collins Street's mighty temples to industry and commerce, such as architect William Wardell's Venetian Gothic-styled bank (1883–7) on the corner of Queen Street, and the Olderfleet and Rialto Buildings (both from 1889).

The Windsor Hotel in Spring Street was built in Renaissance Revival style, opening in 1883 as the Grand Coffee Palace. Such establishments served the moral purposes of Protestant social reformers, or "Wowsers", who between the mid-19th and early 20th centuries agitated for greater state control over liquor licensing, prostitution and gambling. The legacy of their campaigns was felt well into the 1950s, and a law introduced in 1916 requiring the six o'clock closure of hotels was not rescinded until 1966.

Recovery and depression

In the first years of the 20th century, Melbourne, still recovering its tentative self-respect after the lessons of the 1890s, took steps towards establishing its position as the new nation's cultural capital. (It was already the political capital, albeit the temporary one, of the Australian Federation.) In 1906, the Melbourne Symphony Orchestra was formed. Flinders Street Railway Station was built, and the Saturday Half Holiday Act was proclaimed. In the 1920s, the Melbourne tramway system was electrified (although the first electric tram dated from 1906), and the first traffic lights were installed.

On the eve of the Melbourne Cup carnival in 1923, a police strike saw riots and looting in the city as over 600 members of the metropolitan constabulary protested against their being supervised by plain-clothes constables or

"spooks". Culturally conscious Melburnians saw Anna Pavlova dance in their city and heard their own Helen Mitchell, the famed Dame Nellie Melba, sing at their Town Hall. Melbourne University Press was founded in 1928 – and the gangster "Squizzy" Taylor was gunned down in Carlton. Melbourne's suburban frontier spread out to eastern areas such as Heidelberg and Box Hill, and southeast, and towards bayside suburbs like Sandringham and Mordialloc.

When the six colonies became the Commonwealth of Australia in 1901, Melbourne was declared the federal capital and remained so until Canberra was founded in 1927.

The city experienced its second great depression at the beginning of the 1930s. Rather than resulting from over-exuberant land speculation, this economic downturn related more generally to a global crisis of capital, and the fact that the Australian economy had become over-dependent on British investment. Melburnians saw the famous Phar Lap win the Melbourne Cup in 1930, but many were out of work and some had no homes. Unemployment peaked at over 30 per cent in 1932, and many workers were put on sustenance pay ("susso"), labouring on public-works projects such as the Yarra Boulevard, St Kilda Road and the Shrine of Remembrance.

War provides work

By 1933, Melbourne's population had passed the 1 million mark, and economic conditions were slowly beginning to improve. The war years saw the consolidation and expansion of the city's manufacturing sector, with financial outputs doubling. Munitions factories supplied armaments and the Commonwealth Aircraft Corporation's manufacturing facility was based at Fishermans Bend, while food production soared by 20 per cent in response to demand by British markets. World War II saw thousands of Melburnians join their fellow-countrymen fighting with the Allies in Europe,

FAR LEFT: the Federal Coffee Palace on Collins Street West, built in 1886. **TOP LEFT:** the ANZ Gothic Bank from 1887. **ABOVE LEFT:** looking east from the Collins Street/Swanston Street junction in 1920. **ABOVE:** homeless men in Fitzroy *c.*1925. **ABOVE RIGHT:** depression-era family. **RIGHT:** World War II troops departing for Europe.

North Africa and Asia. More than 15,000 Australians were captured when Singapore fell to Japan.

Meanwhile, back home, General Douglas MacArthur and his American troops were stationed in Melbourne in 1942, and by the middle of that year around 30,000 American troops were housed in army camps, in particular Camp Pell in Royal Park. One American soldier, Eddie Leonski – the "Brownout Strangler" – was hanged for the murder of three women. The war years are most remembered for housing shortages, overcrowding and rationing.

Post-war Melbourne

After World War II, Melbourne sustained its fastest period of growth since the gold rush, with expanding industrial production drawing a huge influx of migrants, including thousands of "ten pound poms" lured from the UK with heavily subsidised fares. Perhaps Melbourne's finest moment in the 20th century came in 1956, when the Duke of Edinburgh opened the Melbourne Olympic Games, still known as "the friendly games". They were Australia's finest sporting hour, as the small host nation came third in the final medal tally,

A Radical Change in the Mix

Just as the city's physical form changed rapidly in the post-war period, so did the social make-up of its population. The Australian government adopted a policy of encouraging migration from Europe to provide workers for Australia's developing industries, giving assistance with travel costs and helping the immigrants to settle in Australia, to learn English if necessary and to find employment.

At first migrants came mostly from the Baltic states and other parts of Eastern Europe, many of them war refugees. Then larger numbers began to arrive from the United Kingdom and Ireland under the "assisted passage" scheme. Immigration agreements were also signed with the Dutch, Maltese, West German, Italian, Greek and Austrian governments, sowing the seeds of Melbourne's present multicultural character. In particular, Italian and Greek migrants were attracted to Melbourne in great numbers.

By 1961, the city's population was more than two million. By the early 1970s, more than half of inner-city Fitzroy's residents had been born overseas. The end of the White Australia Policy in 1973 heralded a new era of cultural and demographic change, and from the late 1970s onwards there was a great influx of Asian refugees from Vietnam and Cambodia.

Immigration so transformed Melbourne that, by the end of the 20th century, nearly 30 per cent of its residents had been born overseas.

behind the Soviet Union and the United States.

The long-running annual Moomba Festival opened in 1955; the tradition of the Myer Christmas Windows began thrilling children in 1956; and new planning and design ideas were drawn from the United States as much as from the "mother country".

Suburbanisation took root as car ownership rose, and new industrial developments grew at Broadmeadows and Dandenong. The Housing Commission of Victoria had been established in 1938, and as inner Melbourne strained under the demands for post-war housing, suburban housing estates for low-income Melburnians were developed in outer surburban areas, providing 10 percent of the state's housing needs by the end of the 1940s.

The 1960s were progressive years, and the power of conservative and Church lobbies to affect legislation was beginning to decline. In 1967, public outcry was so great at the hanging at Pentridge Gaol of Ronald Ryan (the last man to go to the gallows in Australia) that capital punishment was eventually abolished in Victoria.

FAR LEFT: emigration from Britain was actively encouraged in the 1950s. **MIDDLE LEFT:** souvenir programme for the 1956 Olympics. **ABOVE LEFT:** cars at a suburban supermarket, 1974. **ABOVE:** a new suburban development at Doncaster East, 1983.

Transformation and decline

In the 1980s, after decades of talk and planning, Melbourne saw the completion of an inner-city underground rail network. As in most other large cities worldwide, there was a tremendous change in the inner-city areas as people realised the disadvantages of living far away from the city centre. The former working-class areas of South Melbourne, Albert Park, Carlton, Fitzroy and North Melbourne all became very desirable places in which to live for the newly affluent middle class. Older residents watched with amusement, shock and then immense irony as their former and very much déclassé suburbs became chic, and working people's cottages became transformed into middle-class villas.

The old Australian dream of one's own home on a quarter-acre block (one-tenth of a hectare) seemed very backward – everyone wanted a trendy villa with a postage stamp-sized garden in Carlton.

Melbourne's Original People

Legislation passed in 1860 swept Aborigines under direct state control. From that point on, the Board for the Protection of Aborigines could dictate where Aboriginal people lived and worked.

An indication of European attitudes in the mid-19th century is revealed in the musings of the Marquis de Beauvoir during a visit to Melbourne in 1866: "A most offensive and horrible group of men and women passed along, with skins as black as a crocodile's, dirty woollen hair, and

low and degraded countenances. They were Aborigines. Ragged old trowsers did not sufficiently hide their repulsive bodies; a miserable appearance of old boots at the end of a bare thigh and leg… a collection of wretched rags on their mean little bodies, uglier than any monkey in the world – such is the aspect of the ancient possessors of this continent; such is the race with which, rightly or wrongly, we dispute the possession of this enormous extent of soil, thrusting them each day farther back into the bush."

After the 1880s, new laws forced those of "mixed blood" off the mission stations, denying their Aboriginality. By 1901, the Victorian census recorded a mere 46 indigenous inhabitants of Melbourne.

From the 1920s, a community was reborn in the inner-city suburb of Fitzroy, as Aboriginal people from across the state gravitated to the city looking for work and support. A number of organisations were formed over the coming decades, promoting Aboriginal rights and seeking social justice and the repeal of discriminatory laws. In 1933, William Cooper founded the Australian Aborigines' League, and in 1938 organised a Day of Mourning as a protest against 150 years of white settlement.

A pan-Aboriginal identity began to develop in Melbourne in the 1960s, and in the 1970s a range of key health, legal and social services were established. By the turn of the new century, there were approximately 15,000 Melburnians of indigenous descent. In Melbourne today, the word "Koorie" is commonly used to identify indigenous groups and individuals, and Koorie culture and heritage is preserved and celebrated through such organisations as the Koorie Heritage Trust (established in 1985) and the Bunjilaka Aboriginal Centre at Melbourne Museum (opened in 2000).

In December 2000, thousands of Melburnians marched in support of reconciliation with Aborigines, and new city landmarks such as a statue of creator spirit Bunjil at Docklands, and Birrarung Marr Park on the Yarra River, celebrate Aboriginal culture and identity. Greater respect and understanding for Koorie culture are hallmarks of the city today, with Prime Minister Kevin Rudd's formal apology to the country's stolen generations in Febrary 2008 a gesture of national reconciliation. The process, however, is far from over. ❑

ABOVE: digging for tubers. **LEFT:** the Corroboree ceremony acts out episodes from the Dreamtime.

But the early 1990s saw Melbourne's fortunes decline dramatically: in the Australia-wide recession, Victoria was the hardest hit. In its capital, factories closed, building societies collapsed amid political scandals, and unemployment increased. Time-honoured institutions such as Mietta's restaurant and George's department store closed their doors, sending shock waves through the city's soul. Melburnians were coming to realise that, having lost the political helm of Australia in the 1920s, they had also lost its commercial and business leadership.

Grand new projects

In 1992, a "radical-conservative" state government was elected, led by Jeff Kennett, under whose leadership a string of grand but sometimes controversial projects were unveiled. The City Link venture connected three major freeways with toll roads, tunnels and a bridge; Albert Park was cleared to hold the Australian Formula One Grand Prix; and the Crown Entertainment Complex (including a casino) was opened at Southbank.

A Labor Party state government unexpectedly came to power in 1999, and continued to change the face of the city into the new century. A new Melbourne Museum campus was opened in 2000, adjacent to the iconic Royal Exhibition Building, which achieved World Heritage status in 2004. The Docklands precinct was developed, and Federation Square gave Melburnians a distinctive new southern gateway to the city in 2002, covering the former unsightly Jolimont railyards with an assemblage of cultural institutions, restaurants and tourist facilities, and a city square paved with strikingly coloured Kimberley sandstone.

> *Between 2000 and 2006 Melbourne sustained the highest population and economic growth rate of any Australian capital city.*

ABOVE: Federation Square is the new heart of the city.
LEFT: re-enactment of 1788, known as Australia Day.

In 2005, the former Spencer Street railway station was redeveloped as Southern Cross Station, winning architectural prizes along the way. More recently the South Wharf precinct has arisen around the new convention centre, which opened in 2009.

A very liveable city

In the early years of the 21st century, with a population approaching four million, Melbourne has, above all, regained its traditional drive and energy. Like any international city of its size and diversity, it faces continued challenges in areas such as traffic congestion, organised crime and climate change. In the noughties, a severe drought tested the city's water supplies, and Melbourne householders were asked to rein in their enthusiasm for watering their lawns and washing their cars.

> *The 2007 opening of the National Synchrotron confirmed Melbourne as a centre for scientific and industrial research, especially in biotechnology.*

Melbourne is used to being in Sydney's shadow, and while its northern neighbour hosted the 2000 Olympic Games, Melbourne continued its tradition as Australia's undisputed sporting capital as host city of the 2006 Commonwealth Games. Comparisons since the 1990s of such factors as climate, public transport, crime rates, cultural diversity and city infrastructure have had Melbourne regularly featuring in the top five on lists of the world's most liveable cities *(see panel on page 28)*. It is an accolade of which Melbourne's residents are quietly proud.

In 1857 William Forster wrote to Henry Parkes that the width of Melbourne's streets and the newness of its architecture gave it a superior position over Sydney. "Will the superiority of Melbourne in point of position," he wondered, "always continue relative to the other colonies?" Over 150 years later, Melburnians, justly proud of their culture and heritage, still like to answer his question in the affirmative. ❑

ABOVE: Bourke Plaza on Collins Street is home to the Australian Stock Exchange. **LEFT:** free rave party at the St Kilda summer festival.

DECISIVE DATES

50,000 BC
The first Australians arrive on the continent, overland from New Guinea (some anthropologists place it even earlier).

1770
Captain Cook lands at Botany Bay, names the territory New South Wales and claims it for Britain.

1788
The First Fleet arrives in Sydney Cove with a cargo of convicts.

1803
Abortive convict settlement at Sorrento.

1835
John Batman makes a "treaty" with the Kulin Aborigines for 600,000 acres (240,000 hectares) of land on the shores of Port Phillip.

1837
A year-old village on the Yarra River is named Melbourne (still part of New South Wales). Surveyor Robert Hoddle plans the Melbourne grid system.

1838
John Pascoe Fawkner prints Melbourne's first newspaper; establishment of the Port Phillip Aboriginal Protectorate; Melbourne Cricket Club is founded.

1848
Melbourne achieves city status.

1851
Victoria officially separates from New South Wales; gold is discovered at Buninyong, near Ballarat, and the gold rush begins.

1853
The University of Melbourne is established; Cobb & Co. coaches founded.

1854
The Age newspaper founded; Australia's first train service runs from Flinders Street to Sandridge (Port Melbourne).

1856
First Victorian Parliament opened; building workers stage a protest that results in the eight-hour day.

1859
Australian Rules Football codified (the oldest code of football in the world).

1860
Population of Melbourne reaches 140,000.

1861
First Melbourne Cup horse race, watched by 4,000.

1867
Alfred, Duke of Edinburgh, first royal visitor to Melbourne, lays the foundation stone of the Town Hall.

1877
The MCG hosts the very first Test match; Australia defeat England by 45 runs.

1880
Bushranger Ned Kelly captured in Glenrowan and hanged in Melbourne;

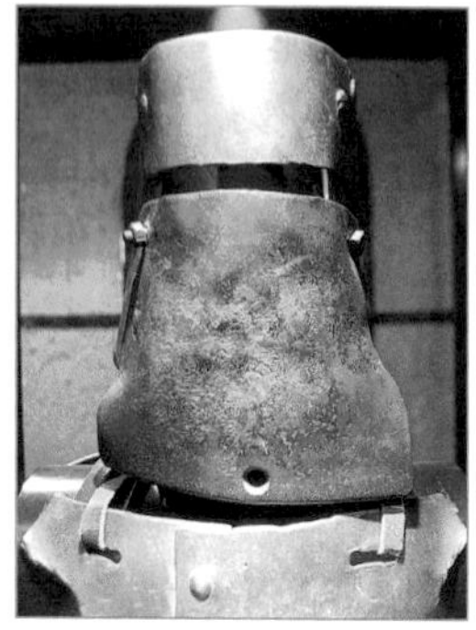

the International Exhibition is held in the city.

1885
Visiting London journalist George Augustus Sala coins the phrase "Marvellous Melbourne".

1888
The Great Centennial Exhibition is held in Melbourne.

1892
The great crash heralds the beginning of the depression years.

1901
Federation of the six colonies into the Commonwealth of Australia. The first Federal Parliament sits in Melbourne.

1906
Melbourne's first electric trams; Melbourne Symphony Orchestra is formed.

1909
French artist Jules Lefebvre's nude painting *Chloé* first goes on display at Young & Jackson Hotel.

1910
Flinders Street Railway Station completed; first aeroplane flight in Victoria, by Houdini at Diggers Rest.

1912
Luna Park opened on the St Kilda foreshore.

1916
Liquor licensing laws force closure of public bars at 6pm. The famous "six o'clock swill" laws were not repealed until 1966.

1918
Alec Wickham (the inventor of the Australian crawl) dives over 30 metres (100ft) into the Yarra River from a cliff at Deep Rock.

1922
Chemist Cyril Callister creates Vegemite, Australia's national food.

1927
Parliament House opens in Canberra, and the Federal Parliament moves there from Melbourne.

1930
Phar Lap wins the Melbourne Cup as economic depression takes hold.

1933
Melbourne's population passes the one million mark, as economic depression recedes.

1942
Melbourne becomes Allied headquarters for the Southwest Pacific, and

thousands of American troops begin to pass through.

1945
Australia embarks on an immigration programme; Melbourne attracts migrants from Greece, Italy and Malta.

1956
Olympic Games held in Melbourne; Australian

television launches; annual Christmas tradition of the Myer Christmas Windows begins.

1958
Construction of ICI Building, Melbourne's first skyscraper.

1964
The Beatles visit Melbourne.

1966
American President Lyndon B. Johnson visits Melbourne; protesters against the Vietnam War throng the city streets.

1967
Last criminal hanging in Australia, held in Melbourne. Capital punishment is abolished in Victoria in 1975.

1970
Span of West Gate Bridge collapses during construction, killing 35 men; Vietnam moratoria organised: 70,000 people march in the city compared with only 20,000 in Sydney; publication of *The Female Eunuch* by the Melbourne-born feminist Germaine Greer.

1972
Freak storm floods city streets, causing cars to float down Elizabeth Street.

1973
The White Australia Policy is overturned, and Melbourne sees a rapid increase in immigration from Southeast Asia.

1986
Picasso's *Weeping Woman* stolen from the National Gallery of Victoria, but later recovered.

1987
Seven people are shot dead in Hoddle Street, Richmond, by a 19-year-old former army cadet.

1988
Opening of Melbourne Park Tennis Centre, home of the Australian Open Grand Slam Championship.

1992
Southgate is completed on the south side of the Yarra River; MCG hosts the Cricket World Cup final.

1996
Melbourne hosts a Formula One Grand Prix for the first time, at the Albert Park circuit; Development of Docklands area commences.

2000
New Melbourne Museum opens in the Carlton Gardens; opening of Docklands Stadium.

2002
Federation Square opens.

2003
Television satire *Kath & Kim*, set in the fictional Melbourne suburb of Fountain Lakes is broadcasted.

2006
Commonwealth Games held in Melbourne.

2007
Stage 3a water restrictions, including a ban on the watering of lawns, introduced to combat effects of severe drought.

2009
173 people perish in Victoria's most lethal bushfires.

CULTURAL CAPITAL

Australia's cultural capital is positively buzzing with creative energy in art, music and theatre. There is something for everyone here, and with the city's relatively compact size, most of it is readily accessible

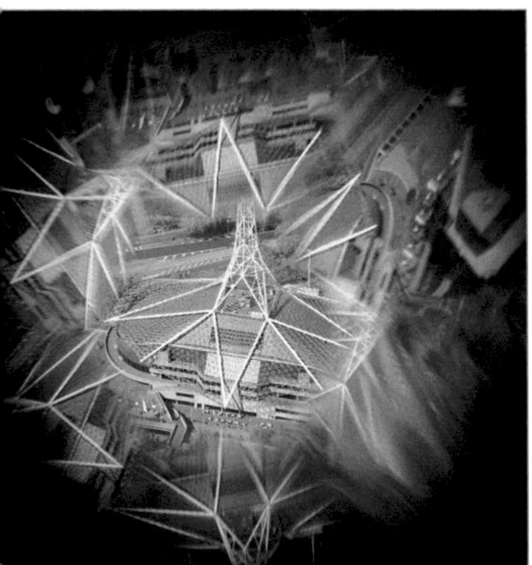

Melbourne combines accessible spaces and venues with a tradition of creativity and vibrancy that makes it Australia's most rewarding cultural and artistic environment. There is something for everyone, from back-lane grunge venues to big shows in theatres and concert halls; from showings of established and emerging artists in tiny, edgy galleries to cutting-edge visual art and historical collections in the city's major art spaces.

As Melbourne is one of the world's great multicultural cities, so its arts draw from all continents and ethnic groups, including the region's indigenous cultures.

Of course, it wasn't always like this. In the early days it was a very Anglocentric society, and although the gold-powered boom of the 1850s onwards attracted a mass influx of fortune-seekers of varying nationalities and backgrounds, and with them new cultural traditions and appetites, the Anglo tradition dominated.

Classical music was always important and played a significant role in the first International Exhibition of 1880. It was an art form that signified a certain respectability – an important attribute in middle-class Melbourne – but it was also very popular. By the beginning of the 20th century, the internationally lauded, Melbourne-born soprano, Dame Nellie Melba, could attract nightly audiences of thousands to theatres in small country towns.

> *"Dancing is the accomplishment which is the most cultivated in the colony."*
> *Clara Aspinall, Melbourne 1860*

Theatre flourished from the beginning, and its fortunes mirrored those around the world, including the hard times induced by the arrival of cinema. Opera and dance, too, have long maintained a strong profile in this most cultured of cities. Their physical legacy can be seen in some gorgeous old theatres, concert halls and other auditoriums.

Today, Melbourne has world-class venues in abundance, with plans to link many of them together in a unique cultural precinct *(see below)*. However, much of the really distinctive and more progressive work takes place in the smaller and less opulent spaces dotted around the numerous lanes of the CBD and inner suburbs. Price is often a misleading guide to the quality of a cultural experience, and some of your most piquant memories of Melbourne may be forged in a strange or unusual smaller space with unheralded creators and performers. Seek out the gold.

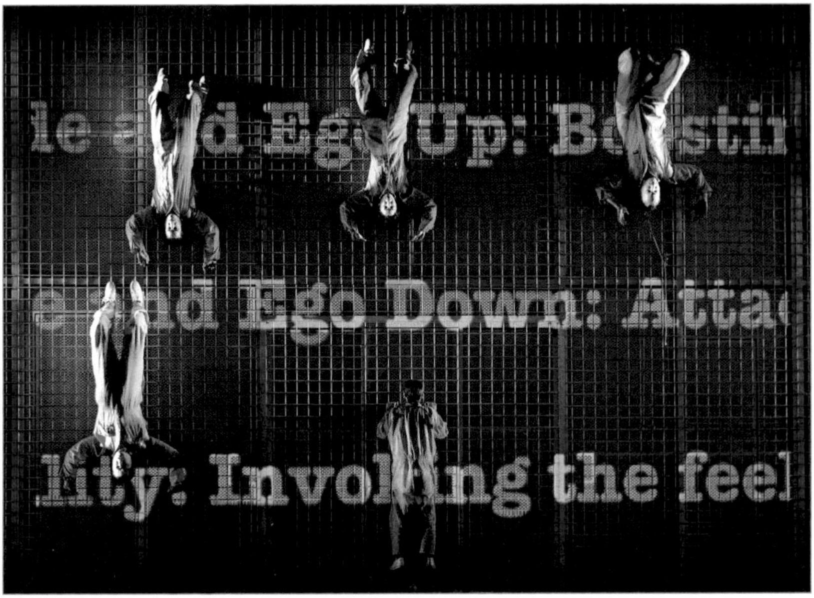

A cultural precinct

Much of the city's artistic activity is focused on a cluster of buildings just to the south of the CBD over Princes Bridge. Back in 2003, Robyn Archer, cabaret chanteuse and then Artistic Director of the Melbourne International Arts Festival, enthused: "A brilliant arts precinct has emerged here... I would define it, brand it and sell it to the world. I would work with descendants of the original owners of the land to try to relate it to the important local iconography of the rainbow serpent, one which stretches from the Malthouse to Melbourne Museum."

What Robyn Archer was both describing and imagining was a coherent and quite remarkable arts precinct starting with the **Malthouse Theatre** on Sturt Street, parallel to St Kilda Road and only a few minutes' walk south from Flinders Street Station, and its modernist companion, the rusty-steel clad **Australian Centre for Contemporary Art** (ACCA). The precinct then coils northwards across the river all the way up to Carlton Gardens and another pairing of modern and historic: the World Heritage-listed **Royal Exhibition Building**, a rare and precious relic

LEFT: the Arts Centre viewed through a fractal telescope on the Eureka Skydeck. **ABOVE:** *Honour Bound* at the Malthouse Theatre. **ABOVE RIGHT:** Victorian Opera's production of *Così fan tutti.*

from the same period of International Exhibitions as the Eiffel Tower in Paris, which has been magnificently restored, and right next door, the contemporary **Melbourne Museum**, featuring a ski-jump roof over a living rainforest, and inside its fascinating collection halls, everything from 3D projections to the stuffed racehorse **Phar Lap**.

Meanwhile, the Victorian State Government has ambitious plans to rationalise the jumbled pedestrian thoroughfares of the Southbank and drive an avenue straight through from the Malthouse to the Arts Centre plaza near the Yarra, thereby bringing most of the arts and culture neighbourhood together.

It is quite a neighbourhood, too. It includes the ABC (Australian Broadcasting Corporation), the **Melbourne Symphony Orchestra**, **Opera Australia**, the **Australian Ballet** and Victoria's leading contemporary dance company, **Chunky Move**, the **Victorian College of the Arts**, the **Melbourne Theatre Company** and a new state-of-the-art **Recital Hall**.

Melbourne's central arts complex – look for the spindly spire – combines three large buildings lining St Kilda Road from the corner of Southbank Boulevard right up to the Princes Bridge: the **National Gallery of Victoria**, international wing, the **Arts Centre,** with its mix of theatres and galleries, and **Hamer Hall**, Melbourne's prime concert space.

North of the river and higher up Swanston Street, the **State Library of Victoria** is one of the city's cultural gems, with its historic circular reading room under a light-flooded dome.

FESTIVALS GALORE

Pulsing through Melbourne's cultural calendar is a series of arts festivals that add an intense shot of extra, often challenging, activity to the already busy scene and bring large crowds into the city. The Comedy Festival in April, the Film Festival in July/ August, the Fringe Festival in September and the Melbourne International Arts Festival in October are the four pillars, but there are many others to choose from.

The Melbourne Fringe Festival, based at the North Melbourne Town Hall, has tentacles all over town, with a huge mix of shows and activities held just before and during the International Arts Festival. *See pages 146–7 for more on festivals.*

The theatre scene

The boom time for fringe theatre was the 1970s, when the Pram Factory and The Australian Performing Group, both in Carlton, produced theatre that was political, nationalistic and experimental. It was also low-budget. Even now, the ripple effect from that renaissance period continues to colour and shape the local scene. Many of the pioneers from that time are still working actors, directors and writers.

David Williamson started out amidst the foment and bravado of those days to become Australia's de facto playwright laureate. One of the hardest goals to achieve in Melbourne now is to write a play and see it produced, although many continue to try. Less literary ways of forging a theatrical piece, through various workshops, improvisation and cross-disciplinary creative input, seem to be closer to the norm in much independent theatre.

The **Arts Centre** manages four performance venues: after its first major reconfiguring, **Hamer Hall** will continue to be the home of the acclaimed Melbourne Symphony Orchestra; the **State Theatre** houses big shows including musicals, ballet and opera; the main-stage **Playhouse** and the smaller, more flexible **Fairfax Studio** are used for theatre. The Melbourne Theatre Company has been the principal user of both these spaces but now also has its own home in Southbank Boulevard. The Arts Centre itself is actively developing new shows with more leftfield artists through its *Full Tilt* programme, which keeps the Fairfax Studio vital and helps to attract a younger audience.

At the Arts Centre, expect mainly big, high-quality productions, name players and often predictable fare. Ticket prices reflect this. The Centre also exhibits art and popular culture in its foyers and the **George Adams Gallery**. Arthur Boyd's large-scale *Shoalhaven* pictures are a special treat.

The **Melbourne Theatre Company** (MTC) is a largely conventional state theatre that relies on a more conservative subscriber and audience base. It only occasionally pushes any artistic boundaries, but usually delivers polished, "professional" performances with high-end staging effects. It does commission plays from local writers but not enough to reflect their number and quality. Often it is the case of "the usual suspects". With relatively short rehearsal periods, and a firmly ensconsed artistic director, the direction and acting have often been uninspiring, but new blood in 2011 may change that.

Many of Melbourne's commercial theatres, after falling into near-total dilapidation, have been restored and now present sure-fire commercial fare and the inevitable big musicals, or provide venues during festivals. **Her Majesty's**, the **Comedy Theatre** and the **Princess Theatre** are in the northeast corner of the city, while the **Athenaeum** and **Regent** theatres are in Collins Street. Over the road from Federation Square is the slightly bizarre **Forum Theatre**, with its beyond-taste interiors (*see page 100*).

The **Malthouse Theatre** started out as The Playbox, with a policy of staging new Australian writing. A change in management introduced a

ABOVE LEFT: the Chunky Move contemporary dance company's production of *Glow*. **ABOVE:** a production of *Hairspray* at the Princess Theatre, a landmark building that is reputedly haunted by a friendly ghost. **ABOVE RIGHT:** Her Majesty's Theatre.

sharply different philosophy and transformed the quality and character of the productions, away from text-based drama to more eclectic works, including cabaret, epic ensemble pieces and virtuoso one-person shows. With a new director starting in 2011, interest is piqued as to where it goes next.

Opera and ballet

Opera Australia brings regular seasons to Melbourne, although not enough fully to satisfy the avid opera community still smarting from the loss of the local Victoria State Opera, subsumed by it some years ago. In recent years, phoenix-like, **Victorian Opera** launched itself with the strong support of the State Government. Its productions offer audiences less well-known works and edgier interpretations. Plans for Melbourne's first home-grown *Ring* cycle are well advanced, with a starting date of 2013.

The **Australian Ballet**, unlike Opera Australia, *is* based in Melbourne, and its productions are lavish, with real depth and star quality. The renowned dancer Rudolf Nureyev often toured with the company. It continues to produce a mixed diet of traditional and contemporary ballet, featuring new works from local and international choreographers.

Chunky Move creates memorable contemporary dance pieces wrapped in daring design. It has studios next to the Malthouse and tours internationally. The company's output is not prolific, but of consistently high quality in conception and performance.

FRINGE BENEFITS

With little or no public subsidy, some of the city's fringe theatres manage to produce challenging and invigorating work that provides balance to the traditional fare of the likes of MTC.

La Mama is still going strong in Carlton after 30 years and clinging to this tiny, potent theatrical space, a crucible for so much new Australian theatre. Experiencing the always varying spatial configuration and the sense of having performers in your lap is worth it alone. La Mama has a second, larger theatre down the road in the former Carlton Courthouse.

Red Stitch Actors Theatre performs in a cramped hall beside a church in St Kilda, although it has been refurbished and expanded slightly. Originally conceived as an actors collective to mount the latest top plays from Europe and America, all the players are professionals working on screen and other stages for money. They demand high standards of themselves, and performance pride runs deep. It is rare to have a dull night with Red Stitch.

45 Downstairs in Flinders Lane is a performance and exhibition space with a strong reputation for attracting quality theatre groups. It recently expanded to more warehouse premises downstairs to offer two playing spaces. Most shows transform these unconventional spaces to produce the unexpected.

Comedy, circus and cabaret

This is a major strand of the performing arts in Melbourne. The **Melbourne International Comedy Festival** is one of the big three laugh fests globally, alongside Edinburgh and Montreal. In April it triggers an explosion of comedy and cabaret in the city, with venues including the Melbourne Town Hall and Trades Hall.

With the **National Institute of Circus Arts** based here, there is no shortage of talented young circus and physical performers. Many of them aspire to, and do, join **Circus Oz**, the pioneering and much-loved local circus company, or **Cirque du Soleil**, the high-end touring company from Canada, whose gleaming tents regularly spring up in the sports precinct. The National Institute of Circus Arts regularly has performances to bring its students to an audience. See the hottest younger performers before they join Cirque du Soleil.

When the **Famous Spiegeltent** is in residence beside the Arts Centre, usually during the last three months of the year, it becomes cabaret central. It's exciting, packed every night and necessary to book.

Elsewhere, there are rich pickings in cabaret and related forms. The **Butterfly Club** in South Melbourne is a minute space but presents good-quality and often edgy work.

Film

A Lumière cameraman filmed the Melbourne Cup in 1896. It is the oldest film held in the National Film and Sound Archive. Furthermore, a magic-lantern unit within the Salvation Army in Melbourne purchased a cinematograph at about the same time, and eventually made hundreds of films here at the dawn of the medium. More than a century later, Central City Film and Television studios in the Docklands are Melbourne's infrastructure stake in the sharply competitive international film and

> *For sitting back in a deckchair, your feet nuzzled by AstroTurf, your hand clutching a drink and a fine film to watch, nothing beats the Rooftop Cinema at Curtin House.*

FAR LEFT TOP: Australian Ballet. **FAR LEFT MIDDLE:** Victorian Opera's *Orphée*. **ABOVE LEFT:** Circus Oz performer. **ABOVE:** the Rooftop Cinema at Curtin House.

video production and post-production industry.

The **Australian Centre for the Moving Image** (ACMI) at Federation Square has been slow to find its imagined high profile and place in Melbourne – the alchemy of building design, location and programming has not quite worked so far. But ACMI is refocusing its state-of-the-art cinemas and high-tech galleries, and runs moving-image art exhibitions and themed seasons of films and discussions. It sustains a sizeable research and curatorial staff, and holds over 40,000 items of film and video, most of them available on loan. When it has big-name temporary exhibitions, the place buzzes; it just

needs to convert these visitors into regulars.

Film buffs and mere movie-lovers flock to the wintertime **Melbourne International Film Festival**. For more local and eccentric film-making, try **St Kilda Film Festival** in early June. But for just going to a flick, there are a number of restored picture palaces, including the **Rivoli** in Camberwell, a beautiful Art Deco complex with a rooftop bar; the **Sun** in Yarraville, with six boutique Art Deco cinemas; and, for a taste of nostalgia 1950s-style with far less opulence, try one of the few remaining drive-ins in Australia at Coburg – three screens on site and the "privacy" of your own vehicle. For rep programming mixed with your Deco, try the Astor in Chapel Street *(see page 189)*.

Art galleries

The **Australian Centre for Contemporary Art** (ACCA), next to the Malthouse Theatre, has no permanent collection but is almost a compulsory destination for visitors wanting a taste of challenging and cutting-edge art. It commissions and invites works from Australian and international artists willing to create specially for that space, including installations that transform the gallery. Each year, ACCA exhibits a group of hot, emerging visual artists under the title NEW.

ABOVE LEFT: board at the Comedy Festival. **ABOVE:** *Collins Street 5pm,* by John Brack, is part of the collection at the Ian Potter Centre. **LEFT:** *Federation Bells.* **ABOVE RIGHT:** *The Public Purse* in Bourke Street.

The **National Gallery of Victoria** has two locations: **NGV: International** in the original building on St Kilda Road, and **The Ian Potter Centre: NGV Australia** at Federation Square. Both have extensive and important permanent collections, and a constant turnover of visiting exhibitions, including major blockbusters.

Melbourne is replete with art galleries. Explore **Flinders Lane** for a range of commercial spaces, and **Gertrude** and **Smith streets** in Collingwood for greater variety and more artist-run galleries. Not far away, in George Street, Fitzroy, is the excellent **Centre for Contemporary Photography**.

Public art

With the development of Docklands in the 1990s came a requirement for developers to set aside a budget for public art, mainly murals and sculptures. This has certainly boosted the number of works around the city environs, not all of them attractive but many that are whimsical and memorable. Keep an eye out for *Forward Surge*, three large, abstract black steel waves between Hamer Hall and the Arts Centre by renowned sculptor Inge King, who has many other sculptures around the city and the suburbs. Or you might trip over the punk bronze dog, *Larry Latrobe*, bump into the elongated *Three Business Men*, or want to reach into *The Public Purse* in Bourke Street

COUNTRY IMPRESSIONS

Eaglemont is only a short train trip from the city. It's worth the ride on the Hurstbridge line to take a walk around the area where pioneering artists of the Heidelberg School, including Tom Roberts, Arthur Streeton and Charles Condor, found the vistas and inspiration to create a kind of Australian Impressionism. There is a detailed artists trail, with pictures to help one to imagine pre-suburban Eaglemont and Heidelberg (www.artist strail.com).

Not far down the road is another treasure, the Heide Museum of Modern Art. This bucolic property was the home of John and Sunday Reed, and a refuge for some notable Australian artists including Sidney Nolan, Albert Tucker and Joy Hester. There is a spicy, layered lore and atmosphere around Heide. A recent expansion makes the gallery even better, while the grounds are dotted with bright sculptures (7 Templestowe Road, Bulleen; www.heide.com.au; tel: 98 50 1500; Tue–Fri 10am–5pm, Sat–Sun noon–5pm; charge).

Mall. Do include a visit to the *Federation Bells* in Birrarung Marr to hear a reinvention of the traditional European bell with the annoying harmonic eliminated from the sound.

Buskers, or "circle performers" as they like to call themselves, are an enjoyable feature of the city, especially on weekends around Southbank. They expect a modest donation, which is fair since they offer quite high-level performance skills and an amusing 20 minutes or so.

Readings and writing

The gold rushes of the mid-19th century and the wealth and confidence they brought Melbourne still resonate in the city's literary life. Local publishing of gazettes, magazines and literature, including poetry, boomed during the rushes. Now Melbourne is the small-press publishing centre of Australia.

One small press – Sleepers – has published several *Sleeper Almanacs,* anthologies of short fiction and non-fiction. To dive into the local writing culture, try one of its regular Sleepers Salons (www.sleeperspublishing.com).

ABOVE: busker gets cocky. **ABOVE RIGHT:** upside down at the bottom of the world at Werribee Mansion.

The **Melbourne Writers Festival** has spread its wings and left the Malthouse Theatre for Federation Square and its larger venues. The springtime programme of conversations with leading Australian and international writers, panel discussions and readings has been remodelled to extend its appeal to a wider and younger audience.

> *For the best in jewellery as art, visit the uncompromising Mari Funaki in her tiny gallery in Crossley Street.*

Finally, **Readings Bookshop** in Lygon Street, Carlton, is a Melbourne institution. A commercial bookstore, it vigorously promotes local writing and publishing, and offers a steady stream of leading local and international authors at its in-store events. ❑

Music City

Melbourne is one of the world's great music cities, especially if your interests lie in the realms of rock, indie, electronica, hip-hop, funk, dance, jazz or folk – anything that works in smallish informal venues. It has its concert and recital halls where the Melbourne Symphony Orchestra and other ensembles present programmes of orchestral, chamber and choral music, and these same halls also welcome artists from other genres. However, it's in its pub and club scene that the city really comes into its own. Grab a free copy of the weekly music papers, *Beat* or *Inpress,* and try not to be overwhelmed by the choices on offer.

Venues come and go, but there are a handful of reliables where you're virtually guaranteed a good night out in premises that are intimate, friendly and yet thoroughly professional. Overseas visitors are often astonished to find big-name international and Australian acts playing rooms perhaps a quarter of the size they would fill in Europe or America.

Granddaddy of the sticky-carpet spaces, although smartened up these days, the **Esplanade Hotel** (or "Espy") in St Kilda is one of Melbourne's quintessential music venues, with an ear-boggling history. Bands play every night across three stages. Try the legendary Gershwin Room, where the SBS television channel stages its show, and *RocKwiz,* or the front room, where there are usually lesser-known acts playing for free. Round the corner, the Bandroom, at the **Prince of Wales**, has bigger draws but is still very much a club venue in atmosphere.

In Richmond, the **Corner Hotel** has it all: a comfortable space, decent sound system, good beer and a superlative booking policy. This is no doubt why the same team books the smaller **Northcote Social Club**, north of the city centre. Northcote, like Brunswick further west (try the **East Brunswick Club** or the **Cornish Arms**), is a suburb with a real buzz to it as it fills with students and bohemians who can't afford to live in St Kilda or Fitzroy.

Fitzroy is packed with good haunts in and around Brunswick Street, while the **Totc** in Collingwood is the archetypal music pub. In 2010 it became the hub of a popular uprising to protect music venues from stifling new licensing restrictions, which at one point saw it close. But people power triumphed and it lives again.

The city centre has the **Hi-Fi Bar** and **The Toff in Town** in Swanston Street, while the laneways have all kinds of attractions. Tiny **Bennetts Lane Jazz Club** is Melbourne's premier jazz venue, and punches way above its weight with high-calibre performers playing every night and the odd international superstar.

For listings, see page 284. ❑

ABOVE: The Cat Empire at the Prince of Wales.
RIGHT: performing at the Ding Dong Lounge.

CULINARY CAPITAL

Melbourne has an extraordinary diversity of restaurants: it's possible to eat a different national cuisine every day of the month. Even more extraordinary is the consistently high standard of food in this quality-conscious city

It has often been said that Melbourne is the most European of Australian cities, and nowhere is this more obvious than in its obsession with food and wine. Melbourne is a place where it is perfectly reasonable to cross town to buy renowned salami, to get into a heated discussion about where to find the best Cantonese duck, to swap stories about chefs as if they were star footie players and to expect that good bread, coffee, wine and produce will always be close at hand. It is a place where proximity to a market can affect property values, and where the Melbourne Food and Wine Festival (one of a dozen or so food-themed events held across the city each year) attracts up to 300,000 people. Food is as important an ingredient in day-to-day conversation as sport and the weather, and the city's food-savvy, quality-conscious population ensures that eating badly can only be a matter of personal choice or sheer bad luck.

There are many reasons for Melbourne's gastrocentric character, but perhaps the most significant factor has been the waves of immigration that have washed over the city at regular intervals since the Chinese first arrived with the gold rushes of the 19th century. Subsequent influxes from Italy, various parts of Eastern Europe, Greece, Spain, Vietnam, Lebanon, India, Ethiopia and elsewhere have all added colour to the food fabric of the city.

LEFT: waffle, waffle, waffle. Melburnians love their food – and love talking about it.

RIGHT: dinner at the Graham in Port Melbourne.

Keeping it real

The main way that these migrants have affected Melbourne's food culture is in having been less inclined – and less pressurised – to tone down their cooking to make it more palatable to local tastes. In recent decades, this has been because Melburnians have come to expect and actively to seek "authentic" eating experiences, but in the past it has been because groups of migrants arrived in numbers significant enough to support restaurants and food stores that chose not to assimilate slavishly.

Not only did these arrivals bring with them a host of new flavours and ingredients – pasta, olives, feta, bok choy, chorizo, calamari,

saffron, star anise – to a largely Anglo-Irish culture, but also an attitude of good food being integral to a good life. Perhaps more than any other factor, it is this attitude that has transformed Melbourne into one of the world's great food cities.

Crucial ingredients

There can be no great cooking without great ingredients, and Melbourne's fortunate geographical position finds it surrounded by fertile countryside with a wide variety of microclimates and soil types producing everything from top-quality meat and dairy to fruit, nuts, vegetables and grains. Easy access to the ocean also ensures a constant and plentiful variety of fresh seafood, and with five wine regions within 90 minutes of the city, getting a bottle of something with which to wash it all down has never been a problem.

A more prosaic part of to the Melbourne food equation is the weather. Unpredictable, often bleak in winter and seldom matching the balmy visions depicted in the holiday brochures, Melbourne's weather often forces its citizens indoors, where the focus is less sun and sand, and more food, wine and conversa-

MARKET FORCES

A great variety of high-quality locally produced food is available from the seven major produce markets that are dotted across the city. Melbourne has a proud tradition of markets, the most famous of which, the 7-hectare (17½-acre) Queen Victoria Market on the western corner of the Central Business District, has been operating since 1878 and attracts more than a million-and-a-half visitors a year. Almost as old, and almost as popular, Prahran Market has been selling fruit, vegetables, meat and fish since 1881, and now also features delicatessens and specialist food shops. Smaller farmers' markets are also sprouting like mushrooms in the city's nooks and crannies.

tion (often about food and wine). It is a final and important part of the recipe that has made eating and drinking an essential ingredient for anyone wanting to know what makes Melbourne tick.

Restaurants and cafés

Melbourne, like most sizeable cities, has its share of high-end dining that can cut it with the big boys, in terms of quality and expense, anywhere in the world. And while restaurants such as modern French Vue de Monde, Cantonese Flower Drum or classic Italian Grossi Florentino provide dining experiences well worth checking out (if your credit card is up for a serious workout), it is on the more egalitarian rungs below the top end that Melbourne's strengths as a food city really come into play.

The diversity of restaurants is remarkable. Name a cuisine – from Balinese to Russian to Ethiopian – and you will be able to find a place that is cooking in that style, doing it well and doing so at a remarkably reasonable price. The easy accessibility to such a broad range of influences has seen local chefs, nurtured by the local scene, creating contemporary dishes that weave multiple influences into a unique and quintessentially Melburnian style. In restaurants such as Richmond's Pearl or Cumulus Inc in the city, you will find ingredients and cooking styles from across the globe, artfully distilled into dishes that pay homage to the ethnic influences central to Melbourne's dining scene, without ever lapsing into the culinary tragedy that is ill-conceived fusion food.

FAR LEFT: demonstrations with stellar chefs are popular during the Food and Wine Festival.
LEFT AND ABOVE: a whole range of produce can be found at Queen Victoria Market.
ABOVE RIGHT: dine in style at the Treasury.

> *The fact that Melburnians take eating out so seriously means that even pub food is generally of a high standard.*

Central lanes and alleys

The CBD is arguably the most interesting place to find a meal. Its famed network of lanes and alleys is home to scores of excellent small restaurants and cafés, many of them hiding away in basements or behind discreetly signed doors.

With these sometimes unprepossessing spaces, good design is at a premium, and a whole industry has sprung up to transform even the dingiest cellar. This occasionally leads to uncomfortable compromises, and there can be a tendency to forget that diners might want to hear what their companions are saying (try Longrain on a Friday night!), but it all adds to the adventure.

Flexibility is the key. In places such as the Spanish-themed MoVida or Bar Lourinha, or

Asian-influenced Longrain and Gingerboy, it is as easy to pop in for a couple of well-selected glasses of wine and to graze among small snack dishes as it is to sit down for the full multi-course dinner experience. Places such as European and Journal continue the city's love affair with dark wood, red wine and great espresso, while for those after the sleekly modern – in design and food – the glass-box dining area at Verge or the spectacular views at Federation Square's Taxi Dining Room will tick the right boxes.

Carlton, Fitzroy, St Kilda and other suburbs

There is plenty beyond the CBD, however, with eating strips in many suburbs taking on their own village-like personality. In Carlton, the renowned Little Italy of Lygon Street has some good Italian food, despite certain stretches of the strip becoming little more than cookie-cutter tourist traps complete with red-checked tablecloth clichés. Toto's, at No. 101, has the distinction of being the first pizza house to open in Australia. Some of the more interesting food on Lygon Street is now found further to the north, at places such as the produce store/restaurant Enoteca Vino Bar and the brilliant little modern Lebanese joint Rumi.

Fitzroy's rapidly gentrifying bohemia has yielded an increasingly curious mix of trashy bars and generic cafés vying for attention with restaurants and cafés that have more on their mind than making a buck. Marios, the much copied but never-equalled Brunswick Street café, perfectly encapsulates retro Fitzroy style, while the always-packed designer pizza joint Ladro, in Gertrude Street, offers a newer version of northside Melbourne cool.

Many of the city's less expensive restaurants advertise BYO (bring your own): you can save money by buying your wine of choice from a shop and paying a small corkage fee.

ABOVE LEFT: Beechworth Bakery now has branches across Victoria. **TOP:** the latte is a staple of café culture. **ABOVE:** sample Chairman Mao's hitherto overlooked culinary expertise in Chinatown. **ABOVE RIGHT:** several restaurants now have open kitchens.

To the south, in bayside St Kilda, the slightly seedy seaside resort ambience provides a great backdrop for some lauded and beautiful-looking restaurants, some with wonderful views, and all with a particular edgy St Kilda style. Cafe Di Stasio shows how well Melbourne does Italian food, while the Stokehouse combines good food, wine and bay views in equal quantities. The Prince of Wales Hotel on Fitzroy Street contains Circa the Prince, one of the city's most stylish dining rooms, serving some of the best European food in town.

Then there is the little Vietnam of Victoria Street, Richmond, the mix of kosher shops and sharp cafés and wine bars in Carlisle Street, Balaclava, and the Middle Eastern strip of Sydney Road, Brunswick, which, despite being increasingly colonised by groovy little cafés pushing caffé latte, is still infused with the aroma of sumac and haloumi.

The best thing about Melbourne's cafés and restaurants is that the standard is set pretty high. In a place where the quality of coffee is a cause for civic pride and a substandard focaccia can mean commercial death, the strike rate is in your favour.

Bars and wine shops

An overhaul of licensing legislation in the late 1980s has given Victoria the most liberal liquor laws in Australia. Freeing up Byzantine rules about where, how and when you can enjoy a glass of wine has see Melbourne develop an enviable bar scene th is as eclectic as the city itself. Whether you e after late-night beers and raucous music in a grungy laneway bolthole, vintage burgundy delivered to your table by a charming waiter, or a decent

MEALS ON WHEELS

The gourmets may sniff, but one of the more enjoyable and idiosyncratic eating experiences is to be had aboard an old W-class tram trundling round the streets of the city and its more picturesque suburbs. The logistics militate against top-notch cuisine, but the wine flows freely and it's a great way to see the city. It's probably best to avoid the early evening sitting, however, as it can feel a little bit rushed.

bottle of plonk to take home as a nightcap, there will be a watering hole to help.

There are clusters of bars in St Kilda and Fitzroy – in fact there are small bars scattered right across the city – but the best place to go bar-hopping is, once again, the CBD. Competition is high with so many bars in close proximity, and the quality – whether you're drinking cocktails or Cabernet – is usually excellent and always interesting.

Two rules: first, remember there is always another bar around the corner, so don't get stuck somewhere that doesn't appeal; second, don't make a rash assessment based on looks. A dimly lit bar with thumping music and private booths such as The Toff in Town might shake its nightclub credentials, but that doesn't preclude being able to get a glass (or bottle) of excellent Alsatian Riesling, an obscure German beer or a single-malt whisky. Much like Melbourne itself, it may take you a minute or two to understand what these bars are on about, but well it is worth it when you take the time.

Outside the city

It is remarkably easy to get out of Melbourne and into the Victoria countryside, the source of much of the city's best food and wine. Many of these regions are less than an hour's drive from the city, and, best of all, the Melburnian foodie obsession has spread into the countryside, so you don't have to leave your inner gourmet behind with the bright lights.

The Yarra Valley, to the northeast of the city, is a remarkably beautiful and abundant place that, while packed to the gills with wineries and food producers – everything from cheese and jam to venison and wild rabbit – manages to retain its tranquil rural character.

To the south of the city is the Mornington Peninsula, another awesomely beautiful area, but this time with rugged coastline and sea

SMALL BEER

It has taken a long time, but boutique breweries are finally gaining some momentum locally. Victoria Bitter, brewed in Melbourne since the 1890s, is Australia's top-selling beer but, sadly, to beer connoisseurs it doesn't actually taste of anything. Its closest local rival, Carlton Draught, suffers from the same malaise. Help is at hand in the shape of several microbreweries in the metropolitan area, notably Mountain Goat Beer in Richmond, the Temple Brewing Company in Brunswick, and 3 Ravens in Thornbury. "Brewpubs", bars that serve beer made on the premises, are also springing up, and there's a High Country Brewery Trail taking in some of the scenic towns towards Beechworth and Bright. Nirvana – or properly cellared real ale from beer engines, as it's also known – has been sighted at the Holgate Brewhouse in Woodend, to the northwest of Melbourne.

views. Again, some excellent wine – Pinot Noir, Pinot Gris and Chardonnay in particular – is made here, and establishments such as Montalto Winery and Olive Grove are on hand to allow you to try local produce washed down with local wine.

The mineral springs and soft beauty of the countryside around Daylesford and the Macedon Ranges drew many homesick Europeans to the area in its early days and continue to be a draw for city dwellers attracted to the quiet pace and the excellent food served at restaurants such as Daylesford's Lake House.

The region surrounding Geelong, Victoria's second-biggest city, has become increasingly renowned for its wine, while Geelong itself has been reinvigorated and is now bustling with new restaurants and food stores.

Further afield the story is the same, with old favourites rising to the challenge and refreshing their menus, while new enterprises spring up, backed by serious money or star chefs, often both. Keep up to date by checking *The Age* for its Epicure section on Tuesdays, or ask a local – you'll be surprised how much they know until you understand that, as we said, this is a town of food obsessives. ❑

ABOVE FAR LEFT: tasting times at Beechworth Brewery. **ABOVE LEFT:** Giant Steps vineyard in Healesville. **TOP:** Montalto is one of many wineries that have gourmet restaurants. **ABOVE:** gold leaf adds the finishing touch to a chocolate tart.

Among the foodstuffs that are unique to Australia are little freshwater crustaceans called yabbies. Look out for yabby chowder, yabby pâté or yabby stir-fry.

Markets and Malls

Discover why Melbourne has the reputation for being *the* place for shopping

From the grand department stores of the Bourke Street Mall to the cluttered cupboard-like spaces of Chapel Street Bazaar, Melbourne has shopping to suit every taste and budget. In recent years there has been a major shake-up in city-centre retailing, which had been losing ground to the suburban shopping malls, typified by Chadstone in the east. New developments such as the QV Centre in Swanston Street and GPO in Bourke Street, as well as a new barn-like mall of factory outlets in Spencer Street, have been accompanied by a revitalisation of the arcades and laneways. Tiny outlets, no matter how quirky or eccentric, find a market for everything from magic tricks to cake-decorating equipment. For fashionistas, it's pure heaven as designers turn the grungiest of spaces into the latest hip emporiums. And then there's Brunswick Street, Toorak, Prahran...

ABOVE: A furious resurgence in city-centre shopping has been fuelled by the opening of the GPO and QV centres, and the extensive refurbishment of the flagging Melbourne Central.
BELOW: The city centre's Victorian-era arcades are a destination in themselves, but once you get over the novelty of the mosaic floors and intricate ironwork, there are some seriously stylish boutiques to be trawled.

LEFT: Melbourne's principal strip of antique stores is along High Street in the eastern suburb of Armadale. Others can be found across the whole city, however, and there are many more around countryside Victoria. Follow the route around the goldfields and scour the crannies in Ballarat, Castlemaine and Daylesford. Pictured is the Den of Antiquities in Yarra Glen.

BELOW: The city is a centre for high-calibre contemporary jewellery. Art glass is another Melbourne speciality. For an overview of the richness of Melbourne and Victorian crafts and design, visit Craft Victoria in Flinders Lane.

ECLECTIC STOCK

There's something somewhere to suit everyone. Just dive in and trust to luck or follow these pointers.

For high-end fashion and accessories – not to mention the ABC Shop for CDs, DVDs and books – the beautifully renovated General Post Office is hard to beat.

The craft markets at St Kilda or Southbank, as well as Queen Victoria Market, have a range of hand-crafted Aboriginal artefacts.

If it's a laughing Buddha it must be Chinatown. Goods from around the globe can be found in various ethnic enclaves.

Fresh produce is the *raison d'être* of Melbourne's famous markets. Try the Queen Vic, Prahran or South Melbourne.

Find footwear in just the right shade of yellow in the city's laneways or the shopping strips of Prahran or Fitzroy.

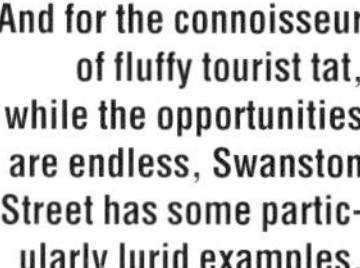

And for the connoisseur of fluffy tourist tat, while the opportunities are endless, Swanston Street has some particularly lurid examples.

46

SPORT

Whether it's Australian Rules football – the game invented in this city – or the nation's favourite horse race, or cricket at the historic MCG, or any of the international events the city has claimed as its own, Melburnians follow sport with a passionate enthusiasm

Sport and Melbourne are inextricably linked. There are two significant historical events that contributed to the city's phenomenal, almost pathological, passion for all things sporty. The first came way back in the 1850s, with the birth of Australian Rules football in parklands then known as Richmond Paddock (one theory is that it was possibly devised as a game to keep cricketers fit during the winter). The second occurred a century later, when Melbourne hosted the 1956 Olympics, whetting the appetite for international events and showcasing the Melbourne Cricket Ground (MCG; *see page 152*).

Jeff Kennett's reign as state premier in the 1990s saw a concerted push to satisfy that appetite and the formation of the Victorian Major Events Corporation, which helped to lure the Formula One Grand Prix away from Adelaide and won the right to stage the 2006 Commonwealth Games. This obsession was evident in the highly charged recapture of the Ashes from England at the end of that year; when tickets went on sale over six months in advance, cricket fans jammed phone lines and websites (thousands were left disappointed). Melbourne successfully bid for the 2007 World Swimming Championships, with the main events staged at Rod Laver Arena in a temporary pool imported from Spain. The championships cost an estimated A$81 million and used 6.1 million litres (1.3 million gallons) of water during the state's biggest drought on record. All for the sake of sport.

> *Some historians claim that Australian Rules football originated from an Aboriginal game called "marn-grook", in which an inflated possum or kangaroo skin was kicked around.*

LEFT: a trip to the footie is a quintessential Melbourne experience. **RIGHT:** be it cricket, rugby or soccer… support for the national team is always enthusiastic.

Aussie Rules footie

But let's start with footie, Melbourne's abiding obsession, as testified by the acres of newsprint and aeons of broadcasting during

the season. The first official match took place between Melbourne Grammar and Scotch College over three weekends in 1858, and the sport quickly became popular. For years it was a parochial activity, with the Victorian Football League the primary competition. This began to change in the 1980s with a series of mergers and relocations that led to the current AFL structure, in which six of the 16 teams are from other states.

The days when the September finals were dominated by Victorian teams are long gone. In fact, no Victorian club won the premiership for six years until Geelong's victory in 2007 – a statistic that worried the locals and caused much longing for the good old days. But regardless of whether Victorian clubs are involved, the Grand Final is always held at the MCG on the last Saturday in September.

The week-long build-up to the big day is huge, starting with the Brownlow Medal count on Monday, right through to the city parade of players on Friday. There's a plethora of breakfasts and lunches scheduled, and Federation Square is taken over all week by a flurry of AFL activities and bands. It's a similar story on the actual game-day, and it's well worth walking down past Birrarung Marr to the ground to get a feel for the colour of the occasion, regardless of whether you've got a ticket. In fact, getting tickets is difficult, even for club members. More than half the stadium is taken

> *Collingwood is the Manchester United or New York Yankees of Aussie Rules: it has a huge fan base, many of whom have only a tenuous link to the club, and everyone else hates them.*

THE NOVICE'S GUIDE TO AUSTRALIAN RULES

Bill Bryson refers to the "transfixing peculiarities" of Australian Rules. So for him, and others like him, here's the lowdown on footie and the AFL (Australian Football League).

- There are 16 clubs – 18 soon – and the top eight sides play-off in a finals series in September.
- Teams consist of 18 players with four interchanges (substitutes who can come on or off at any time).
- There are four goalposts at each end. If the ball is kicked through the two higher middle ones you score six points, but if it is touched, hits a post or goes through the two outer posts, teams score just one point.
- Games consist of four 20-minute quarters, but with time on for stoppages; these invariably last around 30 minutes.
- Players can dispose of the ball by kicking or by handballing, although the handpass requires a clenched fist, not an open hand.
- You can only run with the ball for 10 metres, and then you either have to kick, handball or bounce it.
- You can tackle around the waist, but if you push a player in the back or grab him too high or around the legs, you give away a free kick.
- If you catch (mark) the ball from an opposition kick, you can play on or go back and take your kick.
- If you want to fit in with the crowd, wear a club-coloured beanie and scarf and just yell "ball" every time a player is tackled.

up with AFL and MCC members, so scalpers have a field day marking up the prices on eBay and at the game from around A$130 a seat to A$500-plus. But if you miss out, don't panic. There are plenty of big screens around town. Practically every second household will have a Grand Final day BBQ with their friends.

There are other special occasions. The legendary Essendon coach Kevin Sheedy may have initially upset a few old diggers with his idea of playing traditional rivals Collingwood on the day of reverence for departed war heroes, but the Anzac Day clash between Victoria's two biggest clubs has quickly become one of the must-see games of the season. Crowds at the MCG have averaged in excess of 85,000 for at least a decade, and tickets for the game now sell out early in the week. It is a true blockbuster battle, played with passion and spirit, and the envy of the other 14 clubs.

But it doesn't demand a marquee occasion to lure thousands of locals to the footie. Every weekend during the season (March–September) there are a clutch of games at either the MCG or the Etihad Stadium in Docklands. Many an uninterested sports phobic has been swept along by the skill and grace of the players and the end-to-end quick-scoring nature of the contest. It's a true family game, too, with crowd trouble virtually unheard of and groups of fans proudly showing their colours, happily unsegregated from their rivals. Give it a go.

ABOVE LEFT: fans of Melbourne Victory soccer team.
ABOVE CENTRE: local rivalry: Richmond v St Kilda.
ABOVE: spectating at an AFL game at the MCG.

The Australian Open

Usually staged during the last two weeks of January, this tournament is the first Grand Slam event of the tennis calendar and is staged at Melbourne Park. Most of the big matches are scheduled for Rod Laver Arena or Vodafone Arena, but crowds sporting national warpaint also flock to outside courts and the big-screen beer garden. Attendance over the two weeks now comfortably tops half a million. Tickets go on sale in October: Centre Court sells out early, but you can buy ground passes that give you access to all outside courts on the day for around A$30.

The Australian Grand Prix

South Australians still complain about losing it, but the Grand Prix has become one of Melbourne's major iconic events since being

stolen from Adelaide's streets in 1995. Even the Albert Park resident groups who used to protest against its noisy existence have grudgingly come to accept that one weekend a year they have to wear earplugs in their living rooms. While the Melbourne GP initially pandered to rev-heads, it has become a major corporate party weekend, with the talking points split between which celebrities were spotted in your marquee and whether or not Ferrari won again. There's usually a big-name band performing, too.

Organisers claim that crowds for the four days total around 300,000. Tickets are expensive, most offering four-day packages. The date can vary, but usually it's the first or second event of the season and held in mid-March. There's also talk of it becoming a night race in the not-too-distant future, to tie in better with peak TV viewing in Europe – it has already been pushed back a couple of hours.

The Boxing Day Test

Victorians are also mightily proud of their cricket history. The Melbourne Cricket Club was formed in 1838 and hosted the first match between Victoria and New South Wales (1856) and the first Test between England and Australia (1877). The club has long held control of the MCG, and membership, which gives privileged access to MCG matches and events including football, can involve a 20-year wait. Most suburban and country ovals have a cricket wicket, and members of the national squad are now some of the highest-paid sportsmen in Australia – both signs of cricket's continuing appeal as a national sport.

While the Victorian Bushrangers play most weekends from October, with most home games at either the Junction Oval or the MCG, the sport really heats up with the Boxing Day Test at the MCG followed by a handful of one-day internationals and T20s in January. While the one-day matches may be more festive and rowdy, the purists have long cherished the Test as the main event. The tradition also includes arriving in time to see the first ball, although the switch to a 10.30am start still catches out

ABOVE LEFT: the Australian Open takes over the city in January... **TOP:** ...and the Grand Prix does the same in March. **ABOVE:** day/night cricket at the MCG.
ABOVE RIGHT: race-goers on Melbourne Cup Day, part of the Spring Racing Carnival.

a few diehards. In former days, doting wives would pack Christmas leftover turkey and ham sandwiches for their partner's lunch, but more recently the new grandstands have given rise to corporate boxes or lunches in the numerous dining rooms. On Boxing Day in 2006, a record crowd of 89,155 saw a dead rubber clash between Australia and England.

Soccer and rugby

After decades in which ethnic groups and teams restricted its development, association football has finally got its act together in Australia with a competitive national league. The nation's qualification for the 2006 World Cup finals in Germany and follow-up in South Africa in 2010 also gave the sport impetus. Although Sydney won the first A-League title, Melbourne Victory's second year set new levels of success, and large crowds forced games to switch to Telstra Dome from their initial home at Olympic Park. Victory now share the brand new AAMI Park with 2010 newcomers, Melbourne Heart.

The soccer season begins in late August and

THE SPRING RACING CARNIVAL

Back in the 1970s, horse racing was mainly the domain of bibulous male gamblers, the one exception being Ladies' Day (the Oaks, on the Thursday after Melbourne Cup Day). But racing has grown into one giant spring social, from the first Saturday in October right through to Sandown Cup Day in mid-November – two Saturdays after the Melbourne Cup. In what has been a promotional coup, racing authorities have cornered the female market, with a combination of fashion and champagne, leaving the horses as something of an afterthought. Crowds of women dressed to the nines now flock to the entire spring carnival. And they don't mind which course it is – Caulfield, Moonee Valley or Flemington – so long as one of their clan has access to the members' reserve or an impressive four-wheel drive strategically located in the car park.

The biggest event is still, of course, Melbourne Cup Day, on the first Tuesday in November. It's a public holiday in Victoria, and an unofficial one nationally, with extended lunches and Cup sweeps taking place from Noosa to Fremantle. Though if you want to see the best horses and great races, Derby Day (at Flemington the Saturday before Cup Day) has the gamut, with the nation's best sprinters and stayers on show in a multitude of events. In 2006 it attracted Flemington's biggest ever one-day crowd.

Racing ticks over during the rest of the year at the main tracks around the city. For a completely different atmosphere try a country race meeting, perhaps at a course used only once or twice a year, like the one in the shadow of Hanging Rock.

ends in February, thus avoiding much direct conflict with the AFL. The sport has also caught on at junior level, particularly with girls, and there is now a thriving Goalkick programme for beginners that challenges the AFL's Auskick kids' training programme in popularity.

With a sizeable Kiwi population in Melbourne, there has always been a following for rugby, both League and Union. Pitted against the AFL in the winter, however, Victoria's National Rugby League side, the Melbourne Storm, has struggled to glean large crowds. Even with a winning side in recent years, crowds have remained around the 10,000 mark at Olympic Park and, heavily tainted by a salary-cap scandal in 2010 that saw the team stripped of its trophies, the chances of filling the new stadium look slim.

Rugby Union has flared sporadically down south but the city now claims its first national Superleague side, so it may grow in stature.

The decline of basketball

The boom sport of the late 1980s has been forced to backtrack since then. At one stage, when legendary Australian player Andrew Gaze was at the peak of his crowd-drawing powers, there were five Victorian teams, and the major clashes were capable of filling the 15,000-seat Rod Laver Arena. Now, though, there is only one local side, the Melbourne Tigers, who play at the State Hockey and Netball Centre in Parkville, and around 3,000 spectators turn up. The National League season runs from September to February.

Swimming

The Melbourne Sports and Aquatic Centre *(see page 176)* may spawn new indoor champions, and there is also a booming recreational open-water beach-race circuit during the summer, with most events run by surf lifesaving clubs. Lorne's Pier to Pub, a 1.2km (¾-mile) swim in early January, is the best-known and supported. The 2007 World Swimming Championships took place at the Rod Laver Arena.

> *Yacht clubs abound around Port Phillip Bay, but there's little of Sydney's "How big's yours?" mentality. The Cock of the Bay, Melbourne to Launceston and Melbourne to Hobart are the big races, after Christmas.*

Athletics

Melbourne is not just a spectating city. Running trails are plentiful, with the Botanical Gardens (the Tan Track), Albert Park Lake and Princes Park circuits heavily frequented. There are also longer and tougher running trails for more serious runners at Ferny Creek, Lysterfield and Yarra Boulevard.

As yet, Melbourne does not have a fun run to rival the City to Surf in Sydney, but there are

signs that it soon will have, with the Run for the Kids, first established in 2006 and held the Sunday before Good Friday, attracting almost 30,000 entrants. The Melbourne Marathon, held on the first Sunday in October, is also very popular and nowadays finishes inside Melbourne's sporting mecca, the MCG.

Golf

The city takes great pride in its golf courses and the sandbelt strip from Brighton down to Dandenong is home to many of the finest links in the land, with their slick and true greens the envy of all curators. The finest is the Royal Melbourne, which opened for play in 1901, but Kingston Heath, Metropolitan, Huntingdale, Commonwealth, Victoria and Yarra Yarra all have their admirers. The more recent exclusive club, The Capital, designed by British Open champion Peter Thomson, is less accessible unless you bleed money.

Most private courses will admit interstate and overseas visitors who have a letter of introduction from their home course. For normal hackers, there are plenty of public golf courses not far from the CBD. The closest is in Albert Park, while Yarra Bend in Fairfield is one of the best. Public course green fees are around A$30 (£18.50) for 18 holes. ❑

FAR LEFT: Melbourne Heart vs Melbourne Victory at AAMI Park. **LEFT:** Melbourne Sports and Aquatic Centre. **TOP:** runners at the Tan. **ABOVE:** a round of golf at Apollo Bay. **ABOVE RIGHT:** the World Swimming Championships in Melbourne.

PEDAL POWER

There are two major cycling events on the calendar for recreational riders. Around the Bay in a Day takes place in late October and offers distances ranging from 50–250km (30–150 miles), while the Great Victorian Bike Ride is usually held in late November and can last for around nine days and 500+km (300+ miles). Professional events are staged at the Vodafone Arena, and the Herald Sun Tour runs in mid-October. Visitors can hire bikes from Vault Hire by the Yarra River under Federation Square and have access to a network of cycling trails, including 76km (47 miles) all the way along the Yarra to Warburton.

ARCHITECTURE

In just four decades, Melbourne, grew from a muddy village to become one of the world's great cities. The "Marvellous Melbourne" tag stuck in a manner that would make today's brand consultants green with envy. And it stuck because it summed up a remarkable achievement

The first ride on Melbourne's architectural roller-coaster reached its apogee in the 1880s and 1890s, before economic mayhem saw everyone returning rapidly earthwards. By then, the city centre was well-defined and the suburbs were beginning their inexorable spread. The character of that city still lives on today but filled out with the accretions of a century and, in a nod to symmetry, Melbourne saw another burst of adventurous building activity in the final years of the 20th century.

A Victorian treasure trove

In 1837, under the direction of the Governor of New South Wales, Sir Richard Bourke, and planner Robert Hoddle, central Melbourne was laid out on a grand grid of north–south and east–west streets, each a generous 30 metres (100ft) across. The unrelenting geometry of this plan reflected the attitude of these truly Victorian empire-builders to the landscape's physical contours – that is, Nature must yield to Man.

The Treasury Building of 1858–62 was immediately proclaimed the city's most elegant structure by local newspapers, a title that, in the opinion of many, it has yet to relinquish.

LEFT: art angles. Dramatic lines in the Ian Potter Centre at Federation Square. **RIGHT:** *Architectural Fragment* echoes the portico of the Victoria State Library.

This was an era that revelled in monumental public buildings, exuberantly ornate private villas and splendidly expansive parks and gardens. By the 1850s and 1860s, Melbourne could boast imposing public edifices such as the Treasury Building in Spring Street, the Royal Mint in William Street and the State Library in Swanston Street, all now recognised as among the world's finest examples of Victorian design.

The Treasury Building is generally acknowledged as the work of John James Clark, a 19-year-old junior draughtsman in the Department of Public Works, although its superb facade displays the work of the highly skilled European craftsmen drawn to Melbourne by the

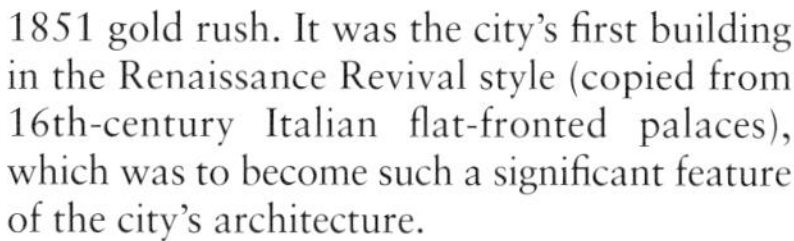

1851 gold rush. It was the city's first building in the Renaissance Revival style (copied from 16th-century Italian flat-fronted palaces), which was to become such a significant feature of the city's architecture.

However, while Melbourne's architectural aspirations were to recreate Renaissance Italy, its cultural priorities and yardsticks remained steadfastly British. The highest compliment that could be paid to Melbourne's Theatre Royal, built in 1842, was that one could see Italian opera "in a style worthy of the English metropolis itself". The Melbourne Club, opened in 1858, aspired to be worthy – both architecturally and ideologically – of a place in London's Pall Mall. Carlton, the suburb that included the site for Melbourne University, founded in 1853, was laid out using London's Bloomsbury as a model, with garden squares and streets of two- and three-storey terraced houses. Melbourne also proudly emulated British cities by expanding its suburbs as quickly as possible, with progress measured by the number of elegant mansions being built in the new wealthy enclaves of South Yarra, Toorak, Hawthorn and Kew. Here, the rich could achieve the Victorian ideal of *rus in urbe* (the countryside in the city) in the privacy of their own gardens.

> *Director of the Royal Botanic Gardens from 1874–1909, William Guilfoyle was responsible for creating a jewel hailed by Sir Arthur Conan Doyle as "absolutely the most beautiful place I have ever seen".*

But the wider population was not forgotten. Melbourne, like all the great cities of Victoria's empire, had to have expansive parks with bandstands and displays of rare and exotic horticultural specimens from all over the world. In the spirit of the age, a disused quarry was transformed into Fitzroy Gardens by

ABOVE LEFT: the Old Treasury Building.
TOP: Government House in the King's Domain.
ABOVE: lush greenery at the Royal Botanic Gardens.
ABOVE RIGHT: the Old Quad at the University of Melbourne. **FAR RIGHT:** cast-iron detailing in Powlett Street, East Melbourne.

James Sinclair, who had previously designed estates for the Russian nobility in the Crimea. Meanwhile, the landscape designer William Guilfoyle had transformed the former bed of a section of the Yarra into the Royal Botanic Gardens, now regarded as one of the world's finest examples of Victorian landscaping.

Building boom

By the 1880s, Melbourne was a mature and confident city. In the burgeoning suburbs, salesmen put an emphasis on style, laying on special trains and free champagne lunches for potential buyers. Building projects sprang up everywhere, with the number of dwellings almost doubling between 1880 (when there were 52,000) and 1890 (93,000). The city was booming and its celebrations of Queen Victoria's golden jubilee, in 1887, were marked, visitors noted, by "an enthusiasm not excelled in any part of the Empire".

INTERNATIONAL AMBITIONS

After the 1850s, Melburnians boasted that their city had everything that London or Paris could offer, except seas of slums. By 1880 and 1881, when the whole world brought its wares to Melbourne's first great International Exhibition, they could truly claim a reputation as a great world city. London's 1851 Great Exhibition had set the pattern for regular displays of homage to the Victorian ideal of industrial progress. When Melbourne's turn came, the city fathers were determined both to build a venue appropriate to the splendour of the occasion and to outdo Sydney, which had hastily thrown together Australia's first International Exhibition the previous year. The Royal Exhibition Buildings in Nicholson Street, Carlton and the surrounding Exhibition Gardens are the lasting result of these lofty ambitions.

The next year, the Victorian government spent £250,000 (10 times the original estimate) on the second great Melbourne International Exhibition, held to commemorate the centenary of British settlement in Australia. Over two million people visited.

The city felt that it had plenty to celebrate. On one day in late January of 1888, £2 million worth of stock was traded on the Melbourne Stock Exchange; the city had electric light, telephones, a well-established rail system and a new tramway network. Melburnians could also experience the novel sensation of riding in hydraulic lifts, a technological prerequisite for the multi-storey red-brick Gothic Revival delights of west Collins Street and the Grand Hotel (now the Windsor) in Spring Street, built for a staggering £110,000 and decorated for an equally extravagant £30,000.

Cast-iron style

The legacy of the four decades of prosperity between the discovery of the Victoria goldfields in 1851 and the end of the land boom in 1891 (which precipitated the great economic crash of 1892–3) was a truly extraordinary range of domestic architecture.

There was something for every taste, from the cool elegance of superb mansions such as Como, Illawarra and Government House, to the florid Italianate grandeur of houses such as Benvenuta in Drummond Street, Carlton, to the graceful uniformity of entire suburbs of terraced houses with their iron-laced verandas.

Labassa, in Manor Grove, Caulfield (open to the public once a month; tel: 9527 6295), is an outstanding example of the opulence of building in boom-time suburban Melbourne, with its mixture of Italianate structure and elaborate French Renaissance detailing. Designed by the German architect John Augustus Bernard Koch in 1890, Labassa was commissioned by Alexander Robertson, who had made his fortune through mining interests and the famous Cobb & Co. stagecoach line. Exterior delights include caryatids at the main entrance and sculpted female figures thought to be copied from the famous Villa Knoop in Bremen, Germany, and inside, the entrance hall has a superb stencilled and hand-painted ceiling.

Cast iron made in local foundries, along with stucco faces, urns and flowers, decorated the mansions of Toorak and South Yarra, as well as the modest workers' cottages of Fitzroy and Collingwood. Home-builders of the time could even buy cast-cement decoration (whether heads, fruit or flowers) off the shelf.

RIPPONLEA

National Trust-maintained Ripponlea, in Hotham Road, Elsternwick, is one of the last great Australian suburban properties from the Victorian era to remain intact, although most of its interior has undergone substantial renovation over the years.

It was designed by architects Reed and Barnes (of Exhibition Buildings fame) as a private Xanadu for merchant and MP Sir Frederick Sargood. It began as a 15-room house in 1868, but the house grew with Sir Frederick's family, ending up with 33 rooms by 1903. Later, a ballroom in the 1920s Grand Hotel style was added.

This polychrome brickwork mansion has a magnificent cast-iron and glass *porte cochère* for carriages depositing guests at the Sargoods' famous "at homes" and balls. The gardens are a paradise of conservatories, ferneries and orchards, and feature an ornamental lake. In 1938, work was carried out to reflect the more informal lifestyle of the time, and the original ballroom was removed to make way for a swimming pool.

By 1920, the Victorian styles were being condemned as symptomatic of a time when, as the 1926 *Australian Encyclopedia* put it, "taste was at a low ebb and cheap ornament popular". Yet the move away from the style had begun earlier. With the 1890s depression, the use of iron decreased, to be replaced by the terracotta and timber characteristic of Australian housing of the Edwardian era. This local adaptation of the Queen Anne style, tempered with Art Nouveau elements, produced the picturesque Australian phenomenon known as Federation.

Camberwell, Essendon, Elwood and St Kilda are full of fine examples of these red-brick, red-tiled fantasies, with their white-painted ornamental timberwork, candle-snuffer spires, octagonal towers, multiple chimneys and polygonal bay windows. The roof was the Federation house's crowning glory, with the architect's imagination the only limitation. Some decorative roof finials display dragons and other mythical beasts, others have Australian motifs: waratahs, gum nuts or kangaroos. Inside, the houses were as homely as their exteriors suggested, with window seats and Art Nouveau stained-glass windows.

ABOVE FAR LEFT: Federation-style house in Camberwell. **ABOVE LEFT:** house buyers put a premium on well-maintained Victorian terraces in the inner suburbs. **ABOVE:** the Melbourne Safe Deposit building in Queen Street is typical of the Gothic Revival style.

The Gothic movement

The international architectural movement known as the Gothic Revival, inspired by the medieval churches of Europe, did not hit Australia until just after the mid-19th century, a good 20 years after it flowered in England. In Melbourne, the style eventually produced many fine churches, such as St Patrick's Cathedral (1860) and St John's, Toorak (1861) – both designed by William Wardell – Wesley Church in Lonsdale Street and St Paul's Cathedral, the last example designed by the great British Gothic Revivalist, William Butterfield. The application of Gothic architecture in the commercial area, funded by land-boom money, has been immortalised in the gloriously exotic office buildings at the western end of Collins Street.

In 1882, William Wardell designed a superb Venetian-inspired Gothic bank and office building, now the ANZ Bank, on the corner of Queen

and Collins streets. It is the kind of building that, according to local architect Granville Wilson, "needs to be seen fronting a canal". It has a 20-metre by 18-metre (65ft by 60ft) banking chamber, with a 9-metre (30ft) hand-painted ceiling decorated in gold leaf. Next door, the former Stock Exchange Building (now also the ANZ), finished in 1890 at a cost of £200,000, is another Gothic extravaganza.

Newman College

A special building of note for architectural aficionados is Newman College (1915–18) at the University of Melbourne. Designed by American architects Walter Burley Griffin and Marion Mahony Griffin (designers of Canberra, Australia's national capital), who were living in Melbourne at the time, the college is a compositional treat. The domed dining room is capped by a *flèche* (spire) and a series of pinnacles, and the college's dramatically low-ceilinged cloister is a unique example of progressive modern architecture in early 20th-century Melbourne. For those especially interested in the work of the Griffins, every effort should be made to see their Expressionist ornamental plaster ceiling at the Capitol Theatre at 109–117 Swanston Street. Now owned by RMIT University, access to this modern-day Aladdin's cave is possible, but as it is a functioning lecture hall, permission is needed.

Modern developments

Griffin and Mahony were part of a wider American influence in Melbourne architecture in the first half of the 20th century. There are skyscrapers in the CBD that could be straight out of Chicago. The Stateside vernacular was appearing in domestic architecture, too, with internal open-planning, borrowed from American suburban styles, appearing in many of the bungalows that were the favoured form from around the 1920s.

Migration after World War II brought an influx of European flavours. But austerity put the brakes on extravagant building and design, except for a few blips such as the 1956 Olympics. The health of the economy always

ARCHITECTURAL HERITAGE

Exquisite pockets of Victorian housing survive all over the city, notably in South and East Melbourne, Fitzroy and Carlton. Architectural gems include Tasma Terrace (the headquarters of the National Trust) in Parliament Place, and terraces in Powlett Street, East Melbourne and St Vincent's Place, South Melbourne.

The best surviving expanse of terraced housing is at Parkville, to the north of Carlton, where the action of conservationists has stymied the worst excesses of well-meaning amateur renovators (and not-so-well-meaning developers who, in the 1960s, were trying to sell the idea of South Parkville as a slum in need of demolition).

impacts on the level of building activity and probably explains the first flush of city skyscrapers in the 1960s and the resurgence in high-profile public and private projects in the 1990s.

With many of Australia's leading architectural firms based here, it's not surprising that Melbourne is rich in modern architecture. Just driving in from the airport, you pass beneath the Constructivist-styled Melbourne Gateway, a giant yellow rod cantilevering over the freeway. The latticework laser-lit spire of the Victorian Arts Centre is not just a beacon for the impressive arts precinct below, but also a symbol of modern Melbourne.

FAR LEFT: soaring development at Southbank. **TOP:** a range of styles and eras in East Melbourne. **ABOVE:** the designers of the QV Centre have consciously referenced the city's laneways. **ABOVE RIGHT:** the Art Deco lines of the Freemasons Hospital.

A string of architectural developments have re-energised the city over recent years. Mitterrand-style building works began in the early 1990s with the Melbourne Central Shopping Centre. With 200 shops spread over two blocks, the futuristic \$1.2 billion complex was the brainchild of Japanese architectural firm Kisho Kurokawa. The shopping centre is built around an 1889 shot tower, itself enclosed by a 20-storey cone of glass. Melbourne Central has been stylishly revamped to become a premier shopping destination.

A very high-profile addition to the city is the internationally acclaimed Federation Square (2002). Located opposite Flinders Street Station, the \$220 million site is the city's new cultural heart and home to the NGV: Australia, ACMI (Australian Centre of the Moving Image) and SBS radio and TV, Australia's multicultural media network. Included in the development are restaurants, the city's main information centre in one of the development's glass "shards", and a glass winter-garden atrium – a 120-metre (130-yard) -long open-ended expanse that slices through the two major building complexes. Designed by LAB Architecture Studio with Bates Smart,

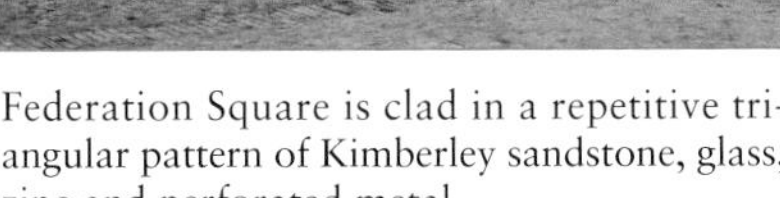

Federation Square is clad in a repetitive triangular pattern of Kimberley sandstone, glass, zinc and perforated metal.

Continuing the list of ambitious recent developments is the Etihad Stadium, a Docklands entertainment and sporting facility that opened in 2000, and the complete redevelopment of the world-famous Melbourne Cricket Ground (MCG), undertaken specially for Melbourne's hosting of the 2006 Commonwealth Games.

The Southgate retail and restaurant complex overlooking the Yarra opened in 1992, with 30 shops and about 40 cafés, bars and restaurants, kick-starting development along the river. The subsequent rejuvenation of the Southbank – including the Crown Casino and entertainment complex with its elegant ovoid tower, Freshwater Place, the Melbourne Exhibition Centre and the new Melbourne Convention Centre – has consolidated what has become one of the most exciting waterfront developments in Australia.

Block Party

Melbourne has many modern office towers worthy of note, among them Rialto Towers (Australia's tallest); 101 Collins Street, with arguably the city's most impressive foyer; the former BHP House at the corner of William and Bourke Streets, which uses black expressed steel on its exterior; the twin towers of Collins Place, designed by Harry Cobb of the US firm IM Pei (architects of the Louvre pyramid); the Telstra Tower in Exhibition Street, with its Piranesi-like interior: and Melbourne's first skyscraper, Orica House (formerly ICI House) in Nicholson Street, completed in 1958 and one of the first curtain-wall buildings in Australia (right).

Residential patterns

Out in the suburbs, the much-treasured Australian dream of a house on a quarter block (0.1 hectares) is beginning to change. Medium-density housing, where two houses are built in a space that originally encompassed one, is fast becoming the norm. This is due in part to economics and in part to government policy. Meanwhile, in the city centre, apartment housing has swamped the landscape, with real-estate pundits suggesting that the market for

FAR LEFT: Federation Square. **TOP LEFT:** footnotes. Paul Carter's word art in the stone paving at Federation Square. **ABOVE LEFT:** Heide Museum of Modern Art. **ABOVE:** the Southgate Centre on the Yarra River.

this type of luxury inner-city housing has reached saturation point.

By way of contrast, Melbourne also sports the Eureka Tower, completed in 2006 and the second-tallest apartment building in the world. Designed by architects Fender Katsalidis, Eureka, on Melbourne's Southbank, soars to 297 metres (975ft) and 92 storeys, with a publicly accessible skydeck that offers tremendous views across Melbourne. The adventurous can even venture into a glass-bottomed cube (a world first) that projects from the tower.

Modern public buildings

Melbourne positively glitters with shiny new public buildings. There are the new museums and galleries, whose architecture trumpets Victoria's proud self-description as "The State of Design". Denton Corker Marshall's Museum of Victoria (2000), to the north of the Royal Exhibition Building, is a triumph of steel and glass. The interior of the State Library of Victoria has had its wonderful picture galleries (full of paintings of early Melbourne) and great Reading Room refurbished. The 1960s bluestone palazzo of the NGV International on St Kilda Road was given a complete refurbishment by international gallery expert Mario Bellini, working with local architects Metier III. Up at the University of Melbourne, Nonda Katsalidis completed the abstract cubic forms of the Ian Potter Museum of Art, while in Sturt Street, South Melbourne, a sculptural tour de force has emerged in the rusted angular forms of the Australian Centre for Contemporary Art (ACCA). Out at suburban Bulleen, the Heide Museum of Modern Art has completed a major refurbishment of its existing galleries and added a new wing.

A recent addition to the growing list of architectural landmarks is Southern Cross Station, designed by the UK firm Grimshaw Architects in association with local architect Daryl Jackson. It is a fitting partner to the Edwardian Baroque pile of Flinders Street Station (1911), but lies at the other end of the city and beneath a wonderful undulating parasol of steel and glass. ❑

START SOMETHING
YARRA

Laneways
pages 126–7

Old Melbourne Gaol
page 107

Melbourne Museum
pages 159, 168–9

Federation Square
pages 97–100, 112–3

Melbourne Cricket Ground pages 151–2

CARLTON & FITZROY
main map 158

THE CITY EAST
main map 98

EAST OF THE CITY CENTRE
main map 154

THE CITY WEST
main map 116

SOUTHBANK
main map 130-1

DOMAIN & BOTANIC GARDENS
main map 140

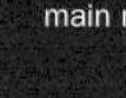

PRAHRAN
main map 190

SOUTH MELBOURNE
main map 172

ST KILDA
main map 180

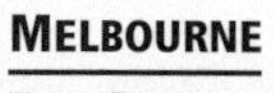

Melbourne Top Sights

Melbourne Zoo
page 165

Eureka Tower
page 132

National Gallery of Victoria pages 99, 130

Royal Botanic Gardens
pages 144–5

St Kilda
pages 179–87

PLACES

The cutaway map opposite shows the neighbourhoods of Melbourne as they have been divided up for this part of the book, in which the major attractions are cross-referenced by number to individual maps

The nucleus of Melbourne, the Central Business District (CBD), was laid out in the earliest days of settlement on a simple grid system perched on the north bank of the Yarra River, at the point where it was most convenient to unload the vessels bringing the city's new inhabitants from the other side of the world. The ships now berth elsewhere, but the grid has remained pretty well unchanged. It doesn't take long to get your bearings in what is a very comfortably sized city centre.

Move beyond the centre and the topography begins to be affected by minor undulations in the land, the curve of Hobsons Bay and Port Phillip Bay, and the increasing agitation of the river. Nonetheless, most of the main arteries of the metropolis stick to a 90-degree grid fanning out into the suburbs.

The Southbank area has been transformed by modern development, as has Docklands, on the western fringe of the CBD, which now contains high-rise apartment blocks, parkland and a sports stadium. The CBD is best tackled on foot, safe in the knowledge that Melbourne's famous tram system is there to take the strain if required. Usually, a café stop for the best coffee in Australia is enough to perk up the jaded visitor.

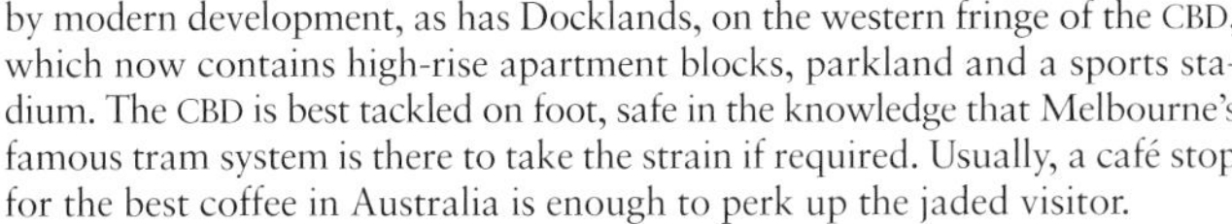

For immediate relief from the urban landscape, you only have to step out of the centre. Beyond the river, itself a place for leisure and relaxation, are roomy stretches of parkland that contribute so much to the character of Melbourne. Immediately to the south, the formal Alexandra and Victoria Gardens link to the more open spaces of the Kings Domain and the magnificently landscaped Royal Botanic Gardens. To the east, the green spaces are largely devoted to the arenas that service the local obsession with sport in all its guises. Then, as you move north beyond the city's first park – Fitzroy Gardens – Carlton Gardens offset the World Heritage-listed Royal Exhibition Building.

Just as important to Melbourne's identity, however – and not just for their formative influence on Dame Edna Everage – are the suburbs. Some of the more historic and colourful are featured on pages 157–95. ❑

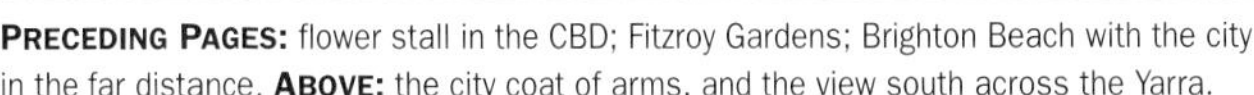

PRECEDING PAGES: flower stall in the CBD; Fitzroy Gardens; Brighton Beach with the city in the far distance. **ABOVE:** the city coat of arms, and the view south across the Yarra.

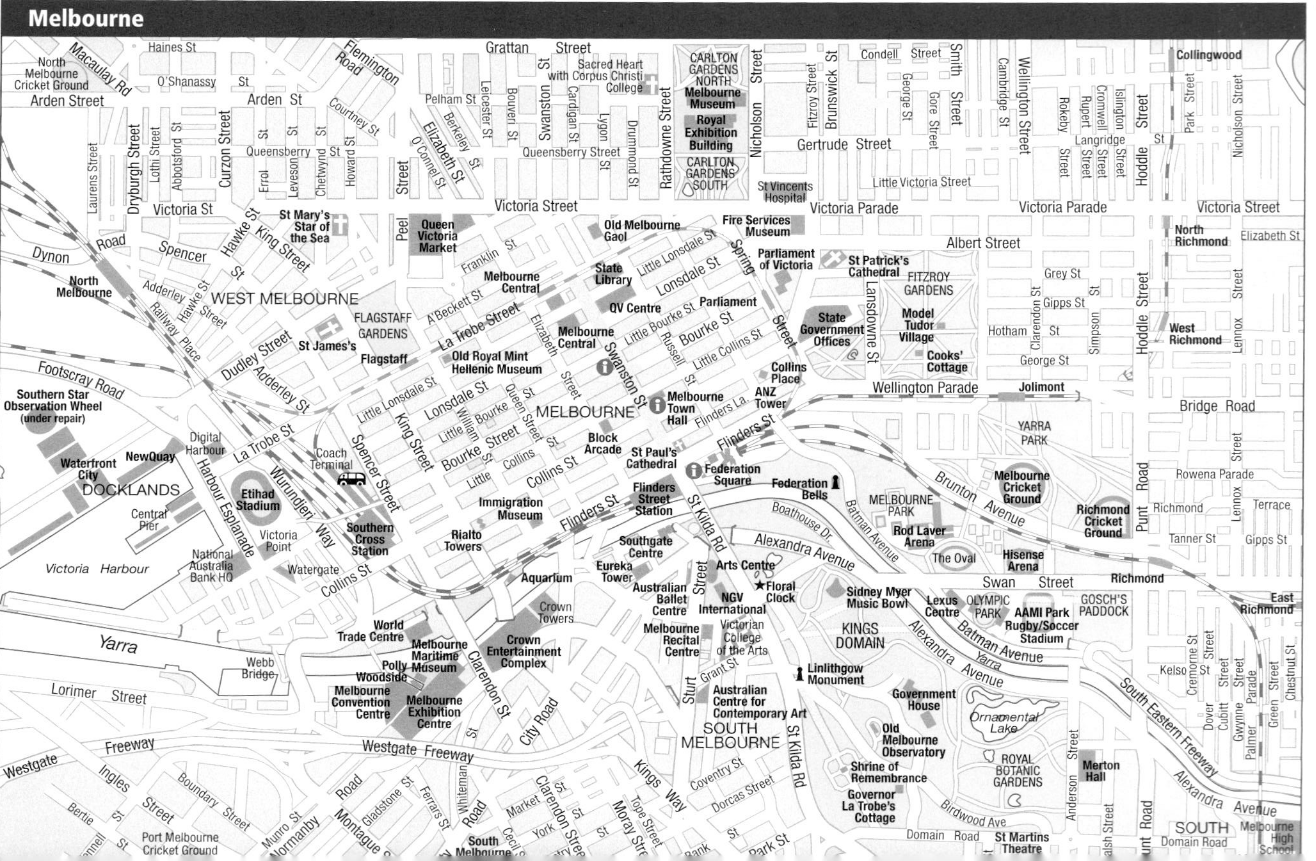
Melbourne
North Melbourne Cricket Ground
Macaulay Rd
Haines St
O'Shanassy St
Arden Street
Arden St
Flemington Road
Courtney St
Grattan Street
Pelham St
Leicester St
Bouverie St
Swanston St
Cardigan St
Lygon St
Drummond St
Sacred Heart with Corpus Christi College
Queensberry St
Queensberry Street
Berkeley St
Elizabeth St
O'Connel St
Laurens Street
Dryburgh Street
Lothian Street
Abbotsford St
Curzon Street
Errol St
Leveson St
Chetwynd St
Howard St
Victoria St
Victoria Street
Rathdowne Street
CARLTON GARDENS NORTH
Melbourne Museum
Royal Exhibition Building
CARLTON GARDENS SOUTH
Nicholson Street
Fitzroy Street
Brunswick St
Condell Street
Smith Street
George St
Gore Street
Gertrude Street
Cambridge St
Wellington Street
Rokeby Street
Rupert Street
Cromwell Street
Islington Street
Langridge St
Hoddle Street
Collingwood
Park Street
Nicholson Street
St Vincents Hospital
Little Victoria Street
Victoria Parade
Hawke St
King Street
St Mary's Star of the Sea
Peel Street
Queen Victoria Market
Old Melbourne Gaol
Fire Services Museum
Albert Street
North Richmond
Elizabeth St
Dynon Road
Spencer St
North Melbourne
Adderley St
Hawke St
Street
Railway Place
WEST MELBOURNE
Franklin St
Melbourne Central
State Library
Little Lonsdale St
Lonsdale St
Spring Street
Parliament of Victoria
St Patrick's Cathedral
FITZROY GARDENS
Lansdowne St
Grey St
Gipps St
Clarendon St
Simpson St
Hoddle Street
West Richmond
Lennox Street
FLAGSTAFF GARDENS
A'Beckett St
La Trobe Street
Elizabeth Street
QV Centre
Parliament
Little Bourke St
Bourke St
Russell St
State Government Offices
Model Tudor Village
Hotham St
George St
St James's
Flagstaff
Dudley Street
Adderley St
Old Royal Mint
Hellenic Museum
Melbourne Central
Swanston St
Little Collins St
Collins Place
Cooks' Cottage
Wellington Parade
Jolimont
Bridge Road
Footscray Road
Southern Star Observation Wheel (under repair)
Little Lonsdale St
Lonsdale St
Queen Street
MELBOURNE
Melbourne Town Hall
Flinders La.
ANZ Tower
Digital Harbour
La Trobe St
Coach Terminal
Spencer Street
King Street
Little William St
Bourke Street
Little Collins St
Collins St
Block Arcade
St Paul's Cathedral
Flinders St
YARRA PARK
Waterfront City
NewQuay
DOCKLANDS
Harbour Esplanade
Etihad Stadium
Wurundjeri Way
Immigration Museum
Federation Square
Federation Bells
Brunton Avenue
Melbourne Cricket Ground
Rowena Parade
Punt Road
Central Pier
Victoria Point
Southern Cross Station
Rialto Towers
Flinders St
Flinders Street Station
St Kilda Rd
Boathouse Dr.
Batman Avenue
MELBOURNE PARK
Rod Laver Arena
Richmond Cricket Ground
Richmond Terrace
Lennox Street
Tanner St
Gipps St
Victoria Harbour
National Australia Bank HQ
Watergate
Collins St
Aquarium
Southgate Centre
Eureka Tower
Alexandra Avenue
Arts Centre
Floral Clock
The Oval
Hisense Arena
Swan Street
Richmond
East Richmond
Crown Towers
Australian Ballet Centre
Street
NGV International
Sidney Myer Music Bowl
Lexus Centre
OLYMPIC PARK
AAMI Park Rugby/Soccer Stadium
GOSCH'S PADDOCK
Yarra
World Trade Centre
Melbourne Maritime
Polly Museum
Woodside
Crown Entertainment Complex
Melbourne Recital Centre
Victorian College of the Arts
KINGS DOMAIN
Batman Avenue
Yarra
Alexandra Avenue
Kelso St
Cremorne St
Webb Bridge
Lorimer Street
Melbourne Convention Centre
Melbourne Exhibition Centre
Clarendon St
City Road
Sturt Street
Grant St
Linlithgow Monument
Australian Centre for Contemporary Art
SOUTH MELBOURNE
Government House
Ornamental Lake
South Eastern Freeway
Dover Street
Cubitt Street
Gwynne Street
Palmer Parade
Green Street
Chestnut St
Westgate Freeway
Old Melbourne Observatory
Shrine of Remembrance
Governor La Trobe's Cottage
ROYAL BOTANIC GARDENS
Anderson Street
Merton Hall
Ingles Street
Boundary Street
Bertie St
Port Melbourne Cricket Ground
Munro St
Normanby
Montague
Road
Gladstone St
Ferrars St
Whiteman Road
South Melbourne
Market St
Cecil St
York St
Clarendon Street
Moray Street
Tope Street
Kings Way
Coventry St
Dorcas Street
Park St
Birdwood Ave
Domain Road
St Martins Theatre
Walsh Street
Punt Road
SOUTH
Domain Road
Alexandra Avenue
Melbourne High School

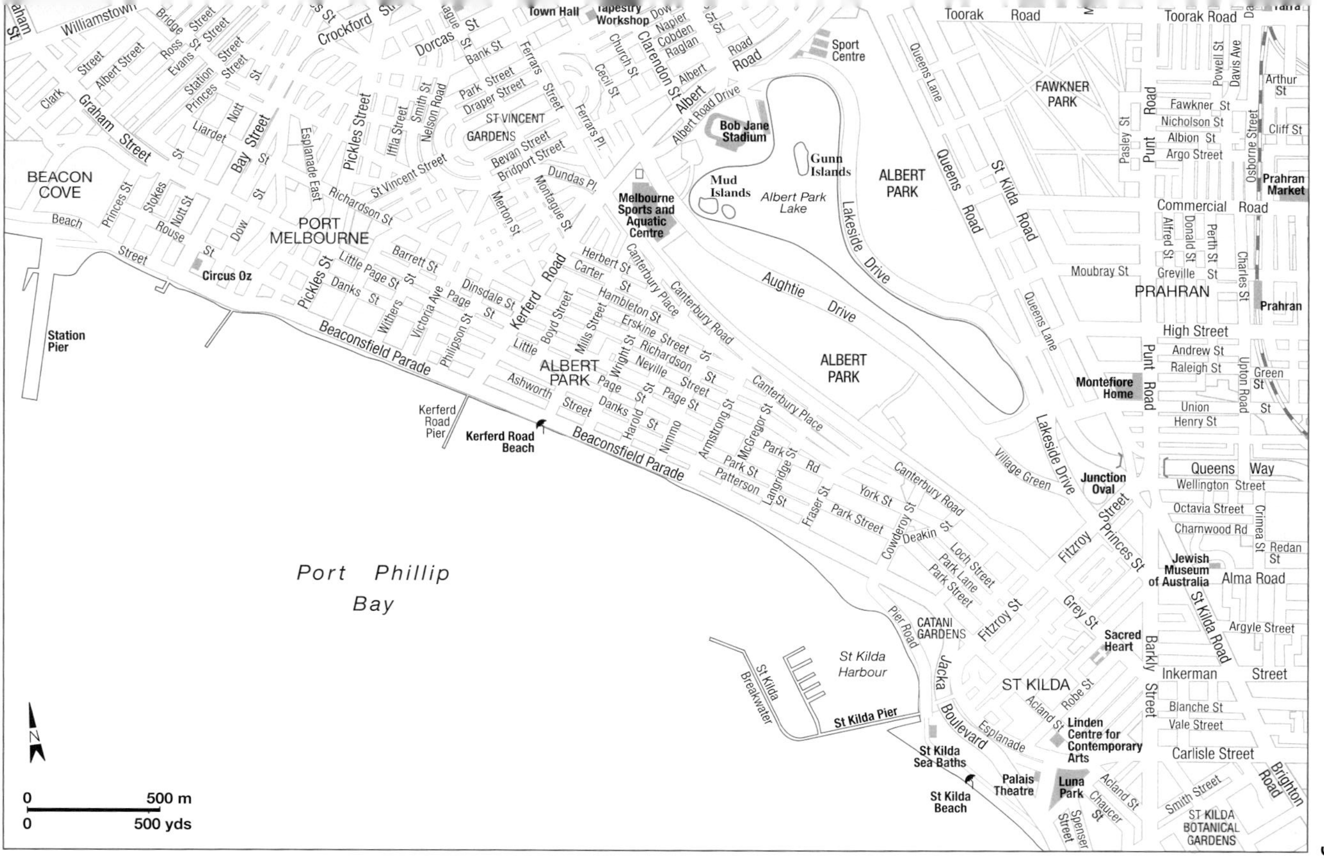
Williamstown
Bridge Street
Ross St
Evans St
Street
Crockford
Dorcas St
Bank St
Town Hall
Tapestry Workshop
Napier
Cobden
Raglan
Road
Toorak Road
Toorak Road
Sport Centre
Queens Lane
FAWKNER PARK
Powell St
Davis Ave
Arthur St
Fawkner St
Nicholson St
Albion St
Argo Street
Cliff St
Osborne Street
Pasley St
Punt Road
Prahran Market
Clark
Albert Street
Station
Princes
Nott
Liardet
Graham Street
Bay Street
Esplanade East
Pickles Street
Iffla Street
Smith St
Nelson Road
Park Street
Draper Street
Ferrars Street
Church St
Cecil St
Clarendon St
Albert
Albert Road Drive
Ferrars Pl.
ST VINCENT GARDENS
Bevan Street
Bridport Street
St Vincent Street
Dundas Pl.
Bob Jane Stadium
Gunn Islands
Mud Islands
Albert Park Lake
ALBERT PARK
Queens Road
St Kilda Road
BEACON COVE
Beach
Princes St
Stokes
Nott St
Rouse
Dow
Street
PORT MELBOURNE
Richardson St
Merton St
Montague St
Melbourne Sports and Aquatic Centre
Lakeside Drive
Commercial Road
Alfred St
Donald St
Perth St
Greville St
Charles St
Moubray St
PRAHRAN
Prahran
Circus Oz
Barrett St
Little Page St
Pickles St
Danks St
Withers
Victoria Ave
Page St
Dinsdale St
Kerferd Road
Herbert St
Carter St
Hambleton St
Canterbury Place
Canterbury Road
Aughtie Drive
Queens Lane
High Street
Andrew St
Raleigh St
Upton Road
Green St
Station Pier
Beaconsfield Parade
Philipson St
Little
Boyd Street
Mills Street
Erskine Street
Richardson St
Wright St
Neville Street
ALBERT PARK
Ashworth
Street
Page St
Danks St
Harold St
Page St
Nimmo
Armstrong St
McGregor St
Park Rd
Langridge St
Park St
Patterson
Montefiore Home
Union
Henry St
Kerferd Road Pier
Kerferd Road Beach
Beaconsfield Parade
Village Green
Junction Oval
Queens Way
Wellington Street
Octavia Street
Charnwood Rd
Crimea St
Redan St
York St
Fraser St
Park Street
Cowderoy St
Deakin St
Loch Street
Park Lane
Park Street
Fitzroy Street
Princes St
Jewish Museum of Australia
Alma Road
Port Phillip Bay
Pier Road
CATANI GARDENS
Fitzroy St
Grey St
Sacred Heart
St Kilda Road
Argyle Street
Barkly Street
Inkerman Street
St Kilda Harbour
St Kilda Breakwater
Jacka Boulevard
ST KILDA
Robe St
Acland St
Blanche St
Vale Street
St Kilda Pier
Esplanade
Linden Centre for Contemporary Arts
Carlisle Street
St Kilda Sea Baths
St Kilda Beach
Palais Theatre
Luna Park
Acland St
Chaucer St
Spenser Street
Smith Street
Brighton Road
ST KILDA BOTANICAL GARDENS
N
0
500 m
0
500 yds

or say
somethi
raging

Recommended Restaurants, Bars & Cafés on pages 108–11

THE CITY – EAST

Using the north–south dividing line of Swanston Street, the eastern side of the city centre rises gently up from Federation Square towards Parliament House. In between there's shopping, the "Paris end" of Collins Street, Chinatown and atmospheric laneways

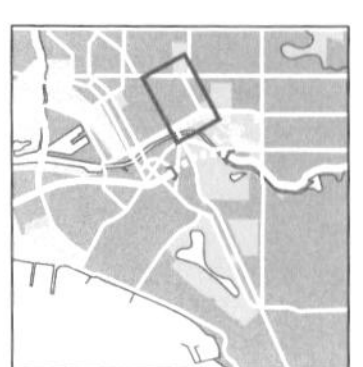

The centre of Melbourne is still defined by Robert Hoddle and his morning's work back in 1837. The boundaries of his grid enclose the Central Business District (CBD) of today and contain a raft of sights and attractions that clamour for a visitor's attention.

Swanston Street is the principal north–south artery and acts as a handy divider to break an exploration of the city centre into manageable chunks. Conceding the pragmatic nature of that split, there are, nevertheless, some generalisations that accurately characterise the eastern side of the CBD. By and large, it has a livelier nightlife than the western half, the political and administrative focus is here, as is the snooty end of Collins Street, and the frenetic delights of Chinatown take up several blocks.

FEDERATION SQUARE

www.fedsquare.com 9655 1900 daily 24 hours free City Circle, 1, 3, 5, 6, 8, 16, 64, 67, 70, 72, 75 Flinders Street

Melbourne's showpiece square was envisioned way back in the mid-19th century, when a pamphlet considered city planning: "In all the western nations, convenience has dictated the desirableness of forming an open space in the centre of the town, for public resort and traffic – whether called a Forum, a Piazza, a Platz or a Market Square... During the heats of summer and the rains of winter they equally offer an agreeable promenade, a pleasant rendezvous for the purposes of business and pleasure, a kind of public exchange for commerce, politics and news." The writer's conclusion was that

Main attractions

FEDERATION SQUARE
ST PAUL'S CATHEDRAL
MELBOURNE TOWN HALL
OLD TREASURY
PARLIAMENT OF VICTORIA
CHINATOWN
STATE LIBRARY OF VICTORIA
OLD MELBOURNE GAOL

LEFT: main piazza at Federation Square.
RIGHT: the free City Circle tram.

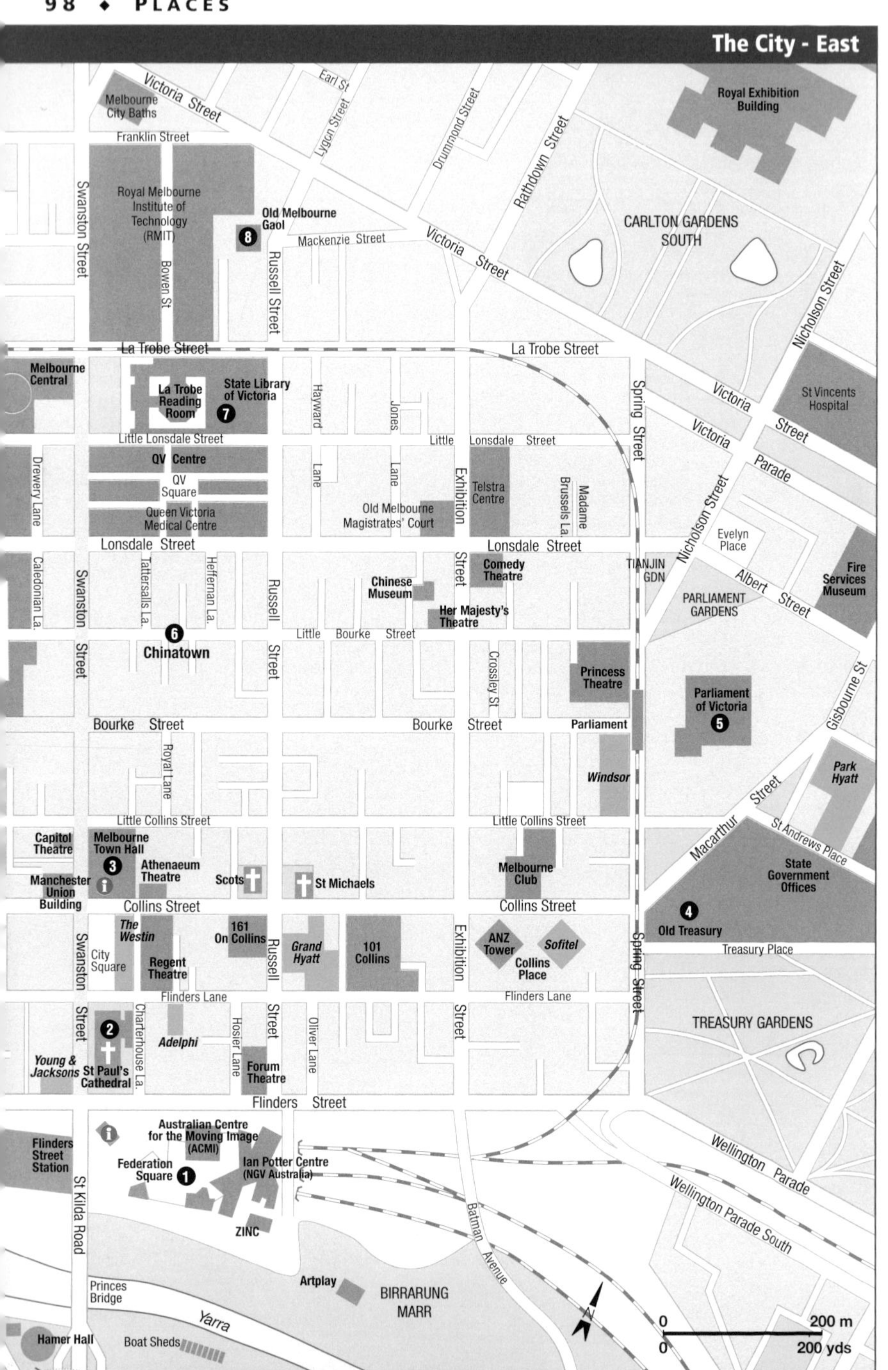
The City - East
Royal Exhibition Building
Melbourne City Baths
Victoria Street
Earl St
Lygon Street
Drummond Street
Rathdown Street
Franklin Street
Royal Melbourne Institute of Technology (RMIT)
Swanston Street
Bowen St
Old Melbourne Gaol
8
Mackenzie Street
Russell Street
Victoria Street
CARLTON GARDENS SOUTH
Nicholson Street
La Trobe Street
La Trobe Street
Melbourne Central
La Trobe Reading Room
State Library of Victoria
7
Hayward Lane
Jones Lane
Spring Street
Victoria Street
St Vincents Hospital
Victoria Parade
Little Lonsdale Street
Little Lonsdale Street
QV Centre
QV Square
Queen Victoria Medical Centre
Drewery Lane
Exhibition Street
Telstra Centre
Brussels La.
Madame
Old Melbourne Magistrates' Court
Nicholson Street
Evelyn Place
Lonsdale Street
Lonsdale Street
Comedy Theatre
TIANJIN GDN
Albert Street
Fire Services Museum
Caledonian La.
Tattersalls La.
Heffernan La.
Russell Street
Chinese Museum
Her Majesty's Theatre
PARLIAMENT GARDENS
6
Chinatown
Little Bourke Street
Crossley St
Princess Theatre
Parliament of Victoria
5
Gisbourne St
Bourke Street
Bourke Street
Parliament
Royal Lane
Windsor
Park Hyatt
Little Collins Street
Little Collins Street
Macarthur Street
St Andrews Place
Capitol Theatre
Melbourne Town Hall
3
Athenaeum Theatre
Manchester Unity Building
Scots
St Michaels
Melbourne Club
State Government Offices
4
Old Treasury
Collins Street
Collins Street
The Westin
161 On Collins
City Square
Regent Theatre
Grand Hyatt
101 Collins
ANZ Tower
Sofitel
Collins Place
Treasury Place
Flinders Lane
Flinders Lane
Charterhouse La.
Hosier Lane
Oliver Lane
2
Adelphi
TREASURY GARDENS
Young & Jacksons
St Paul's Cathedral
Forum Theatre
Flinders Street
Australian Centre for the Moving Image (ACMI)
Flinders Street Station
Federation Square
1
Ian Potter Centre (NGV Australia)
Wellington Parade
Wellington Parade South
St Kilda Road
ZINC
Batman Avenue
Artplay
BIRRARUNG MARR
Princes Bridge
Yarra
Hamer Hall
Boat Sheds
N
0
200 m
0
200 yds

TIP

Melbourne's excellent **Visitor Information Centre** (tel: 9658 9658; www.thatsmelbourne.com.au; daily 9am–6pm), at the northwest corner of Federation Square directly opposite Flinders Street Station, is well staffed with helpful people who know pretty much everything about the city. They can help with maps, brochures, accommodation, car hire and tours around the city or out into rural Victoria.

"Melbourne boasts no large central square" and (rather harshly) that "we have planned our metropolis as we should plan a coal pit".

It may have taken 150 years, but Melbourne finally has its great public space. Federation Square was a massive undertaking, both politically and technically, and there are still arguments over the merits of the design. It is, however, incontrovertibly the de facto public space and it has shifted the whole focus of the city. The idea was embraced by the locals from its opening in 2002, and Federation Square, with its modern architecture, museums and galleries, has become a major destination in itself. Tours from outside the Visitor Centre are conducted Mon–Sat at 2.30pm and take in all the main features (tel: 9928 0096).

Its location means that the Yarra River, which began to fulfil its potential as a cultural, business and sporting precinct in the 1990s, is now properly linked to the Central Business District (CBD). Being smack bang outside Flinders Street Station doesn't do it any harm either.

The sandstone piazza is surrounded by conceptual "shards", or "buildings" as we know them, which house a variety of galleries, performance spaces and restaurants. On the corner of Flinders and Swanston streets is the city's main **Visitor Information Centre** *(see margin, right)*.

The National Gallery of Victoria: Ian Potter Centre

www.ngv.vic.gov.au/ngvaustralia
8620 2222 Tue–Sun 10am–5pm free, except for special exhibitions City Circle, 1, 3, 5, 6, 8, 16, 64, 67, 72, 75 Flinders Street

Deeper into Federation Square, in one of the bigger shards, can be found one of the two main campuses of the National Gallery of Victoria (NGV): the **Ian Potter Centre**. This is a stunning building where, as you travel through its three levels, the walls and

ABOVE LEFT: the view eastwards over the city appears pixellated through the windows of the Ian Potter Centre. **BELOW:** Federation Square Guide.

Transit Lounge, the rooftop bar of the Transport Hotel on the southwestern corner of Federation Square, affords splendid views along the Yarra River and across the city. It's good for first-time visitors getting their bearings and old hands looking for a peaceful break from the urban bustle. The cocktails aren't to be sniffed at, either.

ABOVE RIGHT: The Forum from Exhibition Street. **BELOW:** eating out at the ACMI Lounge.

ceilings seem to be coming at you from all angles, offering a surprise around every corner. The building itself feels like a work of art, but this doesn't detract from the works within.

The first galleries' indigenous art ranges from traditional bark paintings to striking modern canvases. The classic colonials and Australian Impressionists come next, and, as you progress, the works become more contemporary. There are some magnificent exhibts here, and although it's tempting to offer highlights, everyone should find their own favourites. If you feel visually overloaded, the building continually offers spaces to rest, reflect or reconnect to the world outside.

Australian Centre for the Moving Image (ACMI)

www.acmi.net.au ☎ 8663 2200 ⏲ galleries: daily 10am–6pm, cinemas as advertised $ free, except for special exhibitions and cinema 🚊 same as for NGV: Ian Potter Centre

Where the NGV harnesses the energy of the building to support the art, the

Austalian Centre for the Moving Image (ACMI) has taken longer to settle into its space. Exhibition areas, cinemas, a video-games section and interactive video archive booths can all be discovered by visitors. Blockbuster exhibitions on topics such as Pixar animation or Tim Burton vie with arcane video installations. The permanent exhibition, Screen Worlds: The Story of Film, Television and Digital Culture, is a worthy centrepiece and can be sampled on optional guided tours (daily 11am, 2pm; free).

Another museum space opposite the entrance to ACMI failed as a standalone horse-racing attraction and its contents have now been absorbed into the sports museum at the MCG. At the time of writing its future was unclear.

For more on Federation Square see pages 112–13.

Flinders Street

The golden Moorish-style facade of the **Forum Theatre** can be seen peeking out on the corner of Flinders and Russell streets. The extravagant domes and arches, not to mention several dragons, suggest the *Arabian Nights*. However, the interior, while no less theatrical, affects a Roman theme, so the auditorium is dressed with columns, statues and classical arches, while a night sky twinkles overhead. It's used for bands or as a venue for one of the city's numerous annual festivals. Take a look up Hosier Lane for some typically artistic graffiti.

Recommended Restaurants, Bars & Cafés on pages 108–11

ST PAUL'S CATHEDRAL ❷

www.stpaulscathedral.org.au 9653 4333 Mon–Fri 8am–6pm, Sat 9am–4pm, Sun 7.30am–7pm, tours by appointment free City Circle, 1, 3, 5, 6, 8, 16, 64, 67, 72, 75 Flinders Street

Directly across Flinders Street from Fed Square (as you'll come to know it), St Paul's Cathedral now looks very smart after years of renovation work, which included shipping the organ all the way back to the UK for restoration work in 1990. You can enjoy the tessellated floor, stained glass and other features of designer William Butterfield's work (which is more than he ever did, since he resolutely refused to leave England to see it). The cathedral took 11 years to build and was completed in 1891.

Walk along Swanston Street past the statue of Matthew Flinders and pause on the far side of Flinders Lane. Walk up east and you should be able to see the glass base of the rooftop pool of the Adelphi Hotel as it stretches out over the street.

MELBOURNE TOWN HALL ❸

www.melbourne.vic.gov.au 9658 9658 tours Mon–Fri 11am, 1pm; booking essential free 1, 3, 5, 6, 8, 16, 31, 48, 64, 67, 72, 109, 112

Continue along Swanston Street past City Square and the statue of the explorers Burke and Wills *(see pages 27–8)*. The monolithic civic building on the next corner is Melbourne Town Hall, the embodiment of "Marvellous Melbourne" grandeur. Construction of the original building was delayed by labour shortages brought on by the gold rush, and it only lasted for a dozen or so years anyway before it was demolished to make way for something more in keeping with Melbourne's new-found status. This building was completed in 1870 and the portico added 17 years later.

For many years, its barn-like auditorium was the city's main concert hall, as well as being the venue for society balls, and from 2010–11 it reprises the role as Hamer Hall is renovated. It contains a substantial organ of more than 6,000 pipes, which now sees action on only a handful of occasions each year, for everything from the *Messiah* to contemporary jazz. You can see this and the neighbouring council chambers on a free tour. In April the building acts as the central venue for the International Comedy Festival.

Take a seat in the Council Chamber during a free tour of Melbourne Town Hall, or look at the innards of the organ in the main hall and hear it played on special occasions.

ABOVE LEFT: stained glass at St Paul's.
BELOW: Melbourne Town Hall.

It came within a whisker of being demolished after closing as a cinema in 1970, but the beautifully refurbished Regent Theatre lives on as a home for blockbuster theatre and dance.

ABOVE RIGHT: the Windsor Hotel.
BELOW: the atrium at 161 On Collins.

Collins Street

As you head east up Collins Street, the first buildings of note are theatres – the **Athenaeum** on the left and, opposite, the more salubrious **Regent Theatre.** Originally a 3,000-seat picture palace (from 1929), it was rebuilt after a fire in 1947 and renovated as a major receiving house, mainly for musicals, in 1996. Beneath it is the **Plaza** ballroom. You can go on a tour of both that also incorporates the Forum (tel: 9820 0239), but if you get the chance, do at least pop into the foyer to see the mock medieval decor.

Continuing up the hill past the **Scots Church,** built by Dame Nellie Melba's father in 1873, and **St Michaels Uniting Church** (built 1866), designer stores and exclusive boutiques start to proliferate. This is the "Paris end" of Collins Street, so-called after the first street café opened here in the 1950s. The extravagance also extends to some of the office blocks. The building **161 On Collins** has a monumental atrium scattered with glass blocks, and **101 Collins Street** (open weekdays) goes way over the top in its foyer, with abundant marble and gold leaf.

Altogether more restrained and very exclusive, the **Melbourne Club** doesn't even deign to put a sign on its sturdy mansion opposite Collins Place. **Grosvenor Chambers** at 9 Collins Street was once a suite of artists' studios, briefly home to the Australian Impressionist members of the "Heidelberg School". Contemporary art galleries thrive in Flinders Lane, parallel to Collins.

OLD TREASURY ❹

www.oldtreasurybuilding.org.au 9651 2233 Wed and Sun 10am–4pm free City Circle, 31, 48, 109, 112 Parliament

The classical assemblage facing the end of Collins Street is the Old Treasury, built in 1857 to plans by teenage architect J.J. Clark. Its prime purpose was as a repository for the product of the goldfields; the now empty vaults hold displays that trace the impact of gold on Melbourne while mixing in the story of the caretaker's family who lived here in the

Recommended Restaurants, Bars & Cafés on pages 108–11

early 20th century.

Stretching back behind the Treasury are many of the State Government's administrative buildings. Treasury Place is home to a handful of **Premiers' Statues,** part of an initiative by then Prime Minister, Jeff Kennett, to salute former premiers of Victoria who held office for 3,000 days or more. At that stage he was probably not anticipating his own political demise after 2,571 days in the "unlosable" election of 1999.

Walk north up Spring Street for more attractive stacks of stone. The **Windsor Hotel** on the left was built in 1883 and is a throwback to the days of grand colonial hotels. Since then it has accommodated the great and the good, along with several politicians.

PARLIAMENT OF VICTORIA 5

www.parliament.vic.gov.au 9651 8911 tours Mon–Fri 9.30, 10.30, 11.30am, 1.30, 2.30, 3.45pm free City Circle, 31, 48, 109, 112 Parliament

Across the road, in a commanding position looking down Bourke Street, sits the Parliament of Victoria. Its bulk and elevation make it hard to understand how rioters thought they could storm the place in 1860.

The two chambers, in keeping with the Westminster system, were home to the Commonwealth Parliament from 1901 until it was relocated to Canberra in 1927. Tours are available when the house is in recess; if it is sitting, take your chances in the public gallery.

“*The buildings at the eastern end of Bourke Street house... spiritualists, doll-doctors, employment agencies, theosophists, tattooists, and the ravaged and crazy-eyed teachers of elocution, tap-dancing, Pelmanism, zither-playing, Writing for Profit, conjuring tricks and artificial flower-making.*”

Hal Porter looks at life in Melbourne in 1937

BELOW LEFT: Scots Church. **BELOW:** Albert Dunstan, one of four premiers to serve 3,000 days.

As well as Victorian archival treasures, the Old Treasury Building in Spring Street also contains the Victorian Marriage Registry.

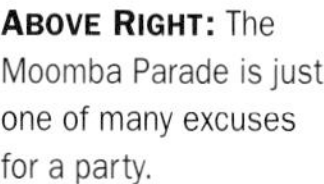

ABOVE RIGHT: The Moomba Parade is just one of many excuses for a party.
BELOW RIGHT: Parliament House.

Spring Street to Exhibition Street

Across Spring Street, the **Princess Theatre** has been operating since 1857. It has its requisite ghost, too – actor Frederick Baker, known as Federici, who died of a heart attack on stage in 1888.

Pass the rather bleak **Tianjin Garden** on your right and turn left down Lonsdale Street. Look out for the entrance to Madame Brussels Lane on the right next to the Department of Human Services Building. It's named after a notorious madam (the Lane, that is) who ran a brothel near here. Continue along the Lane, round a dogleg, and discover some of the few remaining cottages of the area known as "Little Lon" *(see panel, below)*.

Return to Lonsdale Street and continue to the traffic lights, then turn left into Exhibition Street past the **Comedy Theatre** (1928) and **Her Majesty's**, built in 1886 – but with a 1938 interior.

CHINATOWN 6

The ornamental arch at the end of Little Bourke Street announces that you are entering Chinatown. Chinese immigrants and their descendants have occupied this area since the 1850s gold-rush days. Initially only a few stayed in the city, but as

Little Lon

While in the latter decades of the 19th century Melbourne's elite were "doing the block" in fashionable Collins Street, the city's seamier side was to be found in the back lanes off Little Lonsdale Street. It was a quarter of poor artisans and migrant labourers, and developed a reputation for crime and prostitution; Madame Brussels had run a brothel there since 1876. With disquiet being voiced in the community, some of the Spring Street parliamentarians became unstinting in their fact-finding missions; indeed, in 1891 the Parliament's ceremonial mace was reputed to have been mislaid in one of the establishments. In the 1980s, an archaeological excavation of the district enabled historians to appreciate the realities of everyday life in a neighbourhood whose inhabitants were all too easily characterised as "low life". Artefacts from the dig are now on display in the Melbourne Museum and in the Human Services Building in Lonsdale Street.

Recommended Restaurants, Bars & Cafés on pages 108–11

the alluvial gold ran out, many moved back to Melbourne, and the enclave consolidated its economic status through market gardening, furniture-making and laundries. Visitors today will find aromatic shops packed with goods from floor to ceiling, a great array of restaurants and the Chinese Museum.

Chinese Museum

22 Cohen Place; www.chinesemuseum.com.au 9662 2888 daily 10am–5pm charge 86, 95, 96

Founded in 1985 and refurbished 25 years later, this museum covers the history of the Chinese in Australia and is very good on domestic detail and ritual. The centrepiece is the massive Millennium Chinese dragon, which parades through the streets each year during Chinese New Year and Moomba festivals. The journey from China to the goldfields, complete with rolling ship, is another highlight (*see margin, right*). This is the visitor centre for Chinatown and a self-guided walking tour is available.

Along the lanes

In an area packed with narrow alleys and laneways, continue down Little Bourke Street, across Russell Street, and into **Heffernan Lane**. It runs along the side of the old Methodist Mission with its painted "commit no nuisance" signs, an attempt to prevent the deposit of substances both steaming and pungent. Signs, indeed, are the point of this detour. Innocent-looking municipal parking placards carry ever more surreal and delightful homilies or commands. Lonsdale Street at the far end is the historic **Greek Precinct**, although the evidence for this is confined to a few restaurants.

The QV Centre

Across Lonsdale Street, the new **QV Centre** dominates the entire block, although the red-brick **Queen Victoria Medical Centre** has survived. In 1896 a group of female doctors set up a shilling fund to raise money for the first hospital to be run by and for women: 68,000 shillings later, they started building and operated successfully in William Street before moving to this site in 1946.

Downstairs in the Chinese Museum visitors can follow the journey of a migrant from Hong Kong to the goldfields. Feel a ship roll beneath your feet, travel down a mine, and look inside a temple where this figure awaits.

BELOW: life in a cookshop in the goldfields is recreated at the Chinese Museum.

> *I like to lean back on my chair and stare up at the dome. I think in a room like that, you can have the audacity to understand the universe. You can come at knowledge from any angle.*
>
> Playwright Hannie Rayson comes up with another alternative to actually putting pen to paper in the La Trobe Reading Room

ABOVE RIGHT: the La Trobe Reading Room in the State Library. **BELOW:** there is no shortage of upmarket specialist stores in the QV Centre. **BELOW RIGHT:** Queen Victoria Medical Centre.

The QV Centre is one of the largest recent building projects, a mixture of office, residential and retail spaces that echoes the laneways in its design. The passages could do with more character, but the enticement of chocolatiers and other specialist outlets helps people to overcome any aesthetic angst. The internal plaza, QV Square, has yet to establish an identity, but it's still early days.

STATE LIBRARY OF VICTORIA ❼

www.slv.vic.gov.au 8664 7000 Mon–Thur 10am–9pm, Fri–Sun 10am–6pm free 1, 3, 5, 6, 8, 16, 24, 30, 64, 67, 72 Melbourne Central

Next stop up Swanston Street is yet another testament to "Marvellous Melbourne". The State Library of Victoria has occupied this spot since 1853, when it was merely Melbourne Public Library, but it grew to include museum space and the National Gallery of Victoria. Joseph Reed's building is now back to just being a library, and is thriving after a major renovation that culminated in the reopening of the spectacular domed **La Trobe Reading Room**, modelled on the old British Library in London. Visitors are free to wander and will find some stimulating exhibition areas capable of detaining them for hours. The galleries rising around the reading room contain two permanent displays: one on the history of books, the other on the development of Victoria. The latter includes the original body armour worn by Ned Kelly, as opposed to the copies on show in other sites.

Experimedia is a technological playground, with video games and opportunities to experiment with computer-generated music, images and videos. Kids have an area, too. The adjoining café gives you a chance to take it all in.

The RMIT and the City Baths

Continue up Swanston Street to gawp at the distinctive architectural styles of the **Royal Melbourne Institute of Technology** (RMIT). The sculptural green-and-purple frontage

to Storey Hall is supposed to reflect the Irish and suffragette backgrounds of the users of the original building. Along the street, the brightly coloured and textured finish on Building 8 is purely aesthetic.

At the next junction is more Victoriana in the shape of the distinctive **Melbourne City Baths**, where you can swim, have a game of squash or a session in the gym, then wind down in the sauna or spa (tel: 9663 5888; Mon–Thur 6am–10pm, Fri 6am–8pm, Sat–Sun 8am–6pm; charge).

OLD MELBOURNE GAOL 8

Russell Street; www.oldmelbournegaol.com.au 8663 7228 daily 9.30am–5pm charge City Circle, 24, 30 200, 201, 203, 207, 340, 350, 684 train: Melbourne Central

Just one block of the original 19th-century prison remains, but it's more than enough to provide an insight into the conditions that malefactors faced. More than 130 prisoners were hanged here, including Ned Kelly, a copy of whose helmet and armour can be found alongside the gallows, and whose death mask is in one of the cells. His story is enacted in free performances of *Such a Life* every Saturday at 12.30pm and 2pm.

The dingy building is grimly atmospheric as it is, but if you want more, consider a tour by candlelight (Hangman's Night Tours; tel: 13 28 49; Mon, Wed, Fri, Sat 7.30pm, summer 8.30pm; charge) or the monthly overnight ghost hunt (tickets: 13 28 49; www.ticketek.com.au).

Turn right on to Russell Street and admire the sweeping Art Deco lines of the former **Victoria Police Headquarters**, still with its radio mast. The building was the object of an attack by car bombers in 1986.

Finally, the **Old Melbourne Magistrates' Court**, on the corner with La Trobe Street, is a jumble of medieval turrets, battlements and rough-cut sandstone that in 1911 represented the Federation Romanesque style – a style that unsurprisingly failed to catch on in Australia. From here you can take the City Circle tram back to Fed Square. ❑

The Old Melbourne Gaol was last used as a place of detention during World War II for soldiers who went AWOL, or overdid the R&R, or both. Modern-day visitors can themselves be detained in the Police Watch House as an add-on to a Gaol visit.

BELOW: go on a guided night tour at the Gaol.

BEST RESTAURANTS, BARS AND CAFÉS

Restaurants

Prices for a three-course dinner per person with a half-bottle of house wine:
$ = under A$60
$$ = A$60–90
$$$ = A$90–120
$$$$ = over A$120

Arintji Café Bar

Federation Square, City. 9663 9900 L & D daily **$$** [p311, D3]
At this smart, flexible eatery on Federation Square's popular piazza you can snack or dine on clever continent-hopping food that leans towards modern Asian flavours.

Bar Lourinha

37 Little Collins Street, City. 9663 7890 L Mon–Fri, D Mon–Sat **$** [p311, E2]
Perch on a bar stool and work through a list of 20 or more tapas-style dishes inspired by the kitchens of Spain and Portugal. Lively noise levels and interesting wine keep the mood jolly.

Becco

11–25 Crossley Street, City. 9663 3000 L & D Mon–Sat **$$$** [p311, D2]
This buzzy, stylish Italian restaurant tucked down a lane is one of Melbourne's most favoured places for its food, service and the gloomily glamorous bar with its own menu.

Bistrot d'Orsay

184 Collins Street, City. 9654 6498 B, L & D Mon–Sat **$$** [p311, D2]
A Parisian bistrot atmosphere, a menu that encompasses France and the Mediterranean, and close proximity to the Regent and Athenaeum theatres gives d'Orsay a sophisticated, relaxed vibe.

Bottega

74 Bourke Street, City. 9654 2252 L Mon–Fri, D Mon–Sat **$$$** [p311, D2]
A good-looking Italian restaurant where style and comfort combine in a satisfyingly blended package. Expert service and an interesting wine list add the finishing touches.

Cecconi's Cantina

61 Flinders Lane, City. 9663 0222 B & L Mon–Fri, D Mon–Sat **$$$** [p311, E2]
With the large, open kitchen as its dramatic centrepiece and a dark-hued basement location, Cecconi's has the atmospherics down pat. Pricey Italian food ranges from the sublime to the competent.

Chocolate Buddha

Federation Square, City. 9654 5688 L & D daily **$$** [p311, D3]
Communal tables, Japanese decor and splendid views of Federation Square's piazza provide a suitably buzzy background to a menu full of noodle soups, sushi and other tasty Japanese snacks.

Coda Bar and Restaurant

141 Flinders Lane, City. 9650 3155 L & D daily **$$$** [p311, D3]
A relative newcomer, this bold Asian and French mix demands attention, even without the oh-so-trendy surroundings.

Comme Kitchen

7 Alfred Place, City. 9631 4000 B & L Mon–Fri, D Mon–Sat **$$$** [p311, D2]
Tucked at the back of a beautifully renovated Victorian building, Comme Kitchen serves skilfully cooked French and Spanish dishes that sit well with a smart, similarly representative wine list.

Cookie

Level 1, 252 Swanston Street, City. 9663 7660 L & D daily **$$** [p311, C2]
Some go to Cookie just for the excellent cocktails and encyclopaedic wine and beer lists, but down one end of the cavernous space is a modern Thai restaurant dishing up simple, inventive, exciting food.

Cumulus Inc.

45 Flinders Lane, City. 9650 1445 B, L & D daily **$$$** [p311, E2]
As no bookings are taken, it's pot luck whether you get in but it soon becomes apparent what all the fuss is about: perfect snapshots of cutting-edge local cooking.

European

161 Spring Street, City. 9654 0811 B, L & D daily **$$** [p311, E1]

LEFT: Mod Oz food taps into styles of cuisine from around the globe.

An all-European wine list, reliably tasty European bistro favourites, excellent coffee, wood-panelled dining room and 3am closing time have made European one of Melbourne's favourite dining venues.

ezard

187 Flinders Lane, City. 9639 6811 L Mon–Fri, D Mon–Sat **$$$$** [p311, D3]
The low-lit sleek sophistication of this basement restaurant gives no clue to the masterful cooking and huge flavours based on the cuisines of Southeast Asia that come bounding, sculpturally plated, from the kitchen.

Felt

Hotel Lindrum, 26 Flinders Street, City. 9668 1111 B & D daily **$$** [p311, E2]
Located in the small, chic dining room of the small, chic Hotel Lindrum, Felt combines a warm, intimate atmosphere and suitably personable service with a menu of often adventurous modern European cooking.

Flower Drum

17 Market Lane, City. 9662 3655 L Mon–Sat, D daily **$$$** [p311, D2]
Once considered the pinnacle of dining in Melbourne, this Cantonese restaurant may have slipped a little in recent years but still offers fine Chinese food, expert service and an undeniable sense of occasion.

Gingerboy

27–29 Crossley Street, City. 9662 4200 L Mon–Fri, D Mon–Sat **$$** [p311, D2]
Southeast Asian hawker food gets a designer makeover, complete with excellent cocktails and a wine list of Old and New World labels that harmonise well with the abundant hot, spicy, fishy and tangy flavours.

Grossi Florentino

80 Bourke Street, City. 9662 1811 B, L & D Mon–Sat **$$$$** [p311, D2]
This Melbourne Italian institution is three businesses in one, the grand and expensive upstairs restaurant, the '60s-glamorous Grill and the stylishly bohemian Cellar Bar. Three choices offering a win-win (win) situation.

Idea Fine Food and Wine

146–148 Little Bourke Street, City. 9663 8829 L & D daily **$** [p311, D2]
It may not look much from the outside, but this Chinatown restaurant offers pared-back contemporary design, modern Asian food and a lengthy wine list full of interesting and well-priced labels.

Il Bacaro

168–170 Little Collins Street, City. 9654 6778 L & D Mon–Sat **$$$** [p311, D2]
With its sexy Italian good looks, flirtatious Italian staff and skilfully cooked modern versions of classic Italian dishes, il Bacaro has remained a perennial favourite on the Melbourne dining scene.

Il Solito Posto

Basement, 113 Collins Street (enter from George Parade), City. 9654 4466 B, L & D Mon–Sat **$$$** [p311, D2]
Packed to the rafters with city workers during lunch, this laneway Italian restaurant is less frenetic at night, with a more relaxed pace at which to appreciate excellent ingredients, simply cooked.

The Italian

101 Collins Street, City. 9654 9499 L Mon–Fri, D Mon–Sat **$$$** [p311, E2]
After relocating to glittering new premises, The Italian still deftly straddles the old and the new, dishing up rustic Italian cooking with thoroughly modern service and attention to detail.

Izakaya Den

118–20 Russell Street, City. 9654 2977 D Tue–Sat, L Mon–Fri Dec pre-Christmas **$$$$** [p311, D2]
Informal – there are no bookings – Japanese bar with food that's so much more. Enjoy finely honed morsels in ultra-cool surroundings.

Kenzan

Lower Level, Collins Place, 45 Collins Street, City. 9654 8933 L Mon–Fri, D Mon–Sat **$$** [p311, E2]
One of the first Japanese restaurants in Melbourne, Kenzan has remained among the best. Sushi and sashimi are excellent, the specials list always interesting and the service spot on.

The Kitchen Cat

Basement, 115–117 Collins Street, City. 1 300 799 415 L & D Mon–Sat **$$$** [p311, D2]
Antipodean offspring of Jamie Oliver's Fifteen in the UK, Melbourne's Kitchen Cat has the same charitable underpinning combined with simple Mediterranean food, an exemplary wine list, sharp service and a chic basement location.

Kri Kri Mezethopoleion

39–41 Little Bourke Street, City. 9639 3444 L Tue–Fri, D Mon–Sat **$$** [p311, D1]
Focusing on mezedes – lots of small dishes that form a meal – this hospitable Greek restaurant eschews blue-and-white clichés for honest flavours and authentic cooking.

Kuni's

56 Little Bourke Street, City. 9663 7243 L Mon–Fri, D Mon–Sat **$$** [p311, D1]
Consistently good Japanese food arrives from both the sushi bar and the kitchen of this simply

furnished and meticulously maintained long-stayer. Tempura and sashimi mix with less common fare.

Longrain
40–44 Little Bourke Street, City. 9671 3151 L Fri, D daily **$$** [p311, D1]
This is the Melbourne outpost of the modern-Thai Sydney original and is a similarly exciting and stimulating place to eat, not just for the vibrant flavours but for cocktails, cool tunes and undeniable, if rowdy, buzz.

MoMo
Lower Plaza Level, Grand Hyatt Hotel, 123 Collins Street, City. 9650 0660 D Tue–Sat, L Mon–Fri Dec pre-Christmas **$$$$** [p311, D2]
Greg Malouf is one of Melbourne's star chefs and demonstrates why with his Middle Eastern-nuanced menu that is both deft and delicate.

MoVida
1 Hosier Lane, City. 9663 3038 L & D daily **$$** [p311, D3]
It's essential to book ahead at this popular and acclaimed Spanish joint that dishes up authentic tapas to go with its sherry.

Nihonbashi Zen
87 Little Bourke Street, City. 9639 7050 L Tue–Fri, D Tue–Sun **$$** [p311, D2]
This pint-sized Japanese restaurant located in a basement in Chinatown serves up quality staples alongside its speciality, *kushiyaki*, a southern Japanese cooking style of grilling vegetables, meat and seafood.

Nudel Bar
76 Bourke Street, City. 9662 9100 L & D Mon–Sat **$** [p311, D2]
Noodles in all their many forms – from Malaysian laksa to Hungarian spatzli – are Nudel Bar's *raison d'être*, dished up in generous portions in an edgily designed building.

The Press Club
72 Flinders Street, City. 9677 9677 L Sun–Fri, D daily **$$$** [p311, E2]
Greek hospitality and chic city style blend beautifully in this relaxed, elegant restaurant.

Punch Lane
43 Little Bourke Street, City. 9639 4944 L Mon–Fri, D daily **$$** [p311, D1–2]
The interior may feel like a private club, but the robustly flavoured Spanish-influenced food, generous list of wine by the glass, and mouth-watering cheese selection can be enjoyed by all.

Sarti
6 Russell Place, City. 9639 7822 L Mon–Fri, D Mon–Sat **$$** [p311, D2]
Worth a visit for its skilfully cooked Italian food and decently priced wine list alone, Sarti also boasts an excellent outdoor terrace, the perfect place for an aperitif on a warm summer evening.

Shoya
25 Market Lane, City. 9650 0848 L Mon–Sat, D daily **$$** [p311, D2]
There is something for everyone in this four-storey Japanese joint – karaoke rooms, barbecue tables, slick bar, sushi bar and traditional dining areas. The service is erratic, the food regularly sublime.

Society
23 Bourke Street, City. 9639 2544 B, L & D Mon–Sat **$$** [p311, D2]
Eighty years old in 2012, Society continues to attract a crowd, especially after a makeover that has preserved its best features. Tasty, homespun Italian food.

Supper Inn
15 Celestial Avenue, City. 9663 4759 D daily **$** [p311, D2]
This always-crowded late-night institution combines no-frills decor and abrupt service with wonderful Cantonese food.

Prices for a three-course dinner per person with a half bottle of house wine:
$ = under A$60
$$ = A$60–90
$$$ = A$90–120
$$$$ = over A$120

Taxi Dining Room
Level 1, Transport Hotel, Federation Square, City. 9654 8808 L & D daily **$$$** [p311, D3]
Fabulous views from the soaring glass-walled dining room, a head-spinning list of wine and skilfully cooked European and Japanese food.

Verge
1 Flinders Lane, City. 9639 9500 L & D Mon–Sat **$$$** [p311, E2]
The edgy modern decor, including a "glass box" dining room overlooking the Fitzroy Gardens, echoes the modernity of the Japanese-influenced menu here.

Yu-u
137 Flinders Lane, City. 9639 7073 L Mon–Fri, D daily **$** [p311, D2–3]
A serene basement Japanese place, where most of the seating is in comfortable armchairs around a concrete bar behind which traditionally garbed chefs work their magic over smoky yakatori grills.

ABOVE: Japanese restaurants are plentiful in the city.

Bars and Cafés

Breadwell
135 Flinders Lane, City. [p311, D3]
Good, honest, hearty food (yes, they do bread well) served in a buzzy, cluttered and slightly eccentric environment.

City Wine Shop
159 Spring Street, City. [p311, E1–2]
Bottle shop and bar stylishly meld at this popular city watering hole, where you can snack and drink before buying a bottle to take home.

Double Happiness
21 Liverpool Street, City. [p311, D2]
Cocktails with Asian ingredients, hidden nooks and crannies and a kitsch Mao theme make sense of the name.

Gin Palace
10 Russell Place, City. [p311, D2]
Martinis rule at this plush brocade-and-silk joint, but you might also want to try the chocolate fondue with strawberries.

Izakaya Chuji
165 Lonsdale Street, City. [p311, D2]
Packed full of students, this remarkably cheap, no-frills Japanese restaurant makes up in generosity what it lacks in finesse.

Lily Blacks
12–18 Meyers Place, City. [p311, E2]
Potted palms, smartly attired waiters and beautifully constructed cocktails make this feel like a Depression-era speakeasy.

Madame Brussels
Level 3, 59–63 Bourke Street, City. [p311, D2]
AstroTurf and garden furniture inside, a huge balcony with skyscraper views outside, and good wine and cocktails to keep you happy.

Melbourne Supper Club
Level 1, 161 Spring Street, City. [p311, E1]
The bar of choice for night owls combines leather couches, waiter service and brilliant wine until the wee hours of every morning.

The Mess Hall
51 Bourke Street, City. [p311, D2]
Pared-back good looks, great coffee, friendly attitude and interesting food make this a café for discerning eaters.

Meyers Place
20 Meyers Place, City. [p311, E1]
The bar that started Melbourne's laneway trend, Meyers Place still looks great, with its recycled timber and dimly lit split-levels.

Misty
3–5 Hosier Lane, City. [p311, D3]
Down a laneway near Federation Square, Misty keeps its cool with good beer, great tunes and a fashionable yet friendly attitude.

Mr Tulk
State Library, 328 Swanston Street (enter from La Trobe Street), City. [p311, C1]
The State Library's café is a light-filled, book-themed place that serves tasty food and good coffee.

Pellegrini's Espresso Bar
66 Bourke Street, City. [p311, D2]
Pellegrini's has been serving espresso and pasta since 1954. The well-preserved style is worth a visit in itself.

Spice Market
Beaney Lane (off Russell Street), City. [p311, D2]
A bar/lounge/club that melds decorative styles from along the Spice Route to create an over-the-top triumph. Great bar food.

Three Below
3 City Square, Swanston Street, City. [p311, D3]
An atmospheric concrete-and-timber cave at the back of the City Square, Three Below mixes quality alcohol and bar food with understated cool.

The Toff In Town
2nd Floor, Curtin House, 252 Swanston Street, City. [p311, C2]
Turn left out of the lift and you get the Carriage Bar with its private booths; turn right and you enter an atmospheric live-music venue. Both are recommended.

Transit Lounge Garden
Level 2, Transport Hotel, Federation Square, City. [p311, D3]
Perched on the top of the Transport Hotel, this late-night supper club has an outdoor terrace, lengthy wine list and live entertainment.

Transport Public Bar
Ground Level, Transport Hotel, Federation Square, City. [p311, D3]
An often-raucous modern pub with myriad seating options, river views and a huge range of beer.

Federation Square

In the relatively short time since it opened in 2002, "Fed Square" has become Melbourne's defining public space. Now it's hard to imagine the city without it

The basis of the design concept for Federation Square – or at least the cladding on the buildings – is the triangle. This one is split into five constituent parts, which give it the flexibility to wrap its way around the jagged irregular surfaces. It comes in stone, glass, zinc and dramatic conflations of all three to create what we now know to be a "fractal facade". But it's what's inside that concerns most visitors. The National Gallery of Australia: Ian Potter Centre has an interior even more extravagant than the exterior, and a collection of works that easily holds its own in the surroundings. The Australian Centre for the Moving Image (ACMI) is at the cutting edge of cinema and video art, and the Visitor Information Centre, the Edge auditorium and the Atrium complete the package. Fed Square tours delve beneath the surface.

The essentials

corner of Flinders and Swanston streets; www.fedsquare.com
9655 1900
tours Mon–Sat 2pm
free, charge for tours
City Circle, 1, 3, 5, 6, 8, 16, 64, 67, 70, 72, 75
Flinders Street

Below: the Atrium is home to a weekly book market (Sat 11am–5pm), as well as regular wine tasting sessions and displays of fine art and photography. Or you can simply sit back with a coffee and cake.

ABOVE: the sandstone for the surface of the square was specially selected from a quarry in Western Australia and has been cut unevenly to deter skateboarders and cyclists. Oh well…

BELOW: Transport Hotel is the place for a beer or two, but there are several other cafés and restaurants catering to different tastes.

STAGE AND SCREEN

The stage at the foot of the Square is used for all types of open performances and presentations, from big-name rock acts to Cirque du Soleil to welcoming victorious Melbourne sporting teams. Thousands can be drawn to big-ticket occasions, especially if sport is involved. The giant screen above the stage is often used to relay major contests, and there were times during the Socceroos' progress through the 2006 World Cup when, even in the small hours of the morning, the Square's crowd limit was reached and hundreds had to be turned away. In 2010 a bigger arena by the river had to be found. It has now reached the point where there is usually something happening or about to happen in the Square, and a traveller through Flinders Street Station with a few minutes to spare might as well pop over the road to investigate. Even if there's nothing immediately occurring, admission to the NGV Australia collection is free, so why not sample the art?

ABOVE: the Melbourne Jazz Festival is but one of the many international events that make use of the Fed Square stage for free public performances.

24
DECEMBER
Sidney
Myer Music Bowl
FLINDERS STREET STATION
PAKENHAM and CRANBOURNE LINES
FRANKSTON LINE
SANDRINGHAM LINE
WILLIAMSTOWN LINE
ALTONA LINE
ST ALBANS LINE
BROADMEADOWS LINE
LINE
LINE

Recommended Restaurants, Bars & Cafés on pages 124–5

THE CITY – WEST

The main shopping district, the banking and finance centre, the legal precinct and the most famous market in Australia can all be found in the city centre to the west of Swanston Street

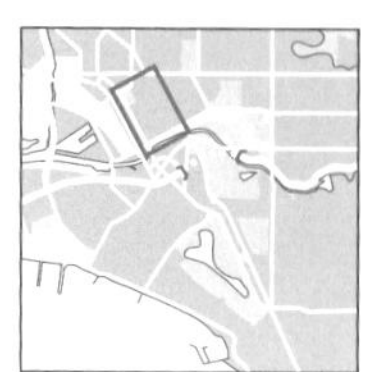

Immediately west of Swanston Street, Melbourne's main downtown shopping area features bulky department stores jostling with intimate laneway boutiques. West of Elizabeth Street, the impression is of a more serious metropolis, where the buildings are austere and unswerving in their dedication to business, banking and the law. The landmarks are there to be ticked off, but a lot of the character of this part of the city comes from the hidden treasures and quiet details to be found down its lanes and alleys.

FLINDERS STREET STATION ❶

The starting point is under the clocks, as it has been for Melburnians for years. Before Fed Square, this was *the* meeting place, indeed *Under the Clocks* is one of the best-known songs by seminal Melbourne band Weddings Parties Anything. The clocks in question are above the main entrance to Flinders Street Station, the iconic centre of Melbourne's rail system. The great yellow facade, the long red-brick and yellow-render aspect along Flinders Street, the tower visible from the south side of the river – all make this Melbourne's best-known and, by many, best-loved building. It was built in 1910, but has that sense of colonial certitude that could have come from 50 years earlier. Some have even suggested that it was intended for an Indian city but the plans got sent here from London by mistake. Fanciful it may be, but you can see how it gained currency.

Across the road is another landmark. During World War II there was a documented instance of prisoners

Main attractions

- FLINDERS STREET STATION
- THE BLOCK ARCADE
- BOURKE STREET MALL
- MELBOURNE CENTRAL
- IMMIGRATION MUSEUM
- FLAGSTAFF GARDENS
- QUEEN VICTORIA MARKET

LEFT: the meeting place under the clocks at the entrance to Flinders Street Station.
RIGHT: the old Rialto Hotel from Flinders Lane, with the Rialto Towers behind.

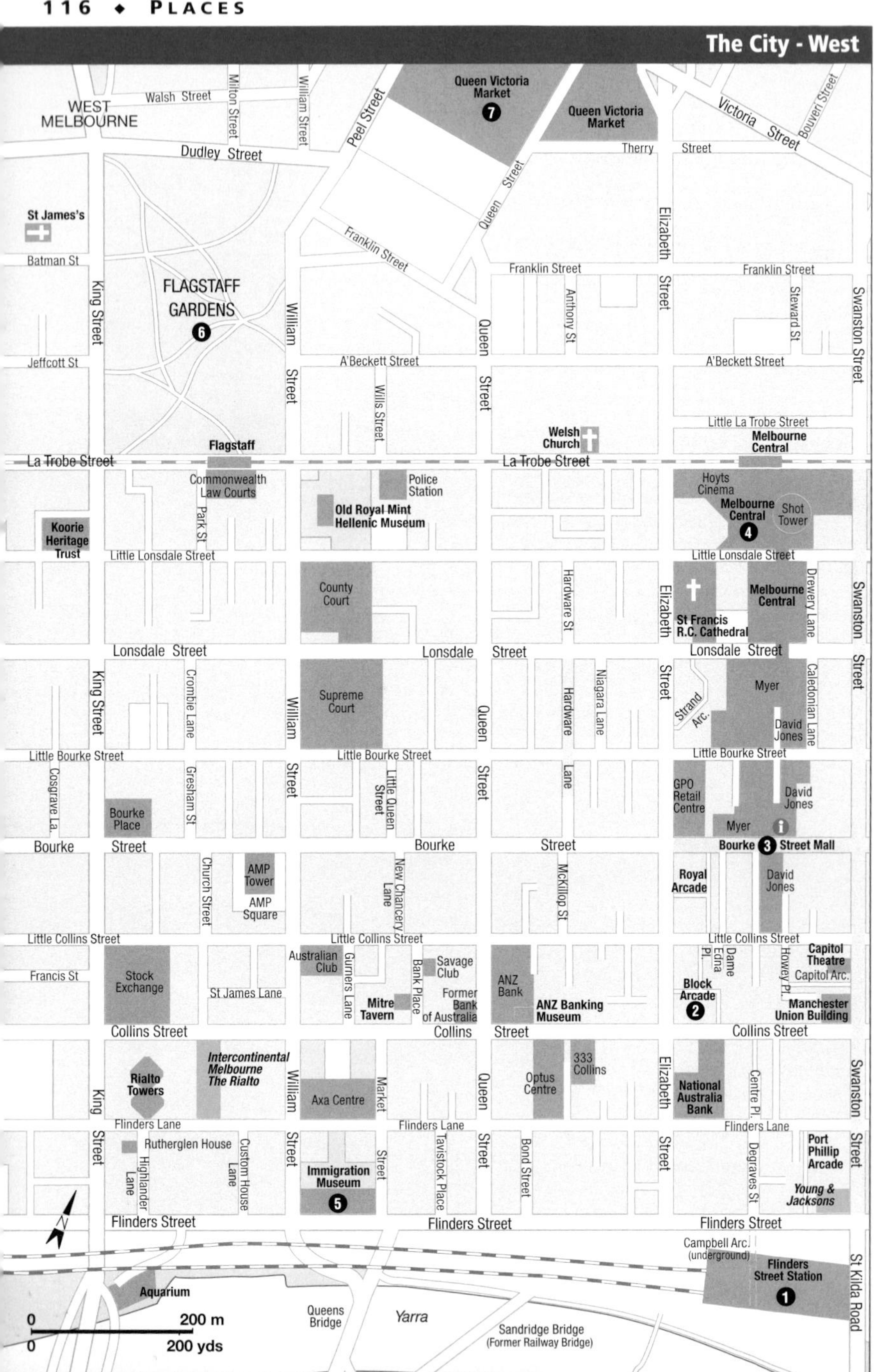
The City - West
Queen Victoria Market 7
Queen Victoria Market
WEST MELBOURNE
Walsh Street
Milton Street
William Street
Peel Street
Dudley Street
Therry Street
Victoria Street
Bouverie Street
St James's
Batman St
FLAGSTAFF GARDENS 6
King Street
Jeffcott St
Franklin Street
Queen Street
Elizabeth Street
Anthony St
Steward St
Swanston Street
A'Beckett Street
Wills Street
Little La Trobe Street
Welsh Church
Melbourne Central
Flagstaff
La Trobe Street
Commonwealth Law Courts
Police Station
Old Royal Mint Hellenic Museum
Hoyts Cinema
Melbourne Central 4
Shot Tower
Koorie Heritage Trust
Park St
Little Lonsdale Street
County Court
Hardware St
St Francis R.C. Cathedral
Melbourne Central
Drewery Lane
Lonsdale Street
Crombie Lane
Supreme Court
Hardware Lane
Niagara Lane
Strand Arc.
Myer
David Jones
Caledonian Lane
Little Bourke Street
Cosgrave La.
Gresham St
Little Queen Street
GPO Retail Centre
Myer
David Jones
Bourke Place
Bourke Street
Church Street
AMP Tower
AMP Square
New Chancery Lane
McKillop St
Bourke 3 Street Mall
Royal Arcade
David Jones
Little Collins Street
Francis St
Stock Exchange
St James Lane
Australian Club
Gurners Lane
Savage Club
Bank Place
Mitre Tavern
Former Bank of Australia
ANZ Bank
ANZ Banking Museum
Edna Pl.
Dame
Howey Pl.
Capitol Theatre
Capitol Arc.
Block Arcade 2
Manchester Union Building
Collins Street
Rialto Towers
Intercontinental Melbourne The Rialto
Axa Centre
Market Street
Optus Centre
333 Collins
National Australia Bank
Centre Pl.
Flinders Lane
Rutherglen House
Highlander Lane
Custom House Lane
Immigration Museum 5
Tavistock Place
Bond Street
Degraves St
Port Phillip Arcade
Young & Jacksons
Flinders Street
Campbell Arc. (underground)
Flinders Street Station 1
St Kilda Road
Aquarium
Queens Bridge
Yarra
Sandridge Bridge (Former Railway Bridge)
0 200 m
0 200 yds
N

Recommended Restaurants, Bars & Cafés on pages 124–5

of the Japanese testing the bona fides of a new arrival to their camp who claimed to be from Melbourne by asking him where he'd find Chloe. The answer is at **Young & Jackson's Hotel**. *Chloé* is upstairs, an 1875 painting of a nude by French artist Jules Lefebvre, and it has been a talking point at the pub since 1909.

Around Flinders Street

Flinders Street is a muddle of cheap cafés and travel agents as you head westwards. **Port Phillip Arcade** isn't the prettiest of its type, but typical in its arcane outlets. You'll find Max Stern & Co., a huge stamp and coin dealer, acting as agents for first issues from countries round the globe. Across the passage there's a cake-decorating specialist, although that is to undersell "Australia's largest retailer of cake-decorating equipment".

Steps lead down from Flinders Street to **Campbell Arcade**, a subway to the station, very 1950s in style and now an ad hoc art gallery. **Degraves Street** has some smart cafés, with tables spilling out across the width of the road and the blue tiles of the Spanish-style Majorca Building giving a touch of colour at the end. It's the beginning of a sweep through a maze of fascinating alleys.

Across Flinders Lane, **Centre Place** has more cafés, but they are smaller and rougher round the edges. It's grungy all of a sudden, with graffiti everywhere, but look closely and there's art to it. Much of it is stencil work, and there are some real touches of talent and wit if you're prepared to look for them. Nothing escapes the paint, so every rubbish bin, lamp-post and junction box gets sprayed.

The covered **Centre Way** is the haunt of small boutiques, and then you are into Collins Street. Cross over, turn left and stride through the doors beyond the mosaic pavement that proclaims "The Block".

THE BLOCK ARCADE ❷

This is one of the most attractive and certainly the most salubrious of all the arcades in the city. When it opened in 1893, its architect, Don Askew, acknowledged the influence of Milan's *Galleria Vittorio Emanuele II*. While not on the same scale as Milan's, or with quite the history, it has the mosaic floor, the glass roof on ornamental iron supports and the luxuriously appointed up-market shops. In not having a branch of McDonald's, it may even be ahead. Instead there are the

With its pink tiled walls and black granite columns, Campbell Arcade – also known as the Degraves Street Subway – is a little piece of the 1950s (it opened in 1955) in central Melbourne. You half expect to find a jukebox amongst the art.

ABOVE LEFT: Centre Place. **BELOW:** tourists photographing graffiti in Centre Place.

Three Businessmen Who Brought Their Own Lunch *is just one of many public sculptures and installations that stem from a commitment by Melbourne City Council to spend 1 percent of its capital works budget on art.*

ABOVE RIGHT: the Royal Arcade. **BELOW:** the Shot Tower inside Melbourne Central.

Hopetoun Tearooms packed with ladies who shop, as they have been for over a century. Wheel round and into **Block Place**, where the cafés and bars get livelier.

In Little Collins Street detour briefly to the right in an act of obeisance to Melbourne nobility. Browns Place was quietly wiped from the map in 2006 and rechristened **Dame Edna Place**. Barry Humphries' greatest creation was acknowledged with silver stars set into the roadway and a ring of lights round the street sign.

Across the road from the Block Arcade, the **Royal Arcade** of 1869 is the oldest in town and best known for the somewhat garish figures of **Gog and Magog**, who strike the hour as required and spend the rest of the time glaring down at bemused children from their stance above the entry.

BOURKE STREET MALL ❸

The Royal Arcade leads to Bourke Street Mall, the epicentre of Melbourne's shopping. To the right are the flagship department stores of Myer and David Jones, and to the left the former General Post Office is

now rebranded as **GPO**. Behind the pillars the building has been opened up to house some very pricey stores. Exit at the far end, head through mundane Strand Arcade into Myer and continue through the store northward, perhaps on the second floor, where bridges ease you over Lonsdale and Little Lonsdale streets into Melbourne Central.

MELBOURNE CENTRAL ❹

This substantial shopping complex was built around an 1889 shot tower (where molten lead was poured through sieves at the top and, as it fell, solidified into lead shot), which now sits in the middle of a multistorey atrium; a small, free museum can be found in the RM Williams store. The centre had a spell in the doldrums until a refurbishment in 2006 revived it, helped in no small part by the introduction of a huge Hoyts Cinema multiplex. Over 300 stores are flourishing here.

Hardware Lane

Exit to Elizabeth Street, go west on Little Lonsdale Street and left into **Hardware Lane**. This is a buzzing, three-block strand of cafés and shops, some of them occupying old warehouses like **Dynon's Building**. It's not as funky as some of the lanes, but it's developing fast.

Turn left on Bourke Street and pass along the Mall all the way back to Swanston Street, dodging the giant *Public Purse* and keeping an

eye on the facades above the shop windows. There's some fine detail, especially above the David Jones store, which mostly goes unnoticed.

Four giant weathervanes mark the corners of the junction with Swanston Street. On the southwest corner, *Three Businessmen Who Brought Their Own Lunch* represent city founding fathers Batman, Hoddle and Swanston, all of whom apparently resembled Mr Bean.

Sample a block of Swanston Street's brashness and turn right into Little Collins Street as far as Howey Place. It's now quite nondescript, but deserves mention for what *used* to be here: Cole's Book Arcade *(see margin, right)*. Towards the end of Harvey Place on the left, an unprepossessing entrance opens up into the **Capitol Arcade** before leading back to Swanston Street *(see panel below)*.

Part of the Union

Just a few steps down Swanston Street another gorgeous building awaits. Taking his cue from Chicago's Tribune Building, the architect Marcus Barlow set about providing Melbourne with its most elegant office block, the **Manchester Union Building** (1932). The graceful lines culminate in a staggered corner tower, in perfect proportion to the whole. It's best seen from up Collins Street. Pass through the foyer, with its marble friezes and ornate polished-copper elevator doors.

Collins Street

It's time for a walk along Collins Street, where the finance houses that grew rich on the back of the gold rush hold sway. They didn't stint in showing off that wealth, either. At **333 Collins**, for example, the Commercial Bank of Australia indulged

From 1883 a small emporium grew and grew until Cole's Book Arcade stretched from Bourke to Collins Street. At its peak it contained over two million volumes. It was unique for its time in evolving as a social hub and quirky place of entertainment; monkeys and other curiosities were used to lure customers.

BELOW LEFT: Capitol Building detail.

Griffin's Capitol Theatre

The entrance foyer and awning to the Capitol Building on Swanston Street give a hint of the blocky 1920s Modernism that makes the **Capitol Theatre** upstairs such an extraordinarily dynamic space. The sculpted plaster ceiling is just astonishing. Two American architects, Walter Burley Griffin and his wife Marion Mahony, the main planners of Canberra, were among the design team of this picture palace, which is now run by RMIT University as a lecture theatre. It is difficult to get into unless you're here March–April, when it's used as a venue in the Melbourne Comedy Festival, or July/August during the International Film Festival. However, you can get a taste on the University's website (www.rmit.edu.au and search for "capitol"). The Griffins completed several commissions around Melbourne, but most of them are long gone. However, Newman College at the University of Melbourne is mercifully intact, since additions over the years have left the main structure largely uncompromised *(see page 165)*.

In the classic idea-on-the-back-of-a-cigarette-packet tradition, the owners of the ubiquitous Mitre 10 hardware chain reputedly got the idea for the name in this tavern. It's unclear whether the '10' reflects the number of drinks involved.

itself with a colossal domed octagonal banking hall in 1891. Hubris perhaps, as it closed down in 1893. The original facade has gone, but visitors can nip in and see the hall during office hours.

The acme of extravagance comes at the ANZ **Gothic Bank** (1887) on the corner with Queen Street. This is Gothic Revival *ad absurdum*. The richly detailed exterior, complete with stained glass and heraldic figures, is mirrored inside in the banking chamber (open banking hours). The Melbourne Stock Exchange (1889) next door now plays host to the ANZ **Banking Museum** (380 Collins Street; www.anz.com; Mon–Fri 10am–3pm; free), which gives the history of banking a bit of oomph with sleek interactive displays.

You can visit the former **Bank of Australia** on the next corner by imbibing at the Treasury Restaurant and Bar *(see page 125)*, part of the hotel that has taken over the building.

ABOVE RIGHT: plaque at the Gothic Bank.
BELOW: Bank Place.

Bank Place

Bank Place's old-fashioned lampposts and historic low-rise structures

ENGLISH SCOTTISH AND AUSTRALIAN BANK AND STOCK EXCHANGE BUILDING

The corner building was erected in 1883/87 as the head office and general manager's residence for the E. S. & A. Bank. Designed by William Wardell it is the finest secular Gothic revival building in Victoria. In 1923 the building was incorporated with the neighbouring Stock Exchange building designed by architect William Pitt in 1888/91.

take you back in time. The **Mitre Tavern** looks like the traditional English pub that its builders were aping. Although this building dates back only to the 1920s, a pub had occupied the spot for 80 years by then, and in its early days had been the domain of the racing and hunting fraternity. Across the road, the plain green building is the home of the **Savage Club**, a members-only establishment but positioned at the less stuffy end of the spectrum. You still won't get in, though.

Legal chambers at the end of Bank Place indicate the beginnings of the law precinct, but first go down Market or William Street to the bottom of the hill, where you'll find the Immigration Museum.

IMMIGRATION MUSEUM

✉ 400 Flinders Street; www.immigration.museum.vic.gov.au
☎ 131 102 ⏲ daily 10am–4.30pm
$ charge 🚋 City Circle, 55, 70, 75
🚆 Flinders Street

Modern Australia is, of course, founded on immigrants, and this building is full of stories of how they all got here. A cutaway of a full-size 19th-century ship graphically reveals the arduous conditions for those aboard the early fleets, and even well into the 20th century most migrants faced several weeks on the high seas. The museum occupies the old Customs House and deftly explains the back story to the cultural mix that is Australia today.

Flinders Lane

From William Street head west along Flinders Lane. Behind the soaring steel and glass of Rialto Towers, note an old red-brick building with a corrugated-iron structure hanging off the back of it. These were the toilets tacked on to the prestigious Rialto Hotel, unaccountably not swept away in its refurbishment.

Further along, the bluestone warehouses denote this as a busy unloading area for the first ships that serviced the fledgling colony until Victoria Dock became the dominant wharf in the 1880s. **Rutherglen House,** down Highlander Lane, is particularly well preserved.

Similarly unreconstructed are some of the men who frequent this area, as is evidenced in the clubs you're about to pass in King Street.

Rialto Towers

On Collins Street two skyscrapers dominate the landscape. The Rialto Towers used to feature an observation deck on level 55. As you might expect, the views were sublime in every direction. However, once the Eureka Tower – higher and loaded with extras – opened on Southbank, the Rialto deck's days were numbered and it closed at the end of 2009.

Display at the Immigration Museum. The Museum occupies the 1858 Customs House that had superseded an 1840s building. It was sited here to serve the Queens Wharf turning basin, the closest place to the city centre that 19th-century cargo ships could navigate.

Former glories

It has always been ebb and flow in this part of the city. Melbourne was riding high and land speculators were forcing prices to astronomical levels when the original **Rialto,** now in the shadow of the towers, was built in 1890–1. Its extravagant Venetian-influenced design by the young architect William Pitt expressed the ambition and confidence of the time. This was replicated in many of the

BELOW: the Immigration Museum.

TIP

The Eureka Skydeck *(see page 121)* may have seen off the observation platform that used to occupy the 55th floor of the Rialto Towers, but that has allowed chef Shannon Bennett to transplant what many believe to be the finest restaurant in Melbourne to a setting befitting its name: Vue de Monde.

neighbouring blocks, including the **Winfield Building** next door that housed the Melbourne Wool Exchange, and the adjacent Olderfleet Building. All of these were earmarked for demolition in the early 1980s until a high-profile campaign won them a reprieve. Look inside the atrium of the Rialto Hotel and see how it aspired to the sophistication of continental Europe.

Drink in the glories of this stretch of Collins Street, but consider how quickly the tide can turn. In 1893 there was a crash, and many of those basking in the silver and property booms were forced out, their reduced status in stark contrast to the luxurious premises they were leaving.

Across the junction with William Street, the area in front of a shabby 1960s insurance block is the site of Melbourne's first general market. Half-hearted statuary commemorating Batman and Fawkner fails to allay the bleakness of the setting.

Law Courts

A walk up William Street gets you acquainted with the monoliths of the

legal district. First up, immediately past Little Bourke Street, is the traditional Victorian splendour of the **Supreme Court**. It has the columns, the dome and the forbidding sandstone walls that underline the gravity of the judicial process.

The **County Court**, next, aims for the same effect, but with concrete. For the **Commonwealth Law Courts**, another block further along on the left, the design has progressed to softened functionalism; splashes of colour and some large-scale artwork

ABOVE RIGHT: grim evidence of colonial maltreatment of Aboriginal people in the Koorie Heritage Trust. **BELOW:** the Royal Mint Building. **BELOW RIGHT:** detail from the Supreme Court.

create a friendlier aspect. It's probably best viewed from the parkland across La Trobe Street.

Facing it on William Street, the **Royal Mint Building**, where Victoria's gold was turned into sovereigns, is surrounded by lawns. Massive coats of arms on the gates somehow lose their lustre when you realise that they're fibreglass. Some of the downstairs rooms are now given over to one of Melbourne's newest attractions, the **Hellenic Museum** (280 William Street; www.hellenic.org.au; tel: 8615 9016; Tue–Thur 10am–3pm; free). Temporary exhibitions are backed up by photo displays of early Greek immigrants.

Turn left along La Trobe and, just down King Street, you'll find the **Koorie Heritage Trust** (295 King Street; www.kooriehertiagetrust.com; tel: 8622 2600; daily 10am–4pm; donation), where a small but affecting exhibition looks at Koorie culture and history in the region. Colourful contemporary Aboriginal art, some of it for sale, can be found in the centre.

Don't miss the astonishing **Russell's Old Corner Shop Luncheon Room** on the corner of La Trobe and King streets. It's been in the same family since 1899 and appears to have seen little change in that time.

FLAGSTAFF GARDENS

Flagstaff Gardens still has a flagstaff at the point where a standard would have been raised to signify the arrival of a ship in the bay in the first days of settlement. In those days this was also the town burial ground. Now it acts chiefly as a recharging spot for neighbouring office workers or parents pestered into taking their offspring to the playgound. A monument to the early settlers can be found towards the top of the hill.

Steps down from the western edge lead to the corner of King and Batman streets, where St James's, the city's first church, is to be found.

QUEEN VICTORIA MARKET

www.qvm.com.au 9320 5822 Tue, Thur 6am–2pm, Fri 6am–5pm, Sat 6am–3pm, Sun 9am–4pm free 19, 55, 57, 59 220, 479, 546

Peel Street runs up from the eastern edge of the Gardens to Queen Victoria Market. With more than 600 traders, you get a lot of market to explore and a huge range of goodies to choose from. The produce stalls dominate, but there are also outlets for clothing, footwear, toys, tourist tat and whatever happened to be in the last container shipment from China. Butchers and fishmongers can be found in somewhat sterile food halls, leaving most of the character to the more careworn deli section, which is worth lingering in for the rich aromas alone. The strip of shops along Victoria Street, under a long stretch of brown-painted veranda, is as lovely as any in Melbourne.

On Sundays there's something of a party atmosphere, as buskers emerge from their lairs and cafés fill up with devotees of brunch with the Sunday papers. ❑

Foodies' tours of Victoria Market comprise two hours of guided wandering through the various halls and involve copious amounts of produce sampling.

BELOW: Queen Victoria Market.

BEST RESTAURANTS, BARS AND CAFÉS

Restaurants

Prices for a three-course dinner per person with a half-bottle of house wine:
$ = under A$60
$$ = A$60–90
$$$ = A$90–120
$$$$ = over A$120

Benito's
445 Little Collins Street, City. 9670 5347 L & D Mon–Fri **$$** [p310, C3]
A popular joint with hip lawyers from the nearby legal precinct, Benito's serves good-quality, rustic Italian food, great coffee and interesting wine in an airy, stylish room.

Bistro Vue
430 Little Collins Street, City. 9691 3838 L & D Mon–Sat **$$$** [p310, C3]
Classic French bistro food is given a modern, humorous twist in a bunker quirkily decorated with French farmhouse flourishes and closely spaced tables.

Bluestone Restaurant Bar
349 Flinders Lane, City. 9620 4060 L Mon–Fri, D Mon–Sat **$$$** [p311, C3]
Downstairs is a cosy bar with couches and less expensive wood-fired pizza, while upstairs the more serious restaurant serves deftly cooked modern European food accompanied by a decent wine list.

Ca de Vin
GPO Building, GPO Lane, City. 9654 3639 L & D daily **$** [p311, C2]
Located in an atmospheric covered laneway off the Bourke Street Mall, Ca de Vin blends casual and quality in equal measures. Noteworthy pizza and dishes to share make this a friendly and communal dining experience.

Caterina's Cucina e Bar
Basement, 221 Queen Street, City. 9670 8488 L Mon–Fri **$$** [p310, C2]
The business crowd love the basement location, clubby decor, classical music soundtrack, deft and discreet service, solid wine list and well-cooked, unthreatening Italian food.

Chillipadi
Menzies Alley (Cnr Little Lonsdale and Elizabeth Streets), City. 9663 5688 B, L & D daily **$** [p310, C2]
A popular haunt for the city's sizeable Asian student population, this restaurant serves reasonably priced, modern Asian food from early until very late.

The Deanery
13 Bligh Place, City. 9629 5599 L Mon–Fri, D Mon–Sat **$$** [p311, C3]
The smart suits gather at this quintessentially Melbourne end-of-a-lane restaurant, with its style-conscious decor and straightforward food with a Middle Eastern lean that plays second fiddle to an excellent wine list.

Gill's Diner
360 Little Collins Street (enter from Gills Alley), City. 9670 7214 L Mon–Fri, D Tue–Sat **$$** [p311, C3]
Great laneway destination in a former garage that retains some of its industrial heritage. Sparky French and Italian food with wines to match.

Hanabishi
187 King Street, City. 9670 1167 L & D Mon–Fri **$$** [p310, B3]
Slightly lacklustre decor masks what many consider to be Melbourne's finest Japanese food. Lunchtime is a bento-box blur but the fine list of specials at dinner is when things get serious.

Maha Bar and Grill
21 Bond Street, City 9629 5900 L Sun–Fri, D daily **$$$** [p311, C3]
Middle Eastern food and ethos in a new outlet from the same team that brought us the Press Club (*see page 110*).

Money Order Office
Basement, 318 Little Bourke Street, City. 9639 3020 L Tue–Fri, D Tue–Sat **$$$** [p311, C2]
Lush, plush basement bar and restaurant where leather chester-

LEFT: Treasury bonding. Lunch at Treasury restaurant.

fields, antiques, wrought iron, killer cocktails and a stylish restaurant cause you to forget the world outside.

MoVida Aqui
Level 1, 500 Bourke Street (entry in Little Bourke Street), City. ☎ 9663 3038 ◷ L Mon–Fri, D Mon–Sat **$$** [p310, C3]
Third in the deservedly popular MoVida series and no sign of any dilution in quality or service. Spanish favourites straight from the charcoal grill.

Salto
530 Little Collins Street, City. ☎ 9629 1500 ◷ B & L Mon–Fri **$** [p310, B3]
There are good sandwiches and focaccia to be had downstairs, but step up into the bistro and you will discover a brief menu of simply superb food with influences from across the Mediterranean.

Sud
219 King Street, City. ☎ 9670 8451 ◷ L & D Mon–Fri **$$** [p310, B3]
With its enthusiastic waiters, a daily changing menu and rustic Italian cooking, Sud heaves during the day and settles into a more relaxed atmosphere after dark.

Syracuse
23 Bank Place, City. ☎ 9670 1777 ◷ B & L Mon–Fri, D Mon–Sat **$$** [p310, C3]
A contender for the most romantic dining room in Melbourne, Syracuse backs up its smoochy style with a superb 350 label-strong wine list and sharply cooked Mediterranean food.

Treasury
394 Collins Street. ☎ 9211 6699 ◷ B daily, L Mon–Fri, D Mon–Sat **$$** [p310, C3]
Located in a beautifully ornate former banking chamber, the Sebel Hotel's restaurant delivers an undeniable sense of occasion whether you are eating a leisurely breakfast, propping up the bar or dining in style.

The Trust
405–411 Flinders Lane, City. ☎ 9629 9300 ◷ B & L Mon–Fri, D Mon–Sat **$$** [p310, C3]
The bar in the ornate and beautifully restored former Port Authority Building might witness the most traffic but the modern European food in the restaurant is also worth checking out.

Vue de Monde
430 Little Collins Street, City. ☎ 9691 3888 ◷ L Tue–Fri, D Tue–Sat **$$$$** [p310, C3]
There are many who would argue that this stylishly spare, expensive, dégustation-only restaurant is the best in Melbourne and, perhaps, the country. The brilliantly conceived modern French cooking may have you shouting *"oui!"*.

Bars and Cafés

Blue Diamond
Level 15, 123 Queen Street, City. [p310, C3]
The best view of any bar in Melbourne, live entertainment, rat-pack cool and great cocktails.

Blufish
16 Centre Place, City. [p311, D3]
Excellent fish and chips cooked in a tiny shop down a laneway.

Degraves Espresso Bar
23 Degraves Street, City. [p311, D3]
One of the original laneway espresso bars, Degraves mixes bohemian atmosphere with good coffee and utilitarian food.

Don Don
321 Swanston Street, City. [p311, C1]
Hearty, cheap and healthy Japanese food, much loved by the student population.

Espressino
68–70 King Street (Collins Street corner), City. [p310, B3]
Ideal for a quick and tasty Italian-flecked lunch. Features bicycles hanging on the walls as decoration.

Federal Coffee Palace
Shop 22–23, GPO, 350 Bourke Street, City. [p311, C2]
A great place to people-watch over snacks and good coffee.

Fo Guang Yuan
141 Queen Street, City. [p310, C2]
Tranquil Buddhist-run teahouse serves vegetarian fare in a suitably serene environment.

Golden Monkey
389 Lonsdale Street (enter from Hardware Lane), City. [p310, C2]
Attractive Asian-themed basement bar with a good list of spirits.

Journal
Shop 1, 253 Flinders Lane, City. [p311, D3]
Communal tables and a library theme combine with simple, interesting food in one of the city's best cafés.

Ortigia
Shop 1, 443 Little Collins Street, City. [p310, C3]
Glamorous pizza joint, complete with Murano glass chandelier, serves traditional pizza.

Tony Starr's Kitten Club
Level 1, 267 Little Collins Street, City. [p311, D2]
Great cocktails and a swinging 1960s vibe make this the place for those who like nostalgia with their imbibing.

Young & Jackson Hotel
Cnr Flinders and Swanston streets, City. [p311, D3]
Iconic pub that has been quenching thirsts since 1861. Fine food, booze and atmosphere.

Laneways and Arcades

One of the joys of Melbourne and the envy of other cities, the laneways are a shopper's delight by day and a hedonist's playground at night

One of the most valuable by-products of the grid that Robert Hoddle staked out when he was planning the new settlement of Melbourne was the network of lanes, originally intended as service roads for the buildings fronting the grand boulevards. They are still that today, but so much more besides. Many of the alleys that had, by the end of the 18th century, become fetid lairs of vice and crime, or simply ad hoc public toilets, are now relatively cleaned up and home to a thriving subculture of bars, clubs and low-rent shops. The key word is "relatively", because much of their atmosphere comes from the residual grime, frequently overlaid with jagged graffiti and street art. The respectable alternatives are the stately Victorian arcades, which are ornate, polished and up-market, but no less atmospheric for that.

If time is tight, prioritise Hosier Lane and Centre Place for graffiti, the Block Arcade for class, Heffernan Lane for its double-take art installation, and, well, that hidden gem you just discovered.

Left: the sun just about penetrates the shabby gloom of Centre Place at lunchtime.

Above: it's possible to traverse several city blocks and barely see any traffic. This has allowed a café culture to thrive; some passages such as Degraves Street (one of the few "streets" that counts as a lane) are lined for almost their entire length by café tables.

Above: the lanes are packed with cafés and restaurants, many with tables spilling out on to the pavements. There are bars, too, but a discreet sign on the door is sometimes the only indicator.

LEFT: these brooches are to be found in a small shop in Centre Place and are typical of the wares on offer in numerous similar enterprises across the city. For big-name shops and chain stores, you'll need to look in the ersatz lanes – more like conventional malls – such as Australia on Collins.

RIGHT: save the planet, or at least save on the planet, in the Royal Arcade. Running from Bourke to Little Collins Street, this is the oldest arcade in the country, having been built from 1869 to 1871, with an extension to Elizabeth Street added in 1902.

ARCADIA

"Doing the Block" was a ritual for Victorian Victorians who had achieved a certain respectability. It entailed promenading along Collins Street between Swanston and Elizabeth streets during recognised hours of the afternoon, with the object of seeing and being seen by the fashionable and affluent. The creation of the Block Arcade in the early 1890s offered an extension to the route and shelter from the elements. The ritual may have fallen into abeyance decades ago, but the spirit lives on in the grandeur of the arcade, with its polished brass fittings, canopied glass roof and intricate mosaic floor. There are echoes, too, of the lost glory days in the enunciations of the society ladies who frequent the Hopetoun Tearooms.

ABOVE: given its status in the heart of Melbourne's "Golden Mile", it is remarkable that there were, albeit briefly, plans to bulldoze the Block Arcade in 1962.

LEFT: on tours of the Block Arcade (Tue, Thur, 1pm; tel: 9650 2777/9654 5244), you'll learn about what was the largest mosaic in the country when laid in 1891–3.

Recommended Restaurants, Bars & Cafés on page 137

SOUTHBANK AND DOCKLANDS

The riverside south of the Yarra and the former docks to its north have been revitalised in recent years. Now mushrooming arts complexes complete for attention with the world's tallest residential building, a massive casino complex and a brand new waterside suburb

The banks of the Yarra south of the CBD and the area curving around to Docklands have undergone rapid change since the 1980s. Whole communities have moved in, the city's tallest building has gone up, an arts precinct has been consolidated and expansion continues. Major investments are being made, new projects mooted, and there's every chance that something in this chapter will be out of date by the time you read it.

THE ARTS CENTRE

100 St Kilda Road; www.theartscentre.com.au 9821 8000 tours Mon–Sat 11am; backstage tour Sun 12.15pm charge 1, 3, 5, 6, 8, 16, 64, 67, 72 Flinders Street

The first thing you see on crossing south from Flinders Street Station on the right-hand side of the renovated Princes Bridge is the concrete drum of one of the city's primary concert venues: **Hamer Hall**. It is part of the **Arts Centre** and can be best appreciated on one of the excellent tours of all the auditoriums in the complex or, better still, the weekly backstage tour.

Hamer Hall is the principal venue for the Melbourne Symphony Orchestra, and also hosts visiting orchestras. Furthermore, it handles jazz, rock and other popular concerts, or at least it will return to doing so after a major overhaul. The design is astonishing. Structural engineers dealt with unstable, waterlogged land by building a huge concrete ark six storeys underground to float on it, and the technical detail of the acoustics is riveting: the seats are padded so that each absorbs the

Main attractions
- THE ARTS CENTRE
- NATIONAL GALLERY OF VICTORIA: INTERNATIONAL
- AUSTRALIAN CENTRE FOR CONTEMPORARY ART
- EUREKA TOWER
- THE SOUTHGATE CENTRE
- MELBOURNE AQUARIUM
- CROWN COMPLEX
- DOCKLANDS
- ETIHAD STADIUM
- SOUTHERN CROSS STATION

LEFT: footbridge over the Yarra.
RIGHT: auditorium of the State Theatre.

From the 1870s the area now occupied by the Arts Centre hosted visiting circuses. Wirth's Circus set up a permanent base here in 1907 and is commemorated in this mosaic.

“

The Yarra “seems to have but little to do with the city... You might live in Melbourne all your life and hardly know that the Yarra was running by your door”

English novelist Anthony Trollope's view in 1871

same amount of sound as the average human body – so there should be no difference between a soundcheck and a performance.

Follow St Kilda Road away from the river. The building with the tapering webbed spire – think ballet dancer in a tutu – houses three theatres. The **State Theatre** (2,085 capacity) is largely for opera, dance and musicals; the **Playhouse** (884) is mostly used by the Melbourne Theatre Company for mainstream programming; the **Fairfax Studio** (376) has more experimental work. Foyers in all the buildings reflect the minerals and landscapes of Australia, and there is first-class art to match. You're free to investigate the public areas whenever the buildings are open.

NATIONAL GALLERY OF VICTORIA: INTERNATIONAL ❷

✉ 180 St Kilda Road; www.ngv.vic.gov.au ☎ 8620 2222 🕒 Wed–Mon 10am–5pm Ⓢ free 🚋 1, 3, 5, 6, 8, 16, 64, 67, 72 🚆 Flinders Street

Next in the stroll along St Kilda Road comes the bluestone bulk of the **NGV: International** – just plain NGV before Federation Square opened up and allowed the collection to be split into Australian *(see page 99)* and international work. The original gallery underwent extensive renovation before reopening in 2003.

ABOVE RIGHT: the Arts Centre, with its distinctive spire.

The results are impressive from the entrance onwards. In fact, the entrance had to remain unaltered. Generations of kids had taken untold enjoyment in sticking their fingers into the water wall that gives the impression from the street that you have to pass through a waterfall to gain access to the building.

Recommended Restaurants, Bars & Cafés on page 137

While not as overtly flamboyant as its other half in Fed Square, there is real pleasure to be had from the building itself. It lures you into parts of the collection you might not normally bother with, and then the curators give you just enough to satisfy your appetite – just what a good gallery should do. The artwork ranges from Ancient Greek and Roman to Aztec, samples a bit of Africa, delves into the Pacific Islands and gives due weight to the European classic works that have underpinned the collection since its establishment in 1861. The visitors lying prone on the carpet in the Great Hall are not simply overwhelmed by choice but taking up the best position – on their backs – to appreciate the stained-glass ceiling by Leonard French.

Handily placed to pick up inspiration from the masterworks at the NGV, the **Victorian College of the Arts** is the next establishment down St Kilda Road. Pass that and turn right into Grant Street. On the left is one of the city's more dramatic buildings, the Australian Centre for Contemporary Art.

AUSTRALIAN CENTRE FOR CONTEMPORARY ART ❸

✉ 111 Sturt Street; www.accaonline.org.au ☎ 9697 9999 ⏲ Tue–Fri 10am–5pm, Sat–Sun 11am–6pm $ free 🚊 1, 3, 5, 6, 8, 16, 64, 67, 72

Rembrandt's Two Old Men Disputing *from the NGV: International collection. Touring blockbuster exhibitions attract many, but it's also rewarding just to dive in and allow serendipity to be your guide. And it's free.*

ABOVE LEFT: walk of art. NGV International.

Southbank and Docklands

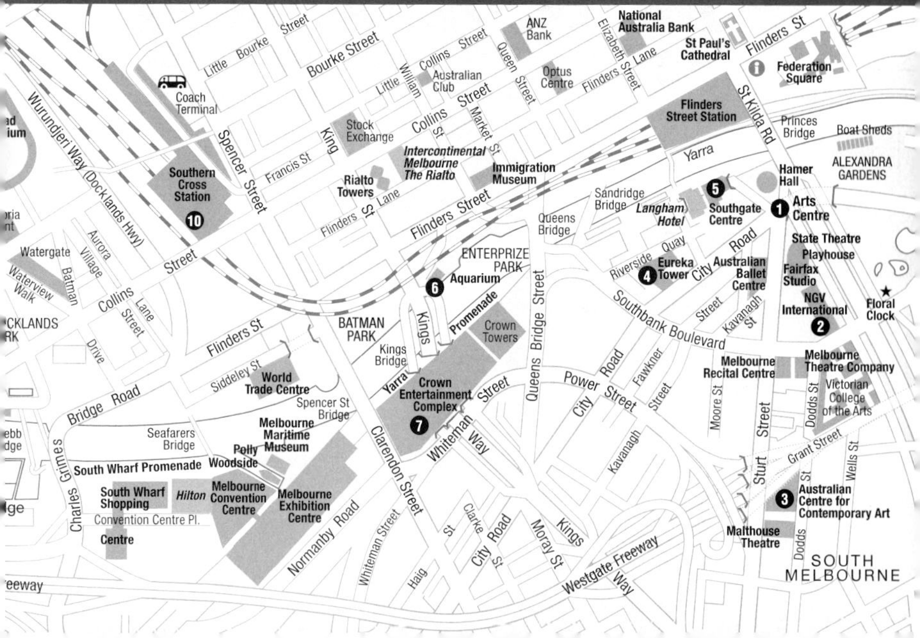

The Malthouse Theatre has occupied this building since 1990. Known as Playbox until 2004, productions always gave a platform to Australian writers, until a move towards less script-based and more international work.

BELOW: the rusted surfaces of ACCA.

It looks like the result of an off-kilter origami exercise, but using steel sheets. Their rusted surfaces suggest the red centre of Australia – Uluru at dusk perhaps – and the rich brown is set off by *The Void*, a brilliant-yellow sculpture whose journey around the city over the years appears to have reached an appropriate end.

Inside, however, the Australian Centre for Contemporary Art (ACCA) is a tad disappointing. After the visceral adventure of the exterior you're faced with a series of white, cubic exhibition spaces. The argument that it constitutes a better showcase for the art is undermined by the Ian Potter Centre in Fed Square. The actual work on display changes regularly and, according to your perception, is either breathtakingly contemporary or tends towards the "Is this really art?" end of the spectrum.

The **Malthouse Theatre** next door, on Sturt Street, occupies part of the former Carlton & United Brewery. It's an appealing conversion, with a large open foyer and café serving audiences for the three performance spaces – the Beckett, the Merlyn and the Tower Theatres – and, indeed, anyone who drops in for a coffee.

EUREKA TOWER ❹

7 Riverside Quay, Southbank; www.eurekaskydeck.com.au 9693 8888 daily 10am–10pm charge 1, 3, 5, 6, 8, 16, 64, 67, 72 Flinders Street

It's time to return northwards to one of Melbourne's newer attractions. You can't miss this one, since the **Eureka Tower** soars upwards as the city's highest structure by some distance. It claims to be the world's tallest residential building and, since 2007, has given non-residents a chance to sample life in the sky with the opening of the **Eureka Skydeck 88**. Predictably, it's on the 88th floor and the views are startling.

If you really want vertiginous thrills, an additional outlay will give you access to **The Edge**. This is a box of glass walls and ceiling with a dark floor. Once it has slid 3 metres (10ft) out from the side of the building, the walls' and floor's opacity suddenly fades to leave clear glass, with an alarming soundtrack of crashing glass and grating machinery. The drop of close to 300 metres (1,000ft) is not for the nervous.

It's not far to the Yarra from here. Development since the 1980s has turned the Southbank area into a humming business, residential and cultural precinct. It's a far cry from the days when Trollope or Finn were making their observations *(see margin, page 130, and panel, right)*.

THE SOUTHGATE CENTRE ❺

3 Southgate Avenue; www.southgate-melbourne.com.au 9699 4311 daily free 1, 3, 5, 6, 8, 16, 64, 67, 72 Flinders Street

One of the first developments of the current boom was the Southgate Centre, opposite Flinders Street Sta-

Recommended Restaurants, Bars & Cafés on page 137

LEFT: the Eureka Tower as seen from the Rialto Tower.

tion. It opened in 1992 with three levels of boutiques and restaurants. The latter have fabulous views over the river, and most have the food to match. Look out for the dramatic split head of *Ophelia*, Deborah Halpern's sculpture coated in brightly coloured mosaic tiles which, for a spell in the 1990s, was the logo for the city in all its tourist promotions. There's a touch of Gaudí, a hint of Picasso – and those who see it as two digits raised at passers-by are too easily offended.

On the quayside at Southgate you can hop on a sightseeing boat *(see Travel Tips, page 270)*, a ferry to Williamstown *(see page 201)* or even take a trip to see a colony of little penguins in Port Phillip Bay.

Crossing the river

Make your way westwards, perhaps dallying with buskers en route, maybe venturing on to the **Rainbow Footbridge** with its graceful modern arch. Alternatively you could wait for the meatier offerings of the **Sandridge Bridge**. This former railway bridge has been given over to pedestrians and cyclists and adorned with *The Travellers*, which is sculptor Nadim Karam's acknowledgement of the waves of migrants to Australia from convict days onwards. Nine steel figures appear to trundle across the bridge while one more, representing Aboriginal people, is anchored to the river bank. Glass panels along one side of the bridge are devoted to each of the home countries of these migrants and provide a fascinating statistical breakdown.

The sculptural celebration of migration was erected here because, for many years, newcomers to Australia, fresh from the boats, came by train into the city across Sandridge Bridge.

This, or the more sober **Queens Bridge** that follows, will take you to the north bank of the river. **Enterprise Wharf** is where the first European explorers landed, just

Keeping it clean

The Yarra River was not always one of Melbourne's feature attractions. As you stroll its banks, crisscrossing with the aid of ever more interesting bridges, consider the days when it was little more than an open sewer and a receptacle for the pungent outpourings from the tanneries that lined its banks ("a fetid, festering sewer, befouled amidst the horrors of wool-washing, fellmongering, bone-crushing and other unmentionable abominations", according to Edmund Finn in 1888). There was also, for good measure, the mortuary that occupied part of the site of Federation Square in the days before refrigeration. Nowadays the only mildly confronting odours are likely to come from one of the firework displays held on the river at the drop of a hat. Litter is caught in one of several traps moored on the water, and a whole team of Parks Victoria rangers works to keep the Yarra pristine for the annual Moomba Birdman Competition and much else besides.

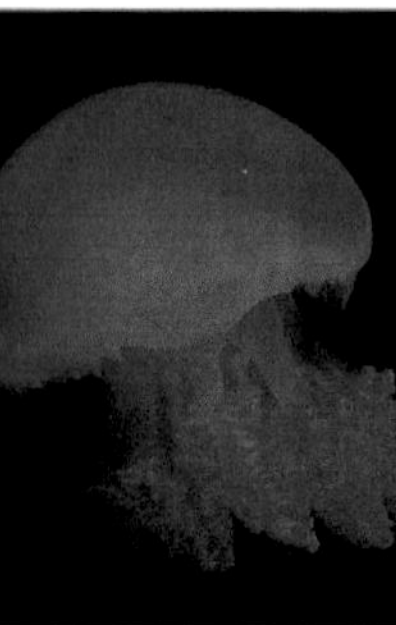

For that 1970s lava-lamp experience, visit the Sea Jellies display on the ground level of the Melbourne Aquarium. Penguins, seals and otters are also on the menu. No, not literally.

ABOVE RIGHT: steam ferry on the Yarra. **BELOW:** tunnel vision. Walking through the Oceanarium at the Melbourne Aquarium.

below the long-gone Rocky Falls. It subsequently became a bustling dock and turning-place for the large sailing ships of the time. Five carved figureheads looking out across the water – *Constellation* by Geoffrey Bartlett – now mark the spot.

MELBOURNE AQUARIUM

Cnr Flinders and King streets; www.melbourneaquarium.com.au 9620 0999 daily 9.30am–6pm, Jan 9.30am–9pm charge City Circle, 70, 75 Flinders Street, Southern Cross

A short walk along the bank takes you to the **Melbourne Aquarium**. This introduction to life in the deep is centred on the vast "Oceanarium", containing over 2 million litres (440,000 gallons) of water and a lively cross section of sea creatures. Walk through to the "Fish Bowl" at its centre and you might be surprised by the sight of visitors who have opted to swim with the sharks (three dives a day, extra charge; non-divers are given a brief diving course by qualified instructors).

CROWN ENTERTAINMENT COMPLEX

www.crowncasino.com.au 9292 8888 daily 24 hours free 96, 109, 112 216, 219, 220, 235, 237, 238 Southern Cross

If you can resist the lure of the café and its views down the river, cross back to the Southbank and the enormous block stretching from Queens Bridge to Spencer Street Bridge. The **Crown Entertainment Complex** is predicated on a massive casino that generates millions for its operators and for the State Government in taxes. However, you're not going to get public support for such a project without a hefty slice of "community benefit", so there are cinemas, performance spaces, a hotel, food halls

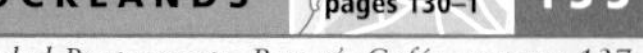
Map on pages 130–1

Recommended Restaurants, Bars & Cafés on page 137

and up-market shops. The restaurants cook up some of the best – and most expensive – food in Melbourne. The main atrium, all lumbering black marble and garish chandeliers, provides a free laser and light show every few minutes that generally evokes a "Was that it?" response. More rewarding are the towers along the river bank that, after dark, spit out fireballs on the hour. Stories of surprised and subsequently flame-grilled seagulls are probably apocryphal.

Melbourne Exhibition and Convention Centre

Locals know the next building, with its dramatic soaring facade, as Jeff's Shed. Technically, it's the Melbourne Exhibition Centre, but its popular sobriquet is testament to the fondness of erstwhile Victorian Premier Jeff Kennett for *grands projets* in the manner of former French President François Mitterrand. For a shed it's remarkably graceful, and you can enjoy the playful use of angles and light in its public areas irrespective of whether you wish to visit whichever exhibition is under way at the time. Beyond it the gleaming new convention centre, opened in 2009, contains 52 meeting rooms, including the 5,550-person capacity plenary chamber.

There's a pleasing contrast to sharp modern lines in the shape of a three-masted iron barque stranded in dock by the river bank. The *Polly Woodside*, which was built in Belfast in 1885 and operated as a cargo vessel, is typical of the ships that sailed into Melbourne in the 19th and early 20th centuries. It's now part of the National Trust-run **Melbourne Maritime Museum** (www.pollywoodside.com.au). Visitors are allowed to clamber over the vessel.

Webb Bridge to Docklands

A walkway continues along the wharf and under a road bridge to **Yarra's Edge**, where apartment blocks have sprung up and a small marina has developed, but it's the **Webb Bridge** that catches the eye. It could equally well be called "web bridge", as its skeletal steel weaving could be the product of an overgrown spider on a ferrous diet. The sculptor Robert Owen (in conjunction with architects Denton Corker Marshall) actually based his design on Aboriginal fishing traps. Either way, its free-flowing form snakes dramatically over the Yarra and leads you towards Docklands.

A path runs through **Docklands Park**, where a children's playground and whimsical sculptures offset the towering office blocks on all sides. The bright primary-colour Lego-like bricks of the new **National Australian**

SHOP

Contrasting shopping opportunities are to be found on Southbank. The Crown Casino complex is full of expensive boutiques for those whose taste, if that's the word, runs to designer labels. Conversely, the adjacent Melbourne Exhibition Centre frequently sees giant warehouse sales of all kinds of goods at bargain prices, while behind the Centre lurks the new South Wharf shopping centre.

ABOVE LEFT: Melbourne Exhibition Centre. **BELOW:** the National Australian Bank offices in Docklands.

Reed Vessel, *by Virginia King, sited in Docklands Park, is one of 25 public artworks in the area that can be seen on* Art Journey, *a self-guided walk that can be downloaded from www.docklands.com.*

ABOVE RIGHT: *Cow Up a Tree* by John Kelly at Docklands.
BELOW: Etihad Stadium viewed from Docklands Promenade.

Bank (NAB) **HQ** loom up on the left before you see the water of **Victoria Harbour**, the focal point of Melbourne Docklands.

DOCKLANDS 8

www.docklands.com.au City Circle, 30, 48, 86 Southern Cross 220

The Promenade runs along the waterfront beside the NAB Building and its cafés and spaces geared to grazing office workers. The primary draw for visitors is across the water at **Waterfront City** and **NewQuay**, where a more extensive collection of bars and eateries is trying to become Melbourne's latest hotspot. For something that was developed from scratch in the 1990s, it has come a long way. Good restaurateurs have been attracted to purpose-built spaces, but even in this gourmet-heavy city, there has to be an extra ingredient to inspire repeat visits. The turnover of businesses suggests that it isn't there yet.

It's worth a look, though, be it for the *Cow Up a Tree*, the stark beauty

of the Bolte Bridge rearing up to the west, or one of the many special events, usually with an aquatic flavour. The completion in 2008 of Melbourne's giant Ferris wheel and its closure for a complete structural overhaul shortly afterwards leaves a question mark hanging over the district.

Etihad Stadium and Southern Cross Station

Docklands is at its liveliest on days when there's a game on at the neighbouring **Etihad Stadium 9**. It was Melbourne's second major sports stadium after the MCG when it opened in 2000. Aussie Rules matches are staged regularly; international rugby, one-day cricket and major concerts occasionally. Major soccer matches are played here too, but regular A League games moved to the city's new rectangular stadium in 2010. It has a retractable roof, often used in ways that defy logic – closed for an international rugby match on a sunny Saturday afternoon, for instance. Ask why on a guided tour.

A pedestrian bridge leads to, and is one of the best places from which to see, **Southern Cross Station 10**. It served the city for years as drab old Spencer Street Station until $700 million saw it transformed into a slab of modern architecture. The defining feature is the vast wavy roof, which was probably the clincher in its winning two Royal Institute of British Architects' prizes in 2007. Shame it leaked under its first exposure to serious rain in 2009. ❑

Best Restaurants, Bars and Cafés

Restaurants

Prices for a three-course dinner per person with a half-bottle of house wine:
$ = under A$60
$$ = A$60–90
$$$ = A$90–120
$$$$ = over A$120

Bhoj Docklands
54 New Quay Promenade, Docklands. 9600 0884 L & D daily **$$** [p302, A4]
Melbourne's smartest Indian restaurant is also one of its best, with deftly cooked dishes from across the subcontinent, sharp service and a wine list that comes with food-matching guidelines.

Livebait
55b New Quay Promenade, Docklands. 9642 1500 L & D daily **$$** [p302, A4]
Seafood is the main event in this waterside restaurant, with its city views and designer Greek-island-café decor, but meat-eaters won't feel neglected as the rustic Mediterranean menu covers both surf and turf.

Nobu Melbourne
Crown Complex, Southbank. 9292 7879 L & D daily **$$$$** [p310, C4]
Modelled on the 57th Street Nobu in New York, this outpost in the southern hemisphere is a glamorously – and expensively – decked out double-storeyed affair that closely follows the Nobu formula of great ingredients and signature dishes.

Pure South
River Level, Southgate, Southbank. 9699 4600 L Sun–Fri, D daily **$$$** [p311, D4]
This conservatively dressed riverside restaurant highlights produce – especially meat – from Tasmania and the Bass Strait islands. Seafood, cheese and oysters also make the cut in simple dishes that make produce the star.

Red Emperor
Upper Level, Southgate, Southbank. 9699 4170 L & D daily **$$$** [p311, D4]
This large, loud Chinese restaurant has great city views, excellent service and some of the best Chinese food in town. There are dishes for the adventurous and the timid, all cooked with equal flair.

Rockpool Bar & Grill
Crown Complex, Southbank. 8648 1900 L Sun–Fri, D daily **$$$$** [p310, C4]
Large, glamorous and expensive, Rockpool Bar & Grill also dishes up some of the best food in town. The menu features many varieties of aged beef, exquisitely fresh seafood and beautifully prepared desserts.

Tutto Bene
Mid-level, Southgate, Southbank. 9696 3334 L & D daily **$$** [p311, D4]
Down-to-earth Italian joint with a great balcony overlooking the Yarra River. Being Melbourne's only *risotteria*, the risotto here is worth a try, but so are the rustically cooked meat dishes and the house-made *gelati*.

Yum Cha Dragon
427 Docklands Drive, Waterfront City, Docklands. 9329 6868 L & D daily **$$** [p302, A4]
Yum cha is available all day at this smoothly kitted-out modern Asian restaurant, as are noodle dishes, barbecued meat and poultry, and a well-priced food-loving wine list.

Bars and Cafés

Bear Brass
River level, Southgate, Southbank. [p311, D4]
Lively riverside bar with great views of the city, plenty of room and a good Aussie wine list.

Bopha Devi
27 Rakaia Way, Docklands. [p302, A4]
Authentic Cambodian flavours and charming service make this casually stylish café one of the dock's best picks.

Mecca Bah
55a NewQuay Promenade, Docklands. [p302, A4]
Tasty, modern Middle Eastern food regularly attracts a fun-loving crowd. It's served in a Moorish-themed dining room overhanging the water.

Sotano
Hilton, 2 Convention Centre Place, South Wharf [p304, A2]
A strong emphasis on *jamón* (ham) and cheese marks out this new wine and tapas bar in the Hilton hotel. Smart interior plus an outdoor terrace.

DOMAIN AND BOTANIC GARDENS

South of the Yarra (east of St Kilda Road) is an expanse of parkland that contains formal gardens, ornamental lakes, historic monuments and memorials, and a fine collection of native and exotic plants

Respite from the urban edges of the CBD can be found south of the river in a series of adjoining public spaces, which together make up the largest green expanse in a city deservedly renowned for its parks and gardens.

Alexandra Gardens

First up, and visible from Princes Bridge on the left, on the walk south from Federation Square, is **Alexandra Gardens ❶**, named after Queen Alexandra, the wife of Edward VII, in 1904. There is nothing particularly remarkable about the space in terms of historic markers or landmark public artworks, but it comes into its own for festivals and major public events.

During Moomba, or Waterfest as we must now call it (*see page 147*), it provides a perfect vantage point for the Birdman Competition, in which a motley collection of the deluded attempt to demonstrate the art of human flight with the aid of more or less professionally constructed wings. The outcome tends to be the same, give or take a couple of metres, but it affords plenty of amusement for the crowds picnicking on either side of the Yarra. Fairground attractions and trapeze structures fill the areas behind the boat sheds, bands play and a village of food stalls cashes in.

On the Yarra

The boat sheds are evidence of the suitability of the Yarra for rowing. Only a few years ago, the hugely successful Australian rowing team, dubbed the "Oarsome Foursome", could be seen training here every

Main attractions

- ALEXANDRA GARDENS
- QUEEN VICTORIA GARDENS
- THE KINGS DOMAIN
- SIDNEY MYER MUSIC BOWL
- GOVERNMENT HOUSE
- SHRINE OF REMEMBRANCE
- LA TROBE'S COTTAGE
- ROYAL BOTANIC GARDENS

LEFT: the Shrine of Remembrance.
RIGHT: Ferris at the bottom of the garden. Funfair in Alexandra Gardens for Moomba.

On warm summer evenings from December to March, people clutching rugs and picnics can be found converging on the Royal Botanic Gardens for a screening at the Moonlight Cinema. Find the programme at: www.moonlight.com.au.

RIGHT: Queen Victoria surveys her gardens.

day. Competitions are held during Waterfest, and the peculiar little hut on the water's edge around the bend towards Swan Street Bridge is used for judging. Even if you've no interest in rowing, the views from the banks back to the city are fabulous.

QUEEN VICTORIA GARDENS ❷

To the south of Alexandra Avenue (which can be tricky to cross: make your way up to St Kilda Road and cross the bridge) lie **Queen Victoria Gardens**. As if she didn't already have enough places named after her, Her Majesty provides the title for

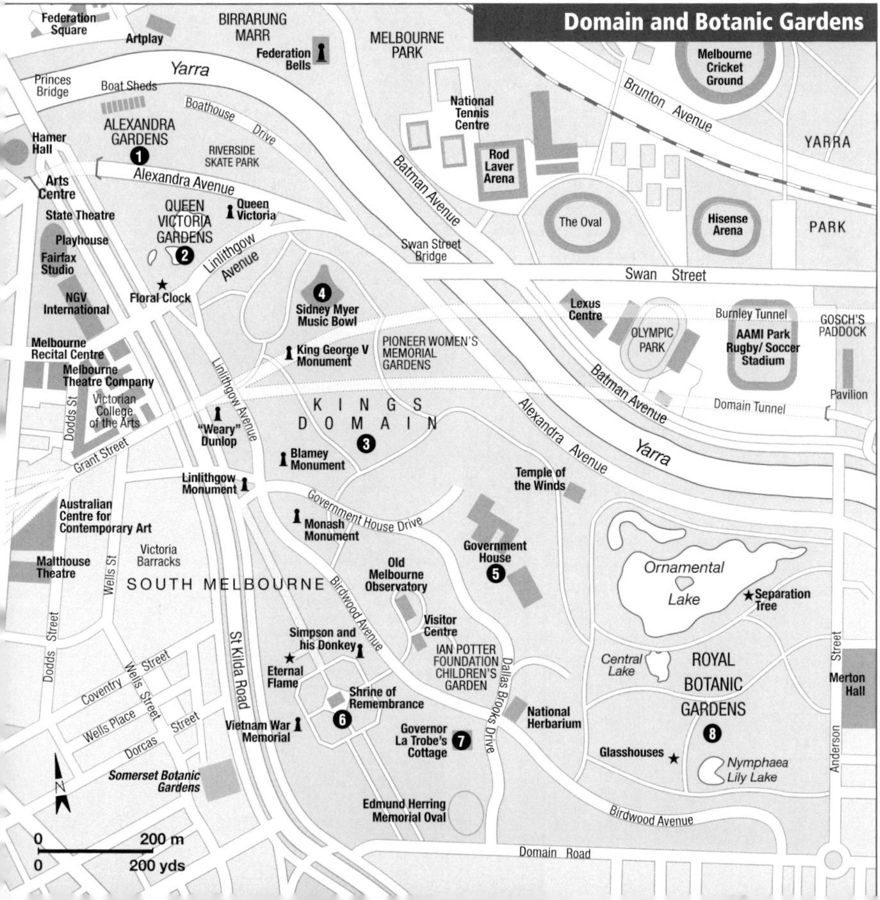

Domain and Botanic Gardens

Federation Square
Artplay
BIRRARUNG MARR
Federation Bells
MELBOURNE PARK
Melbourne Cricket Ground
Princes Bridge
Boat Sheds
Yarra
Boathouse Drive
National Tennis Centre
Brunton Avenue
Hamer Hall
ALEXANDRA GARDENS ❶
RIVERSIDE SKATE PARK
Rod Laver Arena
YARRA PARK
Alexandra Avenue
Arts Centre
State Theatre
QUEEN VICTORIA GARDENS ❷
Queen Victoria
Batman Avenue
The Oval
Hisense Arena
Playhouse
Fairfax Studio
Linlithgow Avenue
Swan Street Bridge
Swan Street
NGV International
Floral Clock
Sidney Myer Music Bowl ❹
Lexus Centre
OLYMPIC PARK
Burnley Tunnel
AAMI Park Rugby/ Soccer Stadium
GOSCH'S PADDOCK
Melbourne Recital Centre
King George V Monument
PIONEER WOMEN'S MEMORIAL GARDENS
Melbourne Theatre Company
Victorian College of the Arts
Dodds St
KINGS DOMAIN ❸
Pavilion
Domain Tunnel
"Weary" Dunlop
Grant Street
Blamey Monument
Temple of the Winds
Linlithgow Monument
Government House Drive
Australian Centre for Contemporary Art
Monash Monument
Government House ❺
Ornamental Lake
Malthouse Theatre
Victoria Barracks
Wells St
Old Melbourne Observatory
SOUTH MELBOURNE
Separation Tree
Birdwood Avenue
Visitor Centre
Simpson and his Donkey
IAN POTTER FOUNDATION CHILDREN'S GARDEN
Central Lake
ROYAL BOTANIC GARDENS
Merton Hall
Eternal Flame
St Kilda Road
Shrine of Remembrance ❻
Dallas Brooks Drive
National Herbarium
Vietnam War Memorial
Governor La Trobe's Cottage ❼
❽
Glasshouses
Nymphaea Lily Lake
Anderson Street
Somerset Botanic Gardens
Edmund Herring Memorial Oval
Domain Road
0 200 m
0 200 yds

Recommended Restaurants & Bars on page 145

this more formal amalgam of beds, lawns, winding pathways and several statues. Stride past the bust of a hirsute Hercules and towards the dominating white statue of Victoria.

On a hillock across the lawn, the old queen gazes out over her domain from a disproportionate plinth in a scene replicated around the globe wherever pink bits used to be splashed on the atlas. Splashing here is limited to the ducks on the ornamental pond below, and a seat affords tranquillity and postcard views across to the city.

With the skateboarders safely corralled in their dedicated space across in Alexandra Gardens, and not quite enough to do for young children, this is the place for those seeking peace. There's a floral clock and statues ranging from Victorian conventional to modern enigmatic. One is both conventional and enigmatic. It is the figure of a man, legs firmly planted, knees bent at right angles and arms stretched out in front of him with hands gripped together. A strained look plays on his face, perhaps because he's about to topple backwards. If you imagine the "hammer", as in the one that athletes throw, it all makes sense. But since vandals removed it, he has remained in an unfortunate state of apparent discomfort.

THE KINGS DOMAIN ❸

Continue southwards across Linlithgow Avenue into Kings Domain, so called because it is the land within the purlieu of Government House, where the King's (or Queen's) representative is ensconced.

Follow the sandy track running parallel to the road, known as the "Tan" – an example of the Aussie penchant for shortening everything into a nickname. The Tan is where Melbourne comes to exercise, or at least city workers on lunch breaks and local residents who can afford the time – and they can afford most things in these parts. Either way, there is always a steady stream of people ranging from the lithe to the languid pounding along in both directions.

Sidney Myer Music Bowl ❹

Avoid being trampled underfoot by strolling up the hill to the Sidney Myer Music Bowl. It's an amphitheatre with an extensive sail roof fanning up from the stage over tiers of fixed seating at the front. When the

The Genie, *a "play sculpture" by Tom Bass, is one of several artworks dispersed around Queen Victoria Gardens.*

ABOVE LEFT: the Kings Domain.
BELOW: having a ball in the Bowl.

The sun shines on the black clouds hanging over the Domain
Even when you're feeling warm
The temperature could drop away
Like four seasons in one day

Neil Finn captures a quintessential Melbourne moment in the Crowded House song *Four Seasons in One Day*

seats finish, lawns continue on up the hill. Big-name performers can attract many thousands to sit on the grass, sup a few beers and watch the lights of the city twinkling away beyond the roof.

The Music Bowl is programmed through the summer by the Victoria Arts Centre, and acts range from the Melbourne Symphony Orchestra, in a season of free concerts, to the Red Hot Chilli Peppers. Just don't be tempted to take an umbrella along on a grey day: they're banned.

On days when there is no show on, the Bowl is open to anyone who wants to wander around. Inspect a couple of sculptures, including one of Sidney Myer, the benevolent patriarch of the Myer Store empire.

Women's Gardens

Follow the high ground southwards and you will find the **Pioneer Women's Memorial Gardens**, an enclosed formal setting that is intended to act as a reminder of the Europe that so many left behind. Just outside the gardens and above its water feature there's a modern bell memorial dedicated to one Tilly Aston. In acknowledgement of her work with the hearing-impaired, it (usually) bursts into sonic activity as you pass and tells a sound-effect-laden story of her life.

BELOW: Government House on Australia Day. **BELOW RIGHT:** water feature in the Pioneer Women's Memorial Gardens.

GOVERNMENT HOUSE ❺

Government House, to the south of the Pioneer Women's Memorial Gardens, was built between 1872 and 1876. It's a homage to Queen Victoria's favourite residence, Osborne House on the Isle of Wight. The Governor still lives and has his offices here (so far, it has always been a man), so access is limited to a couple of hours a week (Mon and Wed, by appointment only; contact the National Trust of Victoria, tel: 8663 7260), or there's free entry for all on Australia Day (26 January), when marquees are set up in the garden, bands play and it's one big party.

Linlithgow Avenue becomes Birdwood Avenue, and the incidence of small war memorials you may have already noticed becomes more frequent. The tribute to Sir Edward "Weary" Dunlop facing St Kilda Road is noteworthy *(see panel, right)*. The memorials are proliferating because this is the vicinity of the Shrine of Remembrance.

SHRINE OF REMEMBRANCE ❻

The best way to approach is to slip down Anzac Avenue at the bottom of Government House Drive – look across to the stern bluestone of

Recommended Restaurants & Bars on page 145

Victoria Barracks over St Kilda Road. This is where the Pacific HQ of Allied Command was based during World War II. Join the avenue that continues along the line of St Kilda Road. The planners positioned the Shrine so that it can be seen along a path from the top of Swanston Street in the CBD.

On the last few hundred metres of the approach, an avenue of poplars, each dedicated to a different regiment, frames the squat stone bulk of the **Shrine** (www.shrine.org.au; daily 10am–5pm; free). It commemorates the fallen of World War I and took seven years to build from 1927.

Every year on Anzac Day (25 April), thousands brave the chill for a dawn service that marks the anniversary of the beginning of the Gallipoli campaign in 1915. Many thousands more march through the city later in the day. As survivors of the wars of the 20th century diminish, it is becoming common for descendants to march wearing the medals won by their fathers and grandfathers.

On 11 November at 11am everything aligns for a beam of light to pass into the inner chamber and illuminate the memorial stone. Apart from when these ceremonies are in progress, visitors can look

ABOVE: guarding the Shrine. **BELOW LEFT:** Anzac Day parade.

"Weary" Dunlop

Sir Edward "Weary" Dunlop (Dunlop – tyres – tired – weary) lived a life that contradicted his sobriquet in every way. Born in 1907, he studied at the College of Pharmacy in Melbourne (top of his class), then gained a medical degree at the University of Melbourne while becoming a champion boxer and playing rugby for the Australian national team. A fellowship with the Australian College of Surgeons followed before he was commissioned in the army medical corps. In World War II he was captured by the Japanese, and his time as leader of the Australian contingent on the infamous Burma–Thailand railway made him a national hero, with astonishing tales of standing up for his men to his captors while, as a doctor, his improvisational skills saved countless lives. After the war he continued in medicine but also became an ambassador for reconciliation with the Japanese. A knighthood and citation as Australian of the Year followed. Weary? Hardly.

Charles Joseph La Trobe lived in this cottage with his family from 1840 to 1854, including the three years from 1851 that he spent as the first Lieutenant-Governor of the newly established state of Victoria.

BELOW: Don't jump! A moment in the Botanic Gardens.

inside the main building and now have the benefit of a whole new exhibition area. This is dug out beneath the Shrine so that the views aren't compromised.

World War II is acknowledged by the eternal flame and a solid column topped by pall-bearers representing each branch of the armed services. The views from the city to the Shrine are reciprocated, especially from the balcony. This also allows excellent sightings of the Observatory Gate complex to the east.

Prefab cottage

Before exploring that, however, continue down Birdwood Avenue. The white building on the right is **La Trobe's Cottage ❼**. It's a plain weatherboard structure sent out from England for the first Superintendent of the Port Phillip District of NSW in 1839, which makes it Victoria's oldest surviving building. It was moved to its current site in 1998. It is open Sundays (Oct–May 2–4pm) or as part of a combined tour with Government House *(see page 142)*.

ROYAL BOTANIC GARDENS ❽

www.rbg.vic.gov.au 9252 2300
daily 7.30am–sunset free

Return to the Observatory Gate entrance to the Royal Botanic Gardens. Visits to the 1863 Melbourne Observatory for daytime solar viewing or night-time peeks at Mars can be booked at the Visitor Centre. This is also the place for tours of the Botanic Gardens, including one that explores the historical and cultural importance of this land to local Aboriginal people.

Just past the Visitor Centre is the **Children's Garden**. Prominence is given to a statue that has been delighting Melbourne children for decades. It features the main characters from a classic Norman Lindsay tale, *The Magic Pudding*. Elsewhere there are pathways and tunnels to entice curious kids, even a fine water spray to walk through. This garden is closed for two months each winter to recover from the children.

The gardens themselves are stunning, a testament to the genius of Baron Ferdinand von Mueller, who,

in 1846, came up with a layout that made the most of a lake left by the fickle trail of the Yarra. The gardens combine native species with the fashionable European imports of the time. Dedicated camellia, herb and cactus gardens are interspersed with a fern gully and segments of rainforest.

It's all very picturesque, so wander through, consult the frequent indicator boards and detour via the Terrace Tearooms, which have one of the prettiest settings in the city next to the ornamental lake. Pass the careworn **Separation Tree**, where Victoria's split from New South Wales was celebrated in 1851, before exiting through Gate H.

It's a delightful walk along the river from here back to Princes Bridge. At weekends the banks are heaving with large groups making the most of the public barbecues, sports fans heading for the MCG, boats sculling along the river and cyclists whizzing along the banks.❑

KIDS

Every summer a group of hardy actors are to be found traipsing through the Botanic Gardens trailing a bunch of children behind them. They are engaged in a promenade performance of *The Wind in the Willows*. Kids love it, and there are subtleties enough to keep adults entertained as well. Book ahead through Ticketmaster (tel: 136 100).

ABOVE LEFT: barbie on the banks of the Yarra. **ABOVE RIGHT:** inseparable under the Separation Tree.

RESTAURANTS & BARS

Restaurants

Bacash
175 Domain Road, South Yarra. ☎ 9866 3566 ⌚ L Mon–Fri, D Mon–Sat **$$$** [p305, D3]
Seafood is the main event at this nicely appointed parkside restaurant, but those needing meat will be as pleased as the piscatarians with the quality.

Botanical
169 Domain Road, South Yarra. ☎ 9820 7888 ⌚ B, L & D daily **$$$** [p305, D3]
The blond and the beautiful love to watch each other at the Botanical, but the superb contemporary food available from morning to nightcap attracts a crowd interested in substance as much as style.

Dish
Royce Hotel, 379 St Kilda Road, City. ☎ 9677 9933 ⌚ B daily, L Mon–Fri, D Mon–Sat **$$** [p305, C3]
Unlike many hotel restaurants, Dish has its own sense of place and style, helped along by a menu of skilfully cooked European-influenced food.

Bars

Belgian Beer Café Bluestone
557 St Kilda Road, City. [p307, D1]
Sit inside in a fully imported Belgian pub or outside under coloured lights in one of Melbourne's best beer gardens. Offers an extensive range of beer plus Belgian-tinged, beer-friendly food.

Observatory Café
Royal Botanic Gardens, Birdwood Avenue, South Yarra. [p304, C2]
Set amongst the Observatory buildings, good coffee and simply cooked café food make this a perfect pitstop pre- or post-stroll through the park. Handy for the Children's Garden.

Prices for a three-course dinner per person with a half-bottle of house wine. ***$*** *= under A$60;* ***$$*** *= A$60–90;* ***$$$*** *= over A$90.*

THE YEAR-ROUND FESTIVAL

If it's... well, any time at all really, it must be festival time. Just follow the crowds and leave your prejudices at home.

Melburnians love an occasion. If there's something good on, they will go and see it. This is evident in both sport and the arts, and begins to explain why the city can sustain so many festivals. Often a carnival will be tagged on to another event, as when huge cultural festivals were attached to the Commonwealth Games in 2006 and the FINA World Swimming Championships in 2007. But most of the time they are annual shindigs that have grown to become regulars in the calendar, attracting audiences from around the country and beyond. October's International Arts Festival and April's Comedy Festival have global reputations, but there are also jamborees for film, food, writers, jazz, flowers and gardens. Alongside these are fringe events, neighbourhood celebrations and parties to mark the various cultures that make up the populace.

CENTRE: street performers delight or blight festivals year round. Here "Chrome" delight as sharks in Birrarung Marr.
ABOVE: the wonderful Strange Fruit is a Melbourne-based performance-art company that appears on its poles in festivals locally and around the world.

ABOVE: Chinese New Year sees the whole of Chinatown, centred on Little Bourke and Russell streets, come to with performances, ceremonies and fireworks. The parade's star participa is the Millennium Dai Loong Dragon, which needs scores of men to carry i

LEFT: most festivals incorporate a fre element as a way of boosting their profile or to justify substantial public subsidy. Either way, there's usually a parade or a performance in Fed Squa

MIDSUMMA MADNESS

Over three weeks at the end of January and into the beginning of February, the Midsumma Festival sets up camp around the city. This is where Melbourne's gay and lesbian population comes out to play – at least, more out than usual – in a series of musical, theatrical and sporting events that culminate in a huge party in Fitzroy Gardens or Alexandra Gardens. It's not as high-profile or flamboyant as Sydney's Mardi Gras, but has built a firm following over two decades and has simply become part of Melbourne life. Sydney may want to make a song and dance about its gay credentials, but Melbourne just gets on with another bout of partying – and in so doing attracts crowds of all ages and persuasions.

BELOW: the annual Moomba parade is a great family occasion in March. The idea that the word means "bottom" in an Aboriginal dialect has gained currency, and, with many activities taking place on the Yarra, we're now supposed to call it Waterfest. But we don't.

ABOVE: the showbag is a great Aussie invention that crops up at various festivals but really comes into its own at the Royal Melbourne Show at the Showgrounds every September. Over 300 varieties of goodie-packed bags are now on sale each year.

Recommended Restaurants & Cafés on page 155

EAST OF THE CITY CENTRE

A stroll along the river east of the CBD takes you through Melbourne's newest public park to a collection of world-class sporting arenas. Just to the north is one of the city's oldest and most attractive areas

Without wanting to overstress the point, Melbourne gives very high priority to sport. Many cities have world-class stadiums and facilities, but surely only Melbourne has them so close to the city centre. From Princes Bridge, south of Federation Square, the skyline to the east is dominated by the Melbourne Cricket Ground. If the wind is in the right direction you can hear the roar of the crowd. There are also all the other venues that make up the Melbourne, Yarra and Olympic Park precincts.

On a more sedate level, East Melbourne has some distinguished early houses and quiet leafy streets, and is flanked by serene Fitzroy Gardens.

BIRRARUNG MARR ❶

Starting from Federation Square, make for the banks of the Yarra River and, with the boat sheds on the opposite bank, follow the water's edge eastwards. Depending on the time of year, or even the day of the week, there may be an outdoor photographic exhibition impinging on the pathway, or perhaps a series of stalls peddling food and drink, linked to that week's festival. Sometimes there's a small Ferris wheel or a tent acting as a venue for the Comedy Festival; perhaps Circus Oz is in town and you can see its Big Top in the distance. You'll rarely be able to walk unhindered towards **Birrarung Marr**, opened in 2002 as Melbourne's first new large public park in over 100 years.

The name means "river of mists" to tribes of the Kulin nation, and great effort has been expended on reflecting the culture of the local Aboriginal peoples whose land this was. Or, it has been argued, is.

Main attractions

- BIRRARUNG MARR
- ROD LAVER ARENA
- MELBOURNE CRICKET GROUND
- POWLETT STREET
- FITZROY GARDENS
- COOKS' COTTAGE
- ST PATRICK'S CATHEDRAL

LEFT: inside St Patrick's Cathedral, Victoria's largest church.
RIGHT: Cooks' Cottage in Fitzroy Gardens.

Aboriginal design at Birrarung Marr.

Metal shields reflect different Kulin groups, engraved steel plates are set into the ground and combine to create an eel in recognition of this important traditional food source, and a scattering of rocks carved with indigenous motifs frame a performance area. You can hear individual stories at panels on the wall of the old red-brick railway building that has been transformed into **Artplay**.

This is a children's centre and gallery where performers and artists run creative programmes. Most require advance booking (tel: 9664 7900). However, behind it and accessible to all, the **Artplay Playground** is a dizzy technicoloured jumble of swings, hammocks, tube slides and novelties yet to be named.

Stay on the river terrace and you'll come across *Angel*, the oddly feline creature with two heads, three legs and bright, glazed tiles all over it.

Up a short flight of steps, the **Federation Bells**, a forest of 39 variously sized bells mounted on poles, sit on the middle terrace. They were set up to mark the centenary of Australia's federation in 2001, and three times a day (8–9am, 12.30–1.30pm and 5–6pm) they clang into life and produce a bit of a tune.

Nearby is the beginning of the **William Barak Bridge**, named after a distinguished indigenous leader who was there to witness the signing of Batman's treaty in 1835. If you follow this for half a kilometre or so (500 yards) over roads and railway tracks you'll come to the MCG.

The sports zone

However, if you stick to the river a little longer, at Swan Street Bridge you can cross over Batman Avenue to gain access to a whole string of other sporting venues. Come here in the second half of January and the area to the left is throbbing with activity because the Australian Open Tennis Championships are in full swing.

The first of the year's four Grand Slam events attracts the finest players in the world. The main auditorium, the **Rod Laver Arena** ❷, is used during the rest of the year for big-name bands, spectaculars such as *Walking With Dinosaurs*, and everything from stunt-bike riding to horse shows. Unless there's something on or you fancy a game of tennis on a championship court (tel:

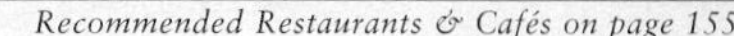
Recommended Restaurants & Cafés on page 155

1300 836 647), there's not a great deal to see, beyond a rather prosaic statue of Rod Laver, which would probably benefit from some of *Angel*'s colourful tiles. The **Hisense Arena**, a little further along, has similar events and used to host the local basketball side, South Dragons, until their demise in 2009.

On the other side of Swan Street, **Olympic Park** is home to athletics. The bubbly white structure further along is the new rectangular stadium **AAMI Park**, where up to 30,000 people can watch the local soccer (Melbourne Victory, Melbourne Heart) or rugby (Melbourne Storm) teams. There's a great light show on match nights, too.

The MCG ❸

One of the best-known structures in Australia, the **Melbourne Cricket Ground** was given a massive makeover in time for the Commonwealth Games in 2006. Even the crusty old members were prised from the original Long Room and now enjoy plate-glass views from the new bar and dining room. Unless you're a member or a friend of one, the only way to get in is on a guided tour, which also takes in the changing rooms, coaches' boxes and the arena itself (Gate 3, Olympic Stand; www.mcg.org.au; tel: 9657 8879; daily on non-event days, 10am–3pm; charge). However, nothing beats being part of the crowd at a cricket match or an Aussie Rules game.

The new **National Sports Museum** incorporates material from the old Olympic Museum, the Cricket Hall of Fame, AFL World and Champions Racing Museum.

From Gate 4 a tree-lined path leads north through Yarra Park. Cross over the railway and Wellington Parade to Powlett Street. This is East Melbourne, one of the earliest areas of settlement for the more prosperous of the first arrivals.

East Melbourne ❹

Random wanderings around the area bounded by Wellington Parade and Clarendon, Albert and Hoddle streets reveal examples of some of the more intricate and ornate imaginings of Victorian-era architects. For a taster, **Powlett Street** contains many treasures, and a few carefully selected sorties down adjoining roads will reveal the best of the rest.

Selling Game Guides outside the MCG before an AFL game.

Far Left: in Birrarung Marr. **Above Left:** tribute to the pioneers of Aussie Rules at the MCG. **Below:** bells up. The Federation Bells.

The MCG

The 'G spends less than half the year as a cricket ground, with Aussie Rules or "footie" taking up the slack. It's a gleaming modern arena with a memorable history

The Melbourne Cricket Ground has long been known as the "people's ground", and, technically, it still is – occupying Crown land leased to the Melbourne Cricket Club (MCC). The club was formed in 1838, three years after settlement, and played its cricket on three other sites before adopting this one in 1853, which wasn't as swampy or prone to flooding as its predecessors.

Interstate matches with Van Diemen's Land (Tasmania) had begun after the state of Victoria was gazetted in 1851, but the first big match on this ground was against New South Wales in 1856. The first game against a touring English team came in 1862, but in those days a handicapping system meant that Victoria fielded 18 men to the tourists' 11. The first recognised 11-a-side Test Match in 1877 saw Australia beat England by 45 runs, a feat that, astonishingly, they repeated to the letter 100 years later in the Centenary Test.

By 1877, Australian Rules football had been codified and was proving to be a popular winter sport. However, concerns about its impact on the cricket pitch meant that it was some years before it was played inside the MCG. Now a minimum of 45 matches are played here each season, including the Grand Final every September. Footie at the 'G has even been recognised in song by Mick Thomas, erstwhile leader of legendary Melbourne band, Weddings Parties Anything:

Is there anywhere you'd rather be
Than with me at the MCG
And if the Saints get done again
By Christ I couldn't care.

Happily for Mick, such an outcome for the Saints (AFL team St Kilda) is less likely these days.

The MCG has led the world by evolving continuously, but there were two spikes: work for the 1956 Olympics included a new grandstand; then from 2002 to 2006 came the biggest upgrade yet. All the stands, apart from the Great Southern Stand of 1992, were torn down and replaced, on time and on budget, for the March 2006 Commonwealth Games. There's more legroom, the seats are more comfortable and only the catering lags behind. This has pushed the notional ground capacity to 100,018, which is some way behind the largest recorded attendance of over 130,000 in 1959 for a Billy Graham crusade, but that did include people on the arena itself.

Rugby (both codes) and soccer are still played here on occasion and there have been some major concerts. *The MCG Anniversary Tapestry* documents much of this and can be seen in the MCC Members' Area during guided tours. On the tour you'll also learn why there's one odd-coloured seat high up in one of the grandstands. ❑

LEFT: Shane Warne in his final test at the MCG.

Recommended Restaurants & Cafés on page 155

George Street – the first cross-street – has some impressive mansions in both directions (and, a block to the right, the comfortable neighbourhood George Street café), but struggles to match the astonishing iron lacework of **Foynes** and **Eastcourt** at 52 Powlett Street. As with other houses nearby, even the gateposts are symphonies in iron. Further along, the shell of the **Cairns Memorial Presbyterian Church** envelops an interesting modern apartment dwelling, while across the road from it a well-preserved Deco block celebrates a different age.

Along Hotham Street to the east, you'll find the magisterial red-brick **Queen Bess Row** (1886) looming up on your left, and a complete mix of architectural eras and styles before you get there. Back on Powlett Street, the house of Eureka Stockade leader Peter Lalor *(see page 225)* at No. 85 is rather overshadowed by **Canterbury Terrace** – Melbourne's longest – over the road. Continue as far as No. 138 for its unusual "opera box" balcony, before doubling back to Gipps Street, where a westward turn will take you past houses once owned by, respectively, Joan Lindsay, author of *Picnic at Hanging Rock* (No. 107 Powlett); Norman Lindsay, best known for the children's book *The Magic Pudding* (No. 155 Gipps); Eugene von Guerard, the renowned Australian Impressionist painter (No. 159), and Frederick Baker, the actor whose ghost haunts the Princess Theatre *(see page 104* ; No. 128). At the end of Gipps Street, cross into Fitzroy Gardens.

FITZROY GARDENS 5

Laid out in the 1850s, this was one of the earliest of the city's public parks. It's a tranquil haven, with stately elm trees providing shade, and little nuggets of eccentricity providing interest. For the first of these walk towards the southwestern corner, and just past the Pavilion Café you'll find the **Model Tudor Village**. This collection of crudely modelled cottages was, as the sign proclaims, sent as a gift by the people of the London Borough of Lambeth to Melburnians who had been so supportive during World War II with, as local legend has it, the gathering of pots of dripping and other

TIP

The Yarra River acts as backdrop and southern boundary to this chapter but is also an attraction in itself. River taxis, shuttle craft, historic steam vessels, floating restaurants and, bizarrely, a boat that looks like a tram compete to draw visitors on to the water. Cruises last from an hour upwards and can be booked at Federation Wharf or at the Southgate Centre on the opposite bank.

BELOW: Foynes and Eastcourt in Powlett Street.

Make a detour to the northeastern corner of Fitzroy Gardens where, across Clarendon Street, the Freemasons Hospital (1936) is one of Melbourne's finest Art Deco buildings.

household surpluses, which were then sent halfway around the world. Seeing the village, it's hard to assess who got the better of the exchange.

Proving that Lambeth didn't have a monopoly on crude modelling, the nearby **Fairies' Tree** attracts children with its carved approximations of elves, animals and, yes, fairies. Continue down the hill for an eccentric enterprise on a much larger scale.

Cooks' Cottage ❻

9419 4677 daily 9am–5pm charge Jolimont 48, 75

Be careful with that apostrophe because this is the dwelling of the parents of James Cook, so it's not the one that the Captain owned or lived in himself. But he did, we are assured, visit in those rare moments when not exploring the world's remote regions in the 18th century. Either way, in what must have been some logistical feat at the time, it was purchased in 1933 and dismantled from its spot in Yorkshire before being transported to Australia and reassembled where it stands today. The handful of rooms are furnished in period style, and there's an attractive four-seasons garden behind.

The **Aboriginal Scar Tree**, or at least its trunk, is beside a pathway leading to the southeastern corner of

ABOVE RIGHT: Fitzroy Gardens. **BELOW:** fairy interesting.

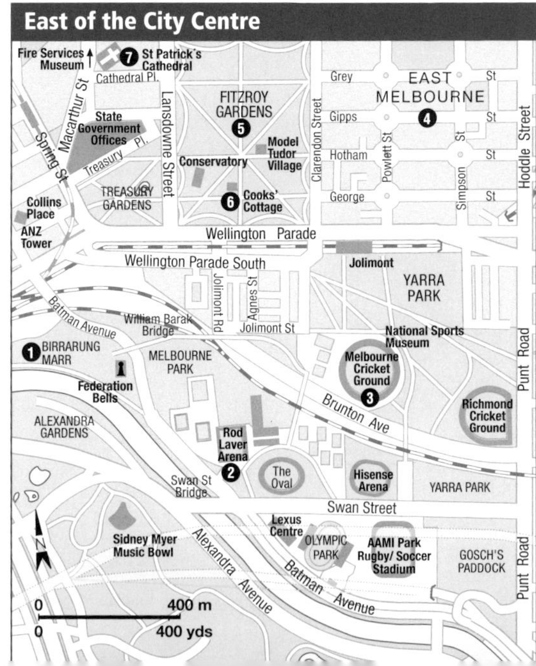

the Gardens, or you can head in the opposite direction for the **Conservatory**. A rare example in these parts of Spanish Mission-style architecture from the 1930s, it houses a regularly changing display of flora while providing respite from the heat or cold, depending on the time of year.

ST PATRICK'S CATHEDRAL 7

Across the road from the north-western edge of Fitzroy Gardens is the focal point for Melbourne's Catholics. It's the largest church in the state and composed on classic Gothic Revival lines, making the most of the indigenous bluestone for its walls and, less predictably, reinforced concrete faced with stone for the three spires, which weren't added until the 1930s. Inside, the soaring columns and arches do their usual trick of humbling the visitor, and are at their best on afternoons when yellow light is flooding the nave and an organist is playing. Major renovations were completed in 1997, and it was then that one of the new gargoyles was found to bear a striking resemblance to Jeff Kennett, the State Premier at the time.

The Fire Services Museum

39 Gisborne Street; www.alphalink.com.au/fsmvic 9662 2907
Thur, Fri 9am–3pm, Sun 10am–4pm charge 12, 24, 30, 31, 109, 112

Diagonally across from the cathedral, some large fiery murals enliven an otherwise dull concrete wall. This is a modern addition to the 1893 Eastern Hill Fire Station. Up Gisborne Street in the old part is the entrance to the **Fire Services Museum**. A rigorously maintained collection of fire engines, equipment and memorabilia from around the world is brought vividly to life by volunteer guides, all of whom are ex-firemen. ❑

At the Fire Services Museum, this man, or one very much like him, will tell you why men would spend all day sitting at the top of a tower, or why Dame Nellie Melba's old car became a fire engine.

ABOVE LEFT: St Patrick's Cathedral.
BELOW LEFT: Cook and his parents' Cottage.

RESTAURANTS AND CAFÉS

George Street Café
65 George Street, East Melbourne.
B & L daily **$** [off p303]
This is an archetypal local corner café where you feel most of the customers are residents in search of a bit of a gossip.

The Pavilion
Fitzroy Gardens. B & L daily **$** [p303, E3]
Solid performer in attractive setting near the Model Tudor Village and the Fairies' Tree. Breakfast is available all day at weekends.

radii
Park Hyatt Hotel, 1 Parliament Square, off Parliament Place.
9224 1211 B & D daily **$$$** [p303, E3]
Before you even lay eyes on the menu, the theatricality of the architecture contributes to the sense of occasion at this high-end eatery. There's a dégustation menu, too.

Prices for a three-course dinner per person with a half-bottle of house wine. ***$** = under A$60; **$$** = A$60–90; **$$$** = over A$90.*

YERING
Station

Recommended Restaurants, Bars & Cafés on pages 166–7

CARLTON AND FITZROY

In their time, these inner-city suburbs have been the haunt of the Establishment rich and the abject poor, of enterprising immigrant communities and academics and bohemians. Today you will find traces of all of these

As Melbourne expanded in the mid-19th century, the area to the north of the CBD was quickly settled for both habitation and light industry, with Fitzroy first out of the blocks. Town houses for professional men were heavily outnumbered by terraces of workers' cottages. All was well until the depression of the 1890s hit, when those who couldn't leave succumbed to poverty and squalor, dragging the suburb down with them. Organised and not so organised crime took hold, further extending the spiral of decline.

A real change in fortunes did not arrive until the middle of the 20th century, when waves of Greek and Italian immigrants, and to a lesser extent Spanish and Yugoslav, arrived after the end of World War II, taking over cheap and dilapidated housing and reinvigorating the local economy.

Little Italy

Carlton, to the west, developed later in the 1800s, its leafy streets and public spaces appealing initially to the well-to-do or those linked to the expanding University of Melbourne, as well as a significant Jewish contingent. However, the same difficulties that had afflicted Fitzroy took hold here. Post-war immigration changed the balance again, and Lygon Street today attracts tourists and locals alike to the city's Little Italy.

Community action saved many of the Victorian terraces from the wreckers, and nowadays prosperous professionals rub shoulders with academics and creatives in the thriving café strips of a thoroughly gentrified neighbourhood.

Main attractions

- ROYAL EXHIBITION BUILDING
- MELBOURNE MUSEUM
- BRUNSWICK STREET
- LYGON STREET
- UNIVERSITY OF MELBOURNE
- MELBOURNE GENERAL CEMETERY
- MELBOURNE ZOO

LEFT: shopping in Brunswick Street, the hub of Fitzroy.
RIGHT: dancing in the street during a city festival.

The Royal Exhibition Building with its splendid dome.

ROYAL EXHIBITION BUILDING ❶

✉ www.museumvictoria.com.au/reb ☎ 13 11 02 ⓒ guided tours daily 2–3pm ⓢ charge 🚊 10, 24, 30, 86, 95, 96 🚌 250, 251, 253, 402, 479

Created by Melbourne Town Hall designer Joseph Reed and opened in 1880 as the ostentatious centrepiece of the Melbourne International Exhibition, the Royal Exhibition Building (REB) was the epitome of Victorian civic pomp and a natural choice for the first sitting of Australia's Federal Parliament in 1901. From its site in Carlton Gardens on the northeastern corner of the CBD, the dome – modelled on the Duomo in Florence – could once be seen from all points of the city, but is at its best closer to, offset by the carefully landscaped gardens. It underwent an extensive renovation in the 1990s, came out gleaming and was rewarded with a UNESCO World Heritage listing in 2004 – at the time the only building in Australia to be so honoured (Sydney Opera House was belatedly recognised in 2007). The building is still used for exhibitions, and you can also gain access on a guided tour.

Carlton and Fitzroy

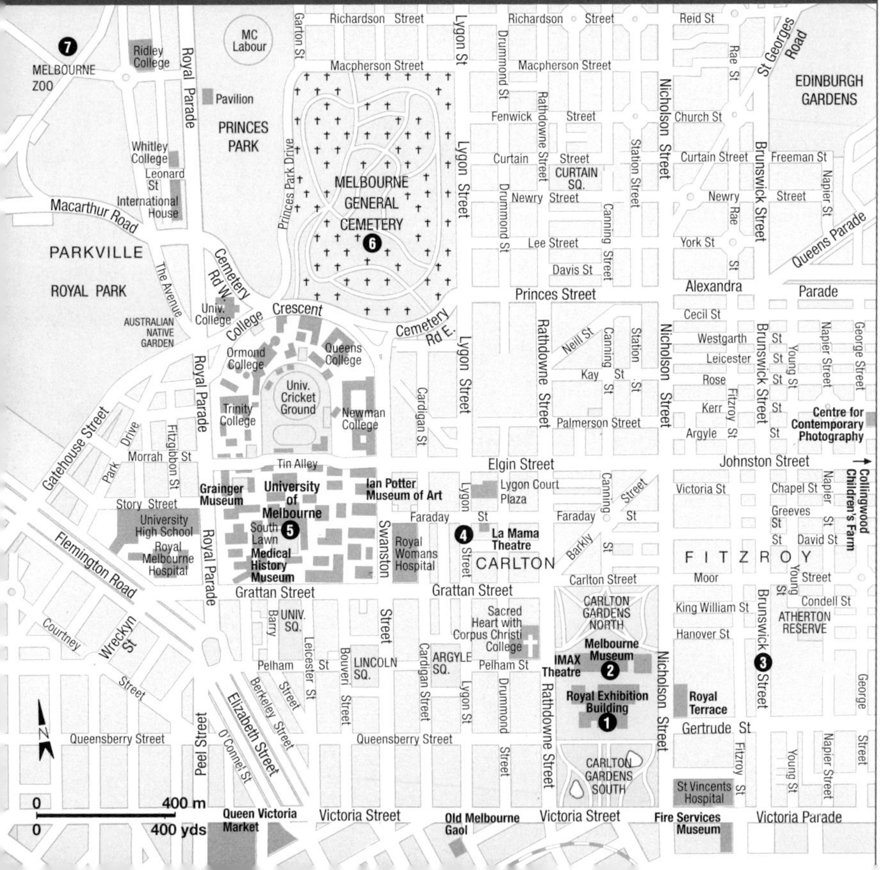

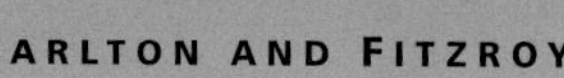

Map on page 158

Recommended Restaurants, Bars & Cafés on pages 166–7

> *...situated in Carlton, a now scruffy but once fashionable suburb of Melbourne*

Ray Lawlor explains the setting of his 1953 play *Summer of the Seventeenth Doll*, which went on to worldwide success and acclaim. It was the first identifiably "Australian" play to break out to a wider audience

MELBOURNE MUSEUM ❷

www.museumvictoria.com.au
13 11 02 daily 10am–5pm
charge as for REB above

Immediately to the north of the REB, the Melbourne Museum is a striking modern construction that seeks to draw together in its airy galleries all the strands that make up the city today. The **Forest Gallery** and **Bunjilaka Aboriginal Centre** give an indication of life before European settlement, while other sections are devoted to evolution and wildlife, scientific advances and the people and events that have shaped the city. An excellent Children's Gallery – the boldly coloured wonky cube off to the side – completes the experience. *For more on the Museum see pages 168–9.*

Around the Museum

From the Museum, turn east towards Nicholson Street for uninterrupted views of some of Melbourne's finest terraces. **Royal Terrace** (50–58 Nicholson Street, between Palmer and Gertrude Streets) was built between 1853 and 1858 in bluestone, and the fact that three-time Victorian Premier John O'Shanassy lived here (1888–9) indicates how fashionable the area was in those days. As with the rest of Carlton, it hit hard times for much of the 20th century, but is now very much back to its former glory.

Head north up Nicholson Street past the Gothic Revival Academy of Mary Immaculate and the Convent of Mercy, the popular backpacker haunt The Nunnery (once home to nuns from the Daughters of Charity, who used to minister to the locals in the 1930s in archaic 17th-century French-style habits), and the Pump House Hotel.

ABOVE LEFT: paintwork in the Royal Exhibition Building. **ABOVE:** two roos outside the Exhibition Building. **BELOW:** canopy over the Living Forest at the Melbourne Museum.

Brunswick Street is notable for its small owner-operated fashion shops. This one has incorporated another common local characteristic: stylish graffiti.

Turn right down Moor Street and you'll begin to pick up a flavour of the diverse history of Fitzroy, where gracious terraces mix with run-down cottages, specialist vendors with utilitarian repair shops.

BRUNSWICK STREET ❸

This thoroughfare has been the hub of Fitzroy from the beginning, the first stores being built in the 1840s. By the end of the 19th century, parades of shops lined the street and many of them are still here, having outlasted various waves of European migrants who have passed through over the years. Brunswick Street is still in a sense Melbourne's fringe; a place where novelty and experiment are not out of place, where it looks as though access to a space, a can of paint and some second-hand furniture can produce a bar or gallery overnight.

The atmosphere is cosmopolitan in the best sense of the word. Grungy second-hand clothes stores mix with cutting-edge restaurants; drinking clubs rub shoulders with Polyester's "Totally Weird Shit" store. An idea of where Brunswick Street sits in Melbourne life can be gleaned from what was, until 2001, its biggest social occasion: the Melbourne Fringe Festival Parade. This raucous, outlandish display of excess and imagination would draw thousands of people to one big street party. Ultimately it outgrew itself, but spend a few minutes browsing here and you'll see why this was the right place for it.

Before diving in, look towards the south. Ungainly blocks of housing-commission flats sit uncomfortably

above the low-rise streetscape, but consider that they were built to replace "The Narrows", a stretch of squalid alleys once considered "probably the most fetid spot in Australia". Further down, St Patrick's Cathedral *(see page 155)* sits squarely at the end of the street, a timely reminder of the higher things in life.

Turning your back on that, contemplate the **Labour in Vain Hotel** on the corner of Moor Street. The name comes from an old pub in England, and the interior, though not quite

ABOVE RIGHT: fine foods in Brunswick Street. **BELOW:** navigating Brunswick Street. **BELOW RIGHT:** housing-commission flats in Fitzroy.

evoking a pre-colonial past, does have a palpable sense of history to it. Bars and cafés become ever quirkier as you head up the street, befitting their young, cool and bohemian clientele.

Students find it cheaper than some of the strips closer to the University, but there's a healthy cross-section of long-time residents, professionals and tourists as well. Property prices are, predictably, creeping up, although some new apartment dwellers appear to be missing the point when they complain about the noisy late-night music venues in the hip suburb they've just chosen to live in.

It's worth a sidetrack to Greeves Street, on the left two blocks up from Moor Street, to appreciate why this collection of 1870s houses was the first streetscape to be listed by the National Trust of Australia, run down though they are.

Artful shopping

Back on Brunswick Street, note the typical Victorian strips of shops with their canopies to protect their customers from everything the Melbourne weather can throw at them, and enjoy the way the uniformity of the buildings has been subverted by some imaginative sculptural look-at-me signage. Most extravagant is the Vasette flower shop coming up on the left with its super-sized flowers and a swarm of bees engulfing the building. The lamp-post-sized bloom gorging itself on a straggler from the swarm is a particular favourite. Further up, Fitzroy Nursery reaps the benefit of commissioning sculptor Deborah Halpern (of *Ophelia* and *Angel* fame) to draw the customers with gates clogged with vivid creatures.

East of Brunswick Street

If you need a break from the bustle and can't find a table in the Fitz

Borsari's corner, where Grattan Street crosses Lygon Street, is named after Italian Olympic gold medal-winning cyclist Nino Borsari. He was racing in Australia when World War II broke out and, stranded, opened a cycle repair shop on this site.

ABOVE LEFT: look flash. **BELOW LEFT:** use flash. **BELOW RIGHT:** flash the readies along Brunswick Street.

KIDS

If you continue east along Johnston Street for a couple of kilometres, signs direct you to Collingwood Children's Farm, a long-term city favourite that has seen generations of kids introduced to the vagaries of domestic and farm animals. There's also a farmers' market every second Saturday of the month.

café, say, or Retro, then take a detour to the right down Kerr Street and discover the peaceful allure of the **Centre for Contemporary Photography** on the corner with George Street (404 George Street; www.ccp.org.au; tel: 9417 1549; Wed–Fri 11am–6pm, Sat–Sun noon–5pm; free). A slew of galleries presents images that have, at some stage of their creation, involved photography. Even when it is closed, you can sample the work after dark courtesy of the Projection Window.

Were you to continue eastwards for a couple of blocks you would hit Smith Street. This is another long shopping strip – a kind of down-at-heel Brunswick Street – where funky shops and shoestring galleries are the hang-outs for those who cherish being part of the next wave.

Johnston Street is the main cross-street in this area and home, as you return west towards Brunswick Street, to a small Spanish enclave of tapas bars and cultural clubs. It's quite a walk west from here but worth it for the sensory extravaganza of Lygon Street that awaits you.

TOP RIGHT: café society in Lygon Street.
ABOVE RIGHT: the long-running home of radical theatre.
BELOW: Readings Bookshop.

LYGON STREET ❹

From the junction with Elgin Street down, this is one of the most atmospheric thoroughfares in Melbourne. It's at its most appealing in early evening, when it plays host to something that comes close to the traditional Italian *passeggiata*. Everyone is strolling, window-shopping, sampling a *gelato*, or contemplating an aperitif. Cafés spill chairs and tables out on to the street, and bow-tied touts (or "spruikers" in the Aussie vernacular) proclaim the merits of their particular restaurants.

There's something about the broad tree-lined street and the human scale of the low-rise buildings that makes you want to linger and sample the modest (by Melbourne standards) accomplishments of the local chefs. Although tourists are targeted, there is a bedrock clientele of first- and second-generation immigrants, academics from the University and city workers who have opted for inner-suburban living.

Readings Bookshop (No. 309) provides intellectual nourishment, along with La Mama Theatre in Faraday Street (www.lamama.com.au; tel: 9347 6142), and the new boutique-style Museo Italiano (199 Faraday Street; www.museoitaliano.com.au; tel: 9349 9000; Tue–Fri 10am–5pm, Sat noon–5pm; free). A block or two west lies the University.

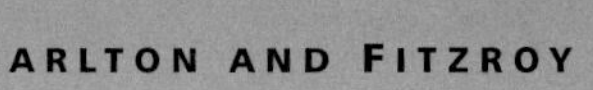

Map on page 158

Recommended Restaurants, Bars & Cafés on pages 166–7

UNIVERSITY OF MELBOURNE ❺

The University was founded in 1853 and looked to Britain for its model, both in terms of structure (collegiate, although with centralised teaching) and environment (neo-classical halls, quadrangles and lawns). Over the years it has been much added to, and discrimination is required to find the gems amongst the hotchpotch.

Approaching from the Swanston Street side, the dynamic facade of the **Ian Potter Museum of Art** is the first thing to grab your attention. What looks like a grab-bag of fragments of classical statuary embedded in the wall goes under the title *Cultural Rubble* and is by Christine O'Loughlin. Inside, a series of spacious galleries house work from the University's collection, including everything from classical antiquities to challenging contemporary art. It hosts touring exhibitions, too (www.art-museum.unimelb.edu.au; tel: 83 44 5148; Tue–Fri 10am–5pm, Sat–Sun noon–5pm; free.)

A collection of a rather different stripe is to be found in the **Grainger Museum** (www.lib.unimelb.edu.au/collections/grainger; tel: 8344 5270). Set up in the 1930s by and for the Australian composer Percy Grainger, it contains documents and artefacts pertaining to his life and career, including manuscripts and instruments, as you might expect, and choice specimens from his collection of pornography and sexual paraphernalia, which you might not.

More or less gruesome, according to your proclivities, is the **Medical History Museum** (www.chs.unimelb.edu.au/programs/jnmhu/museum; tel: 8344 9935; Mon–Fri 10am–4pm; free). A daunting quantity of instruments and devices have been gathered together to illustrate the development of medical science.

The **Old Quad** is the oldest part of the University, and picturesque with it. **South Lawn** nearby is interesting, too, for the ingenuity of its construction. Underneath there's a

EAT

It's not necessarily the best food in Melbourne, but Lygon Street has several landmark establishments, including the country's first pizza restaurant, Toto's (No. 99–101); the historic intellectual hang-out, University Café (No. 257); Jimmy Watson's Wine Bar, one of the first of the genre (No. 333); and Brunetti at 198 Faraday Street, which has spawned a chain of similar cake-centric cafés.

ABOVE LEFT: *Cultural Rubble* at the Ian Potter Museum of Art.
BELOW: Melbourne University campus.

Deadlines

Melbourne General Cemetery is a place for pottering and serendipitous discovery. Key figures from the city's past are here, but there are many other stories to be told

Melbourne Cemetery comprises 43 hectares (106 acres) of gravestones and memorials. It's a fascinating place to delve into the city's past. Try combining random wanderings with the following pointers.

Just beyond the impressive iron gates, the Prime Ministers' Memorial Garden **A** on the right includes the grave of Bob Menzies, Australia's longest-serving Prime Minister (1939–41, 1949–63), as well as a memorial to Harold Holt, the serving Prime Minister who went for a swim off Portsea in 1967 and didn't come back.

Continue eastwards to the hefty Burke and Wills monument **B**, erected to the ill-fated explorers in 1873 *(see page 28)*. A little way up the drive you'll find Sir Redmond Barry **C**, who not only founded Melbourne University but was also the judge who sentenced Ned Kelly to hang, only to book his own spot in these grounds 12 days later.

Across the other side of the path is a memorial to James Galloway **D**, who was central to the campaign to introduce the eight-hour working day. In the grave of Frederick Baker **E** rests, if that's the word, the body of the man known as Federici, the actor who is said to haunt the Princess Theatre *(see page 104)*. Continue eastwards to find Marcus Clarke **F**, author of the seminal convict novel, *For the Term of His Natural Life* (1874). The cream hut ahead is the Jewish Mortuary **G**, and south near the railings is a striking Holocaust Memorial in the shape of a menorah **H**.

Melbourne General Cemetery

World figures

The cemetery is divided according to nationality or religion, and the Chinese section is signalled by the ovens **I** on the junction of Central and East Avenues. Robert Hoddle **J**, the designer of Melbourne's street grid, and John O'Shanassy **K**, whose house we saw in Nicholson Street, are to be found in Central Avenue. Down at the end is Elvis Presley, or at least a memorial to him **L**, which is covered with tributes on his birthday.

More pertinent to Australia is the grave of Walter Lindrum **M**, and what a treat this is. Lindrum was dubbed the "Bradman of billiards" for his utter domination of the sport – he was World Professional Billiards champion from 1933 until his retirement in 1950 – and he now rests beneath a stone billiard table. The grave of Peter Lalor **N**, leader of the Eureka uprising at Ballarat *(see page 225)*, is a sombre reminder of Victoria's tumultuous beginnings.

For more detailed guides track down a copy of the National Trust's *Tour of the Melbourne General Cemetery*, or *The Melbourne General Cemetery* by Don Chambers. ❑

ABOVE: gravestones gently askew in the Cemetery.

car park with a roof held up by Gothic-style columns, which actually serve to provide room for the roots of the trees growing above. The by-product of this is one of the world's more atmospheric car parks.

At the northern end of the campus are the residential colleges. **Trinity College** has a noteworthy chapel – see if you can spot the possums and platypuses inside – and **Newman College** (1918) is lauded as one of the finest designs of Walter Burley Griffin and Marion Mahoney Griffin, the design team responsible for the layout of Canberra. However, in these security-conscious days, getting near it can be tricky.

Cemetery Road marks the northern boundary of the campus and gives a less-than-subtle clue to the next destination.

MELBOURNE GENERAL CEMETERY 6

In the early days of settlement the main city cemetery was on a site now occupied by the Queen Victoria Market. This changed when the Melbourne General Cemetery opened for business in 1853. As with graveyards the world over, a few minutes reading headstones at random can create pictures of lives lived and squandered, of traumas suffered and of perils to our ancestors undreamt of today. Here, along with the unheralded, you'll find some of the key shapers of Melbourne, and indeed the country, many of whom appear elsewhere in this book. For a swift trawl of the highlights, see the panel opposite.

From the west gate of the cemetery, there's a bit of a walk across parkland and down Leonard Street to reach Royal Park, home of Melbourne Zoo.

MELBOURNE ZOO 7

Elliott Avenue; www.zoo.org.au
9285 9300 daily 9am–5pm
charge Royal Park 55

This is one very good zoo. It has evolved from the typical Victorian model – it opened in 1862 – and now consists of a number of habitats ("bioclimatic zones") suited to the animals contained in them. So there's Australian bush, Asian and African rainforests, and smaller areas like the butterfly house, where a handful of the creatures may choose your head for a perch.

The Trail of the Elephants enclosure evokes a Southeast Asian village; the Orang-utan Sanctuary includes a treetop walkway. And then there's the music *(see margin)*. ❑

At summer weekends (Jan–Mar), Melbourne Zoo stays open late for the "Twilights" series of concerts, featuring music across many different genres. Pictured is local legend Joe Camilleri, whose bands have included The Black Sorrows and Jo Jo Zep and the Falcons.

ABOVE LEFT: the colonnade beside the Old Quad.

Culture and Politics in Brunswick

Royal Parade heading north, past Melbourne Zoo, becomes Sydney Road, the main artery of Brunswick, one of the more spirited suburbs of Melbourne. Once the site of a quarry and brickworks before becoming the centre of the textile and other light industries, Brunswick has long been a solid working-class area with a history of cultural variety and political activism. Sydney Road encapsulates all of this. A slew of restaurants and cafés provide global cuisine, reflecting an ethnically diverse population – the post-war flow of Greek and Italian migrants was swiftly followed by contingents from Lebanon, Turkey, China, Vietnam and elsewhere. Struggling artists and students have always appreciated the cheap rents, too, although there are signs of gentrification. For visitors, there are appetising prospects for food, culture (the Mechanics Institute is now an arts centre), music in one of the pubs or political engagement in venues like the Solidarity Salon.

BEST RESTAURANTS, BARS AND CAFÉS

Restaurants

Prices for a three-course dinner per person with a half-bottle of house wine:
$ = under A$60
$$ = A$60–90
$$$ = A$90–120
$$$$ = over A$120

Abla's

109 Elgin Street, Carlton. 9347 0006 L Thur–Fri, D Mon–Sat BYO **$** [p303, D2]
This plainly decorated restaurant is home to the best Lebanese food in the city.

Anada

197 Gertrude Street, Fitzroy. 9415 6101 D daily **$** [p303, E4]
Really a tapas bar but with table sittings (6.15 and 8.30pm) to turn it into a more structured evening. A rewarding taste of Spain.

Arrivederci

191 Nicholson Street, Carlton. 9347 8252 L Mon–Fri, D Mon–Sat **$$** [p303, D1]
There is no written menu at this Italian local, where dishes are dependent on what is available at the market, and the waiters explain the food in theatrical style.

Balzari

130 Lygon Street, Carlton. 9639 9383 L & D daily **$$** [p303, D3]
Wedged amongst the Italian tourist-trap restaurants of Lygon Street is this slice of Mediterranean authenticity, where everything from the dining room to service to flavour is executed with simplicity and style.

Blue Chillies

182 Brunswick Street, Fitzroy. 9417 0071 L & D daily **$** [p303, E2]
Malaysian food is given a modern makeover in terms of both flavour and decor in this popular Brunswick Street joint. Fast service and cheap prices keep the crowd happy.

Builders Arms

211 Gertrude Street, Fitzroy. 9419 0818 L Fri–Sun, D daily **$$** [p303, E3]
A sleek renovation has turned a former rough house into a fashionable venue with good drinks, food and a red, white and black decor that is flashier than a C-grade celebrity at an awards night.

The Commoner

122 Johnston Street, Fitzroy. 9415 6876 L Sat–Sun, D Wed–Sun **$** [p303, E2]
Quirky in a good way, The Commoner combines an appealingly hospitable attitude with food that takes its influences everywhere, from British pubs to Moroccan souks.

Cutler & Co.

55–7 Gertrude Street, Fitzroy. 9419 4888 L Fri and Sun, D Tue–Sun **$$$$** [p303, E4]
This dazzling arrival on the restaurant scene sees chef Andrew McConnell hit new heights in adventurous, contemporary cooking.

Embrasse

312 Drummond Street, Carlton. 9347 3312 D Wed–Sun **$$$** [p303, D2]
Acclaimed dégustation menus and à la carte dishes attain the peaks of French cuisine.

Enoteca Vino Bar

920 Lygon Street, Carlton North. 9389 7070 B & L Tue–Sun, D Tue–Sat **$** [off p303]
Combining a charming, sleekly decorated restaurant with a brilliant Italian produce and wine store, Enoteca Vino Bar is a source of all things quality and Italian.

Esposito

162 Elgin Street, Carlton. 9347 9838 L Mon–Fri, D Mon–Sat **$$$** [p303, D1]
Seafood is Esposito's *raison d'être*, and the

LEFT: Marios in Brunswick Street.

clean-lined space with its fishy art is a great place to indulge. Choose between flavours from Asia or Europe.

Jimmy Watson's
333 Lygon Street, Carlton. ☎ 9347 3985 ⓒ L daily, D Tue–Sat **$$** [p303, D2]
A Melbourne institution, Jimmy Watson's is a wonderfully casual, egalitarian wine bar offering straightforward food, a laid-back attitude and an impressive wine list.

Ladro
224 Gertrude Street, Fitzroy. ☎ 9415 7575 ⓒ L Sun, D daily **$$** [p303, E3]
Make sure to book ahead if you want to get your hands on what many believe is Melbourne's best pizza. The non-pizza dishes are good, too, as is the service and the constantly changing wine list.

Lemongrass
176 Lygon Street, Carlton. ☎ 9662 2244 ⓒ L Tue–Fri and Sun, D daily **$$** [p303, D2]
This stylish, moodily lit Thai restaurant serves traditional Thai food with all the spicy/fishy/tangy/sweet elements you would expect.

Masani
313 Drummond Street, Carlton. ☎ 9347 5610 ⓒ L daily, D Mon–Sat **$$$** [p303, D2]
Masani is old-school Italian at its best – traditional food cooked with care, accented waiters who make a fuss of you and a good-looking, classically decorated room.

Matteo's
533 Brunswick Street, North Fitzroy. ☎ 9481 1177 ⓒ D Sun–Fri **$$$$** [p303, E1]
An adventurous and witty take on Pacific-rim cooking, served in a dining room just within the bounds of good taste.

Old Kingdom
197 Smith Street, Fitzroy. ☎ 9417 2438 ⓒ L Tue–Fri, D Tue–Sun BYO **$** [p303, E2]
The decor – from dusty lanterns to plastic chopsticks – is decidedly no-frills, but the Peking Duck here is amongst the best in town and definitely close to the cheapest.

The Panama Dining Room
Level 3, 231 Smith Street, Fitzroy. ☎ 9417 7663 ⓒ D daily **$$** [p303, E2]
This enormous loft space has great urban views both from the sizeable bar area and the dining section down the back, where classic French bistro food is served with humour.

Pireaus Blues
310 Brunswick Street, Fitzroy. ☎ 9417 0222 ⓒ L Wed–Fri and Sun, D daily **$$** [p303, E1]
Not the place for anybody with sensitive ears, this is a lively taverna with deliciously simple Greek staples and chirpy, cheeky service.

Shakahari
201–203 Faraday Street, Carlton. ☎ 9347 3848 ⓒ L Mon–Sat, D daily **$** [p303, D2]
Shakahari is a vegetarian restaurant that even carnivores could love, so tasty and varied is the food. Dishes draw on the cuisines of Asia, Europe and the Middle East, and change seasonally.

Ying Thai 2
110 Lygon Street, Carlton. ☎ 9639 1697 ⓒ L & D Tue–Sun BYO **$** [p303, D3]
Bright, clattery Thai joint that is a hit with Asian students from the nearby University, who come here for both the cheap prices and the authentic food.

Bars and Cafés

Brunswick Street Alimentari
251 Brunswick Street, Fitzroy. [p303, E2]
Crowded café and foodstore with a great line in Italian and Lebanese food, plus good coffee.

Cavallero
300 Smith Street, Collingwood. [p303, E2] Austerely stylish café and bar.

Gertrude Street Enoteca
229 Gertrude Street, Fitzroy. [p303, E3] A bar for grown-ups that combines good wine, snack food and coffee.

Green Grocer
217 St Georges Road, Fitzroy North. [off p303] Organic café, produce store and wine shop. Scores on all fronts.

Ici
359 Napier Street, Fitzroy. [p303, E2] Leafy, quiet backstreet location and good coffee make this one of Fitzroy's most wanted.

Lygon Food Store
263 Lygon Street, Carlton. [p303, D2] Great produce and panini, accompanied by a bustling vibe.

Marios
303 Brunswick Street, Fitzroy. [p303, E1] A Melbourne classic that serves breakfast all day, comforting pasta, good wine and coffee in retro-cool surrounds.

Markov Place
Markov Place (enter from Elgin Street), Carlton. [p303, D2] Cool, hidden bar with decent food, great drinks and a moodily lit atmosphere.

Tiamo 1
303 Lygon Street, Carlton. [p303, D2] Straight-up Italian café. A home away from home for bohemian types.

MELBOURNE MUSEUM

Roll up for a trailblazing building, galleries ranging from the history of Melbourne to the intricacies of the human mind, and probably the fastest stuffed horse in town

The wonderful Melbourne Museum covers much more ground than its title might suggest. The Science and Life Gallery has the requisite stuffed animals but it's the 3D delights of the Virtual Room or the visceral *Bugs Alive!* exhibition that thrill most visitors. Upstairs, the Mind and Body Gallery provides a study of every aspect of human growth and development, with an especially impressive section on the mind. Kids are spoiled with their own gallery, two playgrounds and an IMAX cinema. And the city itself? *The Melbourne Story* employs glistening exhibition technology to reveal all. *For opening times and more information, see page 159.*

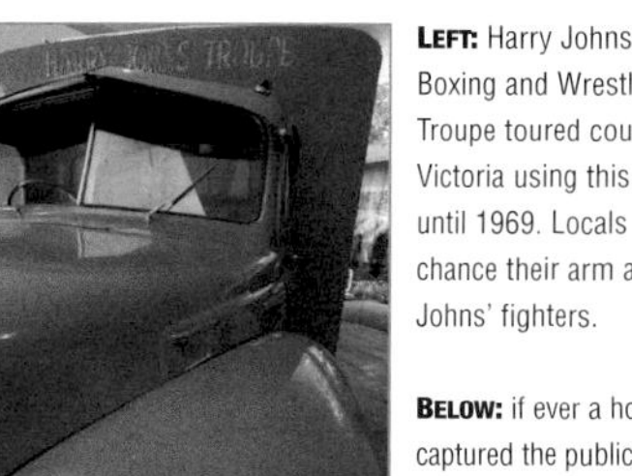

LEFT: Harry Johns' Boxing and Wrestling Troupe toured country Victoria using this truck until 1969. Locals would chance their arm against Johns' fighters.

BELOW: if ever a horse captured the public's imagination, it was Phar Lap during the days of the great depression. He was only six when he died in America in 1932, but by then had won 37 races from 57 starts.

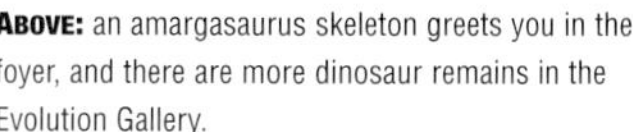

ABOVE: an amargasaurus skeleton greets you in the foyer, and there are more dinosaur remains in the Evolution Gallery.

BUNJILAKA

Curators of the museum's Bunjilaka Aboriginal Centre are well aware of the dilemma of representing Australia's indigenous peoples. Prominence is given to a quote from the Tasmanian Aboriginal Centre: "To be a voyeur on the physical objects of other peoples' cultures is not a way to understand them." In an attempt to deal with this, the curators have turned to that staple of Aboriginal culture: storytelling. At regular intervals there are dark spaces with screens where people speak on film of their history or that of their ancestors; at one point this involves actors engaging in a dialectic exploring the attitudes of Victorian settlers and the people they were displacing. Objects *are* used in this dark, brooding, dramatically lit space, but they are harnessed to illustrate the stories, whether of brutal massacres in the 19th-century colony, or more uplifting tales of those who reconnected with their people, land and culture.

ABOVE: the *Federation Tapestry* is a collective term for 10 separate pieces commissioned to mark the 2001 centenary of Federation. The subject matter ranges from Aboriginal kids' drawings to wry political cartoons. Go to the first floor landing.

LEFT: a Museum guide holds a traditional eel trap in the Bunjilaka Aboriginal Centre. In the background is one of the Lin Onus paintings that combine a reverence for the land with an acute political sensibility. They are on display in the Kalaya Meeting Place.

BELOW: there can't be many museums that incorporate a living forest. This one represents Victoria's mountain woodland and, along a series of pathways, reveals the elemental constituents of earth, fire and water. Try to spot the satin bowerbird in its bower.

Recommended Restaurants, Bars & Cafés on page 177

AROUND SOUTH MELBOURNE

Port Melbourne was the entry point to Australia for generations of immigrants, and the whole area south of the CBD has countless reminders of the 19th century, along with a large, thriving market and state-of-the-art sporting facilities

Main attractions

- STATION PIER
- PORTABLE IRON HOUSES
- SOUTH MELBOURNE MARKET
- CLARENDON STREET
- EMERALD HILL
- MELBOURNE SPORTS AND AQUATIC CENTRE
- ALBERT PARK

As with so much of the rest of Melbourne, the area south of the Yarra River down to Port Phillip Bay was transformed by the gold rush of the early 1850s. Much of the ground was swampy and only a handful of settlers made their homes or livings there. But in 1852, "Canvas City" sprang up to provide makeshift accommodation for the waves of new gold migrants seeking somewhere to spend their first days on a new continent. Its epicentre was the slight rise of Emerald Hill, an area at the centre of today's South Melbourne.

Land sales began at the same time, and soon there was a thriving suburb with hundreds of workers' homes constructed close to the river and wharves. Development spread to the east, and more salubrious dwellings were built around Albert Park and Middle Park, and along the seafront.

Albert Park itself, one of Melbourne's best-known locations thanks to worldwide television coverage of the Formula One Grand Prix that has been held there since 1996, was first designated in 1864. We'll wind up there, but let's begin at Station Pier, where life in Australia has begun for so many over the years.

STATION PIER ❶

This is where a great proportion of the passengers who had endured gruelling journeys from Europe and elsewhere were offloaded. It was at its busiest in the years after World War II, when many thousands, particularly from Italy and Greece, began a new life in Australia.

It's much quieter these days, with just the daily sailings of the ferries to

LEFT: waves of immigrants. New arrivals from Britain at Station Pier in the 1950s.
RIGHT: the beach at Port Melbourne.

The Destinations *installation commemorates the ships that have berthed since the first pier was built in 1854. Key vessels are named along with the date of their maiden voyage.*

ABOVE RIGHT: Contemplating the *Spirit of Tasmania* moored at Station Pier.

Tasmania and the occasional visit from international cruise ships. The 700-metre (760-yard) walk to the pier's end gives fine views around the foreshore to St Kilda and the chance to hobnob with the fishermen perched at the end.

On your return, note a white-and-red beacon in the sea to the left and then return to land to find its twin behind Beach Street, down Beach Vista. Once a ship's pilot aligns these two, the vessel is in the correct channel for the dock.

Destinations is the thrusting sculpture on the traffic island at the pier entrance. The earliest pier carried the steam trains of Australia's first passenger railway, which linked Sandridge (as Port Melbourne was then called) to the site of present-day Flinders Street Station in the city. Sandridge Bridge is now dedicated to the immigrants who took this short journey *(see page 133)*.

When the new Station Pier was

built in 1931, the train terminus moved ashore. Port Melbourne Railway Station has now been restored as a pizza joint, medical centre and a stop for the light rail service.

Beacon Cove

Beacon Cove, the area between Station Pier and the old Princes Pier, is coming to life again with restaurant and apartment development. However, if you continue west to Sandridge Beach, it's unlikely to be busy even on the hottest summer days.

Make your way along the water-

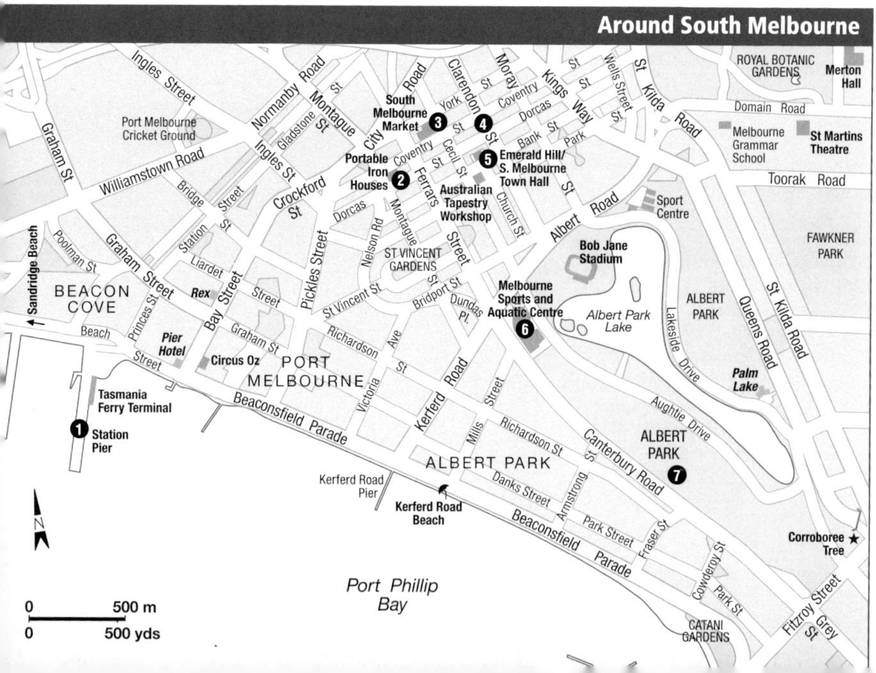

Around South Melbourne

Recommended Restaurants, Bars & Cafés on page 177

front the other way and there's further evidence of the development boom and gentrification that has changed the flavour of the neighbourhood since the 1990s. Old industrial buildings have been demolished or incorporated into new apartment blocks, and a new population of young professionals has moved in. The bars and cafés have followed.

There is still plenty of evidence of the past, though. The Rotunda was erected for troops returning from World War I by the Women's Welcome Home Committee in 1918. The unheralded Seamen's Institute on the corner of Nott Street is another reminder of days past, as indeed is the Pier Hotel at the bottom of Bay Street, along with the old Royal Mail Hotel, now badged as The Local.

Bay Street is a pleasant boulevard without pretensions. The 1860 Post Office used to be the receiving point for all the mail from the ships for the colony. It's now home to the world-renowned Circus Oz, which uses the Naval Drill Hall as rehearsal space.

Further up, on the corner with Graham Street, is the old Police Station, whose lock-up at the back would have held local miscreants prior to their appearance in the 1860 Court House next door. There are some fine late 19th-century shopfronts along Bay Street, although these do rather peter out as you veer right into Crockford Street, which becomes City Road.

Turn right into Montague Street and then left into Coventry Street. Just on the right are some fascinating gems of old Melbourne.

THE PORTABLE IRON HOUSES ❷

399 Coventry Street; www.nattrust.com.au 9645 7517 first Sun of month 1–4pm charge 96

These represent some of the last surviving examples of the cheap prefabricated buildings that were shipped out from Britain in the 1850s to help to deal with the rapid population increase. Dozens of them were erected around here and used as shops and commercial buildings as well as dwellings. There are three

"

Dear old ugly romantic beach; I love every bit of you in a way I will never be able to love St Kilda, or even the surf-washed beauty of Bondi or Manly, or the desecrated strip of blue and gold that is Surfers' Paradise

The heroine of Criena Roan's 1963 novel *Down by the Dockside* eulogises the seashore at Port Melbourne.

BELOW LEFT: one of the Portable Iron Houses... **BELOW:** ...and its bedroom.

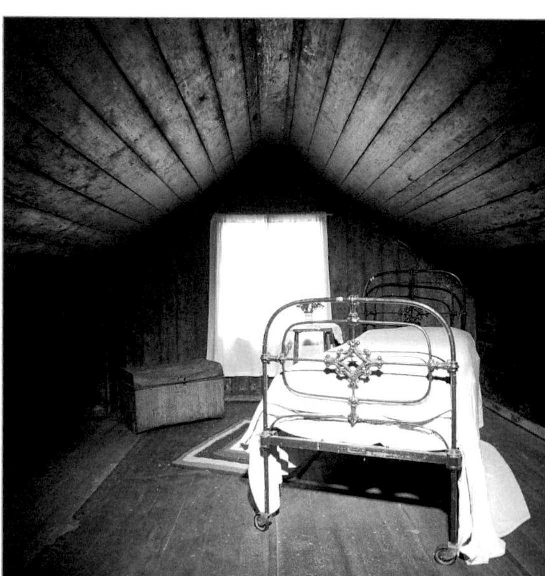

TIP

To locals it's simply the neighbourhood market, but to others from further afield, South Melbourne Market is worth the trek for some of the best dim sum in the city.

on this site, with period furnishings, including the dilapidated Abercrombie House, which was moved here from North Melbourne in 1980, having been occupied until 1976. You may have to go round the back to Patterson Street to see the last, unless you happen to be in town on one of the rare days when the houses are open. Once inside, it soon becomes clear how inappropriate corrugated iron is for the climate of Australia, even in relatively temperate Melbourne.

SOUTH MELBOURNE MARKET ❸

✉ Cnr Cecil and Coventry Streets; www.southmelbournemarket.com.au ☎ 9209 6295 🕒 Wed, Sat, Sun 8am–4pm, Fri 8am–5pm $ free 🚊 96, 112

It's a short walk up Coventry Street and over a bridge to South Melbourne Market. This isn't the most attractive of the city's markets – the building is functional at best – but then, it's not aiming to be anything more than a local resource. The usual fresh produce, flower and deli stalls are supplemented by outlets for clothing, kitchenware and general odds and ends. Surrounding streets are dotted with good cafés and pubs, and enough offbeat shops to create interest. Coventry Street, east of the market, has a mix of antiques, homeware and maternity wear among much else.

ABOVE RIGHT: Clarendon Street. **BELOW:** sign for South Melbourne Market.

Clarendon Street ❹ is the main drag, and it's a remarkably well-preserved one. The street is lined by uniform two-storey blocks, with cream-and-brown-striped awnings intact over the shop windows. Pressed metal ceilings and original stained glass and floor tiles can still be found in some. Turn right and, while indulging in a little window-shopping, attend to the details: the block between Dorcas and Bank Streets, for example, contains some quietly ornate shop fronts. On the eastern side of the street there's a 1909 block heavily indebted to the Glasgow architect Charles Rennie Mackintosh; at the Bank Street junction, look for the hitching posts.

Emerald Hill

Turn up Bank Street and climb the original **Emerald Hill** ❺, which at one time was used as a corroboree site by the Boonerwrung people who used to occupy this land. Today it is

Recommended Restaurants, Bars & Cafés on page 177

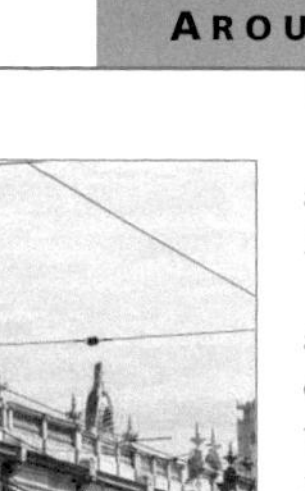

topped by the grandiose **South Melbourne Town Hall**. The Post Office opposite was built in 1912 and now functions as a library.

One block further on, in Park Street, you'll find some exquisitely preserved shop frontages. Behind the splendid ironwork lurks the **Australian Tapestry Workshop**, where some of the world's finest examples of the craft can be discovered. Drop in and see for yourself (262–266 Park Street; www.victapestry.com.au; tel: 9699 7885; Mon–Fri 9am–5pm; free).

Walk down Park Street and left along Montague Street to **St Vincent's Place**. This is where some of those at the top of the heap in gold-rush times built their mansions. It was laid out in 1857 with a nod to the squares of London: magnificent frontages, service access at the back and formal gardens in the communal square at the front. It is still one of the most desirable addresses in Melbourne, even though some of the grand piles are now rooming houses.

Fine gardens are all very well, but there's nowhere to get a coffee – close to a cardinal sin in Melbourne. Relief is to be found around the corner in **Bridport Street**, which has a good selection of cafés and bakeries. The number of outlets seems to have grown exponentially, perhaps a reflection of the number of service industries that have moved into the area: advertising agencies, record companies and motley creatives now proliferate. The Bridport Deli is one of the longer-established enterprises and a good place to start. From here you

South Melbourne Town Hall (1880) is now home to the Australian National Academy of Music and regularly hosts public concerts.

BELOW LEFT: the main workroom at the Australian Tapestry Workshop.

Australian Tapestry Workshop

It may be hidden away in a side street in South Melbourne, but the Australian Tapestry Workshop is a world leader in the craft. A core team of eight weavers works with artists from across the globe to produce tapestries of startling richness, which end up everywhere, from seats of government to private living rooms. The largest work to date is the *Reception Hall Tapestry* in Parliament House in Canberra, which was designed by Arthur Boyd. The best representation locally is the *Federation Tapestry* at the Melbourne Museum, comprising a series of panels by different artists, which together provide an impressive display of what can be achieved in this underexposed medium. Visitors to the workshop will find a quiet hum of activity as weavers beaver away, breaking off now and then to pick up another bobbin of just the right shade, hand-dyed on site, from a palette of 370 colours. There are guided tours on Wednesdays at 11am and Thursdays at 2pm.

With such a substantial proportion of Melbourne's population having some Italian ancestry, it's no surprise that Ferrari obsessives emerge in numbers at the Australian Grand Prix.

ABOVE RIGHT: Melbourne Sports and Aquatic Centre in Albert Park. **BELOW:** jogging beside Albert Park Lake.

can study the disproportionate **Biltmore Building** across the road. Originally a coffee palace in the latter days of the 19th century when temperance was all the rage, it subsequently became a private hotel and was used to accommodate American Army officers during World War II. Their views on temperance are not recorded.

Melbourne Sports and Aquatic Centre ❻

www.msac.com.au ☎ 9926 1555 daily 5.30am–10pm charge 96, 112

Dundas Place curls round towards the corner of Albert Park, where the dramatic white complex of the Melbourne Sports and Aquatic Centre awaits. It opened in 1997 and was upgraded with new outdoor diving pools for the 2006 Commonwealth Games. The 2007 World Swimming Championships were held here, too. If swimming isn't your thing, there are squash courts (which have also hosted world championships) and basketball courts that are used in Australia's national league.

Casual visitors are welcome and kids are well provided for, especially in the various pools where slides, waves and giant inflatables contribute to parental nervousness.

Albert Park ❼

The Sports Centre isn't the only place to get fit around here. Albert Park offers everything from a 5km (3-mile) gentle stroll around the lake to a round of golf. There are opportunities to play tennis or bowls, stadiums for soccer and cricket and several footie ovals. Also, when water levels allow it, the lake fills with sailing dinghies, much to the dismay of the resident black swan population.

Motor-racing fans celebrate in March when barriers go up, grandstands are erected and the Formula One circus comes to town. Some locals still object to the noise and disruption, but others, along with thousands of visitors, relish the carnival atmosphere spiced with adrenalin. It is an expensive day out, though, and workaday fans need to know their place – only corporate sponsors and their guests are allowed access to the best stand on the track.

Driving is allowed in the park, so rev-heads can cover all but a short stretch of the racetrack in their own cars. Mindful of the potential lawsuits, the park authorities have put up some hefty chicane-creating barriers on the main straight. Lap times need to be adjusted accordingly. ❑

BEST RESTAURANTS, BARS AND CAFÉS

Prices for a three-course dinner per person with a half-bottle of house wine:
$ = under A$60
$$ = A$60–90
$$$ = A$90–120
$$$$ = over A$120

Asiana

181 Victoria Avenue, Albert Park. 9696 6688 L Sun–Fri, D daily **$$** [p306, A1]

There is plenty to like about the modern pan-Asian food in this conservatively dressed restaurant, but the lengthy, remarkably well-priced wine list should have you feeling even more satisfied.

The Graham

97 Graham Street, Port Melbourne. 9676 2566 L & D daily **$$** [off p306]

This spruced-up pub is one of the area's gems, combining modern food that takes its influences from across the globe, a lengthy but focused wine list and friendly, highly polished service.

Ido Kitchen

166 Bridport Street, South Melbourne. 9699 8969 L Wed–Sat, D Tue–Sat **$$** [p304, A4]

Vietnamese cuisine burnished to a level rarely found in the eateries dotting the Little Vietnam strip on Victoria Street, in the suburb of Richmond.

Koh Samui

251 Richardson Street, Middle Park. 9696 3080 D daily **$** [p306, B1]

Smart presentation and touches of Malaysia enhance this well-priced Thai restaurant, which combines authentic flavours with a good wine list.

Lamaro's

273–279 Cecil Street, South Melbourne. 9690 3737 L & D daily **$$** [p304, B4]

A beautifully renovated pub on a quiet leafy street, Lamaro's food and service is several cuts above what you'd usually expect in a pub. The sense of hospitality and comfort is reassuringly old-fashioned.

O'Connell's

407 Coventry Street, South Melbourne. 9699 9600 L & D daily **$$** [p304, A3]

Set in a leafy backstreet, O'Connell's has been impressing with its food and service for years. These days it treads the comfort-food path, one that works well with the decor and ambience.

The Point Albert Park

Aquatic Drive, Albert Park. 9682 5566 L & D daily **$$$** [p304, B4]

Views over Albert Park Lake and good wine are part of the attraction, but The Point's best feature is its meat, much of it sourced exclusively for the restaurant from the pristine paddocks of King Island.

Rose Hotel

309 Bay Street, Port Melbourne. 9646 3580 L Sun–Fri, D daily **$$** [off p304]

It seems fitting to have the bay at the end of the street while tucking into some of the best Greek food in Melbourne at this renovated pub.

Tempura Hajime

60 Park Street, South Melbourne. 9696 0051 D Mon–Sat **$$** [p304, A4]

Intimate and exquisite Japanese dining experience with one set menu prepared in front of you. Bookings essential.

Bars and Cafés

Mart 130

107a Canterbury Road. [p306, B1]

Located in a former railway building next to a tram stop, this charming café has some of the best breakfast dishes in town.

Misuzu's

3–7 Victoria Avenue, Albert Park. [p304, A4]

There are several options at this sprawling Japanese café, the best of which is the atmospheric sake bar.

St Ali

12–18 Yarra Place, South Melbourne. [p304, A3]

Backstreet warehouse plays host to hip café with very fine coffee.

Luna Park
PARTY ONS

Recommended Restaurants, Bars & Cafés on page 187

ST KILDA

Round-the-clock revelling in this bayside suburb gives you sun, sand and all the sin you can stomach. There are refined pleasures, too, in the shape of gardens, galleries and gourmet goodies

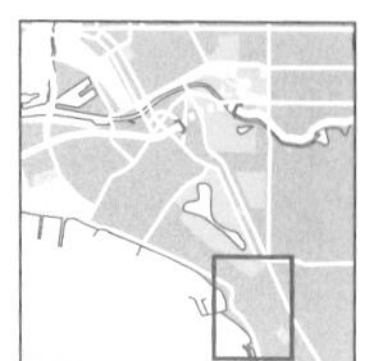

Like seaside suburbs the world over, St Kilda has always had something of a raffish charm that delights most of the time but periodically inclines towards the seedy. The colours are bright, the attractions garish, and there's a whiff of decadence in the air. Little wonder, then, that at the merest hint of sun – and in Melbourne it often is the merest hint – families, students, tourists and anyone else with time on their hands heads down to the Bay for an ice cream on the beach, a cake in Acland Street, a drink in one of the numerous bars and the challenge of trying to keep it all down on one of the more vigorous rides in Luna Park.

And that's only half the story. St Kilda has a justifiable reputation as a hub of throbbing nightlife. A plethora of bars, cafés, restaurants and clubs pulls in anyone with an eye for a good night out. Some of the city's best live-music venues are to be found here, and the tawdry dealings in drugs and prostitution that characterised the area for much of the second half of the 20th century have largely been pushed to the margins.

LEFT: the maw the merrier. Luna Park entrance at night.

RIGHT: in tents activity at the annual St Kilda Festival.

Changing fortunes

Initially established by Melbourne's moneyed founding fathers as a breezy respite from the busy colonial metropolis a few kilometres to the north, the area took its name from the visiting schooner, *The Lady of St Kilda,* in 1841. A brief spell of residential tranquillity began to be eroded in 1857 when a new railway line made the bay readily accessible to day-trippers. The introduction of trams in 1888 brought the crowds who helped to

Main attractions

- LUNA PARK
- THE PALAIS THEATRE
- ST KILDA PIER
- THE ESPY
- FITZROY STREET
- JEWISH MUSEUM OF AUSTRALIA
- LINDEN CENTRE FOR CONTEMPORARY ARTS
- ACLAND STREET
- ST KILDA BOTANICAL GARDENS

Boom and bust: Carlo Catani is remembered for planning the foreshore in the 1850s city expansion.

consolidate St Kilda's role as the city's pleasure gardens.

With the opening of Luna Park in 1912 and the massive Palais Theatre 15 years later, the wealthy saw the writing on the wall and began to leave for more refined neighbourhoods. Some of their mansions were turned into rooming houses, others didn't survive at all. By the time of World War II it was inevitable that St Kilda would become the first destination for American forces hungry for some full-on R&R. The attendant influx of good-time girls and pedlars of every illicit substance imaginable set the neighbourhood's reputation for the ensuing decades.

Development

As the area declined and became more affordable, newly arrived immigrants from Europe, with a strong Jewish contingent, along with students, artists and musicians, began to introduce a bohemian edge and St Kilda reinvented itself again. By the end of the 20th century, the place was oozing trendiness, property prices were skyrocketing and the cycle moved into its next phase. The spate of major development is likely to be only too evident over the next few years and, inevitably, St Kilda's character will evolve yet again.

LUNA PARK ❶

✉ Lower Esplanade; www.lunapark.com.au ☎ 9525 5033 ⌚ Sept–Apr Fri 7–11pm, Sat 11am–11pm, Sun 11am–6pm; Jan–Feb Thur 7–11pm; May–Aug Sat–Sun 11am–6pm $ free, charge for rides 🚊 3a, 16, 96 🚌 PPC1, 606, 623

Luna Park is impossible to miss and a good place to begin. The model was the amusement park at New York's Coney Island, most evidently in the gaping visage of Mr Moon through which all visitors must pass. Restoration work in 2001 saw orig-

BELOW: iced-coffee break on Acland Street.

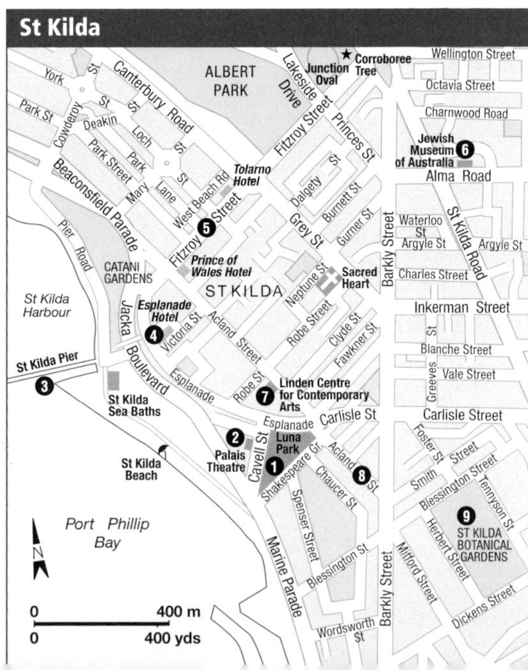

inal attractions such as the (now National Trust-listed) Carousel and the Scenic Railway roller-coaster, which sweeps above and all the way around the perimeter fence, joined by several more technologically advanced rides. Views along the bay can be had from the Ferris wheel or any of the other attractions that hurl you skywards.

The Palais Theatre ❷

This imperious pile next door to the pleasure grounds picks up on the Moorish theme of Luna Park's entrance towers. Beyond the grand marble foyer, Australia's largest theatre seats close to 3,000 people; after years as a picture house and then as a venue for opera, dance and musicals, it has been mostly given over to music following the opening of the various auditoriums in the Victoria Arts Centre in the 1980s *(see page 129)*. All the giants of the Australian scene have played there, along with the likes of Dylan, Springsteen and Sting.

To market, to market

If it's a Sunday, the pavement running up the incline in front of the Palais will be buzzing with people strolling past the stalls of the **Esplanade Art and Craft Market** (www.esplanademarket.com; Sun 10am–5pm; free). The organisers' insistence on craftspeople selling

TIP

If you plan to book tickets for a concert at the Palais Theatre, bear in mind that the seating area that in other countries, and indeed other Australian theatres, is known as the circle, here is termed the "Lounge". Note that it extends up a long, long way from the stage, which may have been fine when the building was operating as a cinema, but doesn't work as well for a live performance.

Above Left: local girls did their bit for the war effort in St Kilda.
Below: the Palais Theatre.

The St Kilda Triangle

The Palais is on the edge of the so-called "St Kilda Triangle", which has been the focus of a series of fierce planning disputes. Things were finally resolved in 2007 after a rearguard action from proprietors of the Palace nightclub – a venue that had generated sentimental attachment because of some of the seminal bands who had played there, but in practice was a grim concrete box with poor sound and worse sightlines – almost won a reprieve. In the end, the global financial crisis meant that the development plans collapsed anyway, but not before all the local councillors who had voted for the development were voted out of office by an ungrateful electorate.

> *I want to see the sun go down from St Kilda Esplanade*
> *Where the beach needs reconstruction, where the palm trees have it hard*
> *I'd give you all of Sydney Harbour (all that land, all that water)*
> *For that one sweet promenade*
>
> Local troubadour Paul Kelly displays an admirable lack of concern about album sales in NSW in one of his best-known songs, *From St Kilda to Kings Cross*

ABOVE RIGHT: Esplanade Market trader with his wares. **BELOW:** sauce pot.

their own works ensures the absence of manufactured or imported tat, and you'll find everything from paintings and ceramics to essential oils, from fearsomely studded dog collars to plaques commemorating various immigrant ships. And, inevitably, there's some assiduously hand-crafted tat.

On the beach

Cavell Street, by the side of the Palais, runs towards the bay. Cross busy Jacka Boulevard to get to the ever-reliable Donovans Restaurant and, beyond that, **St Kilda Beach**. Be wary, though, in crossing the beachside walkway, as there is constant fast-flowing traffic of bikes, skateboarders and in-line skaters.

Regardless of the warblings of Paul Kelly *(see lyric, left)*, the beach, and Port Phillip Bay in general, offers no challenge to the scale or drama of Sydney's Bondi, but it does generate great affection among locals and can get very busy on hot summer days. It's generally clean, with regular needle patrols to rid it of the unwanted detritus of St Kilda's darker side, and there are plenty of kiosks to provide sustenance for the next strenuous hour of sunbathing.

St Kilda Marina can be seen to the south. Machinery-fixated types may wish to wander along to see yachts being lifted up to their "garage" perches on giant forklifts, but for most there is more appeal in heading in the other direction.

Foodie fodder

The **Stokehouse** is a local institution. Upstairs is an acclaimed fine-dining room that has consistently performed well in *The Age Good Food Guide* rankings, while on beach level there's a more informal bistro. It's very popular, so don't necessarily expect to just drop in and get a table. Alternatively, stay on the beach and continue towards **St Kilda Sea Baths**. Following extensive renovation work, the original Edwardian building now houses a mixture of eateries, including the vegetarian canteen Soul Mama, which charges for its dishes according to weight (of the dishes, that is). There is also a pool and fitness centre.

You can't miss **St Kilda Pier** ❸ stretching out into the bay, with the enticing prospect of white-chocolate mud muffins (and much else besides)

Recommended Restaurants, Bars & Cafés on page 187

in the kiosk café at the end. The original kiosk was destroyed by fire in 2003, but from the shore this looks like a faithful replica. Up close you discover that there's a new restaurant lurking behind it. Climb up on to the roof for views around the bay, or carry on around the breakwater until fencing stops you. The fencing is there to protect a colony of little penguins that nest towards the end. Evidence suggests that visitors are required by some arcane bylaw to get their cameras out for views across to the city, with bobbing yachts in the foreground.

Returning beachwards, make for the pedestrian bridge across Jacka Boulevard, which delivers you to the Esplanade opposite the legendary "Espy" (the **Esplanade Hotel**).

The Espy ❹

11 The Esplanade; www.theesplanadehotel.com.au 9534 0211 Mon–Wed noon–1am, Thur–Fri noon–3am, Sat 8am–3am, Sun noon–1am 3a, 16, 96 606

This revered watering hole has seen generations of music fans squelching into its sticky carpets. Legend hasn't prevented it from facing destruction at the hands of developers, though, and the sleek apartment block rising up behind it was the latest quid pro quo to preserve the core of the hotel. The carpets are less sticky these days (OK, non-existent) but the atmosphere's still there, and with live music seven nights a week, much of it free, in three different spaces, there's likely to be something to appeal.

Before crossing over for a beer, you may want to pay homage to Carlo Catani, who was responsible for the Mediterranean-flavoured foreshore design in 1906. His bust backs on to the sea to the right.

Fitzroy Street ❺

The esplanade winds round into Fitzroy Street, a wide avenue of bars, restaurants and cafés that pulses with activity, especially at night. It's hard to miss the clean Art Deco lines of **The Prince hotel**, which contains, in **Circa the Prince**, one of Melbourne's most accomplished high-end

The Espy keeps firmly in the Australian public eye by playing host to the boisterous television show RocKwiz.

Below: cameras out for a classic view.

The Prince hotel is something of a one-stop foodies' goody bag. Circa the Prince has some of the very best cuisine in Melbourne in its stylish, starched dining room upstairs. For more informal eating, try Il Fornaio or Lau's Family Kitchen down below.

restaurants. It is also home to the **Prince Bandroom** – another landmark music venue with bigger names than at the Espy but still in a friendly and intimate setting.

Further along on the other side of the road, the old **Tolarno Hotel** is famous for the murals painted by Mirka Mora in the 1960s, when her husband ran the restaurant here with an art gallery at the back. Her primitive daubs are at the heart of the makeover that has turned an atmospheric informal eatery, very much of its time, into a high-concept dining experience very much of *this* time.

Staying on the northern side of Fitzroy Street, cross the busy intersection with Canterbury Road, pass the old railway station and continue to the edge of Albert Park. Towards the end of the street on the left, past Princes Street, lies **Junction Oval** – officially the St Kilda Cricket Club Ground – where the Bushrangers (Victoria's state cricket team) play some of their matches in the summer. The rest of the year you may be able to catch some footie (Australian Rules) practice.

Corroboree

Follow the perimeter of the park around the corner to find the **Corroboree Tree**, one of the few historic markers of the original Aboriginal occupiers of the area. The tree takes a bit of finding, and its location, through the undergrowth and hard by a road barrier, pays scant respect to its age and significance.

There's a perfunctory plaque nearby. More satisfaction is to be found simply in wandering through the surrounding woodland of native vegetation and finding a shady spot on one of the conventional seats or boomerang-shaped benches.

Return to Princes Street and make your way up the hill past the "Traditional British Pub", which might be more traditional if it had some decent beer. Amid something of a jumble of architectural styles look out for the iron lacework and unrendered brickwork of the old Wesleyan manse at No. 5, and the unsullied Art Deco apartment block on the corner of Dalgety Street. The last house on the left, "Liverpool", was built by Nathaniel Levi, the first

BELOW: the Corroboree Tree. **BELOW RIGHT:** coming up at the Prince Bandroom.

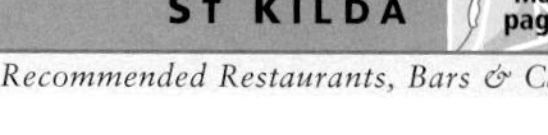

Recommended Restaurants, Bars & Cafés on page 187

Jewish member of the Parliament of Victoria, and this acts as a precursor to the next stop.

JEWISH MUSEUM OF AUSTRALIA 6

26 Alma Road; www.jewishmuseum.com.au 8534 3600 Tue–Thur 10am–4pm, Sun 10am–5pm charge 3, 67 PPC1, PPC2, PPC3

Cross Barkly Street and veer down Alma Road. Just the other side of busy St Kilda Road lies the **Jewish Museum of Australia.** Proudly describing itself as a community museum, it has permanent displays, temporary exhibitions and a strong educational programme. The history of Jewish life, intertwined with the colonisation of Australia, links with the present day and the very visible Jewish community in the streets around here and in East St Kilda and Balaclava.

Mansions

Return along Alma Street to Princes Street and take the first left down Burnett Street. The refined mansion "Oberwyl" has an unusual timber balcony on the first floor and shutters, supposedly to keep out bushrangers. Other impressive period dwellings are interspersed with more modern blocks.

Turn left at the bottom and pass the Church of the Sacred Heart. Next to it, the **Sacred Heart Mission** has long been a respite for the indigent of the area, and several of the old houses in Robe Street to the side come under its auspices. Robe Street has more suburban all-sorts and leads to Acland Street, where a little way along on the right a distinguished white mansion dating from the 1870s now houses the

There is still evidence of the wave of Jewish migrants from Eastern Europe in the great cake shops of Acland Street, such as the Acland Street Bakery.

ABOVE LEFT: city insignia inlaid in the Fitzroy Street pavement. **BELOW LEFT:** the Jewish Museum. **BELOW:** menorah on a ceremonial plate.

Jewish Migration

The first synagogue in Melbourne began with a congregation of precisely 51 in 1841, but numbers boomed with the 1850s gold discoveries. Most of the newcomers were from Britain, and the structures and social systems remained Anglocentric until the 1920s, when Polish Jews began to arrive, followed by exiles from anti-Semitic Nazi Germany. Yiddish language and tradition played a more important role for the new arrivals – a trend that was to continue with the flow of Holocaust survivors from Europe after World War II. Carlton was once the favoured destination, but now around half of the city's diaspora has made its home in the suburbs stretching east and south from St Kilda. The Jewish Holocaust Centre, where all the guides are Holocaust survivors, presents grim but, ironically, life-affirming witness to the wartime horrors (13–15 Selwyn Street, Elsternwick; www.jhc.org.au; tel: 9528 1985; Mon–Thur 10am–4pm, Fri 10am–2pm, Sun noon–4pm; free).

It's changing rapidly as rents rise and the neighbourhood smartens up, but Acland Street and surrounding streets still have their complement of recycled clothes stores and small jewellery and craft shops.

ABOVE RIGHT: blooming marvellous: detail in the Alister Clark Memorial Rose Garden. **BELOW:** Acland Street shop front.

Linden Centre for Contemporary Arts ❼ (26 Acland Street; www.lindenarts.org; tel: 9534 0099; Tue–Fri 1–5pm, Sat–Sun 11am–5pm; free). Here, invigorating work from young and emerging artists is interestingly juxtaposed with the house's original fireplaces, mouldings and wooden floors.

ACLAND STREET ❽

Turn back down Acland Street and it soon gets busy. Pass – if your self-control allows – typical St Kilda manifestations of the cool (Dogs Bar) and the corblimey (Greasy Joe's Bar and Grill), cross Carlisle Street and savour the buzz of the Acland Street strip that epitomises so much of what this suburb is about.

Cafés and restaurants represent the various waves of immigrants who have passed through the area at different periods, with a special emphasis on the extravagantly stocked cake shops that reflect the Middle European origins of their founders. Sadly *Café Scheherazade*, immortalised in a novel by Arnold Zable, is no longer there.

Hair salons and beauty parlours are relentlessly trendy but with a twinkle in the eye: see the outrageous sculptural frontages on numbers 112 and 159. Boutiques keep springing up treading a fine line between *über*-chic design and pointless trash. Some residents bemoan the sweeping away of some older neighbourhood stores, but there's no denying the liveliness of an area in transition.

Cross Barkly Street at the end, turn left and take a right up Blessington Street. Suddenly the parade of cafés is less brash and supremely inviting. You can walk off the excess intake just up the road in the St Kilda Botanical Gardens.

ST KILDA BOTANICAL GARDENS ❾

✉ Blessington Street/Herbert Street
🕒 daily sunrise–sunset Ⓢ free

These gardens suggest a scaled-down version of the concept so popular across the British Empire in Victorian times. The **Alister Clark Memorial Rose Garden** is a tranquil spot, in contrast to the attractive children's play area. There's a modern conservatory (Mon–Fri 10.30am–3.30pm, Sat–Sun 1–4.30pm) and, in the pond in front of it, a wonderfully perverse statue of a man with an umbrella that's too good to spoil with any further description. However, give credit to designers Corey Thomas and Ken Arnold. ❑

BEST RESTAURANTS, BARS AND CAFÉS

Prices for a three-course dinner per person with a half-bottle of house wine:
$ = under A$60
$$ = A$60–90
$$$ = A$90–120
$$$$ = over A$120

Restaurants

Café Di Stasio

31 Fitzroy Street. 9525 3999 L & D daily **$$$** [p307, C3]
Much-loved Melbourne Italian institution keeps the crowds returning with its superbly cooked food, comfortably cosseting room and an atmosphere of smilingly encouraged indulgence.

Cicciolina

130 Acland Street. 9525 3333 L & D daily **$$** [p307, D4]
A no-bookings policy combined with consistent popularity will probably see you waiting for a table at this dark, moody yet hospitable Mediterranean-inspired joint. The buzzy bar out the back is a good place to cool your heels.

Circa, The Prince

2 Acland Street. 9536 1122 B & D daily, L Fri and Sun **$$$$** [p307, C3]
One of Melbourne's most romantically stylish dining rooms also boasts some of the best modern European food in town and a wine list that should have the conoisseurs going weak at the knees.

Donovans

40 Jacka Boulevard. 9534 8221 L & D daily **$$$** [p307, D4]
Looking like a chic, expensive beach house, Donovans' food and service shows great attention to detail. The Mediterranean food is pricey but excellent.

Il Fornaio

2 Acland Street. 9534 2922 B, L & D daily **$** [p307, C3]
This split-level warehouse space is a popular café and bakery during the day, and at night becomes a smart local Italian trattoria serving hearty, restorative food.

Lau's Family Kitchen

4 Acland Street. 8598 9880 L Sun–Fri, D daily **$$** [p307, C3]
This modern Chinese restaurant keeps the menu simple, with good examples of classic dishes. Service is friendly and efficient.

Melbourne Wine Room

125 Fitzroy Street. 9525 5599 L Fri–Sun, D Tue–Sun **$$** [p307, D2]
The public bar of the George Hotel is earshatteringly noisy but, out the back, the Melbourne Wine Room is a haven of muted noise, great modern Italian food and a superb wine list.

Mirka at Tolarno Hotel

42 Fitzroy Street. 9525 3088 L & D daily **$$$** [p307, C3]
The famous murals (by artist Mirka Mora) give this stylish European bar and bistro its name and its air of well-heeled bohemian bonhomie. A perfect place to enjoy bistro classics.

Stokehouse

30 Jacka Boulevard. 9525 5555 L & D daily **$$$** [p307, D4]
Downstairs it's a casual bar serving wood-fired pizza, upstairs it's one of Melbourne's great dining experiences, with a superb view of the bay matched by the robustly delicious Mediterranean-inspired food.

Bars and Cafés

George Lane Bar
1 George Lane. [p307, D2]
Cosy, intimate bar (*pictured above*) with good wine, spirits and cocktails.

Mink
29 Fitzroy Street. [p307, C3]
Enormous list of vodka, curtained private booths and Soviet-themed decor. Located downstairs at The Prince hotel.

Pelican
16 Fitzroy Street. [p307, C3]
A great spot to fill up on tapas and sample a wide range of beers and wines.

SOFT,

Recommended Restaurants, Bars & Cafés on page 195

PRAHRAN TO RICHMOND

This clutch of inner suburbs contains some of Melbourne's most exclusive property and some of its shabbiest, some of the best shopping and some of the cheapest, and a few corners that are just plain eccentric

Main attractions
- ASTOR THEATRE
- CHAPEL STREET
- GREVILLE STREET
- PRAHRAN MARKET
- TOORAK ROAD
- COMO HOUSE
- SWAN STREET
- BRIDGE ROAD

To get a rounded understanding of what makes Melbourne tick, it's necessary to take a look at some of the suburbs. This trawl along a corridor of the inner east has – with a couple of exceptions – no standout individual attractions, but does provide an insight into where Melburnians live and work, and what it is that gives the city its distinctive character. So, beginning in Windsor, we move north through Prahran, South Yarra, Toorak and into Richmond.

ASTOR THEATRE ❶

✉ Cnr Chapel Street and Dandenong Road; www.astor-theatre.com
☎ 9510 1414 ◷ daily screenings
🚊 5, 64, 78, 79

The starting point is one of the most gorgeous cinemas in Australia. The Astor is the epitome of 1930s Art Deco style and has been sympathetically maintained with its original fittings and furnished according to the period. It's hard to draw yourself away from the comfortable foyers, but, once you've bought your home-made cake and drink of choice, the auditorium beckons. Again, it all appears to be original, but fortunately the projection and sound systems are bang up to date. Repertory programming includes a lot of good-value double bills.

CHAPEL STREET ❷

It's a long way from Melbourne to the fishing port of Hoi An in Vietnam, which makes it all the more noteworthy that one of the many tailoring shops in Hoi An has a sign proclaiming its clothes are of "Chapel

LEFT: searching for the groove in Greville Street Records.
RIGHT: foyer of the Astor Theatre in Chapel Street.

Prahran to Richmond

Street quality". For Australians, no other explanation is necessary.

Extending from St Kilda Road in the south right up to the Yarra, Chapel Street is one of Melbourne's best-known thoroughfares. The first section north from the Astor is within the suburb of Windsor, and is the beginning of the retailing stretch. Down here some of the shops are distinctly flyblown and probably not what the Hoi An advertisers were trying to evoke. You may find a bargain, but it might be worth hopping on a tram for a couple of stops to speed you on your way towards the cream stucco bulk of **Prahran Town Hall**.

Prahran

Quite a few of the buildings in this area have seen better days, none more so than the Colosseum Building, identifiable by the Corinthian pillars on its facade and situated just before the Town Hall. This was once a sizeable department store but, after a slow decline, it closed in the 1980s.

Prahran (pronounced Puh-ran) has now been incorporated into Stonnington for administrative purposes,

Recommended Restaurants, Bars & Cafés on page 195

so the Town Hall, whose construction began in 1860, is now officially Stonnington Town Hall. This Victorian Italianate pile is often open for exhibitions or fashion sales. There is a historic courthouse and police station behind it on **Greville Street 3**, but the main reason for taking that route is the eclectic mix of shops and cafés that make this one of the more attractive and fashionable streets in the neighbourhood.

You'll find adventurous handmade jewellery, various fashion boutiques and one of a rapidly diminishing number of independent music stores in the city, Greville Records. Admittedly some of the smaller independent shops are being pushed out by cashed-up chains, but there's still plenty of atmosphere, especially on Sundays when there's a street market from noon to 5pm.

Back on Chapel Street, there are more remnants of former shopping glories: the garish yellow of JB Hi-Fi identifies the Prahran Arcade, where there used to be a couple of dozen shops as well as Turkish baths; some of the old mouldings and fitments remain on the facade and inside. On the other side of the road, Coles occupies the former MacLellan & Co.'s Big Store, another one-stop department store that traded until the 1960s.

The domed towers of what is now Pran Central are local landmarks in the short-lived Edwardian Baroque style that also characterised the Colosseum Building. The shopping complex itself has retained little of the character and detail of the Charles Read Co. emporium that occupied the building until the 1980s.

PRAHRAN MARKET 4

163 Commercial Road; www.prahranmarket.com.au 8290 8220 Tue, Thur, Sat dawn–5pm, Fri dawn–6pm, Sun 10am–3pm free 72, 78, 79

Better to turn left into Commercial Road and cross over to Prahran Market. Locals have been flocking here since 1881, when an earlier market moved from Greville Street, and have now been joined by foodies from much further afield. Fresh fruit and

The exterior of the Prahran Arcade building is looking somewhat "distressed", as the stylists would have it, but the addition of some wacky chandeliers behind the arches has added life.

FAR LEFT: Prahran Town Hall. **BELOW LEFT:** Chapel Street Bazaar. **BELOW:** Prahran Market.

People-watching is best conducted from a café table, and there are plenty of options in Chapel Street. One of the oldest and more character-filled is the compact **Caffe e Cucina** at No. 581.

vegetables, meat and fish have always been here, and now there are delicatessens and specialist comestible traders. Once you've stocked up or just browsed the aisles, grab a coffee in Market Square and, if it's Sunday, enjoy the live jazz. Alternatively, Malvern Road, east of Chapel Street, is stuffed with funky bars and cafés, and is home to Chapel off Chapel, a converted church that's used for theatre, music and exhibitions.

Heading up-market

Chapel Street stores start to become more refined and expensive as you head northwards. Mixing and matching in second-hand shops is out, designer labels are in.

You'll come to a former Baptist church, now functioning as a pub, and shortly afterwards the **Jam Factory**. Only the shell of the factory is left, but the interior designers have taken their cue from the multi-screen cinema that occupies part of the building and created a stage set, with stairways and balconies that just demand that you pose, and pose in more convincing fashion than the rather crude mannequin versions of Marilyn Monroe, Harold Lloyd and other stars of the past.

It's all good practice for the next few blocks, where posing is de rigueur. Shoppers here are ruthlessly casual. Smiles are held long enough to show off dazzling teeth. Skin, often unnaturally taut, is in tones that have you flicking through a mental swatch, trying to identify that particular shade of ochre. Sunglasses are compulsory (because of the teeth).

ABOVE RIGHT: the Jam Factory. **BELOW:** Toorak Village, where status requires ersatz period street lamps.

TOORAK ROAD ❺

The whiff of money gets stronger still as Toorak Road approaches. Follow it to the left and you're in South Yarra, home to many of the fashionistas who haunt the designer outlets. Close to the river and the Royal Botanic Gardens, the houses and apartments here are gated and exclusive, the cars European.

Go the other way down Toorak Road and you'll eventually come to Toorak itself. If ever you were looking for evidence to counter the idea that Australia is a classless society, you'll find it here: mansions proliferate and the security systems are built to ward off anyone without a suitably elevated credit rating. It has

Recommended Restaurants, Bars & Cafés on page 195

always been thus, only the emphasis changes. At one stage it needed to be old money, preferably WASP, now, at least, those barriers are breaking down. Dawdle in one of the arcades off "Toorak Village" (a short section of Toorak Road) and it becomes clear how multicultural Australian money is these days. While you're there, take a peek at some of the city's most expensive shops.

Much of Toorak's cachet came from the presence of the Governor of Victoria in Toorak House until Government House was completed *(see page 142)*. To get some idea of the type of residences that put these suburbs on the map, find your way down Como Avenue.

Como Historic House and Garden ❻

✉ Cnr Williams Road & Lechlade Avenue; www.nattrust.com.au
☎ 9827 2500 ⏲ daily 10am–4pm, winter Wed, Sat–Sun Ⓢ charge

Building began here in 1847, but it was only after the liquor merchant John Brown, who had grown rich servicing the gold rush, bought it in 1852 that Como emerged as one of Melbourne's most elegant mansions, with its distinctive two-storey wrap-around veranda. It enjoyed uninterrupted views across the river and had rather more land to its name than it does now. A subsequent owner added a ballroom and tennis court, and turned it into a haunt of high society. The National Trust took over in 1959 and has done a fine job in restoring and maintaining it in its Victorian splendour. The garden is immaculate.

Some of the old estate now forms **Como Park**, and if you pass through that and cross the busy road, you'll get to the river. If Café Kanteen doesn't distract you, there's a quaint little boat (www.parkweb.vic.gov.au; weekends from January to April) to take you over to **Herring Island** with its Environmental Sculpture Park *(see margin, right)*.

You're about to discover one of Melbourne's secrets. The island was created in 1928 when a new channel for the river was dug out, and it subsequently grew as silt from the Yarra was dumped there. It became a park

The first sculptures on Herring Island were introduced in 1997 as an initiative by the Melbourne International Arts Festival to set up an Environmental Sculpture Park. These included Cairn *by Andy Goldsworthy* (pictured above).

BELOW: Como House.

> *Come shopping in Richmond in September, when the sun has just cleared the clutter of housetops, the spring wind's blowing the blankets airing on the front fences, and Greek pop music wails up from the hallways, half celebration, half lament*
>
> from Barry Oakley's 1977 story *Walking through Tigerland*

ABOVE RIGHT: cut-price Ferrari. **BELOW LEFT:** Dimmeys store. **BELOW RIGHT:** Richmond Hill Cafe and Larder.

in 1994 and saw its first artworks installed in 1997, including *Cairn* by Andy Goldsworthy. It's also a wildlife haven, especially for birds.

Richmond

Back on the "mainland" at the Como landing, follow the river bank back to Chapel Street and cross the bridge into what now becomes Church Street. You are now in Richmond, but this southern fringe is on the non-descript side, so take the tram north. There's a noticeable increase in graffiti and, as with much of the work that decorates the city laneways, it's mostly planned and of a high quality. Indeed, a number of businesses have commissioned artists to cover spare walls. One of those is the palatial **Dimmeys** store, with its beckoning clock tower. Even if you're not in search of bargain-rate mixed goods in the not-quite-junk category, pop inside for an impression of what these old stores once looked like.

SWAN STREET ❼

Dimmeys is in Swan Street, still very much an urban working street with

its share of good-value fashion outlets and salons. Dr Follicles, the barber's shop, will give you a beer while your hair is seen to, or there's good coffee available while you browse the books at the Booktalk Café. Legendary music pub the **Corner Hotel** is one of several places that blossoms at night, as does a strip of Greek restaurants back on the other side of the Church Street intersection.

Bridge Road ❽ runs parallel to Swan Street to the north and is *the* destination for those after designer-wear bargains. Nearly every label you've ever heard of has a factory outlet here, especially on the strip running towards the city. Grab that bargain now and regret it at your leisure in the **Richmond Hill Cafe and Larder**, set up in 1997 by Stephanie Alexander, one of the doyennes of Australian cooking. While the founder may have moved on, the passion and the buzz are still there. ❑

BEST RESTAURANTS, BARS AND CAFÉS

Prices for a three-course dinner per person with a half-bottle of house wine:
$ = under A$60
$$ = A$60–90
$$$ = A$90–120
$$$$ = over A$120

The Argo

64 Argo Street, South Yarra. 9867 3344 L Thur–Sun, D Tue–Sun **$$** [p305, E4]
Hidden in a quiet backstreet, The Argo is worth hunting out. A relaxed attitude is combined with meticulous attention to its modern European food, switched-on service and serious wine focus.

Bacash

175 Domain Road, South Yarra. 9866 3566 L Mon–Fri, D Mon–Sat **$$$** [p305, D3]
Consistently good quality seafood is centre stage in this South Yarra stalwart, which deservedly ranks among Melbourne's best.

Café Latte

521 Malvern Road, Toorak. 9826 5846 B & L daily, D Mon–Sat **$$** [off p305]
Homely, in a well-heeled and fashionable way, Café Latte mixes well-cooked Italian comfort food with a warm and hospitable vibe that keeps the constant crowd happy.

Caffe e Cucina

581 Chapel Street, South Yarra. 9827 4139 B, L & D daily **$$** [p305, E3]
With its dark, timber-panelled good looks and Italian-spouting waiters, Caffe e Cucina does a good job at creating a little bit of Italia south of the river. Reliable food and good coffee add substance to the style.

Da Noi

95 Toorak Road, South Yarra. 9866 5975 D Mon–Sat **$$$** [p305, E3]
There is a menu at this rustically decorated, Sardinian-influenced restaurant, but nobody uses it. Instead they opt for the Chef's Choice and let the kitchen make the call, saving decision-making for the all-Italian wine list.

David's

4 Cecil Place, Prahran. 9529 5199 L & D daily **$$** [p307, E1]
Located in a side-street warehouse space given a low-key fashionable makeover, David's is one of the more adventurous and interesting Chinese restaurants, championing food from Shanghai and tea with health-giving properties.

Fog Bar & Restaurant

142 Greville Street, Prahran. 9521 3155 L & D daily **$$** [p307, E1]
It may look like a nightclub and a place more concerned with good looks than good food, but Fog delivers in the flavour stakes, too, with an eclectic menu of many influences, including from the southern US.

France-Soir

11 Toorak Road, South Yarra. 9866 8569 L & D daily **$$$** [p305, D4]
France-Soir has kept going for more than 20 years because of its consistently good-quality French bistro favourites and an award-winning, French-leaning wine list.

Pearl

631–633 Church Street, Richmond. 9421 4599 L & D daily **$$$$** [p305, E2]
Brilliantly inventive food, much of it borrowing flavour and technique from Southeast Asia, is perfectly matched by smooth service, a sleekly comfortable room and a noteworthy wine selection.

Sushi Bar Aka Tombo

205 Greville Street, Prahran. 9510 0577 L & D Tue–Sat **$$** [p307, E1]
This tiny sushi bar only seats 14, mostly around the bar, where all the action – food- and decor-wise – takes place. However, what it lacks in size it makes up for in superb-quality Japanese staples.

Bars and Cafés

Oriental Tea House
455 Chapel Street, South Yarra. [p303, E4]
All-day *yum cha*, a huge list of teas and even tea cocktails in this groovy former pub.

Red Vault
37–39 Chapel Street, Windsor. [p307, E2]
A cool bar where a sharply dressed crowd get serious about wine.

Spoonful
543 High Street, Prahran. [off p307]
Low-key country style combines with some of the best café food in the city.

BEYOND THE CITY

Venture out of the city for the natural wonders of the Great Ocean Road, the mountains and Wilson's Prom, or sample the rich heritage of the gold towns and the wineries. Pick a day trip or make a longer expedition

Melbourne's 4 million inhabitants represent about 75 per cent of the population of Victoria, so the state feels quite empty once you move beyond the last of the sprawling suburbs. Geelong, the next largest city, has a mere 160,000 inhabitants.

You'll find Geelong in the first of the chapters that follow: a circular route around Port Phillip Bay taking in the Bellarine and Mornington peninsulas, linked by a short ferry trip between Queenscliff and Sorrento. It covers much of Melbourne's weekend playground, with a bucketful of beaches on the tranquil bay or the more boisterous Southern Ocean. Add historic settlements, some outstanding museums, a zoo and a clutch of vineyards, and there's something for everybody.

Apart from the beaches, you can find a similar range of goodies in the Dandenongs and Yarra Valley chapter, where the vineyards take on a much higher profile and there's a famous steam train for good measure.

Both of these journeys can be undertaken in day trips, although they will be very full days if you absorb every one of the highlighted options. For the remaining itineraries you really need at least two days and preferably more.

The Great Ocean Road is one of the world's premier coastal drives, with the Twelve Apostles just one of numerous scenic spots that will fill up your camera's memory card. Amongst other things, there are some beautiful seaside townships, a treetop walkway and a recreated Victorian seaport.

The historic theme park at Sovereign Hill takes you back to the days of the gold rush, which was the crux of Melbourne's development. It's a highlight of a trip through the goldfields that also takes in the craggy beauty of the Grampians, and Echuca, the historic port on the Murray River.

If you're after wildlife, consider the expedition to Phillip Island with its penguins, somnolent French Island and its koalas, and stunning Wilson's Promontory. The final chapter offers a drive into the mountains, mixing Victoria's Alpine resorts with the old stamping ground of the Kelly Gang.❑

PRECEDING PAGES: ski in, ski out accommodation at Mount Hotham. **LEFT:** surveying the annual sandcastle competition on Rye Beach, Mornington Peninsula. The Victorian coast has mile upon mile of glorious, empty beaches. **ABOVE:** wallabies.

R.L.S.S.
L.S.S.

Recommended Restaurants, Bars & Cafés on page 211

AROUND THE BAY

Cyclists can circle Port Phillip Bay in a day, but even with a car you'll be pushed to see everything. Select from picturesque suburbs, a buoyant industrial town, a handful of distinguished Victorian resorts, tranquil beaches, pounding surf and some rather fine wineries

Main attractions

- WILLIAMSTOWN
- WERRIBEE
- GEELONG
- QUEENSCLIFF
- SORRENTO
- ARTHURS SEAT
- MORNINGTON
- BRIGHTON BEACH

Port Phillip Bay is Melbourne's *raison d'être*. Once the first European navigators had worked out a safe passage between the treacherous Heads, it was a matter of where in this vast natural harbour to found a settlement. After some false starts, it was decided upon the mouth of the Yarra Yarra, as it was then called.

As Melbourne has grown over the decades, and suburbs have spread further inland, the bay has taken on the role of playground for the city dwellers. Weekenders flood the roads down to the peninsulas on Friday nights, retirees sell up and move to somewhere closer to the beach.

And where does the Aussie of legend belong if not the beach, surf optional? For that reason the **Mornington Peninsula** on the eastern side of the bay has most of the holiday homes – the beach is better there, especially close to the Heads, where there's a choice between the placid waters of the bay and the driving breakers of the ocean.

The western shores are hardly developed at all until you reach Geelong, a city built on heavy industry, especially textiles and cars. Only in recent years have they really started to concentrate on the possibilities of the waterfront for anything other than a place to load ships.

It is on this side of the bay that this journey begins.

WILLIAMSTOWN ❶

Williamstown, just to the left over the Westgate Bridge, is to all intents a suburb of Melbourne. For a quick jaunt, take a ferry there from Southgate in the city or Port Melbourne.

LEFT: wood-be lifeguards. The Bay Walk Bollards Project on Geelong Waterfront.
RIGHT: Nelson Place in Williamstown, a quiet break from the weekend crowds.

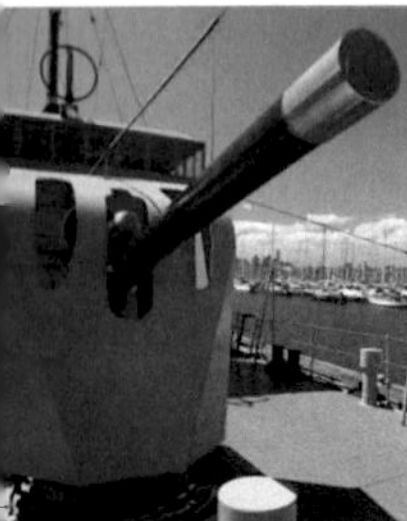

From rusty hulk in 1973, the HMAS Castlemaine *has been fully restored over the last 35 years.*

However you get there, you'll find a lively settlement geared to the needs of visitors who have popped over for lunch and a stroll along the waterfront or a paddle off the beach.

Nelson Place is the focal point, a bustling strip of shops, bars and eateries facing the lawns and mature trees of Commonwealth Reserve and, beyond that, the forest of masts in the marina. Down on the waterfront, walk out on Gem Pier. The grey naval vessel is the **HMAS Castlemaine Maritime Museum** (www.hmascastlemaine.com; tel: 9397 2363; Sat–Sun noon–5pm; charge), a carefully restored World War II minesweeper that undertook escort duty around Australia and in the Pacific.

A flying boat operates from here, or you can just dangle your feet over the edge and enjoy the view across the water to the city. Go south down Nelson Place, behind the shipyards that have driven Williamstown's economy for decades, and you'll come out in **Point Gellibrand Coastal Heritage Park**, where a distinctive **Timeball Tower** sits, enigmatically. A copper ball drops down at 1pm every day, which is useful if you've left your watch, phone or car

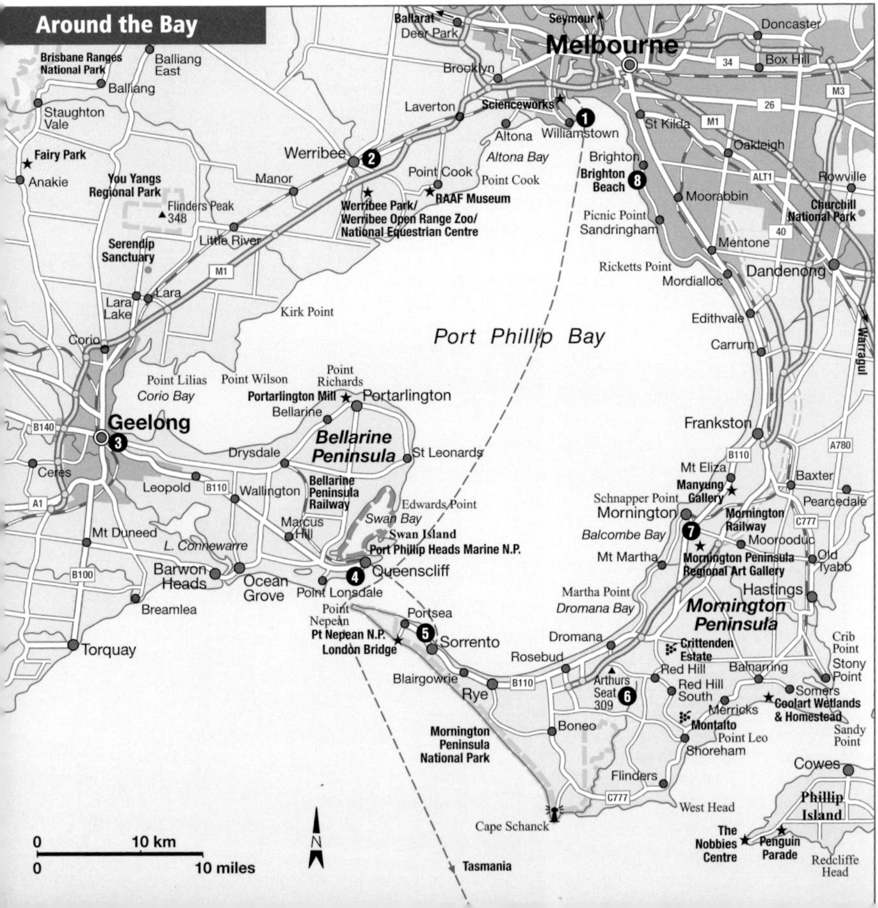
Around the Bay
Ballarat
Deer Park
Seymour
Melbourne
Doncaster
Box Hill
34
M3
26
Brisbane Ranges National Park
Balliang East
Balliang
Brooklyn
Staughton Vale
Laverton
Scienceworks
1
Williamstown
Altona
St Kilda
M1
Oakleigh
Fairy Park
Anakie
Werribee
2
Altona Bay
Brighton
Brighton Beach
8
ALT1
Rowville
You Yangs Regional Park
Manor
Point Cook
Point Cook
RAAF Museum
Moorabbin
Churchill National Park
Flinders Peak
348
Werribee Park/ Werribee Open Range Zoo/ National Equestrian Centre
Picnic Point
Sandringham
Mentone
40
Serendip Sanctuary
Little River
M1
Ricketts Point
Mordialloc
Dandenong
Lara
Lara Lake
Kirk Point
Edithvale
Corio
Port Phillip Bay
Carrum
Warragul
Point Lilias
Point Wilson
Point Richards
Corio Bay
Portarlington Mill
Portarlington
Bellarine
Geelong
3
B140
Bellarine Peninsula
Frankston
Drysdale
St Leonards
B110
A780
Ceres
Mt Eliza
Leopold
B110
Wallington
Bellarine Peninsula Railway
Manyung Gallery
Baxter
A1
Edwards Point
Schnapper Point
Pearcedale
Swan Bay
Mornington
Mornington Railway
C777
Mt Duneed
Marcus Hill
Swan Island
Balcombe Bay
7
Mooroodu
L. Connewarre
Port Phillip Heads Marine N.P.
Mt Martha
Mornington Peninsula Regional Art Gallery
Old Tyabb
B100
Barwon Heads
Ocean Grove
4
Queenscliff
Point Lonsdale
Martha Point
Hastings
Breamlea
Point Nepean
Portsea
Dromana Bay
Mornington Peninsula
Pt Nepean N.P.
5
Sorrento
Dromana
Crib Point
London Bridge
Crittenden Estate
Torquay
Rosebud
Stony Point
Blairgowrie
Red Hill
Balnarring
Rye
B110
Arthurs Seat
309
6
Red Hill South
Somers
Merricks
Coolart Wetlands & Homestead
Montalto
Mornington Peninsula National Park
Boneo
Point Leo
Sandy Point
Shoreham
Cowes
Flinders
C777
West Head
Phillip Island
Cape Schanck
The Nobbies Centre
Penguin Parade
Redcliffe Head
0
10 km
0
10 miles
N
Tasmania

at home, and you happen to want to know when it's one o'clock. Continue along the shoreline and you'll come to the Botanic Gardens and Williamstown Beach.

Scienceworks

2 Booker Street, Spotswood; www.scienceworks.museum.vic.gov.au 9392 4800 daily 10am–4.30pm charge

Three kilometres (2 miles) north of Nelson Place is the impressive Scienceworks Museum. Its modern spaces are combined with an old pumping station, including the huffing steam engines. A whole range of themed exhibits emphasise hands-on learning. The super-sized house is a highlight, and challenges in the sports section include racing against sprinter Cathy Freeman, or at least her image. Admission includes a session in the attached **Melbourne Planetarium**.

Point Cook, a few kilometres south round the bay, claims the **RAAF Museum** (Point Cook Road; www.airforce.gov.au/raafmuseum; tel: 92 56 1300; Tue–Fri 10am–3pm, Sat–Sun 10am–5pm; free). Learn about the history of the world's second-oldest air force, maybe see a flying display (Tue, Thur, Sun 1pm) or study grounded vintage aircraft in a succession of hangars.

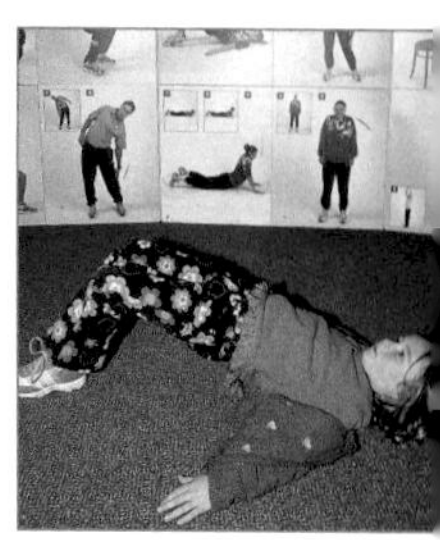

Scienceworks offers many opportunities for visitors of all ages to test both themselves and the displays. Staff lay on a full programme of educational entertainment for children during the school holidays.

WERRIBEE 2

It's easy to spend a day at Werribee by combining two adjacent attractions. **Werribee Park** (www.werribeepark.com.au; tel: 131 963; daily Nov–Apr 10am–6.30pm, May–Oct 10am–5.30pm; free) surrounds the grand Italianate **Mansion**, built from 1874 to 1877 for a prosperous family of pastoralists, the Chirnsides. The audio tour brings life to the

BELOW LEFT: Williamstown's Timeball Tower. **BELOW:** biplane in the RAAF Museum.

Sculptures are carefully set around Werribee Park, many of them winners of the Helen Lempriere National Sculpture Award. They turn the grounds into a kind of sculptural adventure park, as children clamber over the exhibits. The adjacent Victoria State Rose Garden is at its best from November to April.

ABOVE: Werribee Mansion. **BELOW RIGHT:** cause for concern at Werribee Open Range Zoo.

beautifully conserved interior, and the balcony affords views across immaculate formal gardens. The **Victoria State Rose Garden** *(see margin, left)* is also worth a visit (tel: 131 963; daily 9am–5.30pm; free).

Open Range Zoo

The other main attraction – and that's aside from the **Shadowfax Winery** (www.shadowfax.com.au; tel: 9731 4420) and the **National Equestrian Centre** (www.wpnec.com.au; tel: 9741 7672) – is **Werribee Open Range Zoo** (www.zoo.org.au; tel: 9731 9600; daily 9am–5pm; charge). The focus of a visit is a bus ride through the extensive savannah lands where African species dwell in something like a natural state. Enthusiasts can get even closer to the animals by paying extra for the two-hour "Open Vehicle Adventure", or going on one of the walking trails, one of which is amongst Australian wildlife. Summer weekends feature a programme of live African music.

Fairy Park

Wranglers of young children might want to weave across country from Werribee in a westerly direction to **Anakie**, where **Fairy Park** awaits (2388 Ballan Road; www.fairypark.com; tel: 5284 1262; daily 10am–5pm; charge). A pathway winds up a hill – sorry, "magic mountain" – taking in caves and houses where automata grind through salient passages from classic fairy tales. There is, of course, a castle at the top, although this one contains a model-railway layout. The attraction has been going for 50 years now and has rather lost ground to modern theme parks, but most kids seem to like it just so long as something happens when they press the buttons. Camelot, the playground at the end, is a very good mixture of battlements, dungeons and play equipment, but beware of the button labelled "DO NOT PRESS". Twee-averse grown-ups who've had it with musical gnomes may wish to seek solace at the Staughton Vale Vineyard nearby.

GEELONG ❸

Pronounced with a short "ge", as in "genetic", Victoria's second-largest city was, until relatively recently, a utilitarian port and industrial centre that you had to pass through on the way to somewhere nicer. A major development of the waterfront area

Recommended Restaurants, Bars & Cafés on page 211

and a sprucing-up of the town centre has changed all that, and Geelong now makes a pleasant stopover en route to the Great Ocean Road.

First signs on the approach, once you've stocked up at the **Visitor Information Centre** (Princes Highway; www.visitgeelong.org; tel: 52 75 5797; daily 9am–5pm), are for **Geelong Naval and Maritime Museum** (Swinburne Street; tel: 5277 3808; daily 10am–4.30pm; charge), which is packed with model ships and nautical artefacts. Sadly, enthusiastic volunteers can't quite turn it from musty to must-see.

Bollards

Once you reach central Geelong, take a left to the waterfront. Parkland, beach, a pier, a marina, a carousel – there's everything here for a traditional seaside resort, and linking it all, while providing references to the town's history, are a set of wonderful sculpted and painted bollards. For the **Bay Walk Bollards Project**, local artist Jan Mitchell took old wooden pier piles and turned them into life-size figures relevant to the locale. So look out for sailors, lifeguards, a military band, a Koorie family, respectable women, less respectable women, and many more. There are 107 altogether, scattered along the length of the waterfront, and even a couple of escapees in the Botanic Gardens.

If you haven't picked up the free Arts and Culture Walking Trails brochure, there's a detailed guide on sale in the pavilion that shelters the historic working **Carousel** (1892), near to **Cunningham Pier**. There are other, more abstract sculptures here, and seaplane flights to take you over the town or along the Great Ocean Road. South along Eastern Beach lies the distinctive Art Deco **Beach House** restaurant and café, which overlooks the pool, where youngsters happily spend the day throwing themselves off the diving boards.

Botanic Gardens

Climb up the steps to the superb **Geelong Botanic Gardens** (tel: 5227 0387; daily Nov–Mar 7.30am–7pm, Apr–Oct 7.30am–5pm; free). The skilled intermingling of the traditional formal layout of the 1850s

Many museums in Victoria rely on volunteer guides. Geelong's National Wool Museum is fortunate in having a small pool of retired textile workers to operate the historic carpet loom.

BELOW: more of the entertaining Geelong Bay Walk bollards.

Detail from Eugene von Guérard's View of Geelong, *which the City of Geelong purchased from Andrew Lloyd Webber in 2006 for $3.8million. It now hangs in Geelong Gallery.*

ABOVE RIGHT: classic Victorian architecture on Hesse Street, Queenscliff.
BELOW: more bangers for your buck at the Ford Discovery Centre.

with the Australian native border of the 1960s was augmented in 2002 with the opening of the 21st Century Garden. Volunteers conduct guided tours on Wednesday at 10.30am and Sundays at 2pm (Friends of Geelong Botanic Gardens; www.friendsgbg.com; tel: 5222 6053).

National Wool Museum

The centre of Geelong has a few appealing streetscapes, and one of them, Moorabool Street, includes the **National Wool Museum** (26 Moorabool Street; www.nwm.vic.gov.au; tel: 5272 4701; Mon–Fri 9.30am–5pm, Sat–Sun 1–5pm; charge). Now, at the risk of offending shepherds and shearers, a wool museum is not a promising prospect. So reason suggests it must be pretty good to survive and thrive. And reason is correct. Start with a sturdy 1870s wool store, open up the interior with dramatic ramps and walkways, tell the story of the wool industry with imaginative displays, add a working carpet loom, sundry other machinery and retired wool-industry workers, and the outcome

is a living museum where the enthusiasm of the staff is almost palpable. Don't miss the extraordinary sock-making machine, either.

Other sights in Geelong

In Little Malop Street, along the side of the Town Hall, **Geelong Gallery** (www.geelonggallery.org.au; tel: 52 29 3645; daily 10am–5pm; charge) does the city proud with an extensive collection that began in 1900 with British and European art and some Australian works, but soon concentrated on local output, such as Frederick McGubbin's esteemed *A Bush Burial* (1890). The 2006 acquisition of Eugene von Guérard's

Ford and Geelong

Ford began its Australian operation at Geelong in 1925 and has been here ever since, providing an important economic stimulus to the region. The first Ute (a variant on the pick-up truck) came from here, as, since 1960, has the Falcon. The engine plant, slated for closure in 2010, was reprieved and the company link with the town is still strong. The **Ford Discovery Centre** (12 Gheringhap Street; www.forddiscovery.com.au; tel: 5227 8700; Wed–Mon 10am–5pm; charge) has examples of the company's vehicles from the very beginning up to the present day, and includes racing cars and hybrids along with the production vehicles. It could do with less of the corporate promotional nonsense, but enthusiasts will enjoy it.

View of Geelong (1856) was a proud moment.

Round the corner, the **Ford Discovery Centre** celebrates the contribution to the town's prosperity by the massive Ford factory with examples of the company's vehicles *(see panel, below left)*.

East of the city, the Bellarine Peninsula has some pretty villages, a couple of low-key but popular beach destinations in **Barwon Heads** and **Ocean Grove**, and the burgeoning settlement of **Portarlington**, where vineyards, local mussels and the venerable **Portarlington Mill** (Turner Court; www.nattrust.com.au; tel: 52 59 2804; Sept–May Sat–Sun noon–4pm) make the case for a visit.

However, the standout destination is Queenscliff.

QUEENSCLIFF ❹

It's a Victorian resort in the grandest of traditions. You only need to walk along Hesse Street or Gellibrand Street to appreciate how privileged the elite clientele of the **Queenscliff Hotel**, say, or the **Vue Grand** must have felt when they passed through the doors of such distinguished establishments. Current fashion sees them dubbed "boutique" hotels.

Fort Queenscliff (King Street; www.fortqueenscliff.com.au; tel: 52 58 1488; tours Sat–Sun and school holidays, 1pm, 3pm; charge) on Shortland Bluff is a hefty structure designed to deter an anticipated Russian invasion in the 1860s (it was the era of the Crimean War). There are a couple of lighthouses here and another down the road at Point Lonsdale on the cliffs. Much more modern is the new marina with its view tower.

Finally, the **Bellarine Peninsula Railway** (Queenscliff Station; www.bpr.org.au; tel: 5258 2069; Sun, more often during holidays; charge) runs steam-train services for joy rides and for the popular Blues Train events. On the latter, passengers listen to live blues bands in each of the four carriages, changing at each of the evening's stops until they've had the opportunity to hear all of the artists (www.thebluestrain.com.au; tel: 132 849; Aug–May Sat, some Fri; charge).

A ferry will take you and your car over to the Mornington Peninsula in a 40-minute voyage during which there is a good chance of seeing dolphins surfing the bow wave. Occasionally in winter, a whale will appear (www.searoad.com.au; tel: 5258 3244; daily 7am–6pm on the hour). Disembark at Sorrento.

A ferry runs between Queenscliff and Sorrento.

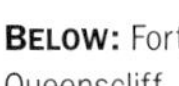

BELOW: Fort Queenscliff.

When at the stately end of Sorrento's Ocean Beach Road, it is a requirement to stop at **Just Fine Food** on the left for a vanilla slice. It's part of coming to Sorrento. They may, as is claimed, be the best slices in the state, and sales of 1,000 a day tend to support this.

ABOVE CENTRE: Sorrento's Ocean Beach. **BELOW:** The Baths restaurant on the edge of Port Phillip Bay, Sorrento.

SORRENTO ❺

Situated on the narrow peninsula defining the southern rim of Port Phillip Bay, Sorrento offers a choice of beaches. There are some fine stretches of sand along the calm waters of the bay, or you can opt for the more rugged and bracing Ocean Beach on the southern coast.

The linking Ocean Beach Road begins with imposing Victorian sandstone structures that give way to modern shops and restaurants. It's a street where you can stroll along, indulge in a little shopping, or perhaps just sit in the shade with a coffee and watch the fashionable city dwellers let their hair down. It can get very busy in summer, particularly at weekends, but otherwise it's pleasantly low-key. In this regard it's much like the rest of the peninsula.

If you tire of this and of poking around in rock pools, go out on one of the boats that promise swimming with dolphins and seals; the combination of adrenalin and emotion will soften even the flintiest of hearts (Moonraker, Sorrento Pier; www.moonrakercharters.com.au; tel: 5984 4211; Oct–Apr daily, 9am or 1pm; charge).

Portsea, towards the end of the peninsula, is where the super-rich have their houses and where the helipad sees more use than the garage. There are more lovely beaches, a golf course – one of more than a dozen this side of the bay – and a famous pub, the Portsea Hotel.

Dramatic **Cheviot Beach** gained notoriety as the site of Harold Holt's last swim. The Australian Prime Minister went for a dip in 1967 and was never seen again. The Harold Holt Swim Centre, in one of Melbourne's eastern suburbs, commemorates the man, apparently without irony.

The tip of the landmass is within **Point Nepean National Park**, a

Recommended Restaurants, Bars & Cafés on page 211

former fort and quarantine station, and you can now visit the site with the aid of a "transporter" service that runs from the visitor centre (tel: 5984 1586; daily 10am–5pm; free). Shell middens (the detritus of thousands of oyster meals) attest to long-standing Aboriginal occupancy of the land. Return through Sorrento and note **Sullivan's Cove**, where the first European settlers came ashore in 1803 *(see page 32)*.

North around the bay

The road stays close to the coast all the way to Mornington, passing through a host of settlements, all with beaches and mostly low-key features. **Blairgowrie** and **Rye** both have spectacular ocean beaches, which extend all the way down to **Cape Schanck**, marked by a historic **Light Station** from which there are gaspworthy views over Bass Strait (tel: 5988 6184; tours daily 10am–5pm; charge). There is also easy bushwalking and abundant wildlife. The easiest road access is directly south from Rosebud.

Continue along the bay to **Dromana**. Another long, safe sandy beach is on offer, but your eyes will inevitably be drawn to the looming bulk of **Arthurs Seat** ❻, the highest point on the peninsula, just up from the shore. You might be able to reach the summit by taking the **Arthurs Seat Chairlift** (a dispute over the lease stymied its operation at the time of writing). Alternatively, you can always drive up. Either way, the views both at the top and on the way up make it worthwhile.

This is a good point at which wine enthusiasts should head inland through rolling hills towards **Red Hill** and **Red Hill South**, where there are dozens of vineyards to investigate, some of them with exceptional eateries attached. Highlights might include **Crittenden Estate**, in its tranquil lakeside setting (25 Harisons Road, Dromana; www.crittendenwines.com.au; tel: 5981 9555; daily 11am–4pm, dinner Fri–Sat), or **Montalto**, for its kitchen and its sculpture trail (33 Shoreham Road, Red Hill South; www.montalto.com.au; tel: 5989 8412; daily 11am–5pm).

If you get down as far as the shores of Western Port, then a visit to **Coolart Wetlands and Homestead**, near Somers, is recommended (Lord Somers Road; www.parkweb.vic.gov.au; daily 10am–5pm; free). The 1895 red-brick mansion is noteworthy, but

Since 2003, the acquisitive Montalto Sculpture Prize has helped to expand the collection on the vineyard's sculpture trail.

BELOW: horse riding on Rye Beach.

At the Mornington Railway, a squad of volunteers has restored an old steam locomotive that now undertakes the short run to Moorooduc.

the true appeal lies in the wetland habitat that attracts birds in their thousands in the winter and spring breeding season.

However, back on the bay, it's an attractive ride around the coast to **Mount Martha**, where the beautiful sand is augmented by gaily painted beach huts.

MORNINGTON ❼

Mornington, 7km (4 miles) to the north, has a quaint harbour with a small fishing fleet. The pier is likely to be peopled by anglers and is worth walking down for the views across the bay, with Melbourne's towers just visible glinting on the horizon. A particular highlight is the **Mornington Railway**, which operates a steam train on a short route and infrequent timetable (Pentecost Road; www.morningtonrailway.org.au; tel: 5978 8792; first three Sundays each month, call for times).

The **Mornington Peninsula Regional Art Gallery** (Dunns Road; http://mprg.mornpen.vic.gov.au; tel: 5975 4395; Tue–Sun 10am–5pm; charge) has half a dozen exhibitions a year and its own collection, which specialises in Australian art from the late 1800s onwards.

It's necessary to cut inland at this point to continue north for the home run to Melbourne. Mount Eliza's **Manyung Gallery** (1408 Nepean Highway; www.manyunggallery.com.au; tel: 9787 2953; Mon–Tue 11am–3pm, Wed–Fri 10am–5pm, Sat–Sun 9am–5pm) can be interesting, and is one of several commercial spaces in the region.

Make haste through Frankston and stay on the Nepean Highway until turning on to the Beach Road at Mentone. It becomes the Esplanade in **Brighton**. Slow down after the junction with South Road and at Dendy Street pull into the car park on the left. Prepare yourself for one of the iconic sites of Melbourne: the bathing boxes on **Brighton Beach** ❽. They change hands for astronomical sums and instil sufficient pride in their owners to keep them immaculately painted in their fairground colours. From here it's a short drive on to St Kilda and back to the city. ❑

BELOW: Brighton Beach huts.

BEST RESTAURANTS, BARS AND CAFÉS

Prices for a three-course dinner per person with a half-bottle of house wine:
$ = under A$60
$$ = A$60–90
$$$ = A$90–120
$$$$ = over A$120

Flinders

Flinders Hotel

Cnr Cook and Wood Streets, Flinders. 5989 0201 L & D daily **$**

Choose from the local-filled public bar, the family-friendly bistro or the serious diner restaurant at this versatile and interesting small-town pub.

Main Ridge

La Baracca Trattoria

T'Gallant Winemakers, 1385 Mornington–Flinders Road, Main Ridge. 5989 6565 L daily **$$**

A converted farm shed is the main dining room at this rustic, Italo-centric vineyard restaurant that serves great local produce on wood-fired pizza and home-made pasta.

Merricks

Salix

Willow Creek Vineyard, 166 Balnarring Road, Merricks North. 5989 7640 L daily, D Fri–Sat **$$**

Local ingredients – everything from mussels to cherries – and skilled, interesting cooking taste even better with the elevated views over the vineyard from the casual, comfortably upholstered dining room.

Queenscliff

Athelstane House

4 Hobson Street, Queenscliff. 5258 1024 B, L & D daily **$$**

The light and spacious dining room of this restored 1860s guest-house takes a simple, breezy approach to food using good ingredients, cooked with skill.

Kelp Café

67 Point Lonsdale Road, Point Lonsdale, Queenscliff. 5258 4797 B, L & D daily **$**

The pared-back modern decor reflects the cooking in this popular seaside café, from breakfast through to dinner, when the seafood really shines.

The Queenscliff Hotel

16 Gellibrand Street, Queenscliff. 5258 1066 L & D daily **$$$**

This grand old Victorian hotel is not only big on nostalgic atmosphere, it also serves up decent food in its sheltered courtyard or grand candlelit dining room.

Red Hill

Montalto

33 Shoreham Road, Red Hill South. 5989 8412 L daily, D Fri–Sat (in summer Mon–Sat) **$$$**

The fabulous views from the glass-and-timber building, gardens full of sculpture, picnic areas and dishes favouring local produce make this one of the Mornington Peninsula's best picks.

Vines of Red Hill

150 Red Hill Road, Red Hill. 5989 2977 L Thur–Mon, D Fri–Sat (extended hours in summer) **$$$**

With its Tuscan-inspired dining room and terrace, menu of Mediterranean-flavoured food and countryside hush, Vines is an ideal place for slow grazing over a bottle or two.

Waurn Ponds

Pettavel Winery and Restaurant

65 Pettavel Road, Waurn Ponds (south of Geelong). 5266 1120 L daily, D Fri **$$$**

Pastoral views through walls of windows, a five-course dégustation menu showcasing local produce, and friendly, well-paced service.

Bars and Cafés

Fork to Fork at Heronswood
105 Latrobe Parade, Dromana.
Feast on rare and heirloom produce pulled from the garden of this historic estate with brilliant sea views. Menu changes often.

Portsea Hotel
3746 Point Nepean Road, Portsea.
The food is fairly standard pub fare, but having a beer on the lawn by the sea is not to be missed.

Red Hill Brewery
88 Shoreham Road, Red Hill South.
Funky microbrewery that serves great beer along with beer-friendly food on a sunny terrace.

Recommended Restaurants, Bars & Cafés on page 221

THE GREAT OCEAN ROAD

The cliff-hugging road through the state's most spectacular coastal scenery is one of the world's great drives. It will take you from Victoria's surfing capital, past stunning beaches and rock formations, to charming resorts and fishing ports

Main attractions
- TORQUAY
- AIREYS INLET
- LORNE
- APOLLO BAY
- CAPE OTWAY
- THE TWELVE APOSTLES
- WARRNAMBOOL
- PORT FAIRY

The coast road running from Torquay all the way along to Warrnambool must count as one of the most beautiful stretches of road in Australia, if not the world. Its genesis came during World War I, when public works projects were being planned in anticipation of the return of diggers from the battlefields of Europe. The Great Ocean Road Trust began to solicit donations in 1918, the year that the first survey detail began work, and the following year rock-blasting in Lorne marked the beginning of construction.

From then until the grand opening in 1932, hundreds of men worked in often gruelling conditions to create a marvel of engineering that thousands enjoy today. It stands as both a memorial to those who lost their lives in the Great War and a successful job-creation scheme that ultimately employed almost 3,000 ex-servicemen.

TORQUAY ❶

Torquay lies 39km (24 miles) south of Geelong and, if you stick to the main B100 road, appears to be an unprepossessing collection of surf-wear factory outlets best left to rabid wave riders. But the story changes as soon as you turn off towards the sea. Before that, however, pull into the **Visitor Information Centre** (Surf City Plaza, Beach Road; www.visitgreatoceanroad.org.au; tel: 5261 42 19; daily 9am–5pm). One look at the volunteers staffing the bureau and it becomes clear that surfing is everything in this part of the world, although other states may wish to debate its claim to be the surf capital of Australia.

LEFT: the Great Ocean Road between Lorne and Apollo Bay.

RIGHT: suited up for an afternoon in the surf at Torquay.

It helps your feet grip the surfboard. And more besides, if this display of surfing wax at the Surfworld Museum is any guide.

For a crash course in the subject, try the adjoining **Surfworld Museum** (www.surfworld.com.au; daily 9am–5pm; charge). For what is essentially a tarted-up collection of surfboards and other paraphernalia, it has been put together with a sizeable amount of wit and imagination. Non-surfers should find more than enough to keep them interested – like the sliced-open kombi van or the wacky collection of board wax – and enthusiasts will be rapt.

After that it's time to hit the beach for the real thing. **Fisherman's Beach** and **Front Beach** are ideal for surfing, beginners upwards, windsurfing and parasurfing. Pure surfing starts to the south of Point Danger and round in **Half Moon Bay**. The car park at **Point Danger**, by the ANZAC memorial, is a good spot for spectators to catch the action as well as being a scenic viewpoint in its own right.

Torquay is an attractive low-key resort, but it is starting to change: two new upmarket hotels are opening, and the town's population is expected to double over the next decade.

Perhaps the best-known surfing destination in Australia, **Bells Beach** is just a few kilometres down the road. Rincon and Winkipop may sound like Teletubbies to the layman, but to aficionados they are just two of the "breaks" that make this beach so special, and that attract world-class competitors to the Rip Curl Pro Event every April. There

BELOW: Bell's Beach.

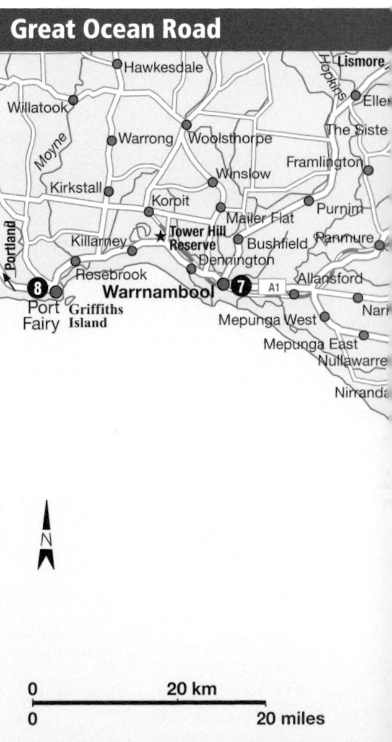

Recommended Restaurants, Bars & Cafés on page 221

are various spots for non-surfers to get a view of the action.

The next promontory to the west, **Point Addis**, provides tremendous views in all directions and is just the place to dawdle and enjoy a lovely walk to the beach, although the "optional dress bathing" may take some by surprise.

The road continues through **Anglesea**, a modest resort with the requisite gorgeous beach, surf and a golf course popular with kangaroos.

AIREYS INLET ❷

Aireys Inlet doesn't have the golf course but more than makes up for it with **Split Point Lighthouse**, which looks just like every lighthouse should: sheer white with a red roof. You can see inside it, too (www.splitpointlighthouse.com.au; tel: 1800 174 045; tours daily 11am–2pm; charge). There's a 300-metre (330-yard) circuit track that crams in several views to die for, including one over the mass of **Eagle Rock**, a limestone stack thrusting up from the sea that acts as a precursor to the Twelve Apostles. The old Lighthouse Stables are now handy tearooms – a good place to recover from the 300-metre hike, or a fuelling station for the other walks, ranging from 45 minutes to three hours, which start from the car park. The shorter walk takes in a replica of an 1860s bark hut settler's home.

Continuing westward, look out for the houses imaginatively suspended or cantilevered high in the hills to take advantage of the views. After an arch, which commemorates the war dead, the road begins to get tighter and windier. It's a pleasure to drive and, unsurprisingly, motorbike riders see the road as something of a challenge. Be cautious because, despite tight speed limits, there's a history of the madcap few treating it as a time trial and coming to grief on vehicles just like yours.

Split Point Lighthouse was built in 1891 and automated as early as 1919.

Great Ocean Road

Geelong
Melbourne
Torquay
Bells Beach
Anglesea
Point Addis
Aireys Inlet
Split Point Lighthouse
Pt Addis Marine N.P.
Great Otway National Park
Lorne
Point Greyon
Erskine Falls
Otway Range
Wye River
Kennet River
Point Hawdon
Wongarra
Skenes Creek
Apollo Bay
Great Ocean Road
Otway Fly Tree Top Walk
Cape Otway
Cape Otway Lighthouse
Colac
Camperdown
Lake Corangamite
Loch Ard Gorge
The Twelve Apostles
Port Campbell
Port Campbell N.P.
Princetown
Twelve Apostles Marine N.P.
Point Reginald
Peterborough
Bass Strait
SOUTHERN OCEAN

The pier at Lorne is a quiet, romantic place most of the time, and then once a year, in January, grabs the spotlight as thousands turn up for the Pier to Pub swimming competition across the bay.

LORNE ❸

Lorne is a very popular resort that, despite the physical constraints of the hills and the sea, is still managing to grow. A few years ago, a quiet place of a few houses and shops appeared to be completely unbalanced by the mass of the Cumberland Resort Hotel. Now the Cumberland is just one of many and, accordingly, fits in much better. Once you hit the beach you can forget all about such things and just concentrate on sea, sand and swimming.

Or maybe drive inland, either to Teddy's Lookout for views of a blissful stretch of the Great Ocean Road, or up to the **Erskine Falls**, set attractively in a fern gully. You can walk on fairly level ground to the top of the falls or, if you're feeling energetic, to the base and back up again.

APOLLO BAY ❹

It's another 45km (28 miles) down the coast to Apollo Bay. This is another popular resort, but without the pretensions or prices of Lorne. Or, to be fair, the classy restaurants and chic drinking holes. It's more scuffed and relaxed here, and what it does have, unsurprisingly, is great beaches. Venture down to them first thing in the morning and you will find row upon row of anglers communing in silence.

There is also a harbour where you can watch the crayfish being landed in the morning before buying it fresh from the store nearby. Just back from that, the local golf course gets busy with players who want a sea view with their game.

The road cuts inland a little bit further on and rises up into the hills of the **Great Otway National Park** before dropping down to the sea again, fleetingly, at Glenaire.

Cape Otway ❺

Before that though, turn off to Cape Otway and keep your eyes peeled for koalas in the trees beside the winding road to the **Cape Otway Lighthouse**. The lighthouse, built in 1848, is the oldest in Australia and marks the entrance to Bass Strait, separating the mainland from Tasmania. It is open to visitors, as is the neighbouring **Telegraph Office** and sundry other

BELOW: ancient forest at Great Otway National Park.

Recommended Restaurants, Bars & Cafés on page 221

buildings in the complex. The views are as splendid as you would expect (www.lightstation.com; tel: 5237 92 40; daily 9am–5pm; charge).

Return to the Ocean Road until taking the C155 at Lavers Hill. Continue as far as Beech Forest Road and look for signs to the **Otway Fly** (www.otwayfly.com; tel: 5235 9200; daily 9am–5pm; charge). There's something magical about walking along steel walkways high off the ground through the canopy of a temperate rainforest. It gives you a completely different perspective on the local country and gets you much closer to the birds that are only specks from the ground. Add to that the frisson that comes with the slight swaying of the structure as you walk along it, and you have one exciting excursion – especially if you haven't visited one of the similar enterprises elsewhere in Australia.

The Twelve Apostles ❻

Time to return to the Great Ocean Road, which takes a while to rejoin the coast, but that only heightens the drama of the next stop, the world-renowned **Twelve Apostles**. This is what everybody comes to see, and – in an attempt to manage the numbers – there is now a **Twelve Apostles Centre** next to a sizeable car park north of the road, and a path through a tunnel to get to the coastal viewpoints. The stacks staggering into the distance, pounded by waves from the Southern Ocean, never fail to amaze. And remember, it's an evolving landscape. As recently as September 2009, another of the stumps collapsed into the sea, leaving only a small mound of rubble (and, actually, just seven Apostles).

There are several more stopping-

There's a small airfield behind the Twelve Apostles Centre where a clutch of helicopters await tourists who want an aerial view of the coastline. Or, to cut down the lengthy drive from Melbourne, make the trip in a flying boat from the waterfront at Geelong.

ABOVE LEFT: tiptoe through the treetops at the Otway Fly.
BELOW: a pair of Apostles.

The roaring winds and pounding waves of the Southern Ocean have eroded the soft limestone of the cliffs to create spectacular formations.

points as the road continues westwards. Many are linked to shipwrecks, a constant peril along this coast. **Loch Ard Gorge**, for instance, is named after the vessel that came to grief here in 1878. Three months at sea since leaving England and cruelly close to its destination, it went down with just two of the 54 on board surviving. It's a beautiful spot, especially if you take the steps down to the beach.

Pass through the expanding **Port Campbell**, where ever more accommodation services the flood of tourists, and make a point of stopping for at least two more rock formations. At **London Bridge** spare a thought for the tourists marooned on a brand new island when the main arch collapsed in 1990; at **The Grotto**, clamber down into the cave and see the sea eating away at another arch.

WARRNAMBOOL 7

It's time for the road to take another detour inland before returning to the ocean at **Warrnambool**, the largest town on this stretch of coast and a very good family holiday destination. Aside from the beach-based activities of surfing, swimming, fishing and sailing, you can add some extra adrenalin at the **Lake Pertobe Adventure Playground** (Pertobe Road; daily; free), where huge slides, flying foxes, paddleboats and a maze are amongst the offerings.

The big ticket attraction here is to be found in the complex behind the **Visitor Information Centre** (Merri Street; tel: 5559 4620/1800 637 725; daily 9am–8pm), so follow the big yellow-and-blue "i" signs, pick up the brochures you need, and then clear a few hours for Flagstaff Hill.

Flagstaff Hill

Merri Street; www.flagstaffhill.com
5559 4600/1800 556 111
daily 9am–5pm charge

In essence it's a historic fishing-port theme park. Starting with an audio-visual history lesson, you progress through a beautifully designed display area that includes treasures from the wreck of the *Loch Ard*, including a

BELOW RIGHT: Loch Ard Gorge.

Getting Wrecked

Hundreds of ships have been lost in Victorian waters over the last two centuries, many of them on the treacherous rocks of the stretch of coast running westwards from Cape Otway. The "Shipwreck Coast" has accounted for numerous vessels that have failed to "thread the needle" – find the gap between King Island and the mainland to enter Bass Strait on the run in to Melbourne. Rough seas, bad weather and rudimentary navigational equipment proved a fatal combination for many of the world's trading ships, as well as a good proportion of local craft ferrying goods and passengers around Australia. The *Loch Ard* is by far the most famous victim by dint of the gorge to which it gave its name and, more recently, the *Shipwrecked* sound and light spectacular at Warrnambool's Flagstaff Hill. The story of an eventful three-month voyage round the world brought to a tragic end just hours before its completion is not atypical.

Recommended Restaurants, Bars & Cafés on page 221

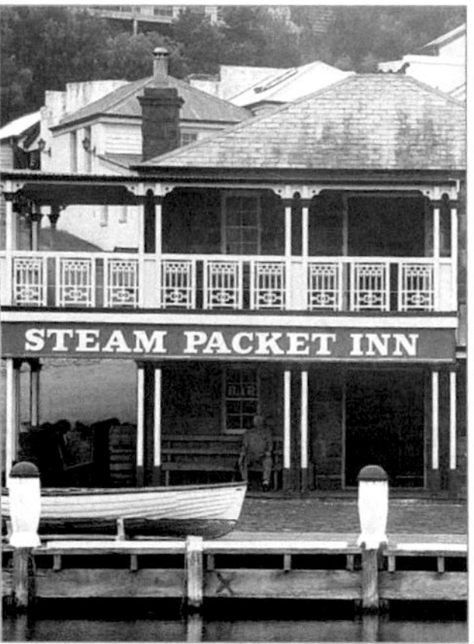

remarkable life-sized earthenware peacock intended for display at the 1878 Great Exhibition in Melbourne.

Step outside on to a hillside sloping down towards the bay and Lake Pertobe. Here a 4-hectare (10-acre) maritime village loosely recreates the Warrnambool of the late 1800s. All the usual buildings are ticked off as you stroll down the coiling main street until, at the bottom, you arrive at a port. The whole site is peopled with characters willing to share their stories or demonstrate some arcane lore of the shipwright or bartender.

Every night at dusk you can experience *Shipwrecked*, which tells the story of the final voyage of the *Loch Ard*. It is an impressive sound, light and laser show, incorporating extraordinary projections on to a curtain of water.

Other attractions

Warrnambool Art Gallery (cnr Liebig and Timor Streets; tel: 5559 4949; Mon–Fri 10am–5pm, Sat–Sun noon–5pm; free) has a range of works from the last 200 years and a small section devoted to European art that was part of the founding bequest by local merchant Joseph Archibald.

If you're around in winter (June to September), then you'll be spending time at **Logan's Beach**, where a hefty viewing platform has been set up to take advantage of the annual arrival of a group of Southern Right whales who calve here and then use the area as a nursery *(see margin, right)*.

Tower Hill Reserve

Just 14km (9 miles) beyond Warrnambool on the Great Ocean Road, **Tower Hill Reserve** occupies the

Whales visit the coast off Warrnambool regularly, and if you're in luck you may experience the thrill of seeing a mother and calf frolicking in the surf. The presence, or otherwise, of the whales is closely monitored: call the Visitor Information Centre (see page 218) to see if any are in the area.

ABOVE LEFT AND CENTRE: Flagstaff Hill. **BELOW:** Warrnambool Art Gallery.

Map on pages 214–15

There are few, if any, better gigs to play than Port Fairy, for the quality, size and support of the crowds. Port Fairy? – it doesn't get any better than that.

Greg Champion on the Port Fairy Folk Festival

ABOVE RIGHT: wind-shaped trees at Anglesea. **BELOW:** a snoozing koala at Tower Hill.

crater of a dormant volcano. It's packed with wildlife, and if you don't see at least one koala in the wild here on one of the five self-guided walks, you should contact your optician. Keep looking at the upper branches of the eucalypti, and the chances are that the furry blob in a handy fork in the tree will be a snoozing koala.

Tower Hill has long been an Aboriginal stamping ground, and the Robin Boyd-designed **Worn Gundidj Visitor Centre** (www.worngundidj.org.au; tel: 5561 5315; Mon–Fri 9am–5pm, Sat–Sun 10am–4pm) maintains the tradition with sales of art and craft objects. Check here, too, for guided walks.

PORT FAIRY ❽

Port Fairy is the perfect place to finish this journey. The natural harbour at the mouth of the Moyne River first attracted whalers in the early 1900s, and the town grew up slowly behind it. The port was always known as Port Fairy, but the town began life as Belfast and reflects an Irish presence that can be traced through to today.

It's an attractive town, whether for a walk along the wharf as the day's catch is landed, or a stroll along streets lined with listed buildings. Usually the pace is gentle and there is plenty of time to have a drink in the oldest licensed pub in Victoria, the **Caledonian Hotel**.

However, on Labour Day weekend thousands arrive for the **Port Fairy Folk Festival** (www.portfairyfolkfestival.com; tel: 5568 2227), the largest such event in the country. There are two other music festivals during the year, and the level of artistic activity is disproportionate to the size of the town.

Meanwhile, unaffected by all this, a colony of mutton birds (short-tailed shearwaters) take over **Griffiths Island** between September and April to hatch their young. Venture down there at dusk for the startling experience of hundreds of the creatures whirring past you in near darkness as they head unerringly for the same burrow to which they return every year.

To return to your own burrow, the quickest way back to the start of this route is the Princes Highway through Warrnambool and Colac. ❑

BEST RESTAURANTS, BARS AND CAFÉS

Aireys Inlet

A La Grecque

60 Great Ocean Road, Aireys Inlet. ☎ 5289 6922 ⏲ B, L & D daily Nov–Apr, hours restricted in winter **$$**

Ocean views, carefully cooked Greek food, Mediterranean-themed decor and a warm, hospitable attitude create a little touch of Paros.

Anglesea

Furio's

95 Great Ocean Road, Anglesea. ☎ 5263 3616 ⏲ B & L daily, D Sat **$$**

Without too much fanfare, Furio's manages to tick all the boxes for locals and tourists alike. Good Italian food.

Apollo Bay

Chris's Restaurant

280 Skenes Creek Road, Apollo Bay. ☎ 5237 6411 ⏲ B, L & D daily **$$$**

The chef makes the most of his Greek background and puts the emphasis on fresh local seafood to corner the top end of the market at this hilltop eyrie.

Lorne

Ba Ba Lu Bar and Restaurant

6a Mountjoy Parade, Lorne. ☎ 5289 1808 ⏲ B, L & D daily, hours reduced in winter **$$**

Spanish delicacies are the speciality here, and how you take them is up to you, with tapas available for the grazers and full plates for making a night of it.

Port Fairy

Dublin House Inn

57–59 Bank Street, Port Fairy. ☎ 5568 2022 ⏲ L & D daily **$$**

European-style food is dished up with flair in this atmospheric, former merchant-trader building, built in 1855. A decent, mostly Australian wine list completes the picture.

Merrijig Inn

1 Campbell Street, Port Fairy. ☎ 5568 2324 ⏲ D Mon–Sat **$$**

Beautifully cooked, contemporary Mediterranean food is teamed with an excellent wine list of Old and New World labels to create one of the area's best dining experiences.

Portofino On Bank

26 Bank Street, Port Fairy. ☎ 5568 2251 ⏲ D Mon–Sat, daily in Jan **$$$**

A favourite of locals and tourists alike, this cosy restaurant has a suave wine list, a deftly cooked Mediterranean-inspired menu and attentive, informed service.

Prices for a three-course dinner per person with a half-bottle of house wine:
$ = under A$60
$$ = A$60–90
$$$ = A$90–120
$$$$ = over A$120

Torquay

Growlers

23 The Esplanade, Torquay. ☎ 5264 8455 ⏲ B, L & D daily **$**

Something of a scatter-gun approach to the menu, but quality is high in this relaxed if slightly chaotic foreshore eatery.

Scorched

17 The Esplanade, Torquay. ☎ 5261 6142 ⏲ L Wed–Sun, D Wed–Sat **$$**

Sleekly modern good looks and great water views through pine trees are fine, but Scorched backs up the style with the substance of a clever wine list and a range of contemporary food.

Warrnambool

Pippies by the Bay

Flagstaff Hill, 91 Merri Street, Warrnambool. ☎ 5561 2188 ⏲ L & D daily **$$**

Seasonally driven dishes, many of them containing locally sourced produce, are worthy competitors to the beautiful view of tranquil Lady Bay. Does a dinner-and-show deal with Flagstaff Hill.

Bars and Cafés

Aqua Restaurant & Bar

150 Mountjoy Parade, Lorne.

Standard continent-hopping café fare and cheery if forgetful service are helped along by great views of the ocean.

La Bimba

125 Great Ocean Road, Apollo Bay.

Water views, a bohemian sense of style and a friendly attitude keep La Bimba popular with visitors and locals alike.

Kafe Kaos

54–56 Mountjoy Parade, Lorne.

Kaos indeed. A riot of colour, which extends to the food, keeps the smaller and louder members of the family happy in this popular nosh house.

Kosta's

48 Mountjoy Parade, Lorne.

Perhaps not the greatest food in town but the relaxing Greek-tavern ambience is worth a look.

BALLARAT

Recommended Restaurants, Bars & Cafés on pages 238–9

THE GOLD TOWNS AND BEYOND

The wealth from the 1850s gold rush helped to build a chain of distinguished towns and cities to the north and west of Melbourne. The region also offers the more tranquil options of the Grampians National Park or mucking about in boats on the Murray River

Main attractions
- BALLARAT
- MARYBOROUGH
- AVOCA
- ARARAT
- THE GRAMPIANS
- MALDON
- CASTLEMAINE
- BENDIGO
- ECHUCA
- HANGING ROCK
- KYNETON
- DAYLESFORD

The discovery of gold near present-day Ballarat in 1851 was the catalyst for the transformation of Melbourne and the development of the newly created state of Victoria. Melbourne's grand 19th-century buildings would have been rather less grand without the influx of wealth and people that gold engendered.

Rural Victoria was even more radically affected, with several sizeable towns growing rapidly in what had until then been largely empty bush. Of course those heady days couldn't last for ever and, in the slowdown, many of the boom towns gently subsided into torpor, subsisting on agriculture, logging or whatever else could be scraped from the ground.

However, that meant that there were few resources available to fund any post-war modernist rush to sweep away the past and replace what might have been decreed outdated buildings with elegies in concrete and steel. Today we can reap the benefits. Dotting the countryside north and west of Melbourne, town after town is packed with beautifully preserved or renovated colonial architecture. As tourists latch on to this wealth of history, there is greater incentive to preserve even the ropiest of miners' lean-tos for posterity.

BALLARAT ❶

Where better to start than Ballarat, where the adventure began. After an easy 110km (68-mile) drive from Melbourne along the Western Freeway, follow the sporadic signs to the Visitor Centre – don't panic when you don't see a sign for several blocks as there's always another one

LEFT: Ballarat Railway Station epitomises the pomp of Goldfields architecture.
RIGHT: the Contemplation Room in the Eureka Centre.

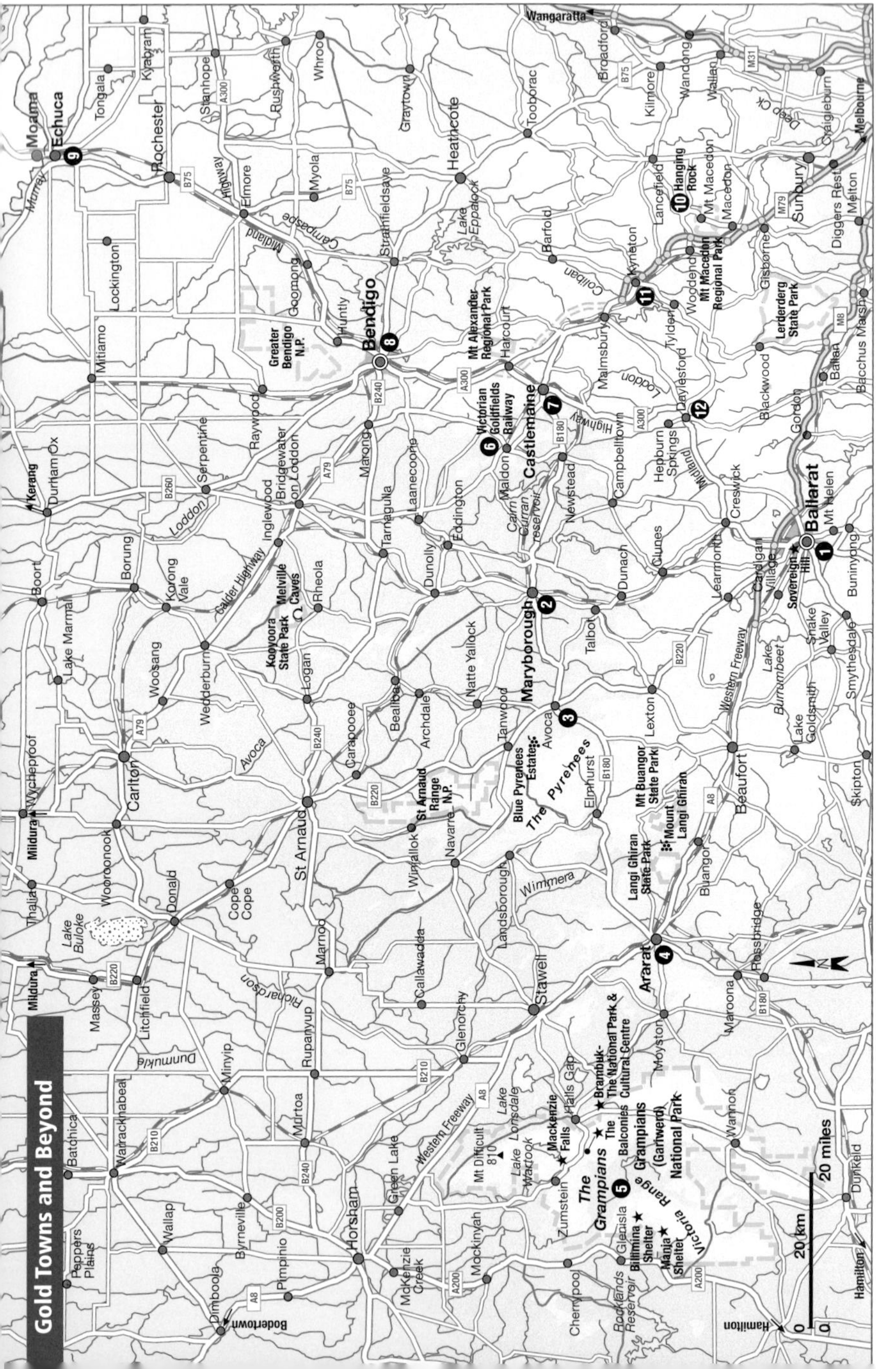

Gold Towns and Beyond
Echuca
Moama
Murray
Tongala
Kyabram
Stanhope
Rushworth
Whroo
Rochester
Elmore
Midland Highway
Campaspe
Myola
Graytown
Heathcote
Tooborac
Broadford
Wangaratta
Kilmore
Wandong
Wallan
Deep Ck
Craigieburn
Melbourne
Hanging Rock
Lancefield
Mt Macedon
Macedon
Sunbury
Diggers Rest
Melton
Gisborne
Woodend
Mt Macedon Regional Park
Kyneton
Coliban
Barfold
Lake Eppalock
Strathfieldsaye
Lockington
Goornong
Huntly
Bendigo
Greater Bendigo N.P.
Mt Alexander Regional Park
Harcourt
Tylden
Malmsbury
Lerderderg State Park
Bacchus Marsh
Ballan
Blackwood
Daylesford
Loddon
Castlemaine
Victorian Goldfields Railway
Mitiamo
Raywood
Marong
Serpentine
Kerang
Durham Ox
Bridgewater on Loddon
Inglewood
Laanecoorie
Eddington
Maldon
Cairn Curran reservoir
Newstead
Campbelltown
Hepburn Springs
Creswick
Gordon
Ballarat
Mt Helen
Buninyong
Sovereign Hill
Cardigan Village
Learmonth
Clunes
Dunach
Tarnagulla
Dunolly
Maryborough
Talbot
Boort
Borung
Korong Vale
Calder Highway
Melville Caves
Rheola
Kooyoora State Park
Lake Marmal
Woosang
Wedderburn
Logan
Bealiba
Archdale
Natte Yallock
Tanwood
Avoca
Lexton
Western Freeway
Lake Burrumbeet
Snake Valley
Smythesdale
Lake Goldsmith
Beaufort
Skipton
Wycheproof
Carlton
Avoca
St Arnaud
Carapooee
St Arnaud Range N.P.
Blue Pyrenees Estate
The Pyrenees
Elmhurst
Mt Buangor State Park
Mount Langi Ghiran
Langi Ghiran State Park
Buangor
Navarre
Winjallok
Landsborough
Wimmera
Mildura
Wooroonook
Donald
Cope Cope
Thalia
Lake Buloke
Marnoo
Massey
Litchfield
Richardson
Callawadda
Stawell
Ararat
Rossbridge
Maroona
Moyston
Brambuk-The National Park & Cultural Centre
Halls Gap
Glenorchy
Dunmunkle
Minyip
Rupanyup
Murtoa
Warracknabeal
Batchica
Lake Lonsdale
Mackenzie Falls
Lake Wartook
The Balconies
Grampians (Gariwerd) National Park
The Grampians
Mt Difficult 810
Western Freeway
Green Lake
Zumstein
Victoria Range
Wannon
Dunkeld
Hamilton
Horsham
Byrneville
Wallap
Peppers Plains
Pimpinio
Dimboola
Bordertown
McKenzie Creek
Mockinyah
Cherrypool
Rocklands Reservoir
Glenisla
Billimina Shelter
Manja Shelter
20 km
20 miles
0

Recommended Restaurants, Bars & Cafés on pages 238–9

just when it begins to feel like you've made a wrong turning (unless you have made a wrong turning).

The Eureka Centre

It's worth persisting, because you end up at the **Eureka Centre**, part-museum, part-info centre, and soon to be reconstituted as the Australian Centre for Democracy at Eureka. The building is being massively expanded, better to tell the story of Eureka Stockade. It will also once again house the visitor information centre, which is in the town centre in the meantime. The **Visitor Information Centre** (www.visitballarat.com.au; tel: 5320 5741/1800 446 633; daily 9am–5pm) promotes enough local walks, drives and attractions to satisfy even the most hyperactive visitor for several days.

The Eureka Centre itself is built on the site of the stockade at the heart of the rebellion of 1854 *(see panel, below)*. It's well worth seeing the **exhibition** (www.eurekaballarat.com; tel: 5333 1854; daily 9am–4.30pm; charge) for its effective use of audio-visual techniques to tell the story of the uprising and its aftermath; the narrative subtly shifts to the wider implications for democracy and workers' rights in a nascent Australia. After considering this in the Contemplation Room, there's a path to follow outside, taking in an 1880s memorial to those who lost their lives, a 2004 sculptural *Eureka Circle* and a wonderful kids' stockade

ABOVE: privates on display at Sovereign Hill. **BELOW LEFT AND RIGHT:** Ballarat's Eureka Centre.

The Eureka Stockade

The colonial authorities milked the miners on the Ballarat goldfields with a hefty tax of 30 shillings a month on a plot measuring 3.6 square metres (39 sq ft). Ruthless and sometimes violent military police were on hand to collect it, but the miners, denied any democratic representation, could do little about it. Dissatisfaction was compounded by the murder of one of their number and the acquittal of the perpetrator, the owner of Bentley's Hotel. A mob burnt down the hotel and two men were arrested for the crime. Negotiations to deal with this went nowhere, and, led by Irishman Peter Lalor, miners made a bonfire of their licences. The Eureka flag was raised and a stockade built to deter reprisals. On 4 December 1854, six soldiers and 24 miners died in the ensuing attack. Although 13 miners were sent for trial, they were acquitted in the face of popular outcry. Shortly afterwards, gold licences were abolished and full (white) male suffrage introduced.

The Eureka flag incorporates the constellation of the Southern Cross in its design. It is still used by the union movement as a symbol of the fight for workers' rights.

BELOW: Ballarat Fine Art Gallery.

for the little ones to play in.

The next stop is a rollicking theme park that combines living history with a good deal of entertainment.

Sovereign Hill

✉ Bradshaw Street; www.sovereignhill.com.au ☎ 5337 1100 ⏲ daily 10am–5pm $ charge; various ticket and accommodation packages

Follow the brown-and-white tourist signs to discover an entire 1850s township complete with diggings and gold mine, all spread across 25 hectares (62 acres). A huge team of fully costumed staff stay in character to make the experience as authentic as possible. After that it's down to you to make the most of it. You can start by panning for gold (the real thing is discreetly sprinkled along the creek bed to provide an incentive), go down the mine, ride in a horse-drawn carriage, catch a show in the theatre or just prop up the bar in one of the hotels, perhaps with one of the soldiers from the local squad for company.

There's enough to fill a whole day here, and if you want more, the *Blood on the Southern Cross* sound-and-light show is 80 minutes well spent after dark as the Eureka Stockade story is retold in a lavish spectacle (tel: 5337 1199; times vary, see the Sovereign Hill website; charge). There are even hotel rooms available if you can't bear to leave.

There is an interesting **Gold Museum** (daily 9.30am–5.20pm; charge, or admission with Sovereign Hill ticket) outside the entrance, although it does seem somewhat static after the histrionics of Sovereign Hill itself.

Downtown Ballarat

The real city of Ballarat is chock-full of magnificent buildings that testify to the value of the gold being dug out nearby. Try some of the self-guided walks or, at the very least, take a stroll down Sturt and Lydiard streets, where the greatest concentration of landmark structures is to be found. Look out in particular for the **Mechanics' Institute** (1859), the **Mining Exchange Building** (1865), several hotels,

Recommended Restaurants, Bars & Cafés on pages 238–9

especially the refurbished **Craig's Royal Hotel**, and **Her Majesty's Theatre** (17 Lydiard Street; www.hermaj.com; tel: 5333 5800), which has been staging shows since the 1860s. It is often possible to look inside the auditorium.

Ballarat Station is monumental in scale, and it's worth continuing to the level crossing to see the original signal box and old-style wooden signals, which, sadly, have huge black crosses bolted on to them, no doubt to prevent train drivers from following their commands (although one might hope that modern-day drivers could tell the difference between these and the standard electric signals).

Ballarat Fine Art Gallery (40 Lydiard Street; www.balgal.com; tel: 5320 5858; daily 9am–5pm; charge) is the country's largest regional gallery, spread through a conjunction of original Victorian structures and striking modern spaces. It has strong representation from all eras, especially the Heidelberg School *(see page 55)*. The original Eureka flag is housed here, too.

The Eureka trail continues to **Ballarat Old Cemetery** (Macarthur Street) where some of the key protagonists are buried. There is an interesting Chinese section, too.

The Botanical Gardens

To the east of the city centre, **Ballarat Botanical Gardens** (Wendouree Parade; tel: 5320 5135; daily; free) follows the basic layout of its original design from 1858, but with some notable additions: the dramatic, jagged Robert Clark Conservatory (1995) is in keen contrast to the classic Statuary Pavilion of 1888. Within the gardens, the Prime Ministers' Avenue is a collection of bronze busts of every Australian Prime Minister. The Tramways Museum (tel: 5334 1580) runs short trips along Wendouree Parade at weekends.

Lake Wendouree

The gardens are situated on the shore of **Lake Wendouree**, originally created to supply Ballarat's water in 1851. It has been a place of recreation ever since and took its place in the spotlight by hosting the 1956 Olympic rowing and kayaking events. The recent long-term drought reduced it to the swamp that it was before European settlement, but the 2010 floods have helped to refill it.

Completists might want to investigate **Kryal Castle**, a "Medieval Castle" located to the east of Ballarat, or perhaps **Gold Rush Golf**, inaccurately described as "Ballarat's No. 1 family entertainment centre".

The Prime Ministers' Avenue in Ballarat Botanical Gardens provokes idle speculation as to the political significance, or otherwise, of who has been freshly targeted by the birds in their "spot the Prime Minster" competition. Today it's Paul Keating.

ABOVE LEFT: autumn in Ballarat Botanical Gardens. **BELOW:** Maryborough Railway Station (the town is round the back).

TIP

The Grampians Grape Escape festival at the beginning of May sees a series of events across the region tied in with local produce and wines. Pick from tastings, live music and cookery demonstrations.

BELOW: Ararat.

The C287 road north will take you to **Clunes**, an attractive village where it is worth spending a few minutes ambling along the untarnished gold-rush-era streets. Life appears to have passed the place by, although it is now marketing itself as a "book town" in a bid to attract visitors.

MARYBOROUGH ❷

Fifty kilometres (31 miles) further on sits **Maryborough**, a place once notoriously described by Mark Twain in the 1890s as "a station with a town attached". The **railway station** is still the signature building, but its bulk, now untroubled by passenger trains, has been largely given over to a huge antiques store and café.

The town centre has the requisite number of historic administrative buildings, and the **Central Goldfields Art Gallery**, housed in the distinctive fire station (1860), has a small collection of its own, as well as revolving exhibitions by local and contemporary artists (Neill Street; tel: 5460 4588; Thur–Sun 10am–4pm; free).

AVOCA ❸

Avoca, to the west of Maryborough, has a main street full of character and is known for the country race meetings that take place three times a year and draw crowds as much for the quality of the food and wines as the racing. And here is the clue to Avoca's year-round appeal: it is handily placed for the **Pyrenees Wine Region.**

The region's reputation was made on the back of full-bodied Shiraz and Cabernets, but white varietals are also making their presence felt, as you will discover if you drop by any of the cellar doors in the area. There are 16 establishments to choose from, but you could do worse than have a look at **Blue Pyrenees Estate** (Vinoca Road; www.bluepyrenees.com.au; tel: 5465 1111; Mon–Fri 10am–4.30pm, Sat–Sun 10am–5pm) or **Mount Langi Ghiran** (80 Vine Road, Bayindeen; www.langi.com.au; tel: 5354 3207; Mon–Fri 9am–5pm, Sat–Sun 10am–5pm).

ARARAT ❹

Ararat, 64km (40 miles) west of Avoca, is on the western edge of the goldfields and is well stocked with its quota of grandiose Victoriana. The gleaming white stucco of the **Town Hall** (1898) on Vincent Street articulates civic pride; elsewhere, copious iron lacework and robust stone reflects the affluence of the times. The unusual feature of this

Recommended Restaurants, Bars & Cafés on pages 238–9

town, however, is that it was founded by the Chinese community – the only conurbation that can make such a claim in Australia.

The **Gum San Chinese Heritage Centre** (31–3 Lambert Street; www.gumsan.com.au; tel: 5352 1078; daily 10am–4.30pm; charge) tells the story of how several hundred Chinese miners on the long walk from Robe in South Australia to Ballarat happened upon a rich seam of alluvial gold and founded a settlement. Visitors can pan for gold here themselves, as well as learn about Chinese culture and its role in the region's development through various interactive exhibits.

Ararat Gallery (Town Hall; tel: 5352 2836; Mon, Wed–Fri 10am–4.30pm, Sat–Sun noon–4pm; charge) specialises in contemporary textiles and fibre art.

THE GRAMPIANS 5

As a break from pounding the streets of a succession of gold towns, continue westwards on the C222, climb up into the hills and down to the friendly clutches of **Halls Gap**, the main settlement in the **Grampians National Park**. Halls Gap is surrounded by mountains bearing little resemblance to their namesakes in Scotland, after which their first European discoverer, Major Thomas Mitchell, named them in 1836. The cocooning effect seems to shut out the cares of the world.

This is a place to surrender yourself to nature, and there's an awful lot of it. Copious species of trees and wildflowers come in and out of bloom throughout the year, and there is rarely any silence as the abundant bird

The Brambuk Aboriginal Cultural Centre opened in 1990. Architect Greg Burgess designed this "fusion of organic and holistic architecture". No, us neither.

ABOVE LEFT: Mackenzie Falls.
BELOW: The Balconies viewpoint in the Grampians.

> *In it, I spent the happiest days of my childhood, free at last of unchildish anxieties; and when, of a sleepless night, my thoughts turn homewards, it is usually in these carefree, sunlit surroundings that I find myself...*
>
> Henry Handel Richardson (Ethel Richardson's pen name) on her upbringing in Maldon

RIGHT: a cottage auditions for a chocolate box in Maldon. **BELOW:** candles provide the light in Carman's Tunnel Gold Mine... **BELOW RIGHT:** ...along with the guide's headgear.

and animal life makes its presence felt. Koalas are regular occupants of the trees at Halls Gap, and, as you tackle any of the dozens of bush tracks on offer, there's every chance of surprising something furry or feathery.

Before venturing too far, check out what's on offer at the **Visitor Information Centre** (Grampians Road; www.visitgrampians.com.au; tel: 5356 4616/1800 065 599; daily 9am–5pm) or at **Brambuk – The National Park and Cultural Centre** (2km (1¼ miles) north on Grampians Road; www.brambuk.com.au; tel: 5361 4000; daily 9am–5pm).

Next to the latter, and not to be confused with it, is a remarkable building with a wavy roof, the **Brambuk Aboriginal Cultural Centre** (www.brambuk.com.au; tel: 5361 4000; daily 9am–5pm; free), where the history and culture of the five Aboriginal communities who have links with the area are explained. A multimedia presentation tells of the creation of Geriwerd, as the area is known to the Koorie people.

There are occasional performances and demonstrations on the ceremonial ground outside, and guided tours can be arranged to some of the Aboriginal rock-art sites in the park. There's also a short loop walk, which acts as an introduction to the local flora.

Mackenzie Falls

There are numerous walks and drives catering to all interests and fitness levels. Deservedly popular destinations accessible by car are **Mackenzie Falls** – a short hike down a set of steps to the base, or an easy stroll to a lookout at the top; Lake Wartook, where the landscape flattens out for once; and **The Balconies**, where a 20-minute walk through fire-damaged forest is rewarded with staggering views

See a movie and then stay the night at the Theatre Royal in Castlemaine.

across Victoria Valley. At **Zumstein** you can follow a short loop walk, but the main draw is the mob of kangaroos that congregates in the late afternoon.

Probably the most impressive Aboriginal art site is at **Billimina Shelter** on the western side of the park, and the **Manja Shelter** (with more hand stencils than any other rock-art site in Victoria) can be found in the same area.

MALDON ❻

Suitably revived, it's time to return to the central goldfields. Head back through Maryborough and continue on the B180 until the turn-off for **Maldon**, one of the marvels of Victoria. The whole town is listed as "notable" by the National Trust, and there are times, especially first thing in the morning or at night when there are no vehicles about, when a walk under the awnings of gently sloping Main Street feels just the same as it would have a century or more ago. It's weathered enough to feel lived in – faded shop signs and rusting corrugated iron see to that – and there's an almost complete absence of new development.

Get a walking guide from the **Visitor Information Centre** (93 High Street; www.maldoncastlemaine.com; tel: 5475 2569; daily 9am–5pm) and savour the riches to be found on every street. It's not a destination for great activity, but visitors can climb the hill above town and relish the view from **Mount Tarrengower Lookout Tower**, or potter among the ruins of the **North British Mine** and then enjoy the tales of the misfortune that dogged the miners in a guided tour

ABOVE LEFT: Restorers Barn in Castlemaine. **ABOVE CENTRE:** detail on the old police station. **BELOW:** Castlemaine Art Gallery.

Once the brewery decided to take its XXXX to Queensland, Castlemaine's best-known product in a red-and-yellow can became souvenir rock.

of the candlelit **Carman's Tunnel Gold Mine** (Parkin's Reef Road; tel: 5475 2656; Sat, Sun and school holidays, 1.30pm, 3.30pm; charge).

Above all, though, Maldon is a place to kick back, browse in the shops, look at the pictures in **Penny School Gallery** (11 Church Street; www.pennyschoolgallery.com.au; tel: 5475 1911; Wed–Sun 11am–5pm; free) and people-watch from a café or in the Grand Hotel. You can also hop on a steam train here: the **Victorian Goldfields Railway** runs between Maldon and Castlemaine (www.vgr.com.au; tel: 5470 6658; Wed, Sun, call for details.)

CASTLEMAINE 7

Castlemaine, while busier than Maldon, is still only a country town. The **Visitor Information Centre** (44 Mostyn Street; www.maldoncastlemaine.com; tel: 5471 1795; daily 9am–5pm) is to be found in the historic **Market Building** (1862), where there is also a somewhat verbose exhibition about local gold extraction, and an ever-changing art exhibition. Most of the key attractions are within walking distance, so collect the customary self-guided tour map and get perambulating.

Note the statue of Roman goddess Ceres perched above the Market Building's facade on Mostyn Street and then soak up the history, while keeping an eye on the contents of the buildings you're reading about, for Castlemaine is developing quite a reputation as an arts-and-crafts centre, and many unprepossessing shop fronts have treasures within. The most remarkable emporium in town is the atmospheric **Restorers Barn** (129–133 Mostyn Street; www.restorersbarn.com.au; tel: 5470 56 69; daily 10am–5.30pm). It's part-builders' supplies, part-antique store and part-junk shop. The staff wear old-fashioned aprons and you can find everything from… well, just go and have a look.

Other highlights include the **Theatre Royal** (30 Hargraves Street; www.theatreroyal.info; tel: 5472 11 96; call for times and programme),

RIGHT: detail from The Midland Hotel in Castlemaine.
BELOW: an 1850s family panning for gold.

Recommended Restaurants, Bars & Cafés on pages 238–9

which has been operating since 1854. Do go and see a film in the glorious auditorium if you get a chance. You can even stay in a room backstage if it's available.

Castlemaine Art Gallery (14 Lyttelton Street; www.castlemainegallery.com; tel: 5472 2292; Mon–Fri 10am–5pm, Sat–Sun noon–5pm; charge) is not large, but has some exquisite works from all eras of Australian art, with the emphasis on Australian Impressionism and landscape painting. The **Historical Museum** in the basement fulfils its purpose but feels a little poky by comparison.

Get an overview of the town from the **Burke and Wills Monument** at the top of Mostyn Street (Burke lived locally), and then traverse sleepy residential streets to **Buda Historic Home and Garden**, a grand old property that stayed in the Leviny family for 118 years and has been preserved as it was in 1981 when the last members moved out. It has a lived-in feel that gives an authenticity missing from some of the better-preserved historic houses (42 Hunter Street; www.budacastle maine.org; tel: 5472 1032; Wed–Sat noon–5pm, Sun 10am–5pm; charge).

The town was built on the proceeds of the world's richest shallow alluvial goldfield, and in **Castlemaine Diggings National Heritage Park** are to be found many remnants of the relentless search for gold in the 19th century, such as mine shafts, mullock heaps and the Pennyweight Cemetery. There is also evidence of the original occupiers of the land, the Jaara Jaara people, in the shape of scarred trees. **Mount Alexander Regional Park** to the north has similar remains of old diggings.

BENDIGO 8

Bendigo, 38km (24 miles) north of Castlemaine, is the largest town in the region, and this is reflected in some of the grandest public buildings – all hulking stonework, soaring columns and mansard roofs. The epitome of flaunted civic wealth is the **Town Hall**, dripping with plaster mouldings and gold leaf. Tours are sometimes available and can be booked through the **Visitor Information Centre**, based in the historic Post Office (51–67 Pall Mall; www.bendigotourism.com; tel: 5434 6060; daily 9am–5pm). Don't miss the extravagance, both inside and out, of the **Shamrock Hotel** across the road from the Information Centre.

There are two good ways to get an introduction to Bendigo: one is to

Bendigo's Visitor Information Centre has a packed display area – verging on a museum – that reveals the town's history in entertaining fashion.

ABOVE LEFT: get a crash course in the history of Bendigo at the Visitor Information Centre. **BELOW:** the house at Buda Historic Home and Garden.

The Bendigo Explorer pass offers discounted entry to four of the city's main attractions: the Talking Tram, Central Deborah Gold Mine, Golden Dragon Museum and Bendigo Pottery. Buy one at the Visitor Information Centre or online at www.bendigotourism.com

climb to the top of the **Rosalind Park Poppet Head Tower** for 360-degree views, making sure to look down to the Bendigo Heritage Mosaic on the ground below; the other is to take a ride on one of the Bendigo Tramways **Talking Trams**, which wind their way through the city streets – or "heritage streetscape" as they put it – while a running commentary fills in the background detail (www.bendigotramways.com; tel: 5442 2821; call for times; charge). The tram ticket lasts for two days, includes admission to a Tram Museum, and allows you to hop on and off the trams at will.

Mines

At one end of the tram route lies the **Central Deborah Gold Mine** (76 Violet Street; www.central-deborah.com; tel: 5443 8255; daily 9am–5pm; charge). Here, once you've been kitted out in overalls, a miner's hat and lamp, you can go on a guided tour deep underground – and even have a go with a drill as you search for gold.

If, after that, you want still more active learning, then the **Discovery Science & Technology Centre** (7 Railway Place; www.discovery.asn.au; tel: 5444 4400; daily 10am–4pm; charge) promises – and delivers – "100% hands-on science", with permanent attractions such as the 7-metre (23ft) vertical slide and the Thong-a-phone, an arresting musical concept for non-Australians.

The Chinese have always made an important contribution to Bendigo, indeed they constituted 20 percent of the population in the1860s, and this is recognised in a whole precinct centred on the **Golden Dragon Museum** (1–11 Bridge Street; www.goldendragonmuseum.org; tel: 5441 5044; daily 9.30am–5pm; charge). Mannequins illustrate aspects of life on the diggings, and Sun Loong, apparently the biggest ceremonial Chinese dragon in the world, winds its way up a ramp around the circular main hall. It's all rather static, though, and the lighting is terrible. More rewarding is a visit to the **Yi Yuan Classical Chinese Garden** in front of the museum, which takes its cue from the Imperial Palace in Beijing (entry with museum ticket). Plans are in

BELOW: a dragon frieze in the Yi Yuan Classical Chinese Garden.

place for an eight-storey pagoda.

The 1860s **Chinese Joss House** (Emu Point, Finn Street; tel: 5442 1685; Sun 11am–4pm) can be found at the eastern end of the Talking Tram route and is still used as a temple.

Finally, there's yet another superb regional gallery. **Bendigo Art Gallery** (42 View Street; www.bendigoartgallery.com.au; tel: 5434 6088; daily 10am–5pm; donation) includes some 19th-century European paintings alongside Australian works of all eras. Its old building is counterpointed by a sleek 2001 extension.

To the Murray

There's a good argument that, having come this far, it would be churlish not to continue up to the great Murray River, which defines Victoria's northern border. It's an 86km (53-mile) drive to the historic town of **Echuca** ❾, where you should make straight for the river and Murray Esplanade. The original wharf of what was Australia's largest inland port was built in 1865 and originally 1.2km (¾ mile) long. Although it has lost a few metres since then, it's still an impressive sight, with the huge red-gum piles that support the structure dwarfing the paddle steamers that still chug up and down the Murray.

Wharf air

To get on to the wharf you need a ticket for **Port of Echuca** (52 Murray Esplanade; www.portofechuca.org.au; tel: 5482 4248; daily 9am–5pm; charge), which includes admission to the Cargo Shed Museum, a couple of railway trucks, the secret underground bar of the Star Hotel and the preserved upstairs rooms of the Bridge Hotel. Crucially, it also includes a river cruise on one of the three paddle steamers that call the wharf home.

There are still a few original Murray steamers operating at Echuca. There are several others that do good impressions.

Above Left: historic steam engine at Port of Echuca. **Below:** the Murray River at Echuca.

Discover just why Holden cars have been, and still are, central to Australian life at the National Holden Motor Museum.

ABOVE RIGHT: one of the penny-arcade machines at Sharp's. **BELOW:** a scene from *Picnic at Hanging Rock.*

Even if you don't follow that path, it is recommended that you take at least one voyage on the Murray to savour the vistas of river red gums sweeping down to the banks on either side, with just the chugging of the engine and the screeches of river birds to interrupt the idyll. There are plenty of options available: a dinner cruise, an overnight trip, perhaps just an hour on a restored steam-driven vessel. You can even rent houseboats for weeks at a time.

The car-free section of Murray Esplanade is a 19th-century time capsule, with horse carriages plying their trade. **Sharp's Magic Movie House and Penny Arcade** in the old Bond Store (Murray Esplanade; www.sharpsmoviehouse.com.au; tel: 5482 2361; daily 9am–5pm; charge) has non-stop screenings of old silent films and early slot machines for which you are provided with a supply of old pennies.

Elsewhere in town, the **National Holden Motor Museum** (7–11 Warren Street; www.holdenmuseum.com.au; tel: 5480 2033; daily 9am–5pm; charge) has over 40 examples of Holden vehicles by this home-grown car manufacturer and national treasure, while the **Great Aussie Beer Shed** (377 Mary Ann Road; www.greataussiebeershed.com.au; tel: 54 80 6904; Sat–Sun and hols 9am–5pm; charge) displays over 16,000 beer cans from around the world.

If you're really feeling brave, you could cross the border into New South Wales and Echuca's sister city, Moama. Otherwise return south on the Northern Highway all the way through Heathcote, where a visit to one of the local wineries may be rewarding, and take a right on the C326. Join the Calder Freeway towards Woodend and after a few kilometres turn off for Hanging Rock.

HANGING ROCK ⑩

This haunting volcanic outcrop will be familiar to anyone who has seen Peter Weir's enigmatic film, *Picnic at Hanging Rock*, based on the novel of the same name by Joan Lindsay. Climb to the top for views and drop into the Discovery Centre to learn about what you've just been climbing. People not traumatised by the film might want to consider a guided night walk (www.hangingrock.info; tel: 5429 9631).

Kyneton ⑪, which developed as a staging post on the route from Melbourne to the goldfields, sits on the Campaspe River. It has some lovely

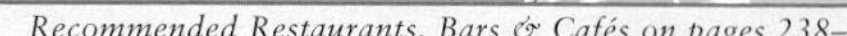

old bluestone buildings and, in Piper Street, an attractive historic stretch of cafés, shops and antique emporiums. In fact you can hardly move for antique stores unless you go to the **Botanic Gardens** (Mollison Street; tel: 5422 0333; daily; free), which were originally curated by Baron Ferdinand von Mueller, the guru behind Melbourne's Royal Botanic Gardens.

Continue north to **Malmsbury**, which is notable for the bluestone **viaduct** built in 1859 to traverse the Coliban River.

DAYLESFORD ⓬

West on the C316 lies Daylesford, a delightful settlement set just above a lake. In recent years the town has thrived on the pink dollar and turned into a chic, sophisticated weekend retreat for Melburnians.

The **Visitor Information Centre** (98 Vincent Street; www.visitdaylesford.com; tel: 5321 6123; daily 9am–5pm) is in the old fire station at the beginning of the main street. The brochures here all seem to be geared to pampering the visitor, whether it's upmarket eating or exotic spa treatments.

Visitors have been coming here and to neighbouring **Hepburn Springs** since the late 1800s to partake of the rejuvenating mineral waters from the springs that abound in the district. The bucolic hills and lakes reinforced its appeal, so it's advisable to book ahead year-round if you want accommodation, especially at weekends.

The lake

Vincent Street, with its spruced-up stone frontages, is the focal point and tailor-made for browsing or idling over a coffee. Exercise can be had by walking round the pretty **Daylesford Lake** or climbing up Hill Street to **The Convent**, an imposing institution that houses seven separate galleries of paintings, ceramics, glassware, jewellery and the like, as well as a café and bar.

From Daylesford you can be back in Melbourne in a couple of hours. ❑

Boating, fishing and jogging occupy the active at Lake Daylesford. The rest kick back with a latte and enjoy the view.

ABOVE LEFT: Deco style in Daylesford. **BELOW:** the hillside setting elevates the church above the indulgences of Daylesford.

BEST RESTAURANTS, BARS AND CAFÉS

Prices for a three-course dinner per person with a half-bottle of house wine:

$ = under A$60
$$ = A$60–90
$$$ = A$90–120
$$$$ = over A$120

Restaurants

Avoca

Pyrenees Pies, Pizza & Takeaway

120 High Street. 5465 3280 B, L & D daily **$**

Spend a month in Avoca and try a different pie every day, taking in a variety of local fauna, including crocodile.

Ballarat

The Boatshed Restaurant

27a Lake Wendouree Foreshore, Ballarat. 5333 5533 B, L & D daily **$$**

For a restaurant that makes much of its views, times have been hard, with Lake Wendouree being a long-term casualty of the drought (although floods in 2010 helped to counteract the effects). The food needs to be good to make up for it and, on the whole, the simple dishes turned out round the clock in this atmospheric building do the trick.

Phoenix Brewery

10 Camp Street, Ballarat. 5333 2686 L Mon–Fri, D daily **$$**

Running across three floors, including a cellar tapas bar, expect sharp contemporary cooking.

Bendigo

The Bridge

49 Bridge Street, Bendigo. 5443 7811 L & D daily **$$**

This old country pub looks more like a city slicker, with its clean lines and modular chairs, and has a contemporary European-leaning menu and sharp wine list to match.

GPO

60–64 Pall Mall, Bendigo. 5443 4343 L & D daily **$$**

The choice of hip young Bendigoans, GPO combines robustly flavoured café food with a drinks list as fond of beer as it is of wine.

Whirrakee Restaurant

17 View Point, Bendigo. 5441 5557 L & D Tue–Sun **$$$**

The place to go for grand dining. The food is delivered with aplomb, conviction and a pronounced French accent.

Wine Bank on View

45 View Street, Bendigo. 5444 4655 L & D daily **$**

The wine comes first here – there are literally hundreds to choose from – with able support in the form of tapas, bruschetta and light meals.

Castlemaine

Empyre Hotel

68 Mostyn Street, Castlemaine. 5472 5166 B, L & D Wed–Sat **$$**

This spectacularly well-restored building houses a café by day and, four nights a week, a fine-dining establishment where the modern Australian cooking is presented with attention to detail and great finesse.

Daylesford

Farmers Arms Hotel

1 East Street, Daylesford. 5348 2091 L Sat–Sun, D daily **$$**

Keeping one eye firmly fixed on its country-pub roots, the Farmers Arms nevertheless has upped the ante both in terms of the simple but stylish food and the locally leaning wine list.

Lake House

King Street, Daylesford. 5348 3329 B, L & D daily **$$$**

Considered one of the finest country restaurants in Australia, Lake House combines lovely views over gardens and water with superb service, a cosseting room and deftly cooked dishes that favour local ingredients. Popular with weekenders who book a room to stumble back to.

Perfect Drop Wine and Food Lounge

5 Howe Street, Daylesford. 5348 3373 L Sat–Sun, D Wed–Mon **$$**

LEFT: coded message at Oscar W's, Echuca.
RIGHT: Maldon's Grand Hotel.

Offers a sophisticated take on wine-bar eating with a strong reliance on local produce.

Dunkeld

Royal Mail Hotel

Glenelg Highway, Dunkeld. 5577 2241 L & D daily **$$$**

Sitting at the foot of the spectacular Grampians, the Royal Mail augments the great views with well-cooked, contemporary food and a lengthy and award-winning wine list.

Echuca

Left Bank

551 High Street, Echuca. 5480 3772 D Tue–Sat **$$**

Housed in a former bank, this warm-hued, welcoming restaurant with its contemporary European food is amongst the area's best. Sit outside on warm evenings for a quintessential country experience.

Oscar W's

101 Murray Esplanade, Echuca. 5482 5133 L & D daily **$$**

The setting on the wharf above the Murray River is a big attraction, but the finely crafted food more than holds its own. Kids are fed well, with not a chicken nugget in sight.

Kyneton

Annie Smithers Bistrot

72 Piper Street, Kyneton. 5422 2039 L Wed–Sun, D Thur–Sat **$$**

This bluestone building houses a restaurant with its heart in provincial France, in terms of both the dishes and the attitude of preferring the best local, seasonal ingredients.

Royal George Hotel

24 Piper Street, Kyneton. 5422 1390 L Thur–Sun, D Wed–Sat **$$**

This gold-rush-era hotel has been given a spruce up, but retains the charms of open log fires and a comfortable lounge area. The menu is dotted with local ingredients and leans towards the Mediterranean.

Maldon

De Vere Café & Restaurant

24 High Street. 5475 2504 L & D daily **$$**

The best option at night if you're looking for something other than a pub. Could do with a hint more inspiration.

Grand Hotel

26 High Street, Maldon. 5475 2213 L & D daily **$**

Unpretentious dining in this delightful historic pub (1888). The menu covers the usual bases, with local produce at compelling prices.

Bars and Cafés

The Vines Café and Bar

74 Barkly St, Ararat.

A beacon for local foodies, the Vines mixes café staples with some quietly adventurous offerings, all in an open, friendly space.

Café Companis

5 Camp St, Ballarat.

Attached to the Ballarat Fine Art Gallery in Lydiard Street, Café Companis is a bonus for art lovers and accomplished enough to draw even diehard philistines.

L'espresso

417 Sturt Street, Ballarat.

Some would say that L'espresso's main strength is its coffee, but its simply cooked café food has a following with the locals, too.

Mason's Café and Food Store

32 Drummond St North, Ballarat.

A café linked to a food-store has to guarantee the finest ingredients and know how to handle them. Mason's scores on both counts.

Cliffy's Emporium

30 Raglan Street, Daylesford.

Half-food store, half-café, this Daylesford favourite does atmospheric, old-fashioned general store brilliantly.

Perfect Drop

5 Howe Street, Daylesford.

A popular but cosy wine bar where you can snuggle down into a chesterfield and peruse a wine list heavy with bottles from local vineyards.

La Trattoria

350 Hepburn–Newstead Road, Shepherds Flat.

Head to the Lavendula Swiss Italian Farm in Hepburn Springs for this charming, casual café. Housed within a barn on a lavender farm, it serves simple, tasty Italian-leaning food.

2 NBD
CLEARANCE
45m

Recommended Restaurants, Bars & Cafés on page 247

THE DANDENONGS AND THE YARRA VALLEY

To the east of Melbourne is a range of bluffs adorned with mountain-ash forests, fern gullies and formal gardens. Added attractions include a steam railway, a wildlife sanctuary and one of the world's great wine regions

Main attractions

PUFFING BILLY
RHODODENDRON GARDENS
WILLIAM RICKETTS SANCTUARY
MOUNT DANDENONG
WARBURTON
HEALESVILLE
YARRA GLEN

Only an hour out of the centre of Melbourne, the Dandenong Ranges provide a wonderful antidote to the city. Winding roads climb up to an area of rich forest and sumptuous gardens, with the odd settlement to service the day-trippers and holiday-makers who flock here, especially at weekends. This is not serious mountain country – Mount Dandenong is only 634 metres (2,080ft) high – but that doesn't lessen the enjoyment of a warm fire in an old weatherboard hotel in the winter months, or the fresh breezes that take the edge off the heat of summer.

Just down from the hills there's another of Victoria's most popular attractions: the Yarra Valley, with its rolling landscapes and enticing vineyards. There are dozens of cellar doors vying for your custom, and in their efforts to stand out, a good number have added on high-class restaurants or cafés, and even the odd art gallery.

It's only 35km (22 miles) to the Dandenongs, and the first stop – if you're not waylaid by the charms of Ramsay Street *(see panel, page 242)* – is the headline tourist draw of the area, Puffing Billy.

PUFFING BILLY ❶

Belgrave Station; www.puffingbilly.com.au 9757 0700 daily, see website for timetable charge

The Dandenongs were first opened up in the 1870s by loggers and prospectors, and within a few years timber and farm produce was flowing down to the city. However, the bullock drays employed for the task

LEFT: Puffing Billy trundles through the Dandenongs.
RIGHT: conductor awaits Puffing Billy at Belgrave Station.

A drive-in cinema complete with working screen is typical of the detail at the Emerald Lake model railway.

were stymied in winter by the muddy tracks. The answer was a narrow-gauge railway, which came into service in 1900 and ran until halted by a landslide in 1953. Puffing Billy is the last remnant of that era, and is only running now because of years of restoration work by the Puffing Billy Preservation Society. Thanks to them, thousands of visitors now trundle through the hills every year, legs dangling out over the sills.

Lakeside Station serves Emerald Lake Park, a gorgeous spot for a picnic or a spell in a pedal boat. There's also a sizeable model-railway exhibit if you haven't been sated by the real thing (www.emeraldlakepark.com.au; tel: 5968 3455; Tue–Sun 11am–4pm; free).

Gardens galore

Back on the road, the trail north through soaring mountain ash touches on a series of historic formal gardens. **George Tindale Gardens** (Sherbrooke Road; daily 10am–5pm; free) makes the most of its hilltop setting and is very English in style; **Alfred Nicholas Gardens** is noted for its water features, including an ornamental lake; and the **Pirianda Gardens** tumble gracefully down steep terraces. However, the cream of the collection is to be found in Olinda.

Neighbours

It may be just another soap in Australia, but such is the global following – especially in the UK – of the *Neighbours* TV show that an industry has developed to satisfy the needs of curious fans. Various organised tours run to "Ramsay Street", where the outdoor scenes are shot, and there's even a weekly *Neighbours*-themed pub quiz. A tour isn't really necessary as anyone can drive to the residential cul-de-sac of Pin Oak Court, off Weeden Drive in Vermont South. If there's no filming in progress, all the action is confined to a bored security guard and a stream of excited British fans.

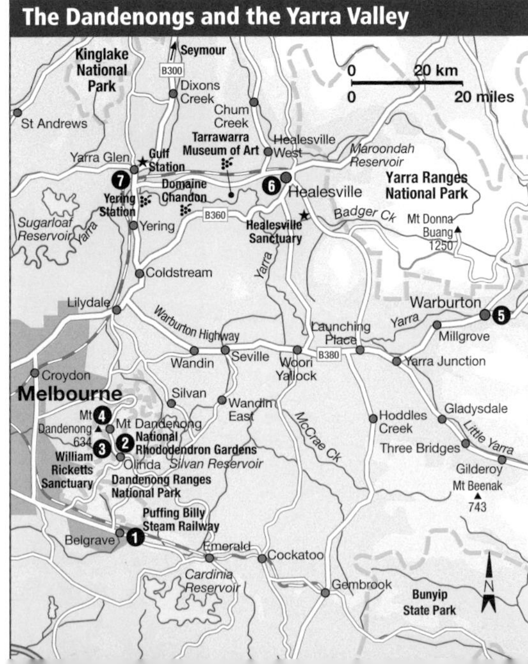

Recommended Restaurants, Bars & Cafés on page 249

NATIONAL RHODODENDRON GARDENS ❷

The Georgian Road, Olinda; www.parkweb.vic.gov.au 131 963 daily 10am–5pm free

A self-guided walk reveals much treasure in these 40 hectares (100 acres) spread through a valley and along a hillside. Backed by mountain ash and opening up to reveal magnificent views across the Warburton Ranges, these gardens feature camellias, azaleas, hydrangeas and a fern gully, as well as the rhododendrons. In spring they're magnificent.

During peak season, a free shuttle bus ferries visitors through the gardens and a café is open. At other times, try Olinda itself as this pleasant township is more than adequately supplied with cafés.

Continue northwards on the Mount Dandenong Tourist Road for 4km (2½ miles) to reach one of the region's more eccentric attractions.

WILLIAM RICKETTS SANCTUARY ❸

www.parkweb.vic.gov.au 131 963 daily 10am–4.30pm free

The eponymous sculptor lived and worked here for nearly 60 years before his death in 1993. In a lush fern gully he created a series of dun-coloured ceramic sculptures that celebrate and romanticise Aboriginal people and culture, while also incorporating winged creatures looking suspiciously like fairies. The 92 figures emerge from rocks and the undergrowth as if they were of the earth itself – a kind of literal interpretation of Aboriginal links to the land. Many visitors find this an affecting and spiritual place. Others detect a flaky mysticism that would not be out of place on an overindulgent prog-rock album cover from the 1970s.

Continue north, then double back on Ridge Road to the left to reach the heights of Mount Dandenong.

It can vary, but October is usually the best time to visit the National Rhododendron Gardens at Olinda. This is also when the Rhododendron Festival is held.

BELOW: Ricketts in the thickets.

There are countless picnic sites around the Dandenongs, but watch out for over-friendly kookaburras who try to steal your sandwiches.

MOUNT DANDENONG ❹

Terraces here provide sweeping views back towards Melbourne, and the circular building that surmounts them houses a bistro and function centre. The complex goes under the title of **Skyhigh Mount Dandenong** (26 Observatory Road; www.skyhighmtdandenong.com.au; tel: 9751 0443; Mon–Thur 9am–10pm, Fri 9am–10.30pm, Sat 8am–11pm, Sun 8am–10pm; charge) and includes a maze, a "Giant's Chair" and "Percy Possum's House". It's all pretty desperate, and yet it appears to be doing better than previous enterprises that have occupied this site.

WARBURTON ❺

If there's time, consider a detour of 20km (12 miles) or so eastwards to Warburton, a picturesque little town set in the Upper Yarra Valley along the banks of the river. There are few attractions as such, but it's a fabulous place for walking, cycling and horse riding. The **Yarra Ranges National Park** nearby preserves more swathes of mountain ash and

features the occasionally snow-capped Mount Donna Buang.

Afterwards, it's time to follow the river back to the west and investigate the better-known stretches of the Yarra Valley. From this direction, the gateway is Healesville.

ABOVE RIGHT: Percy Possum's House. **BELOW:** wombats are quite common all over Victoria. **BELOW RIGHT:** Healesville's Grand Hotel.

HEALESVILLE ❻

The town has some fabulous old hotels and punches above its weight for food and drink; mind you, it has to given the level of competition from the wineries.

However, the place is best known for the **Healesville Sanctuary** (Badger Creek Road; www.zoo.org.au; tel: 5957 2800; daily 9am–5pm; charge). As part of a triumvirate with Melbourne Zoo and Werribee Open Range Zoo, Healesville concentrates on native Australian fauna and shows them off in something approximating a bush setting. It's a great place to familiarise yourself with all the bouncing, leaping and, indeed, biting creatures of Australia. Make the most of the Platypus House to see these ofte-elusive creatures, or enjoy a display of some of the many birds of prey, including the

Recommended Restaurants, Bars & Cafés on page 247

majestic wedge-tailed eagle. Ensure you also have a look at the Australian Wildlife Health Centre, where you can watch the progress of the inmates from first admission up to and including the operating theatre. Special activities include a behind-the-scenes tour with one of the keepers (weekends and public holidays 2pm; charge) or a guided walk through protected tribal land adjoining the sanctuary on the Burra Burra Yan Indigenous Walking Tour (Sat 1pm; charge).

YARRA GLEN 7

The town at the heart of Yarra Valley wine country is quite low-key, apart from an impressive Victorian-era hotel and a handful of antique shops. However, a kilometre up the road there's a historic gem waiting to be discovered.

Gulf Station

Melba Highway; www.gulfstation.com.au 9656 9800 daily 10am–4pm charge, free with National Trust card

This pioneer farm was originally built in the 1850s using a timber slab construction and is now preserved, with all its outbuildings intact, as a working farm complete with livestock. The house of the founding Bell family remains in all its shabby glory, and visitors get a very real

KIDS

Healesville Sanctuary has a daily programme of supervised encounters with its animals and birds that will appeal to children of all ages.

ABOVE LEFT: raptor over the knuckles at Healesville Sanctuary. **ABOVE:** the Den of Antiquities store in Yarra Glen. **BELOW:** Gulf Station.

Perhaps this is the true precursor to the water-cooler. The Furphy water cart, first made in the 1880s, offered such fertile ground for idle rumour that in Australian slang a "furphy" is a tall story.

ABOVE RIGHT: Tarrawarra Museum of Art. **BELOW:** working on the wine in the Yarra Valley.

sense of the sheer amount of hard work entailed in running an enterprise on this scale. Many of the animals are the same breeds that would have lived on a 19th-century farm, including Clydesdale horses for the heavy work. It's a fascinating destination and, even without the academic element, the setting is sublime. Though beware the manic goat that treats its hutch as a dry run for the days when it will be free to leap across mountain crags. In vain, one feels. A serious renovation is being undertaken at Gulf Station so do check it's open before setting off.

The Yarra Valley vineyards

There's little doubt about the prime motivation of most visitors to the Yarra Valley. Its reputation as one of Australia's great cool-climate wine areas brings connoisseurs and rank amateurs from around the world. The big-name producers are here, outposts of multinational companies co-exist with smaller operations that have been absorbed into conglomerates, and just a few boutique wineries remain blissfully independent.

For visitors it's a case of choosing between the slick, bus-party-friendly destinations such as Domaine Chandon or Yering Station, and the quieter, more low-key estates where you can sip a few glasses over a plate of cheese. However, don't expect to pick up cellar-door bargains. Prices are just as high here as in the bottle shops, indeed sometimes higher, while many sellers now make a charge for tasting as well.

Some have taken a tangential approach: **Tarrawarra** has built a sparkling **Museum of Art**, which is well worth a look irrespective of whether you want to research the wine (Yarra Glen Road; www.twma.com.au; tel: 5957 3100; Tue–Sun 11am–5pm; charge). Its bedrock collection is modern Australian, from the 1950s onwards, almost all from the Museum's founders, Eva and Marc Bessen. This material is then augmented for individual exhibitions, of which there are at least four every year.

Having your own car allows spontaneous cellar-door visits, but there are also guided tours that allow you to taste without worrying about the consequences for your driving licence. The Visitor Centre in Melbourne's Federation Square has piles of leaflets. If you want to stay, Chateau Yering is the luxury option in the area, with an up-market restaurant as an extra incentive. ❑

BEST RESTAURANTS, BARS AND CAFÉS

Coldstream

Bella Vedere

Badger's Brook Winery, 874 Maroondah Highway, Coldstream. 5962 6161 B & L Wed–Sun, D Fri–Sat **$$**

Located in a house in the middle of a vineyard, Bella Vedere has its own bakery, an open kitchen with chefs willing to chat, and carefully cooked, locally sourced food.

Stones of the Yarra Valley

14 St Huberts Road, Coldstream. 9739 0900 L Wed–Sun **$$**

This restaurant in a smartly renovated, light-filled 1850s barn is an ideal place for the long, slow lunch. Simply prepared food, much of it served on platters to share, adds to the feeling of relaxed conviviality.

Dixons Creek

De Bortoli Winery & Restaurant

58 Pinnacle Lane, Dixons Creek. 5965 2271 L Thur–Mon, D Sat **$$**

There's nothing fashionable about this winery restaurant, but who needs fashion when you have skilfully cooked Italian food, excellent estate wines and an impressive cheese-maturing room?

Healesville

Giant Steps/Innocent Bystander

336 Maroondah Highway, Healesville. 5962 6111 B, L & D daily **$**

There is plenty to do (and eat) at this impressive winery/brewery/bistro with wood-fired pizza oven/bakery/cheese shop that manages to wear all its hats with equal aplomb. They also roast their own coffee beans.

Healesville Hotel

256 Maroondah Highway, Healesville. 5962 4002 L & D daily **$$**

This beautifully renovated pub not only features an acclaimed restaurant with a lauded wine list, but has an attached café and food store that does things in a more casual but equally stylish fashion.

Mount Rael Retreat

140 Healesville–Yarra Glen Road, Healesville. 5962 1977 B Sat–Sun, L & D Thur–Sun **$$**

Superb views over the Yarra Valley from this hilltop retreat are the attractive backdrop to this casually stylish restaurant that sits squarely in the modern-Australian category. Locally sourced food and attentive staff.

Sassafras

Ripe

376–378 Mount Dandenong Tourist Road, Sassafras. 9755 2100 B & L daily **$**

There is no sign to flag Ripe's existence, but it is well worth tracking down because this cosily crowded café and food store puts a unique and tasty spin on all the best local produce. Highly recommended.

Tarrawarra

Cru Restaurant

97 School Lane, Tarrawarra. 5962 6966 L Thur–Sun, D Thur–Sat **$$**

A Tuscan-style building set in a vineyard, with tremendous views across the surrounding mountains. A superb place for a long lunch, sampling the estate wines as you go.

Yering

Eleonore's at Chateau Yering

42 Melba Highway, Yering. 9237 3333 L Sat–Sun, D daily **$$$**

Lavishly decorated, expensive Eleonore's feels like a step back in time – complete with classical music soundtrack and intricate, elaborate food – but it does it so well that you may wish you'd packed the crinolines.

Prices for a three-course dinner per person with a half-bottle of house wine:
$ = under A$60
$$ = A$60–90
$$$ = A$90–120
$$$$ = over A$120

Bars and Cafés

Cucina Rossa
Bianchet Winery, 187 Victoria Road, Lilydale.
European peasant food is given a Yarra Valley spin using local ingredients in this room with a view.

TarraWarra Estate Restaurant
311 Healesville-Yarra Glen Road, Yarra Glen.
This sleek wine bar and café is the perfect pit stop after checking out the art in the Tarrawarra gallery or sampling the vino at the cellar door.

Yering Station Wine Bar
38 Melba Highway, Yarra Glen.
This light-filled, glass-walled space can get noisy when crowded, but the view and the food are well worth braving the rumpus to enjoy.

Wine Tasting in Victoria

The Yarra Valley is just one of a number of wine-growing regions in the state that are fully geared to welcoming visitors for a tasting session and gourmet lunch

The first vines were brought over to the Melbourne area from Van Diemen's Land (now Tasmania) in 1834, and viticulture spread somewhat haphazardly across the state from then on. The gold rush saw a cluster of vineyards in the less-than ideal conditions of central Victoria, but with price as a driving factor it made sense at the time. Now, more than 150 years down the track, there are still pockets of wine-growing across the state, and almost any drive through rural Victoria will take you past signs offering cellar-door sales and tastings. Standards are generally high, so there's not much risk in picking a gate at random and diving in.

Above: wine tourists are travelling around the region in such great numbers that most vineyards now make a charge for tasting sessions, although some will offset the cost against any subsequent purchases.

Left: there is more variety in wine production in Victoria than anywhere else in the country, but overall conditions favour the lighter varietals, which just happens to be where demand is increasing most rapidly. There are quirks, though, so the area around Glenrowan in the northeast, where it's getting warmer, is renowned for its "stickies" (sweet dessert wines).

FRENCH CONNECTION

As wine tourism becomes big business, many of the larger wineries cater to visitors on a semi-industrial scale, with sizeable tasting rooms and a variety of eating options. At Domaine Chandon, in the Yarra Valley, there are regular free guided tours of the cellars and the wine-making equipment, with an in-depth explanation of the manufacturing of the sparkling wines for which the company is justly famed. As with many of the other local enterprises, the operation is part of a large conglomerate – in this case linked to the French Moët & Chandon brand – but is given a considerable degree of autonomy in the actual wine-making. This means that a lot of bright, ambitious young wine makers have been attracted to the region and are making the most of the cool climate where Pinot Noir, Chardonnay and Riesling varieties thrive. The outcome is some of the finest wine in the country.

ABOVE AND LEFT: the attractive setting of the Yarra Valley, along with its proximity to Melbourne, makes it the most popular of the wine areas, but visitors can still find plenty of quiet boutique wineries where the atmosphere is informal and the service friendly.

ABOVE: James Halliday, the godfather of Australian wine writers, was a founder of the Coldstream Hills vineyard and still provides the photos featured on the labels.

LEFT: fine dining is a common lure to draw customers to particular vineyards. Try Montalto, near Red Hill, or Chateau Yering.

Recommended Restaurants on page 255

PHILLIP ISLAND AND WILSONS PROMONTORY

Three contrasting islands, the southernmost point of mainland Australia and wonderful opportunities for wildlife-spotting along the way make this one of Melburnians' favourite regions to head to when escaping the city

A few times each year, Phillip Island roars to the sound of racing machinery, but for the most part it's a relaxed holiday destination, best known for its penguin parade. Peace prevails at Wilsons Prom in some of the most beautiful and dramatic scenery in the state, and if even that gets too busy, then cut yourself off from the rest of the world on French Island. But before you reach any of these, there's a rewarding stop along the South Gippsland Highway at Cranbourne.

THE AUSTRALIAN GARDEN 1

off South Gippsland Highway, Cranbourne; www.australiangarden.com.au 5990 2200 daily 9am–5pm charge

Opened in 2006 under the aegis of the Royal Botanic Gardens and still a work in progress, the Australian Garden is all about native flora. See plants in their various habitats, learn how to use them in a domestic setting and enjoy them in a series of natural sculptures carved out of the land. The centrepiece (literally), *Red Sand Garden*, has great crescents of earth splaying out from a rusted steel *Escarpment Wall Sculpture*. This red centre is encircled by smaller, lusher plots. There are also four exhibition gardens and areas devoted to specific terrains.

It's another 72km (45 miles) to Phillip Island, but you may be tempted to stop at **Wildlife Wonderland** (Bass Highway; tel: 5678 2222; daily 9am–sunset summer, 10am–5.30pm winter; charge). It used to be called the "Big Worm", after the Giant Gippsland earthworm that can grow up to a metre long, but there are

Main attractions

- THE AUSTRALIAN GARDEN
- CHURCHILL ISLAND HERITAGE FARM
- COWES
- PENGUIN PARADE
- FRENCH ISLAND
- WILSONS PROMONTORY NATIONAL PARK

LEFT: close in on koalas at Phillip Island's Koala Conservation Centre, or see them in the wild on French Island. **RIGHT:** the Australian Garden at Cranbourne.

As luck would have it, the pelican-feeding is right over the road from the bars of the San Remo Hotel.

now none living there, and we're left with a musty display and cramped enclosures of native fauna outside.

Just before crossing the bridge to Phillip Island, check your watch: if it's approaching noon, pull into **San Remo** and enjoy the spectacle of dozens of agitated pelicans jostling for position at their daily feed by the jetty.

PHILLIP ISLAND

Its international profile is probably highest with fans of bike racing, but in Victoria, Phillip Island is favoured for its beaches and wildlife – especially penguins.

Churchill Island Heritage Farm ❷

www.churchillisland.org.au
5956 7214 Apr–Sept 10am–4.30pm. Oct–Mar 10am–5.30pm
charge

Samuel Amess, formerly Mayor of Melbourne, bought Churchill Island, off the north of Phillip Island, in 1872 and built the homestead that is still in pristine condition. It's in a beautiful garden setting with farm buildings scattered behind it, animals to pet and a working blacksmith's shop. Walking and cycle tracks ring the island.

Return to Phillip Island Road for the **National Vietnam Veterans Museum**, opened in 2007 (25 Veterans Drive; www.vietnamvets-museum.org; tel: 5956 6400; daily 10am–5pm; charge) which tackles the difficult topic of Australia's 10-year involvement in that war.

A short detour down Back Beach Road will get you to the **Phillip Island Grand Prix Circuit**. Apart from hosting two rounds of international motorbike racing each year and the ever-popular V8 touring car event, the circuit is a tourist attraction in its own right. Sample a guided tour, kart racing or even a "hot lap" in a touring car (www.phillipisland

Phillip Island and Wilsons Promontory

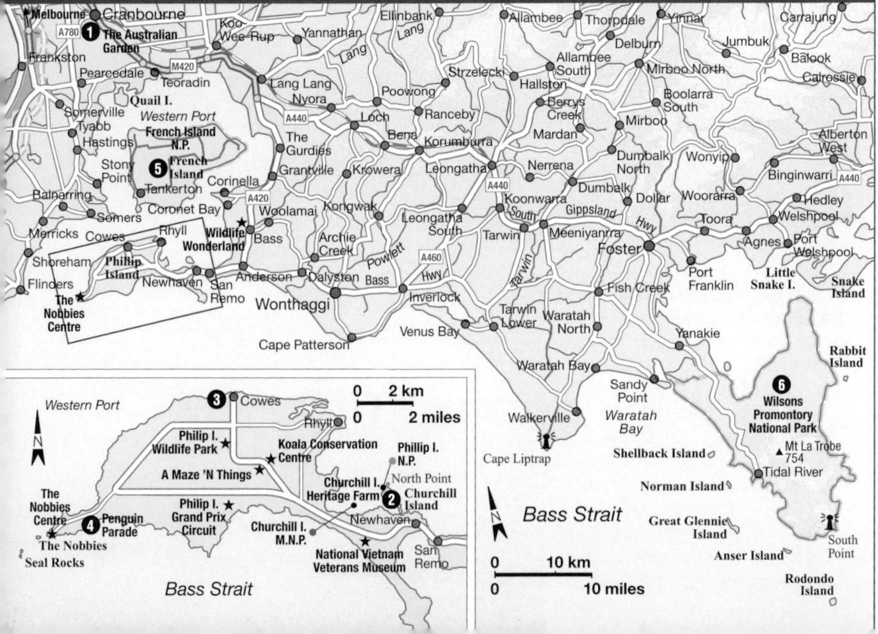

Recommended Restaurants on page 255

TIP

You can save money by buying a Three Parks Pass to cover the Churchill Island Heritage Farm, the Koala Conservation Centre and the Penguin Parade. Details can be found at any of these destinations.

circuit.com.au; tel: 5952 2710; tours 11am, 2pm; charge).

The **Koala Conservation Centre** (tel: 5951 2800; daily 10am–5pm; charge) is irresistible as a concept. Visitors stroll on boardwalks through eucalypti within inches of the cuddly marsupials, who are so used to visitors that they occasionally ruffle a child's hair in passing. And it has "conservation" in the title, so visiting is pure altruism. Watch out, though, for the odd venomous copperhead snake sleeping beside a path.

For a broader selection of furry creatures, as well as feathers and scales, try the **Phillip Island Wildlife Park** further up the road (tel: 5952 2038; daily 10am–5.15pm; charge). If all this nature palls, there is an amusement park across the road from the Koala Centre offering a maze and various hands-on thrills, all under the straining pun of **A Maze 'N Things** (www.amazen things.com.au; tel: 59 52 2283; daily 10am–5.30pm; charge).

Cowes ❸

Named after the resort on England's Isle of Wight, Cowes has all of Phillip Island's shops, services and restaurants, and much of the accommodation, too. The road leads down to the jetty, once the main point of entry to the island, but now hosting a few ferries and sightseeing boats. There are two fine beaches here that can get busy at holiday times, but with 24 others around the island it isn't hard to escape the crowds. The seas to the north are tranquil, those to the south the domain of surfers.

However, Cowes isn't the focus for most visitors, the wildlife is, especially along at the island's western tip.

Above Left: inside the homestead at Churchill Island. **Above:** peacock faces a long wait for the blacksmith on Churchill Island. **Below:** lookout at the Nobbies Centre.

While the Penguin Parade can get fearfully crowded, is it really likely that any of them would actually try to stow away to make a better life elsewhere?

The Nobbies Centre

✉ www.nobbies.org.au ☎ 5951 2800 ⓒ Dec–Feb 10am–8pm, Mar–May 11am–5pm, June–Aug 11am–4pm, Sept–Nov 11am–6pm ⓢ free

This modern centre, with commanding views across Seal Rocks and Bass Strait, looks a little like an airport terminal. In late afternoon the parallels are uncanny as busloads of tourists mill around the café, shop or exhibition area giving off a slight air of killing time. The centre's "interactive seal cameras" show the mammals in a reality-TV setting. In addition, there is a network of boardwalks leading down towards the sea and **Seal Rocks** where, depending on the time of year, thousands of seals may be frolicking in the surf or just snoozing. Binoculars come in handy for your own interactive seal-viewing experience, or there are coin-operated ones beside the Centre.

ABOVE RIGHT: Seal Rocks.
BELOW: little penguins, also known as blue or fairy penguins.

THE PENGUIN PARADE ❹

✉ www.penguins.org.au ☎ 5951 2800 ⓒ daily around sunset ⓢ charge

Grandstands on Summerland Beach hold hordes of tourists drawn nightly to the spectacle of little penguins (the official species name) emerging from the sea and waddling up the sand to their burrows in the dunes. Sometimes there are thousands of the creatures, other times only a few dozen, but the thrill of spotting those first white blobs emerging from the surf usually makes up for the lengthy wait in the perishing wind that blows off Bass Strait. Sit on the edge of the bleachers and you may find a penguin scrambling over your foot to get home.

If all this activity is too much for you, the antidote lies just over the water from Cowes (or from Stony Point on the Mornington Peninsula).

FRENCH ISLAND ❺

It was the captain of French ship *Le Naturaliste* who named French Island in 1802 (in French, obviously) and the name stuck even though nobody bothered to live there for another 40 years. Farming, particularly of chicory, was the mainstay; plans to introduce heavy industry in the 1960s were shelved, and today there are only 70 or so people living on a landmass considerably larger than Phillip Island. Over 70 per cent of it is now designated as National Park. Kylie Minogue was the best-known property owner on the island but she's now sold up.

Only locals can take cars over, so either take a bicycle or go on one of the two organised tours (French Island Eco Tours; www.frenchisland

ecotours.com.au; tel: 0429 177 532; and French Island Bus Tours; www.frenchislandtours.com.au; tel: 5980 1241). As you rattle along gently undulating dirt roads spotting countless koalas and acknowledging the very occasional car coming the other way, you'll hear timeless tales of local characters. Enjoy access to the former **McLeod Prison Farm**, soak up the solitude, and spot numerous bird and animal species that you'll spot only rarely on the mainland.

WILSONS PROMONTORY ❻

www.parkweb.vic.gov.au 131 963 daily 24 hours free

It's 127km (79 miles) from Phillip Island to the main settlement in **Wilsons Promontory National Park**. **Tidal River** has a store, a café, a few cabins, a campsite and the Visitor Centre. In holiday periods, book accommodation far in advance.

Drink in the beauty of the setting: the smoothly flowing river, the beach strewn with boulders flecked with orange lichen, the hills rearing up in the background, and wildlife everywhere, including some wombats who recognise the campsite as a primary food source.

Dozens of walking tracks criss-cross the 50,500 hectares (125,000 acres) ranging from the straightforward ambles to **Squeaky Beach** and **Lilly Pilly Gully** to demanding multi-hour hikes, such as the one to the lighthouse at the southern tip. Allow as much time as you can and you'll begin to understand why so many Victorians have such affection for the Prom. ❑

Fierce winds create wonderful patterns with the tea trees at Wilsons Promontory National Park.

RESTAURANTS

Big Fat Greek Bar and Grill

9 Beach Road, Rhyll. 5956 9511 D Thur–Mon **$**

Busy seaside diner comes up trumps with simple, succulent platefuls. Strong on seafood.

Caldermeade Farm Café

4385 South Gippsland Highway, Caldermeade. 5997 5000 L daily **$**

Between observing milking demonstrations and the animal nursery you can refuel with hearty home-made pies, ploughman's lunches and a variety of dairy-driven drinks.

The Foreshore Bar & Restaurant

11 Beach Road, Rhyll. 5956 9520 L & D daily **$$**

Unpretentious café food, friendly staff and excellent sea views add up to a relaxed and pleasant dining experience.

Grand Ridge Brewery

Main Street, Mirboo North. 9778 6996 L & D Thur–Mon **$**

Stop by for one of Grand Ridge's clean green (and delicious) beers, or combine beer-guzzling with straightforward beer-friendly food in the bistro.

Harry's On the Esplanade

17 The Esplanade, Cowes. 5952 6226 B Sun, L & D Tue–Sun **$$**

Plenty of seafood on the menu in this laid-back bayside bistro, but carnivores are also well catered for. Has its own bakery as well.

Koonwarra Fine Food and Wine Store

South Gippsland Highway, Koonwarra. 5664 2285 B & L daily, D Sat **$**

Buy newspapers, post letters, stock up on provisions or kick back in the café that likes to flaunt its local and organic credentials.

*Prices for a three-course dinner per person and a half-bottle of house wine. **$** = under A$60; **$$** = A$60–90; **$$$** = over A$90.*

Recommended Restaurants, Bars & Cafés on page 265

THE MOUNTAINS

In winter it's a playground for snowboarders and skiers. The rest of the year, Victoria's high country offers picturesque walking trails, rock climbing and watersports, as well as historic towns, steam trains and Australia's most celebrated criminal

Main attractions
- MARYSVILLE
- LAKE EILDON NATIONAL PARK
- MOUNT BULLER
- BENALLA
- GLENROWAN
- BEECHWORTH
- YACKANDANDAH
- BRIGHT
- MOUNT BUFFALO NATIONAL PARK
- FALLS CREEK
- MOUNT HOTHAM

The Great Dividing Range extends down almost the entire eastern rim of Australia from northern Queensland, until it expires just past the Dandenongs east of Melbourne. Its southernmost ridges constitute Victoria's high country, a region of mountainous terrain with an Alpine climate that attracts winter-sports fans for a few months of the year (June–September, and occasionally October) and dedicated hikers and pleasure-seekers for the rest of the time.

MARYSVILLE ❶

The closest ski fields to Melbourne are only a couple of hours' drive from the city along the Maroondah Highway. The first snow is to be found at Lake Mountain Alpine Resort, but facilities there are limited and there is no accommodation. Until recently, the place to stay was Marysville, a favourite honeymoon destination in the 1920s and subsequently a sleepy but attractive Alpine township. That all changed on Black Saturday (*see panel*). Now all that greets the visitor is a town being rebuilt from scratch. Two years on from the fire, just a quarter or so of the plots of land have been built on.

Limited accommodation is available but it will be some time before a full infrastructure is in place. While there is a push to support such communities, visitors need to be aware that facilities are still severely limited. Contact the Visitor Centre for updates (www.marysvilletourism.com; tel: 5963 4567). Surviving attractions don't run much beyond **Steavenson Falls**, with its 83-metre (272ft) -high cascade, and **Bruno's**

LEFT: early winter snow in Mount Buffalo National Park. This subalpine park, created in 1898, is ideal for walking, cross-country skiing and canoeing.

Black Saturday

On Saturday 7 February 2009, some of the worst bushfires on record roared through great swathes of Victoria and took the lives of 173 people. Years of drought combined with a baking-hot summer had turned much of the country to tinder. As temperatures headed above 47°C (116°F), winds whipped up, some gusting over 120kmph (75mph). Several dangerous, but to that point manageable, bushfires began to run out of control. Blazes jumped control lines and embers were blown hundreds of metres, setting off more spot fires that soon combined to create unstoppable fire fronts roaring across thousands of hectares. Houses, farmland and forests were razed and entire settlements were destroyed. The Kilmore fire, as it became known, devastated Kinglake, Strathewen, Flowerdale and other townships to the north of Melbourne. When it combined with the Murrindindi blaze to the east, it virtually wiped out Marysville, where 34 people perished. Further east, in Gippsland, vast areas of forest were destroyed and much of Wilson's Promontory was affected. Over 1,200 homes were lost across the state and, as well as the human toll, wildlife was decimated and millions of acres of forest and bushland were destroyed.

Vehicle tyre chains are available from most ski-equipment hire stores.

Sculpture Garden, where terracotta figures dotted along riverside pathways are testament to an artist's irrepressible eccentricity.

Around Marysville

Lake Mountain is another 19km (12 miles) into the hills (entry fee during the snow season). For much of the year there's a network of fine bushwalking routes, but the place really comes into its own in the winter.

The only skiing option is cross-country, which requires a very different technique from downhill. Once the skills are mastered, there are some beautiful routes through snow-covered gum trees with sporadically placed picnic spots. For non-skiers the toboggan runs are a must.

Cathedral Range State Park, just 10km (6 miles) north, is relatively unexplored. Jagged sedimentary rock looms over paddocks and woodland. Fire damage was extensive here but walking trails and campsites at lower levels were quickly reinstated.

It's 30km (19 miles) further to **Alexandra**, home of the **Timber Tramway and Museum**, which

The Mountains

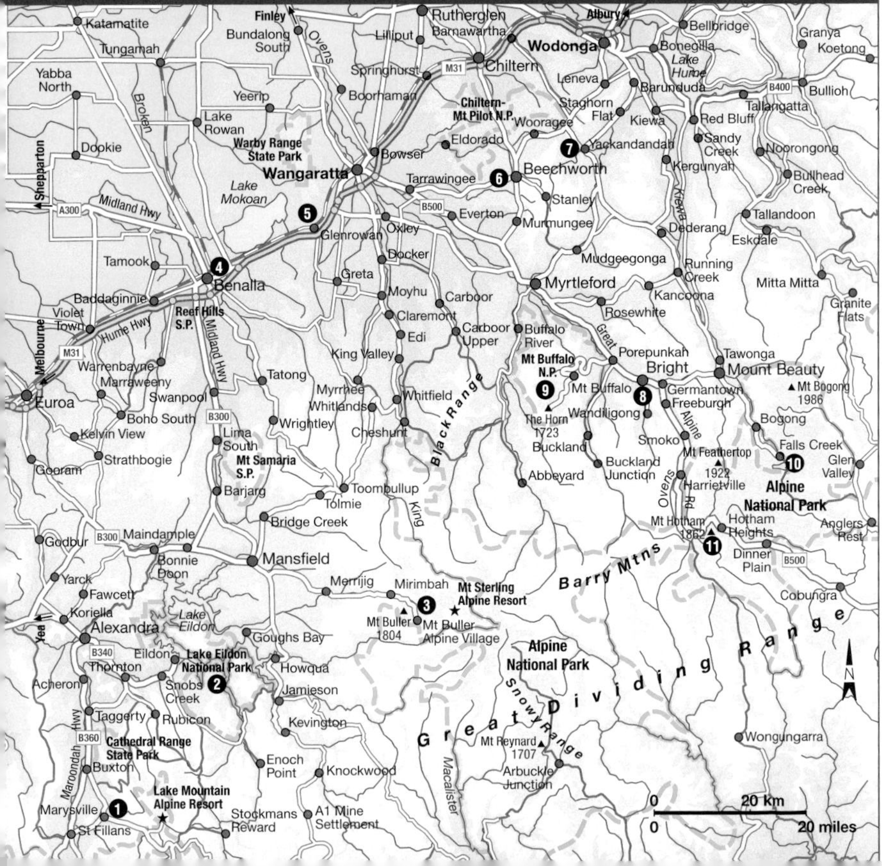

Recommended Restaurants, Bars & Cafés on page 265

preserves some of the old timber-industry narrow-gauge railway system and operates steam trains from the old station (Station Street; www.alexandratramway.org.au; tel: 5772 2392; weekends, call for schedule; charge for trains).

LAKE EILDON NATIONAL PARK ❷

Alexandra is a jumping-off point for Lake Eildon National Park, 30km (19 miles) to the east. This artificial lake was established as a reservoir and source of hydroelectric power after World War II, and the town of Eildon began as a settlement for workers constructing the dam. It soon became a holiday spot for anglers, watersports enthusiasts or simply lovers of dramatic scenery. Many of the houseboats moored in clumps around the lakeside are available to rent (www.lakeeildon.turbo.net.au).

The severe and persistent drought that has afflicted Victoria for several years has had an adverse effect on tourism, although it has revealed some of the old structures, such as Merlo Homestead, which were submerged in the 1950s.

The Maroondah continues north-east to **Mansfield**, a town that sees itself as the launch-point for the High Country. Much is made of the hardy colonial pioneers pitching themselves against the elements and the harsh country, struggling from one rough-hewn mountain hut to the next. Some of the huts are still there and act as focal points on a network of hiking trails. Horse riding will get you even closer to that settler spirit. The eye-catching **Visitor Centre** (175 High Street; www.mansfield-mtbuller.com.au; tel: 5775 7000/1800 039 049; daily 9am–5pm) has informative displays, including an intricate felt mural illustrating early pioneer days.

MOUNT BULLER ❸

Many visitors to Mansfield are simply passing through on their way to the ski slopes, 49km (30 miles) to the east. As the road climbs, the scenery changes from rolling pastureland to wooded hills and eventually full-on mountains, with the asphalt corkscrewing impressively around the rock face.

In winter there's a charge for entry to Mount Buller (see www.mt

TIP

There are three colour-coded bus routes in Mount Buller, and a light at the top of the bus's windscreen tells you which one it's on. For newcomers, a good way to get your bearings is to hop on to one of these buses and sit tight as it follows each of the three routes in succession.

ABOVE LEFT: aerial view of Mount Hotham.
BELOW LEFT: detail of the felt mural in Mansfield.
BELOW: installation at the Mansfield Visitor Centre.

The terrain around Merrijig, en route to Mount Buller, may look familiar to domestic visitors because this is where the 1982 film of The Man from Snowy River, *based on the classic "Banjo" Paterson poem of the same name, was shot.*

BELOW: polar bear at Mount Buller's ABOM. **BELOW RIGHT:** Buller boys on the piste.

buller.com.au for rates). Park your car at the base of the village, and a shuttle bus takes you up to the centre, where more free buses will transport you around the settlement. Odds are that a friendly driver will point out the landmarks and show you where massive bushfires came within a whisker of the resort.

Buller's hub is close by the bus station at the **Village Square**. The Bourke Street ski run ends just above it and the **Kooroora Hotel**, where tales of exploits on the snow are lubricated into myth – the hotel draws in all-comers with its roaring fires. Beneath the grey clock tower, the Visitor Information Centre, an offshoot of the one in Mansfield, is open in the winter (tel: 5777 7600; Mon–Fri 8am–5pm, Sat–Sun 8am–6.30pm) and supplies weather forecasts and snow reports. For the rest of the year, the Post Office is the place to go.

Victoria's ski resorts don't have quaint Alpine chalets the way Europe's do, but Buller probably comes closest to creating that atmosphere. There are lodges and hotels at all standards and several hostelries to wind down in at the end of a hard day on the slopes. **Bourke Street** is like a main street for skiers. Occupying a prime position on it is ABOM, an accommodation complex that caters on an industrial scale to anyone who parks their skis or snowboards at the door. A stuffed polar bear, a moose head in the bar downstairs and other bizarre adornments create a quirky atmosphere.

The skiing caters for every degree of expertise, as you would expect in Victoria's largest resort. Snowboarders make up an increasing proportion of visitors, especially off-peak when prices are lower.

Mount Sterling

Buller's sister destination has plenty of fine cross-country ski trails and no fees to use them. There's no accommodation, but Buller is only half an hour away. On Mount Sterling, as at Buller, there are magnificent views from the walking trails in the summer.

Return through Mansfield and join the Midland Highway north to Kelly country, where the infamous bushranger lived out his short life.

BENALLA ❹

First stop is Benalla, Ned's home town, which has a Ned Kelly Trail. **Benalla Art Gallery** (Bridge Street; www.benallaartgallery.com; tel: 57 62 3027; daily 10am–5pm; free) has a tapestry of Sidney Nolan's *Glenrowan*, depicting Ned's fateful date with the law, and a painting of one of his gang by Albert Tucker. Kelly aside, the gallery has a strong collection of modern Australian work and an expanding Aboriginal component. Its lakeside setting is in itself enough to justify a visit.

At the **Costume and Pioneer Museum** (14 Mair Street; www.benalla.vic.gov.au; tel: 5762 1749; daily 9am–5pm; charge), the spread of historic artefacts includes the portable cell that held Kelly briefly, and a section devoted to a genuine hero, Sir Edward "Weary" Dunlop *(see page 143)*, who grew up nearby.

GLENROWAN ❺

Glenrowan is dominated by Ned Kelly. Literally so, as there's a giant 6-metre (20ft) effigy of the man staring down the main street. This was the site, after all, of the Kelly gang's last stand, and you can learn about that day (28 June 1880) by following the plaques in the Glenrowan Heritage Siege Precinct. Wandering around the old railway station and other key sites, a visitor equipped with the free Ned Kelly Touring Route brochure and an imagination can create a powerful picture of historic events. Those without the requisite tools can visit **Kelly Land** (Gladstone Street; www.nedkellysworld.com.au; tel: 5766 23 67; daily 9.30am–4.30pm; charge), where computerised robots help to re-enact key events in the Kelly story. A slew of other museums and souvenir shops vie for your attention, but it's time to take your own stand and move on.

BEECHWORTH ❻

East, beyond Wangaratta, is one of the best-preserved and most attractive towns in the state. The roads that meet at the main intersection, Ford and Camp streets, are lined with gorgeous 19th-century shops, banks and hotels, all built on the proceeds of the gold rush. Everything in town is immaculately maintained, and yet, despite the crowds of visitors at weekends and holiday times, it just about retains a sense of a living, breathing community.

First stop has to be the **Town Hall**, which contains the **Visitor Information Centre** (103 Ford Street; www.beechworthonline.com.au; tel: 5728 8065; daily 9am–5pm) where, along with the usual services, book-

Skiing in Australia carries nothing like the social baggage that it does on other continents, so – here particularly – people will drive up for an afternoon in the most casual of warm clothing, verging on what the local parlance would term "daggy".

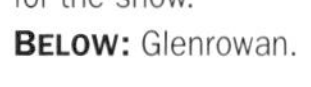

ABOVE LEFT: dressed for the snow.
BELOW: Glenrowan.

Operating the Morse signalling equipment at Beechworth's Telegraph Station.

ABOVE RIGHT: echoes of history in Beechworth. **BELOW RIGHT:** Ned Kelly: The Guide.

ings can be made for a range of guided tours, including one led by an ersatz Ned Kelly. They also sell tickets for the old justice and administration buildings grouped across the road, or the Historic and Cultural Precinct as it is termed.

Look for a row of vibrant sandstone buildings and start with the **courthouse,** where so many of Kelly's family and gang were arraigned. The holding cells, judge's and jury rooms and the court itself are open, accompanied by a soundtrack of historic proceedings (Ford Street; daily 9am–5pm; charge). Next door in the **Telegraph Station** you can get the operator to send a message by Morse code anywhere in the world for a small fee. There's also a collection of telecommunications equipment and a brief AV history of the town (daily 10am–4pm; charge).

A Chinese Cultural Centre in one of the cottages has closed down but evidence of the importance of these migrants to the area can be inferred from the **Chinese Burning Towers** in the cemetery down the road. A couple of lock-ups and some early

offices complete the Ford Street part of the precinct.

In Loch Street you'll find the old-fashioned **Robert O'Hara Burke Memorial Museum** (daily 10am–5pm; charge), whose main claim to fame is the reconstruction of a historic streetscape at night. There's only desultory attention to detail, though, and in a town with such stunning original streetscapes, it is easily bypassed.

The Kelly Gang

The exploits of the Kelly gang captured the popular imagination from the very beginning. By the time of Ned Kelly's execution in November 1880, the event could draw a crowd of several thousand to Melbourne Gaol, even though there was no chance of seeing the man or of determining whether he really did utter the final words: "Such is life." Kelly's journey to the scaffold began with his upbringing in a poor Irish family well known to the police, took in a spell in the company of renowned bushranger Harry Power, and gained full momentum when he was joined by his brother Dan and various associates on a string of robberies. The deaths of three constables in a shoot-out at Stringybark Creek in northeastern Victoria led to a huge manhunt, which, after further daring robberies, culminated in the siege at Glenrowan. Kelly took a larrikin disrespect for authority to murderous levels, and in so doing generated the myth that sustains a whole industry today.

Otherwise, just meander. Drop into **Tanswells Commercial Hotel**, or investigate a relative newcomer to town, Bridge Road Brewers, who operate the **Beechworth Micro Brewery** (Ford Street; www.bridgeroadbrewers.com.au; tel: 5728 27 03; Wed–Mon 11am–6pm).

Once you're sated with history or beer, walk down to **Lake Sambell** or take the Gorge Scenic Drive.

YACKANDANDAH ❼

It may only be 27km (17 miles) away, and it may be listed in its entirety by the National Trust, but Yackandandah attracts a fraction of the numbers that visit Beechworth, so you can enjoy its historical ambience without too much competition. Drop into the **Information Centre** in the Athenaeum (High Street; www.uniqueyackandandah.com.au; tel: 6027 1988; daily 10am–4pm), grab the leaflet A Walk in High Street and embrace the history and the quiet. Look out for a reconstructed miner's hut just before the courthouse in William Street.

Around the township there's evidence of gold diggings in the scenic walks to **The Gorge**, and **Karrs Reef Goldmine** up in the hills can be inspected on guided tours (tel: 0408 975 991, or book through Visitor Centre; Sat–Sun 10am, 1pm, 4pm; charge). The ambitious, once armed with a licence, can pan for gold in a number of locations locally.

After Yackandandah, make your way down to **Myrtleford** to join the Great Alpine Road winding its way south towards Bass Strait. It's a picturesque route through lush arable land, the occasional vineyard and Alpine pasture.

A good base for exploring this area and the local mountains is **Bright ❽**. It's a small town with a range of walks along the Ovens River and beyond. The presence of some of the best restaurants in the region is further inducement to stay here.

MOUNT BUFFALO NATIONAL PARK ❾

Drive 45 minutes northwest of Bright to this walker's paradise, with over 20 signed hiking tracks. There are spectacular views to be had, many requiring no more than a short stroll from your vehicle, and then there are the limpid blue waters of **Lake Catani**, which don't even require that

They were hanging a man up at Bright
He had been a temperance light
When they showed him the rope
He said "I do hope
That it isn't inclined to get tight".

1907 limerick by John Shaw Neilson

BELOW: Yackandandah Public Hall.

TIP

It is compulsory to carry snow chains for your vehicle in winter on the higher mountains and passes, so factor in local hire rates if you can't justify buying your own set. Four-wheel-drive vehicles are not exempt.

small effort – you can see them as you drive past. In winter, there's cross-country skiing in Cresta Valley.

Mount Buffalo Chalet is one of the few relatively old accommodation options in any of the mountain resorts. It was built in 1909 and managed to survive the devastating bushfires of summer 2006–7, which is more than can be said for the Cresta Lodge, which was completely destroyed. Operational disputes mean that the Chalet is not open at the time of writing.

Falls Creek ⑩

Serious devotees of the snow tend to head east through pleasant **Mount Beauty** and up another corkscrewing road to Falls Creek. There are no historic lodges here, indeed first impressions are of lots of concrete, but as you get deeper into the village there is some interesting architecture embracing local stone and wood. The skiing includes both downhill and cross-country, and can be superb. The clientele tends towards the moneyed. As ever, in summertime the hikers take over. The Visitor Information Centre on Bogong High Plains Road is the fount of all information on conditions, accommodation and so on (www.fallscreek.com.au; tel: 5758 1202 or 1800 033 079; daily 8am–5pm in season).

Top Right: Mount Buffalo Chalet. **Middle Right:** equipment hire in Bright.
Below: snowboarding at Mount Hotham.

Mount Hotham ⑪

Stay with the Great Alpine Road, and south of Bright you can't avoid climbing all the way up to **Mount Hotham**, the highest ski fields in the state (www.hotham.com.au; tel: 57 59 4470). It's an exposed route over the ridge and conditions can become treacherous in winter. The vistas across miles of Alpine peaks make it worthwhile, though.

At Hotham itself there's good, challenging skiing and quite an emphasis on snowboarding, as befits one of the first resorts to encourage the sport. There's plenty of accommodation available on the mountain, but many use **Dinner Plain**, 11km (7 miles) further on, as a base. Dinner Plain is a purpose-built resort with a rare dedication to incorporating traditional materials and styles in an attempt to reference early High Country structures. The outcome is a much more village-like atmosphere that generates keen loyalty in its residents and visitors. This is also the centre for the region's cross-country skiing. ❑

BEST RESTAURANTS, BARS AND CAFÉS

Beechworth

Provenance

86 Ford Street, Beechworth. 5728 1786 L Sun, D Wed–Sun **$$$**

The old Bank Restaurant has been stripped back, brought up to date and is now home to the region's most adventurous contemporary eatery.

Wardens Food & Wine

32 Ford Street, Beechworth. 5728 1377 B & L Wed–Sun, D Wed–Sat **$$**

Once a corner pub, this has morphed into a smartly attired, wooden-floored Mediterranean restaurant that takes pride in using local produce alongside an extremely impressive wine list and excellent coffee.

Bright

Sasha's of Bright

2d Anderson Street, Bright. 5750 1711 D daily **$$**

Duck is the word at this Eastern European-leaning restaurant, as evidenced by the whiteboard tally that keeps a running count of how many have been consumed since Sasha's opened.

Simone's Restaurant

98 Gavan Street, Bright. 5755 2266 D Tue–Sat **$$**

Brilliant Italian food and a homely ambience combine in this family-run restaurant where the seasonal and regional rule. This is one of the region's best.

Buckland

Villa Gusto

630 Buckland Valley Road, Buckland. 5756 2000 D Wed–Sun **$$$**

Five-course modern Italian dégustation menus that change daily are the feature of the restaurant at this five-star Tuscan-style resort. The wine list alone is worth the trip.

Mooroopna

Teller

108 McLennan Street, Mooroopna. 5825 3344 B Sat–Sun, L & D Wed–Sun **$$**

Beautifully cooked, adventurous food that borrows from Asia and Europe is served in a former bank, with carpets and banquettes decked out in earthy tones. Due to move to new premises in nearby Shepparton in 2011.

Myrtleford

Range

258 Great Alpine Road, Myrtleford. 5752 2885 L Thur–Sun, D Wed–Sat **$$**

A stylish dining room with an open fire and views of Mount Buffalo, offering nicely cooked food that uses regional ingredients, sourced as locally as possible, as a starting point for dishes inspired by Asia, Europe and the Middle East. There is also an outdoor terrace for summer dining.

Tawonga

Roi's Diner

177 Kiewa Valley Highway, Tawonga. 5754 4495 D Thur–Sun **$$**

A relaxed, hospitable attitude, a dining room full of mismatched furniture and eccentric art, and a (blackboard) menu full of brilliant, rib-sticking Italian food make Roi Rigoni's establishment the ideal place for the ski crowd.

Prices for a three-course dinner per person with a half-bottle of house wine:
$ = under A$60
$$ = A$60–90
$$$ = A$90–120
$$$$ = over A$120

Bars and Cafés

Bright Brewery
121 Great Alpine Road, Bright.
A range of European-style beer made with fresh mountain water. Beer-friendly snacks.

Food Wine Friends
6 Ireland Street, Bright.
Produce store, wine shop and café bringing together the best of the Alpine region.

Milawa Cheese Factory
Factory Road, Milawa.
This bakery, restaurant and cheese shop offers a little something for everybody.

theartscentre.com.au
MELBOURNE
RACV
MELBOURNE
RACV

INSIGHT GUIDES

MELBOURNE

Travel Tips

TRANSPORT

GETTING THERE AND GETTING AROUND

Although Melburnians would be offended to hear it, their city is a long way from anywhere – a 12-hour drive from Sydney, for instance. That's why most visitors arrive by air. But once in Melbourne, getting around is pretty easy. The city is compact enough to explore much of it on foot, and the public-transport system is reasonable despite some locals' complaints. There are efficient buses and trains, plentiful taxis and, most distinctively, the famous trams, ancient and modern, in a variety of fetching colours.

GETTING THERE

By Air

International Flights

Almost all foreign visitors travel to Australia by air. Melbourne is one of the major international tourism gateways, so there are daily flights arriving from Asia, Europe and North America. More than 40 international airlines currently fly to the city.

Fares to Australia vary widely, so it pays to shop around before buying a ticket. Budget domestic airlines Jetstar and Pacific Blue (a subsidiary of domestic carrier Virgin Blue) now fly to New Zealand, Asia and Pacific destinations and have regular sales online where you can snap up cheap fares. A relatively recent budget entry into the market is Tiger Airways (a Singapore Airline subsidiary), with direct flights from Singapore.

Domestic Flights

There are three main domestic carriers. Qantas, Jetstar and Virgin Blue fly direct to Melbourne Airport (Tullamarine) from all the state capitals. Pushy newcomer Tiger Airways offers budget flights from eight destinations to Tullamarine and seven to Avalon airport, which is 55km (34 miles) southwest of the city centre – fares to Avalon airport tend to be slightly cheaper, though it is a 55-minute bus ride to the city. Jetstar also flies to Avalon, from Sydney and Brisbane.

Each of these airlines regularly offers discounted fares for midweek departures, and there are frequent price wars.

Flight times are about an hour from Sydney and Hobart, 80 minutes from Adelaide, 2½ hours from Brisbane and approximately 4½ hours from Darwin.

Regional Express (Rex) operates flights to smaller interstate destinations including Burnie and King Island in Tasmania, Mount Gambier in South Australia, Albury on the border with New South Wales, and Mildura in Victoria. However, as Victoria is the smallest state of mainland Australia, it tends to be just as fast and convenient to travel to most destinations in the state by road or rail.

By Bus

The biggest long-distance bus company, with the most services, is Greyhound Australia. Firefly also operates daily express services to Melbourne from Sydney and Adelaide. While the standard of buses is high, distances are enormous in Australia. It will take approximately 12 hours by bus from Sydney, whereas a flight will only take one hour.

The main bus station is Southern Cross Terminal on Spencer Street, where you can connect with city train, tram and bus services. V/Line, also based at Southern Cross Station, operates bus and train services to and from regional Victoria.

Firefly Express
Tel: 1300 730 740
www.fireflyexpress.com.au

Greyhound Australia
Tel: 1300 473 946
www.greyhound.com.au

V/Line
Tel: 136 196
www.vline.com.au

By Train

The principal rail lines of Australia follow the east and south coasts, linking Melbourne's Southern Cross Station to neighbouring capital cities. CountryLink has daily train services from Sydney. From Adelaide, Great Southern Railway's Overland (which links to the famous Ghan and Indian-Pacific routes in Adelaide) operates three times a week in each direction. V/Line operates regional services throughout Victoria as well as interstate services to Canberra and Adelaide.

CountryLink
Tel: 132 232
www.countrylink.info

The Overland
Tel: 132 147
www.gsr.com.au

V/Line
Tel: 136 196
www.vline.com.au

By Sea

If you're coming from Tasmania, ferries offer a leisurely overnight journey between Devonport and Port Melbourne. *Spirit of Tasmania I* and *II* make overnight crossings seven days a week. In peak periods there is also a daytime crossing in both directions. The trip takes about 10 hours. Fares depend on the time of year, accommodation and vehicle size.

Spirit of Tasmania
Tel: 1800 634 906
www.spiritoftasmania.com.au

Getting Around

From the Airport

Melbourne Airport is 22km (14 miles) from the city centre. A taxi takes 20–30 minutes and can cost around A$40–50. This includes a A$2 vehicle fee for taxi passengers leaving the airport.

For around half that price, Skybus operates a daily 24-hour bus service between the airport and Southern Cross Station. Buses depart every 10–15 minutes during the day and every 30–60 minutes overnight. Sunbus Melbourne meets all incoming flights and provides hotel transfers to the CBD and inner suburbs.

Avalon airport is 55km (34 miles) from the city, on the main road between Melbourne and Geelong. Avalon Airport Transfers operates services that meet arrivals and drop off passengers at Southern Cross Station. The journey takes approximately 55 minutes. Drop-offs are also available to accommodation in the CBD and inner suburbs for an additional cost.

Avalon Airport Transfers
Tel: 5278 8788
www.sitacoaches.com.au/avalon

Skybus
Tel: 9335 3066
www.skybus.com.au

Sunbus Melbourne
Tel: 02-9666 6777
www.sunbusmelbourne.com.au

Public Transport

Melbourne's integrated public-transport system, called Metlink or the Met, is among the best in Australia. A good way to introduce yourself is to visit the MetShop located at Melbourne Town Hall, on the corner of Swanston and Little Collins streets, where you can find all the information you could ever need.

There is a wide range of tickets (Metcards) for unlimited travel over various periods (eg hourly, daily, weekly) and throughout the various zones of the city (zone 1 is big enough for most visitors' purposes). A Metcard can be used on metropolitan trams, buses and trains (excluding airport services). You can purchase them on board trams and buses, at train stations and at stores displaying a blue "Metcards sold here" sign. Note that the ticket-vending machines on trams only take coins. Concessions are only available to holders of an approved Victorian Concession Card or children aged 14 and under. After you purchase a Metcard, you must validate it in the machine on board the bus or tram, or at the train station. For visitors staying more than a few days, it's worth buying and charging up a Myki card (www.myki.com.au). This touch-on-touch-off card is the most cost-efficient way to use the city's integrated transport system.

As in most Australian cities, Melbourne's public transport tends to curl up and go to sleep

Major Airlines

Qantas
Tel: 131 313
www.qantas.com.au

Jetstar
Tel: 131 538
www.jetstar.com.au

Virgin Blue (and Pacific Blue)
Tel: 136 789
www.virginblue.com.au

Tiger Airways
Tel: 9335 3033
www.tigerairways.com

Air New Zealand
Tel: 132 476
www.airnewzealand.com.au

Emirates Airlines
Tel: 1300 303 777
www.emirates.com

Singapore Airlines
Tel: 131 011
www.singaporeair.com

United Airlines
Tel: 131 777
www.united.com

Regional Express
Tel: 131 713
www.rex.com.au

YARRA CRUISES

Taking a boat trip on the Yarra can include a romantic interlude on a gondola or an evening excursion to see little penguins. Standard voyages tend to head upriver as far as Herring Island in Richmond, or down to Docklands and Westgate Bridge, and some go on to Williamstown. The main starting point is by the Southgate Centre or at Federation Wharf (below Fed Square), and the two principal operators are: **Melbourne River Cruises** (www.melbcruises.com.au; tel: 8610 2600) and **Williamstown Bay and River Cruises** (www.williamstownferries.com.au; tel: 9506 4144).

soon after midnight. An hourly NightRider bus service operates from Swanston Street (between Collins Street and Flinders Lane) between 12.30am and 4.30am on Saturday and Sunday mornings. The easiest late-night option for visitors unfamiliar with the city would be hailing a taxi.

For information on all public transport in Melbourne contact Metlink, tel: 131 638; or visit www.metlinkmelbourne.com.au.

Trams

Melbourne's iconic trams form the basis of the public transport system. There are about 750 trams, venturing as far as 20km (12 miles) out of the city.

Trams are an excellent option for getting around the CBD and to inner-city shopping precincts and attractions. The free City Circle tram (Sun–Wed 10am–6pm, Thur–Sat 10am–9pm) operates in both directions around the outer edge of the CBD (including along Spencer, La Trobe and Flinders streets). It stops at or close to some of Melbourne's major tourist attractions, including Federation Square, Melbourne Aquarium and the Melbourne Museum.

Trains

The metropolitan train service connects an underground city loop to the outer suburbs. Flinders Street Station is the hub for metropolitan services, while Southern Cross Station is the place to connect with regional train and bus services.

Southern Cross Station Information Desk
Tel: 9619 2587

Buses

Buses are the secondary form of public transport, often taking over when trams and trains are out of service. Melbourne City Tourist Shuttle is a free service that stops at key attractions. It operates daily between 9.30am and 4.30pm, and you can hop on and off at any one of the 13 stops. Information about the shuttle is available from the Melbourne Visitor Centre at Federation Square.

Taxis

Melbourne's yellow taxis are easy to spot and are an affordable way to get around the inner city if you are in a group. You can hail them in the street if the rooftop light is on. Taxi ranks can be found at major hotels, train stations and shopping malls.

The meter should be clearly visible. There are surcharges for phone bookings, between midnight and 5am, departing from the airport taxi rank and for using the CityLink freeway or other tolls. Drivers are entitled to ask for money in advance after 10pm.

Embassy Taxis
Tel: 131 755
Silver Top Taxis
Tel: 131 008
Yellow 13 CABS
Tel: 132 227

Driving

Visitors from overseas can drive in Victoria if they have an International Driving Permit or a current licence from home, provided it is in English (or you have an English translation).

Traffic drives on the left in Australia. Most of Victoria's road regulations are based on international rules and it is simply a matter of following the signs and sticking to the specified speed limits. VicRoads can provide information about road rules and licensing. Here are some rules that drivers should be aware of:

- Drivers must give way to the right, unless otherwise indicated, to pedestrians, and to all emergency vehicles.
- The speed limit in built-up city and suburban areas is 50kph (30mph) and on country roads 100kph (60mph) unless otherwise indicated.
- It is the responsibility of the driver to ensure that everybody in the vehicle is wearing a seatbelt at all times (or they are appropriately restrained in the case of children and babies).
- There is a 0.05 percent blood alcohol limit for drivers, which is widely enforced by the use of random breath tests carried out by the police. Random drug tests are also performed.
- Street parking is always in the direction of travel.
- U-turns are permitted at traffic lights in Victoria (except where there is a "NO U-TURN" sign).
- Drivers may only overtake a tram on the left. It is illegal to drive past the rear of a stopped

tram – drivers must stop level with the rear of the tram and wait for the doors to close.

Hook Turns

Melbourne is the only city in Australia where vehicles can be required to perform a hook turn to turn right. This is only applicable at some intersections and is designed to give trams priority. These intersections are clearly marked with a sign saying "Right turn from left only" *(as pictured, below left).*

To make a hook turn, put on your right indicator, enter the intersection in the far left lane and wait on the far left-hand side of the road. Wait until the lights in the street you want to enter have turned green before making the turn to the right.

VicRoads
Tel: 131 171
www.vicroads.vic.gov.au

Breakdown Services

The Royal Automobile Club of Victoria (RACV) provides roadside service to members and has reciprocal arrangements with many motoring organisations from overseas and interstate. They can also supply you with maps and travel information. Most car-hire outlets arrange their own roadside service, but the RACV is a good point of contact for all sorts of motoring advice.

RACV
Tel: 131 111
www.racv.com.au

CityLink

Melbourne has a handful of freeways for which tolls are charged. Visitors can buy a 24-hour pass or a weekend pass (valid from noon Friday to midnight Sunday), but there are no toll-booths on the roads themselves. Payment must be made online (www.citylink.com.au), by phone (tel: 132 629) or over the counter at Australia Post outlets in Victoria. You must pay the fee by midnight within three days of travel, after which fines are incurred.

Car Hire

Many visitors choose to rent a car for day trips and longer excursions into the countryside.

If you have not organised car hire as part of a package, you should shop around for the best deal: the smaller independent operators tend to be cheaper. Major car-hire companies have offices at Melbourne and Avalon airports and in the city centre.

An important point to consider is insurance. Many companies have an excess charge ranging from A$700 to A$1,500, which means you pay that amount in the case of an accident. You may choose to pay a little bit extra per day to reduce the figure. When you are getting a quote from the company, ask for the full amount including insurance and charges for extra items such as baby restraints. Many companies do not insure vehicles for off-road travel, which means the driver is liable.

Vehicle Hire Companies

Atlas Rent A Car
Tel: 1800 808 122
www.atlasrent.com.au

Avis
Tel: 136 333
www.avis.com.au

Britz Campervan Rentals
Tel: 1800 331 454
www.britz.com.au

Budget
Tel: 132 727
www.budget.com.au

Europcar
Tel: 131 390
www.europcar.com.au

Hertz
Tel: 133 309
www.hertz.com.au

Holiday Autos
Tel: 1300 554 507
www.holidayautos.com.au

Thrifty
Tel: 1300 367 227
www.thrifty.com.au

Cycling

Melbourne's inner-city terrain is generally flat, which makes it an easy city to explore by bike. An extensive system of cycle paths also makes it one of the most bicycle-friendly cities in Australia. Helmets are compulsory and riders must ensure they have lights attached to the bike for riding at night. Familiarise yourself with Victoria's road rules if you plan to ride on the roads.

Melbourne has a number of trails where you can explore the city and barely come into contact with the busy roads. The Capital City Trail leads you in a wide loop around the city, past notable landmarks. Bicycle Victoria and the Melbourne Visitor Centre can supply maps and further information.

Bikes can be taken on trains free except during peak times (Mon–Fri 7–9.30am and 4–6pm), when a small fee applies.

Melbourne Bike Share picks up on an idea seen in other cities across the world. Bright blue bikes are available in docking stations around the city and for a small fee can be released for short excursions. The only flaw is the legal requirement to wear a helmet in Victoria, which rather undermines spontaneity.

Bicycle Victoria
Tel: 8636 8888
www.bv.com.au

Melbourne Bike Share
Tel: 1300 711 590
www.melbournebikeshare.com.au

Rentabike and Real Melbourne Bike Tours
Tel: 0417 339 203
www.rentabike.net.au

St Kilda Cycles
11 Carlisle Street, St Kilda
Tel: 9534 3074
www.stkildacycles.com.au

Accommodation

Some Things to Consider Before You Book the Room

Melbourne has all sorts of accommodation dispersed throughout the city. "Designer" or "boutique" hotels with fashion-conscious interiors as well as a range of apartment-style options are growing in popularity. The latter can often provide more space and facilities for the same price as a hotel. Out of town, prices tend to be lower, but a lot of tired hotels and motels are being smartened up for moneyed weekenders and tourists. Multi-day cottage or unit rentals can offer some of the best value.

Overview

Unlike central business districts in some cities, Melbourne's goes beyond a corporate wasteland and remains a lively centre with an excellent choice of facilities seven days a week. All of these are within walking distance or an easy tram ride if you choose to stay close to the city centre.

That being said, there are some lively precincts outside the city if you prefer to get away from the hustle and bustle. The seaside suburb of St Kilda is popular with visitors. There's plenty of moderate and budget accommodation here, and it's a particular favourite with backpackers.

In the city, budget-priced hotels lie mainly at the Spencer Street end, around Southern Cross Station. The new blocks rising around the Docklands development are increasing apartment availability in that area, too. The inner north, including Carlton and Fitzroy, also tends towards budget and moderate accommodation options, and it's only a short tram or taxi ride to the city. Upmarket hotels are generally found in the eastern half of the city centre near some of the city's key theatres and shopping streets. Luxury lodging also tends to dominate in the upmarket suburb of South Yarra.

It is almost unheard of for television and basic tea- and coffee-making facilities not to be provided in accommodation of all levels. If they are not in your room, try the communal room(s).

With more than 23,000 rooms in the city, you should be able to find last-minute accommodation throughout the year. However, you should play it safe and book ahead during busy periods, which include Christmas, Easter and major sporting events – especially the Grand Prix (March), AFL Grand Final (September), Australian Tennis Open (January) and the Spring Racing Carnival (November). Official Visitor Information Centres (identifiable by a yellow "i" on a blue background) offer advice on accommodation types and can often make bookings on your behalf. The classifieds and travel section of *The Age* newspaper on Saturdays can be a good source for new and offbeat places.

Most accommodation providers have their own websites. One of the easiest ways to book is online, where you can get cheap, last-minute deals through specialist "clearing houses" for unsold rooms. If you are looking for the cheapest deal possible and are willing to put in some effort, a worthwhile tactic can be looking up last-minute prices at these clearing houses, then contacting the hotel direct to see if it can undercut this, effectively saving you the commission.

You may well get a bargain at the following websites:
www.stayz.com.au
www.wotif.com
www.lastminute.com.au
www.needitnow.com.au
www.standbyrates.com.au
www.tripadvisor.com.au

ACCOMMODATION LISTINGS

CITY CENTRE, EAST OF SWANSTON STREET

Adelphi
187 Flinders Lane
Tel: 8080 8888
[p311, D3]
www.adelphi.com.au
An ultra-modern designer hotel in the heart of the city. Spectacular views from the rooftop bar and the pool cantilevered over the street. **$$$**

Grand Hyatt Melbourne
123 Collins Street
Tel: 9657 1234 or 131 234
[p311, D2]
www.melbourne.grand.hyatt.com
Ostentatious display of brass and marble right down to the huge black marble bathrooms. Popular with business conventions. **$$$$**

Hotel Grand Chancellor
131 Lonsdale Street
Tel: 9656 4000
[p311, D2]
www.ghihotels.com
Comfortable rooms, close to Melbourne Cricket Ground and the shopping district. **$$**

Hotel Lindrum
26 Flinders Street
Tel: 9668 1111
[p311, E2]
http://mirvachotels.com
The epitome of the contemporary boutique hotel. If you don't have style beforehand, you will after a stay here. **$$$**

The Park Hyatt
1 Parliament Square, off Parliament Place
Tel: 9224 1234
[p311, E1–2]
www.melbourne.park.hyatt.com
Surprisingly tranquil for somewhere so close to the action of the state government and CBD. In radii it has one of the last destination restaurants in a hotel. **$$$$**

The Sofitel
25 Collins Street
Tel: 9653 0000
[p311, E2]
www.sofitelmelbourne.com.au
Guest rooms start on the 36th floor and offer sweeping views across Melbourne and Port Phillip Bay. The fancy restaurant has returned and the bar and café at the top still welcome visitors who want the view without the room. **$$$$**

The Victoria Hotel
215 Little Collins Street
Tel: 9669 0000
Freecall: 1800 331 147
[p311, D2]
www.victoriahotel.com.au
Budget, standard and superior rooms are offered in this good, mainstream hotel. Within walking distance of the CBD. **$$**

The Westin
205 Collins Street
Tel: 9635 2222
[p311, D2]
www.westin.com.au
Facing City Square in Swanston Street, it's hard to get more central than this. Combine that with sleek interiors and fine service. **$$$$**

The Windsor
111 Spring Street
Tel: 9633 6000
[p311, E2]
www.thewindsor.com.au
This majestic National

Trust building is one of the few in Australia originally built as a hotel. Intended to provide the most luxurious accommodation in town. Compact rooms, old-world interiors and high tea at 3pm. **$$$$**

CITY CENTRE, WEST OF SWANSTON STREET

Batman's Hill Hotel
623 Collins Street
Tel: 9614 6344
[p310, B4]
www.batmanshill.com.au
Here you'll find old-fashioned, friendly style behind an elegant, historic exterior. **$$$**

Intercontinental Melbourne The Rialto
495 Collins Street
Tel: 9620 9111
Freecall: 1800 221 335
[p310, C3]
www.intercontinental.com
A stunning makeover has returned this 1891 classic of Venetian Gothic architecture to the position of being one of the city's great hotels. **$$$$**

Jasper Hotel
489 Elizabeth Street
Tel: 8327 2777
Freecall: 1800 468 359
[p310, C1]
www.jasperhotel.com.au

This contemporary boutique accommodation is located next to the popular Queen Victoria Market. **$$$**

PRICE CATEGORIES

Price categories are for a double room without breakfast:
$ = under A$80
$$ = A$80–130
$$$ = A$130–200
$$$$ = over A$200

Oaks on Market
60 Market Street
Tel: 8631 1111
[p310, C3]
www.theoaksgroup.com.au
Good value for central apartments. **$$$**

Pensione Hotel
16 Spencer Street
Tel: 9621 3333
[p310, B4]
www.pensione.com.au
A modern hotel with simple but good rooms. **$$**

Robinsons in the City
405 Spencer Street
Tel: 9329 2552
[p310, A2]
www.robinsonsinthecity.com.au
With only six rooms, this is Melbourne's smallest boutique hotel. Emphasis is on personal service and home comforts. **$$$$**

Vibe Savoy
630 Little Collins Street
Tel: 9622 8888
[p310, B3]
www.vibehotels.com.au
This intimate 1920s hotel promotes an elegant, club-like atmosphere. **$$$**

SOUTHBANK AND DOCKLANDS

Crown Promenade Hotel
8 Whiteman Street, Southbank
Tel: 9292 6688
Freecall: 1800 776 612
[p310, C4]
www.crownpromenadehotel.com.au
This 39-floor hotel towers above the Yarra River and a vast casino and entertainment complex that includes cinemas, restaurants and live entertainment. **$$$$**

Docklands Apartments – Grand Mercure
23 St Mangos Lane
Tel: 9641 7503
[p302, B4]
www.docklandsserviced apartments.com.au
Sleekly comfortable to match the setting. **$$$**

Hilton Melbourne South Wharf
2 Convention Centre Place, South Wharf
Tel: 9027 2000
[p304, A2]
www.hilton.com/south-wharf
Sizeable modern block with every facility, built to service the new convention centre. **$$$$**

The Langham
Southgate Avenue, Southbank
Tel: 8696 8888
[p311, D4]
www.melbourne.langhamhotels.com.au

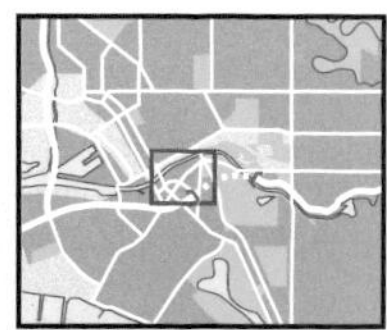

Central to the Southgate Development, this high-rise promotes an aura of untrammelled luxury with the bonus of exceptional city views. Has a private promenade to the shopping district. **$$$$**

Quay West Suites
26 Southgate Avenue, Southbank
Tel: 9693 6000
Freecall: 1800 800 193
[p311, D4]
www.mirvachotels.com
Well-appointed apartments with spectacular views across the Yarra River. **$$$$**

MELBOURNE PARK, EAST MELBOURNE

Albert Heights Serviced Apartments
83 Albert Street, East Melbourne
Tel: 9419 0955
Freecall: 1800 800 117
[off p303]
www.albertheights.com.au
Modern apartment units, all facing a central garden courtyard and spa pool. The units are functional but tasteful and well-equipped. **$$**

Georgian Court
21–25 George Street, East Melbourne
Tel: 9419 6353
[off p303]
www.georgiancourt.com.au
Comfortable B&B situated on a tree-lined street, across from the beautiful Fitzroy Gardens and just a short walk to the city centre. Has 31 rooms and dinner available most nights. **$$**

Hilton on the Park Melbourne
192 Wellington Parade
Tel: 9419 2000
Freecall: 1800 222 255
[off p303]

www.melbourne.hilton.com
Luxury suites with modern styling and views across the Melbourne

Cricket Ground or Fitzroy Gardens. On the eastern edge of the CBD. Walking distance to Melbourne Park and the city centre. Has an outdoor heated pool and makes a point of the opening windows in its bedrooms. **$$$$**

Quest East Melbourne
48 Wellington Parade, East Melbourne
Tel: 9413 0000
[arrow off p303]
www.questeastmelbourne.com.au
Serviced apartments a short jog away from the MCG and the sports precinct. **$$$**

CARLTON AND FITZROY

Downtowner on Lygon
66 Lygon Street, Carlton
Tel: 9663 5555
[p303, D3]
www.downtowner.com.au
Carlton is the cosmopolitan location of this hotel near the University. Stylishly decorated rooms. Guests have access to the Melbourne City Baths. **$$$**

Melbourne Big4 Holiday Park
265 Elizabeth Street, Coburg
Tel: 9354 3533
Freecall: 1800 802 678
[off p302]
http://melbourne.vic.big4.com.au
Most caravan and campsites are located on the city outskirts, so you should book ahead for this one just 9km (6 miles) north of the city centre. Powered, unpowered or en suite sites with private facilities available. **$**

Melbourne Metro YHA
78 Howard Street, North Melbourne
Tel: 9329 8599
[p302, C3]
www.yha.com.au
Huge property with fine facilities, with its rooftop lounge a particular selling point. Breakfast and dinner service, plus internet access and bicycle hire. **$**

The Nunnery
116 Nicholson Street, Fitzroy
Tel: 9419 8637
[p303, E2]
www.nunnery.com.au
Converted Victorian building close to the city, with comfortable heated rooms, good facilities and a friendly atmosphere. Includes some dormitory-style sleeping for A$30. **$**

Quest Carlton Clocktower Apartments
255 Drummond Street, Carlton
Tel: 9349 9700
Freecall: 1800 062 966
[p303, D2]
www.clocktower.com.au
Stylish apartments in bustling Lygon Street area. **$$$**

Quest Royal Gardens
8 Royal Lane, Fitzroy
Tel: 9419 9888
[p303, E2]
www.questroyalgardens.com.au
More apartments from the ever-reliable Quest chain. Phone for great deals in quiet periods. **$$$**

Vibe Hotel Carlton
441 Royal Parade, Parkville
Tel: 9380 9222 [arrow off p302]
www.vibehotels.com.au
Clean, bright, modern and ideally placed for the University and Melbourne's Italian neighbourhood. **$$$**

PORT MELBOURNE, SOUTH MELBOURNE, MIDDLE PARK AND ALBERT PARK

Jackson's on Middle Park
404 Richardson Street, Middle Park
Tel: 9534 7615
[p306, C2]
www.middle-park.com/Jacksons
Just two rooms in this Victorian single-storey house in a leafy suburban street. Fifteen-minute tram ride away from CBD, five minute ride from St Kilda. **$$**

PRICE CATEGORIES

Price categories are for a double room without breakfast:
$ = under A$80
$$ = A$80–130
$$$ = A$130–200
$$$$ = over A$200

La Maison de Babette
4 Garton Street, Port Melbourne
Tel: 9645 6067
[off p304]
http://lamaisondebabette.com.au
French-style B&B in an old Victorian home, handily placed between the city, the beach and Albert Park. **$$**

Sweeny Luxury Cottage
24 Brooke Street, Albert Park
Tel: 0438-250 050
[p304, A4]
www.melbourneboutiquecottages.com.au
Original artwork and even a choice of pillows

in this beautifully appointed two-storey house. The proprietors have another property slightly further out in Elwood. **$$$$**

ST KILDA

Base St Kilda
17 Carlisle Street
Tel: 8598 6200
[p307, D3]
www.basebackpackers.com/stkilda
Modern accommodation priding itself on girl-only dorms with clean bathrooms. Offers private singles and doubles. **$**

Easystay@Acland St
65 Acland Street
Tel: 9536 9700
[p307, D3]
www.easystay.com.au
One of a six-strong St Kilda chain ranging from simple motel rooms to family apartments. **$$**

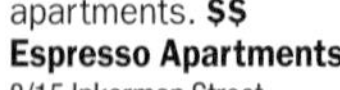

Espresso Apartments
8/15 Inkerman Street,
Tel: 9055 4633
[p307, D3]
www.espressoapartments.com.au
Warehouse-style executive apartments available for short-, medium- or long-term rental. More under the umbrella to be found in other Bayside suburbs. **$$$**

Medina Executive St Kilda
157 Fitzroy Street
Tel: 9536 0000
[p307, D2]
www.medina.com.au
Self-contained, contemporary apartments with great views across Albert Park to the city. **$$$$**

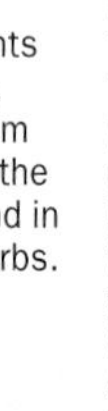

Novotel St Kilda
16 Esplanade
Tel: 9525 5522
[p307, C3]
www.novotelstkilda.com.au
Hideous building from the outside but once you're inside, the views across the bay are second to none. **$$$**

Olembia Guest House
96 Barkly Street
Tel: 9537 1412
[p307, D3]
www.olembia.com.au
Cosy and friendly guesthouse with good facilities, parking and a pleasant lounge. **$**

The Prince
2 Acland Street
Tel: 9536 1111
[p307, C3]
www.theprince.com.au
Ultra-modern luxury hotel with innovative restaurant and bars.

Forty individually designed rooms in neutral colours, spa and reading room. **$$$$**

St Marine Boutique Hotel
42 Marine Parade
Tel: 9534 1311
[p307, D4]
www.stmarine.com.au
Both rooms and apartments are available in this Edwardian-style hotel overlooking St Kilda beach. **$$$**

Tolarno Hotel
42 Fitzroy Street
Tel: 9537 0200
[p307, C2/3]
www.hoteltolarno.com.au
Bright, vibrant rooms reflect Mirka Mora's artwork in the restaurant below. Buzzing location. **$$$**

PRAHRAN, TOORAK, SOUTH YARRA AND RICHMOND

The Como Melbourne
630 Chapel Street, South Yarra
Tel: 9825 2222
Freecall: 1800 033 400
[p305, E3]
www.mirvachotels.com.au
Many of the rich and famous wouldn't stay anywhere else. The Como wins awards year after year for its attention to comfort and uniquely designed suites. Located in the fashionable South Yarra district, famous for its fine restaurants and boutiques. **$$$$**

The Lyall
14 Murphy Street, South Yarra
Tel: 9868 8222
[p305, E3]
www.thelyall.com
Award-winning, incredibly stylish boutique hotel and spa to tempt even the most jaded. **$$$$**

Manor House Apartments
36 Darling Street, South Yarra
Tel: 9867 1266
[p305, E3]
www.manorhouse.com
Well-furnished apartments in the exclusive restaurant and shopping district of South Yarra. **$$$**

The Olsen
637–41 Chapel Street, South Yarra
Tel: 9040 1222
[p305,E3]
www.artserieshotels.com.au/Olsen
The third in the art series chain opened in 2010 and continues the theme of high luxury accompanied by extensive displays of the eponymous artist, in this case John Olsen. The Cullen can be found down the road at 164

Commercial Road, Prahran. **$$$$**

Prahran Village Guest House
39 Perth Street
Tel: 9533 6559
[p307, D1]
www.guestlink.com.au
Slightly out of the way, but this B&B makes up

for it with four luxuriously appointed rooms and an apartment. **$$$**

Richmond Hill Hotel
353 Church Street, Richmond
Tel: 9428 6501
[p305, E1]
www.richmondhillhotel.com.au
Mid-range hotel in an attractive heritage setting. **$$**

AROUND THE BAY

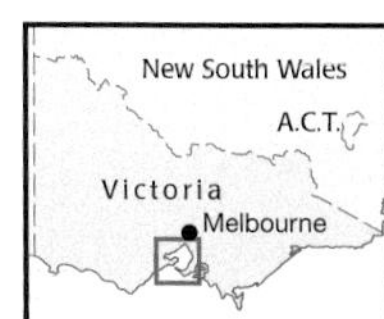

Cape Schanck

Cape Schanck Lighthouse
420 Cape Schanck Road
Tel: 9567 7900
Self-contained old lighthouse-keeper cottages. **$$$**

Geelong

Pevensey House
17 Pevensey Cresent
Tel: 5224 2810
B&B in a wonderful 1892 mansion. **$$$**

Queenscliff

The Queenscliff Hotel
16 Gellibrand Street
Tel: 5258 1066
www.queenscliffhotel.com.au
If you're going to stay in a Victorian-era resort then you won't find a better representative of the era than this. **$$$**

Rye

Blue Moon Cottages
12 Blakiston Grove
Tel: 9775 4722
www.bluemooncottages.com.au
Three cottages at this location, along with others in Rye and Sorrento, make this a good first port of call if you're in search of quality beach houses. **$$$$**

Sorrento

Oceanic
231 Ocean Beach Road
Tel: 5984 4166
www.oceanicgroup.com.au
Historic hotel with standard rooms now joined by modern apartments next door. **$$**

Werribee

Sofitel Mansion & Spa
Werribee Park K Road
Tel: 9731 4000
www.mansionhotel.com.au
Boutique hotel with contemporary styling and garden views at the heart of a historic estate. **$$$$**

Williamstown

Quest Williamstown
1 Syme Street
Tel: 9393 5300
www.questwilliamstown.com.au
Self-contained apartments on the waterfront. **$$$**

GREAT OCEAN ROAD (TORQUAY TO PORT FAIRY)

Aireys Inlet

Aireys on Aireys
19 Aireys Street
Tel: 5289 6844
www.aireysonaireys.com.au
Five comfortable two-storey cabins in a peaceful woodland setting consisting of over an acre. Ideal for families. Beaches and public tennis courts within walking distance. **$$$**

Apollo Bay

Seaview Motel and Apartments
6 Thomson Street
Tel: 5237 6660
www.seaviewmotel.com.au
Clean, modern accommodation within easy reach of the sea. Choose from two-bedroom family apartments, self-contained studio apartments and motel units without cooking facilities. **$$**

Lorne

Cumberland Lorne
150 Mountjoy Parade
Tel: 5289 4444
Freecall: 1800 037 010
www.cumberland.com.au
Offers suites with wonderful views and complimentary recreational activities, right in the

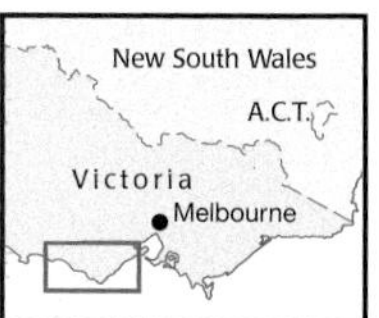

PRICE CATEGORIES

Price categories are for a double room without breakfast:
$ = under A$80
$$ = A$80–130
$$$ = A$130–200
$$$$ = over A$200

heart of this friendly town. **$$$$**

Qdos Treehouse
35 Allenvale Road
Tel: 5289 1989
www.qdosarts.com
Japanese minimalism in a relaxed bushland setting. Adjacent to the Qdos arts venue. **$$$**

Port Fairy

Merrijig Inn
1 Campbell Street
Tel: 5568 2324
Freecall: 1800 682 324
www.merrijiginn.com
Cosy accommodation in Victoria's oldest inn. **$$**

The Victoria
48–50 Bank Street
Tel: 5568 1160
www.thevictoria.com.au
This new development behind the historic pub has well-appointed apartments where detail is everything. **$$**

Torquay

Crowne Plaza Torquay
100 The Esplanade
Tel: 5261 1500
Freecall: 1800 000 867
www.ichotelsgroup.com
Huge new surf-coast hotel with every amenity and then some. Includes a restaurant, lounge bar and summer café. **$$$$**

Warrnambool

Surfside Holiday Park
Pertobe Road
Tel: 5559 4700
www.surfsidepark.com.au
Cottages, units and camping facilities in a pleasant setting handy for Flagstaff Hill and seeing endangered Southern Right whales. **$**

Wattle Hill

Moonlight Head Lodge
Parkers access road (off Great Ocean Road)
Tel: 5237 5208
www.moonlighthead.com
An architectural wonder surrounded by nature and dedicated to hedonism. Rates begin at A$3,500. **$$$$**

GOLD TOWNS, THE GRAMPIANS AND ECHUCA

Ballarat

Craig's Royal Hotel
10 Lydiard St South
Tel: 5331 1377
www.craigsroyal.com.au
One of the magnificent gold-era pubs in the centre of Ballarat. The rooms have been refreshed to a very high standard. **$$$**

Bendigo

Comfort Inn Shamrock
Corner of Pall Mall and Williamson Streets
Tel: 5443 0333
www.hotelshamrock.com.au
Grandiose country hotel dating from the gold-mining period. Ornate roof and balconies. Inexpensive "traditional" rooms plus de-luxe suites. **$$$**

Castlemaine

Campbell Street Lodge
33 Campbell St
Tel: 5472 3477
http://campbellstlodge.com.au
Sound motel that never quite lives up to its listed building. **$$**

The Empyre
68 Mostyn Street
Tel: 5472 5166
www.empyre.com.au
Period boutique hotel that also houses an accomplished restaurant. The six suites feature original French furniture from the 1800s. **$$$$**

Daylesford

Lake House
4 King Street
Tel: 5348 3329
www.lakehouse.com.au
A luxurious lakeside retreat in "Spa Country", with a fine country restaurant. **$$$$**

Echuca

Echuca Gardens
103 Mitchell Street
Tel: 5480 6522
www.echucagardens.com
This B&B/cottage doubles as the local YHA and offers good value in both guises. **$**

Maldon

Clare House
99 High Street
Tel: 5475 2229
www.clarehouse.com.au
Beautiful Victorian villa providing bed and breakfast right in the heart of this time-capsule township. Warm welcome from the owners. **$$$**

PRICE CATEGORIES

Price categories are for a double room without breakfast:
$ = under A$80
$$ = A$80–130
$$$ = A$130–200
$$$$ = over A$200

DANDENONGS AND THE YARRA VALLEY

Healesville

Healesville Hotel
256 Maroondah Highway
Tel: 5962 4002
www.yarravalleyharvest.com.au
Seven simple but chic bedrooms await those who've enjoyed the gourmet treats in the pub below. **$$**

Sanctuary Park Cottages
85 Badger Avenue
Tel: 5962 6240
www.sanctuarypark.com.au
Private cottage accommodation decorated in Australian style, across the road from Healesville Sanctuary. **$$$**

Olinda

Como Cottages
1465 Mt Dandenong Tourist Road
Tel: 9751 2264
www.comocottages.com
Rustic, self-contained bed-and-breakfast cottages in a lush setting that cater for couples and groups. Within walking distance of local villages. **$$$**

Yarra Valley

Chateau Yering
42 Melba Highway
Tel: 9237 3333

www.chateauyering.com.au
A touch of Victorian splendour in the grounds of an acclaimed vineyard. **$$$$**

PHILLIP ISLAND AND WILSONS PROM

Cowes

Amaroo Caravan Park and YHA Hostel
Corner of Church and Osborne Streets
Tel: 5952 2548
www.amaroopark.com
In the main town, this friendly hostel and caravan park is the best budget option by far. **$**

Quest Phillip Island
Corner of Bass Avenue and Chapel Street
Tel: 5952 2644
www.questphillipisland.com.au
Modern apartments with every facility, in a central location. Part of an ever-reliable chain. **$$$**

Waratah

Bayview House
202 Soldiers Road, Waratah North
Tel: 5687 1246
www.bayviewhouse.com.au
B&B or self-catered accommodation in a modern house with views across farmland

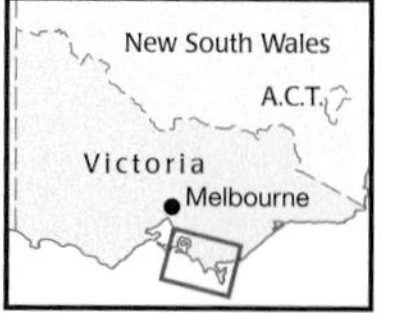

to Wilsons Promontory. Set in three acres of gardens. **$$$**

THE MOUNTAINS

Beechworth

Provenance Restaurant & Luxury Suites
86 Ford Street
Tel: 5728 2223
www.theprovenance.com.au
Stylish B&B rooms with an award-winning restaurant attached. **$$$$**

Bright

Barrass's John Bright Motor Inn
10 Wood Street
Tel: 5755 1400
Reliable, good-value motel close to the centre of town. **$$**

Luxury Townhouses
Bright Motor Inn, 1 Delany Avenue
Tel: 5750 1433
www.brightmotorinn.com.au
Part of the otherwise undistinguished Bright Motor Inn, these houses live up to their name and throw in the best location in town, right by the river. **$$$$**

Falls Creek

Julians Lodge
18 Slalom Street
Tel: 5758 3211
www.julianslodge.com
Long-running and still one of the best. **$$$**

Mansfield

Mansfield Motel
3 Highett Street
Tel: 5775 2377
www.mansfieldmotel.com.au
See how a bog-standard motel can be transformed into a smart, modern facility. **$$**

Mount Buller

Hotel Pension Grimus
224 Breathtaker Road
Tel: 5777 6396
www.pensiongrimus.com.au
A friendly, great-value lodge. All rooms have spa baths. Families welcome. **$$$**

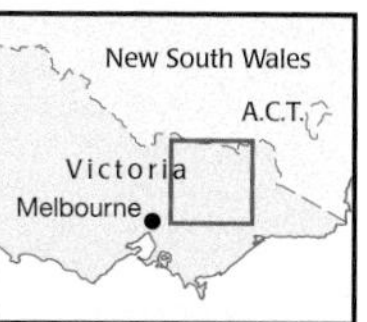

Mount Hotham

Arlberg Resort
Mount Hotham
Tel: 5986 8200
www.arlberghotham.com.au
A sizeable apartment block that sells itself on being value for money. Includes swimming pool, spa and steam room. Ski and board hire available. **$$$$**

SHOPPING

BEST BUYS

Melburnians have taken shopping seriously for a long time, as evidenced by the large number of elegant 19th-century arcades and venerable open-air markets across the city, and also by today's giant precincts and chic boutiques. Every area has its own retail flavour, whether it's Collins Street for high-end fashion and jewellery, Bourke Street for grand department stores, Flinders Lane for local designers' latest creations, Richmond for factory outlets or Fitzroy for alternative style and retro fashion.

WHAT TO BUY

Aboriginal Art

In Australia, Aboriginal artists sell their work in art centres, specialist galleries and craft stores, and through agents. Each traditional artist owns the stores to his or her particular stories, motifs and tokens.

Bark paintings are the most common form of Koorie (Aboriginal) art, but look out for contemporary works on board, boomerangs and didgeridoos. Indigenous fabric designs by artists such as Jimmy Pike are eagerly sought.

Flinders Lane is home to a number of private galleries selling Aboriginal art by renowned artists. The shop at the Koorie Heritage Trust in King Street has an excellent range of affordable Aboriginal crafts and gifts, including didgeridoos, boomerangs, clothing and ceramics.

Gallery Gabrielle Pizzi
Level 3, 75–77 Flinders Lane
Tel: 9654 2944
www.gabriellepizzi.com.au

Flinders Lane Gallery
137 Flinders Lane
Tel: 9654 3332
www.flg.com.au

Koorie Heritage Trust Shop
295 King Street
Tel: 8622 2600
www.koorieheritagetrust.com

Fashion

Australians are generally renowned for their relaxed style, but in Melbourne you'll notice the locals raise the style stakes a notch or two, with a lot more people dressing up and experimenting with their individual look. Akira Isogawa, Saba, Alannah Hill, Collette Dinnigan, Wayne Cooper and Zimmerman are some of the biggest names in Australian fashion that are worth looking out for. You will find their

boutiques in the city centre and along Toorak Road and Chapel Street in South Yarra.

Food and Drink

Local delicacies include cheese and wine. The deli section at the Queen Victoria Market is an excellent place to discover and taste delights from local producers. Australian wine can be bought at any pub or bottle shop; you can also get some fine bottles direct from the cellar door in the Yarra Valley.

Crown Lager, Victoria Bitter, Carlton Draught and Melbourne Bitter are the major local beers.

Mountain Goat is a successful local microbrewery specialising in ales that are a favourite with discerning drinkers. 3 Ravens is an emerging microbrewery that specialises in some fine ales, although they are harder to come by and generally found in the city and inner north.

Souvenirs

You will find an abundance of souvenir outlets along Swanston Street and plenty of cheap souvenirs at the outdoor section of Queen Victoria Market. More upmarket souvenirs and gifts, including opals, handmade crafts, clothing and jewellery, can be found at Southgate shopping centre on Southbank. Melbourne's markets are another good spot for buying unique, locally made gifts and souvenirs.

WHERE TO BUY

City

Melbourne sees itself as Australia's major fashion centre. In the city centre, a lot of the shopping is in the vicinity of Bourke Street Mall, which is home to the major department stores Myer and David Jones, as well as book, music and fashion stores. Shopping centres include the Melbourne Central complex, with its multi-level glass atrium, and GPO, the refurbished Post Office on the corner of Bourke and Elizabeth streets. Collins Place offers more than 40 stores, Collins two3four is a well-designed modern complex that boasts the largest bookshop in the city, and Australia on Collins features more than 60 stores, many with imported fashions. For the cost-conscious, factory outlet malls are located adjacent to Southern Cross Station and the new conference centre.

Melbourne has several famous shopping arcades. The oldest, the Royal Arcade, dates from 1870 and, along with the intimate Block Arcade, is one of Melbourne's landmarks *(see page 118)*.

Shopping Secrets (www.shoppingsecrets.com) is an innovative shopping guide to Melbourne in a compact deck of cards. Each card includes a description of a store and a map of its location. Available from good bookstores.

Melbourne Central
Corner of La Trobe and Swanston streets

GPO
Corner of Bourke and Elizabeth streets

Collins Place
45 Collins Street

Collins two3four
234 Collins Street

Australia on Collins
260 Collins Street

Royal Arcade
308 Little Collins Street

Block Arcade
282 Collins Street

Inner City

In South Yarra and Toorak, Chapel Street and Toorak Road are for the well-heeled only. The Windsor end of Chapel Street and Greville Street in Prahran are where you will find funkier designers and second-hand stores. Younger, alternative designers tend to congregate along Brunswick Street, Fitzroy, and on Smith Street in Collingwood. Richmond has a popular strip of factory outlets on Bridge Road and bargain clothing shops where you can also buy clothes by young designers. Chadstone is the largest shopping centre in Australia and still growing.

Chadstone Shopping Centre
341 Dandenong Road,
Chadstone
Tel: 9563 3355
www.chadstoneshopping.com.au

Department Stores

Melbourne's main department stores are Myer and David Jones. They both offer an extensive range of goods, from fashion and accessories to hardware and homeware. Target, Big W and KMart fill a similar role at the lower end of the price spectrum.

Myer
314 Bourke Street Mall
Tel: 9661 1111

David Jones
310 Bourke Street Mall
Tel: 9643 2222

Target
236 Bourke Street
Tel: 9653 4000

Big W
QV Village, corner of Swanston and Lonsdale streets
Tel: 9650 7355

KMart
Corner of Victoria and Burnley streets, Richmond
Tel: 9421 0100

Tours

Shopping tours have become one of the city's biggest tourist draws: they usually include lunch and can take in Melbourne's famous factory outlets and seconds shops. Or you can choose a tour that will lead you to those harder-to-find local designers who are often hidden in Melbourne's labyrinth of laneways.

Hidden Secrets Tours
Tel: 9663 3358
www.hiddensecretstours.com
The Lanes and Arcades Tour leads you to more than 50 local designers and speciality shops.

Markets

Markets are very popular and are a great place to soak up the local atmosphere. There's the lively Queen Victoria Market, or the comprehensive Prahran Market, which attracts the Melbourne gourmets. Craft markets such as the Rose Street Artist's Market in Fitzroy and the Shirt and Skirt Market at Abbotsford Convent are where you can uncover up-and-coming design talent.

Queen Victoria Market
513 Elizabeth Street
www.qvm.com.au
Tue and Thur 6am–2pm, Fri 6am–5pm, Sat 6am–3pm, Sun 9am–4pm
Historic market with great atmosphere. Wander the delis and produce sections while snacking on a bratwurst. Lots of cheap clothing and souvenirs in the massive open-air section.

Prahran Market
163 Commercial Road, South Yarra
Tue, Thur and Sat dawn–5pm, Fri dawn–6pm, Sun 10am–3pm
Locals flock here for fresh food and gourmet produce. Free face-painting and live music on Sundays.

Rose Street Artist's Market
60 Rose Street, Fitzroy
Sat–Sun 11am–5pm
The place for the latest from Melbourne's emerging designers.

Shirt and Skirt Market
Abbotsford Convent, 1 St Heliers Street, Abbotsford
Third Sunday of every month 10am–4pm
Fashion designers showcase their latest creations in the beautiful setting of the convent.

Camberwell Market
Station Street, Camberwell
Sun 6.30am–12.30pm
A Melbourne institution. Browse the abundance of bric-a-brac, second-hand fashion and collectables. More than 350 stalls.

Ceres Organic Market
Corner of Roberts and Stewart streets, Brunswick East
Wed and Sat 9am–1pm

Food and craft market held every Wednesday and Saturday morning. Featuring organic produce and local artisans selling a range of items, including handmade clothing, natural skincare products and recycled goods.

Federation Square Book Market
Federation Square
Sat 11am–5pm
Pick up some new or second-hand reading material at Australia's only weekly book market.

South Melbourne Market
Corner of Cecil and Coventry streets, South Melbourne
Wed and Sat–Sun 8am–4pm, Fri 8am–5pm
Lots of fresh food as well as clothes and gifts.

St Andrews Community Market
Kangaroo Ground, Kinglake Road, St Andrews
Sat 8am–2pm
Leafy setting for this vibrant craft and produce market on the outskirts of Melbourne. There's also food and entertainment.

St Kilda Esplanade Arts and Craft Market
St Kilda Esplanade
www.stkildamarket.com
Sun 10am–5pm
Soak up some sun, fresh sea air and beachside views while browsing about 150 stalls selling handmade arts and crafts.

Sunday Market at the Arts Centre
St Kilda Road, Southbank
Sun 10am–4pm
Bustling market that specialises in local handmade goods.

ACTIVITIES

THE ARTS, NIGHTLIFE, EVENTS AND FESTIVALS, KIDS, SPORTS, OUTDOOR ACTIVITIES AND TOURS

Sydneysiders might disagree, but Melbourne has a good claim to be Australia's cultural capital. Whether your tastes veer towards concerts, ballet or opera, theatre, comedy or cabaret, rock, jazz or electro, you'll have no problem in finding live performances to satisfy them. There's a wide choice, too, when it comes to art, film and other cultural festivals. And that's not to mention the city's obsession with sport. Whether you want to play, watch or gamble on it, Melbourne can accommodate you.

THE ARTS

Art Galleries

Melbourne is passionate about its art and culture. If you are too, there are more than 100 public and private galleriesin which to lose yourself. The National Gallery of Victoria's collection is split between two sites: at Federation Square you will find the Ian Potter Centre, which is dedicated to Australian art, while a short walk away, on St Kilda Road, you'll find the international collection.

Flinders Lane is home to many commercial galleries, including artists' studios and indigenous art collections. If you are exploring the city on foot, you will notice that a lot of Melbourne's art is outdoors, in the streetscape.

Hidden Secrets Tours have an Art and Design walk taking in some of the best of the public artworks on Melbourne's streets, or you can pick up a free *Art Walk* brochure from the Melbourne Visitor Centre at Federation Square for a self-guided tour. On a three-hour Walk to Art tour, you will get an introduction to Melbourne's art world and be led to some of the harder-to-find galleries and design studios.

For the latest on Melbourne's subculture, subscribe to the weekly *Three Thousand* e-newsletter, or browse its archives at www.threethousand.com.au.

One of the best ways to find out what's going on is to buy a copy of *Art Almanac*, a monthly booklet with listings of galleries and exhibitions, or the similar bi-monthly *Art Guide Australia*. Both cost A$4 and are available from galleries, some bookshops and newsagents. You can also find listings online at www.art-almanac.com.au.

Hidden Secrets Tours
Tel: 9663 3358
www.hiddensecretstours.com
Art and Design Walk every Saturday.

Walk to Art Tours
Tel: 8415 0449
www.walktoart.com.au
Every Wednesday and Saturday or an express tour on Friday.

Some of Melbourne's most renowned galleries are:

NGV International
180 St Kilda Road
Tel: 8620 2222
www.ngv.vic.gov.au/ngvinternational
Open Wed–Mon 10am–5pm
An extensive collection of international art from around the globe.

Ian Potter Centre: NGV Australia
Federation Square
Tel: 8662 1555
www.ngv.vic.gov.au/ngvaustralia
Open Tue–Sun 10am–5pm
Excellent collection of Aboriginal and Australian colonial art, as well as more modern work.

Melbourne Museum
Carlton Gardens, Nicholson Street, Carlton
Tel: 131 102
www.melbourne.museum.vic.gov.au
Open daily 10am–5pm
Home to Melbourne's IMAX

theatre and Australia's icon of horse racing, Phar Lap.

Koorie Heritage Trust
295 King Street
Tel: 8622 2600
www.koorieheritagetrust.com
Open daily 10am–4pm
Galleries feature emerging and established Aboriginal artists. Guided cultural tours are also available.

Heide Museum of Modern Art
7 Templestowe Road, Bulleen
Tel: 9850 1500
www.heide.com.au
Open Tue–Sun 10am–5pm
Bucolic setting for newly refurbished and extended gallery.

The Australian Centre for Contemporary Art
111 Sturt Street, Southbank
Tel: 9697 9999
www.accaonline.org.au
Open Tue–Fri 10am–5pm, Sat–Sun 11am–6pm

ACMI (Australian Centre for the Moving Image)
Federation Square
Tel: 8663 2200
www.acmi.net.au
Open daily 10am–6pm

City Lights
Centre Place and Hosier Lane
Open 24 hours a day, rain or shine
Stencil graffiti and works by local and international artists on the laneway walls are illuminated by lightboxes at night.

Strips of contemporary galleries are mushrooming in the inner suburbs, with Gertrude and Smith streets in Collingwood leading the way. Visit:
www.gertrude.org.au
www.ccp.org.au

Concerts

The Melbourne Symphony Orchestra (www.mso.com.au) performs at a variety of locations, including the Melbourne Town Hall and the Arts Centre from March to October, while chamber-music concerts can be heard at the new Melbourne Recital Centre.

Much of Melbourne's rock and jazz scene is found in its thriving pub venues. Listen to the gig guide on the FM stations 3RRR (102.7 FM), 3MMM (105.1 FM) and 3PBS (106.7 FM). The Esplanade Hotel (The Espy) and the Prince of Wales Bandroom, both in St Kilda, have for years been a good bet for rock music, as have the Corner Hotel in Richmond and the Hi-Fi Bar in the city. The Northcote Social Club is another popular venue to see local and visiting acts. The cutting-edge jazz venue is Bennetts Lane in the city.

Cover charges vary widely depending on the night of the week and the band that is playing (from around A$10, but free on some nights).

The best listings for Melbourne's lively music scene can be found in the Entertainment Guide (EG) in *The Age* newspaper every Friday, or the free weeklies *Inpress* and *Beat.*

The Esplanade (The Espy)
11 The Esplanade, St Kilda
Tel: 9534 0211
www.theesplanadehotel.com.au

Prince of Wales Bandroom
29 Fitzroy Street, St Kilda
Tel: 9536 1168
www.princebandroom.com.au

Corner Hotel
57 Swan Street, Richmond
Tel: 9427 9198
www.cornerhotel.com

Hi-Fi Bar
125 Swanston Street
Tel: 9654 7617
www.thehifi.com.au

Northcote Social Club
301 High Street, Northcote
Tel: 9489 3917
www.northcotesocialclub.com

The Tote
71 Johnston Street, Collingswood
Tel: 9419 5320
www.thetotehotel.com

Bennetts Lane Jazz Club
25 Bennetts Lane
Tel: 9663 2856
www.bennettslane.com

Theatre

Melbourne is noted for its high-quality performances of comedy, theatre and music. There are always theatre productions at the city's major arts venue, the Arts Centre, which has three theatres. Other major commercial theatres include the grand Princess Theatre, Her Majesty's and the spectacularly refurbished 2,160-seat Regent Theatre.

The Melbourne Theatre Company is the major drama company, performing at the Arts Centre and in its new spaces around the corner in Southbank Boulevard. More adventurous work can be found at the Malthouse, Red Stitch and La Mama.

The best listings for Melbourne's lively performing arts scene can also be found in the Entertainment Guide (EG) in every Friday issue of *The Age* newspaper or the free weekly street press: *Inpress* and *Beat*. For theatre, the quickest way to find out what's on and where is to use the online service Theatre Alive (www.theatrealive.com.au). Melbourne's main venues for plays, musicals, dance and opera:

The Arts Centre
100 St Kilda Road
Tel: 9281 8000
www.theartscentre.com.au
Australia's and the world's leading companies perform here, including the Royal Shakespeare Company and the Sydney Dance Company.

Princess Theatre
163 Spring Street
Tel: 9299 9800
www.marrinertheatres.com.au
A historic venue where big-budget productions such as *Phantom of the Opera* and *Cats* are staged.

Her Majesty's
219 Exhibition Street
Tel: 8643 3300
www.hmt.com.au
Musicals, opera and ballet are all performed in this historic theatre.

Regent Theatre
191 Collins Street
Tel: 9299 9800
www.marrinertheatres.com.au
After being through numerous reincarnations, the lavishly restored Regent Theatre reopened for musicals and concerts in 1996.

The Forum
Corner of Russell and Flinders streets
www.marrinertheatres.com.au
This theatre hosts contemporary music of all styles except when acting as a venue for the comedy or film festivals.

The Malthouse
113 Sturt Street, Southbank
Tel: 9685 5111
www.malthousetheatre.com.au
A beacon for contemporary Australian theatre.

Red Stitch
2 Chapel Street, St Kilda
Tel: 9533 8083
www.redstitch.net
One of Melbourne's leading independent theatre companies.

La Mama
205 Faraday Street, Carlton
Tel: 9347 6142
www.lamama.com.au
Nurtures new and unconventional theatre talent.

Dance

The national company, the Australian Ballet, is based in Melbourne and runs regular seasons at the Arts Centre and elsewhere. Chunky Move concentrates on modern dance and more experimental work, runs dance classes and workshops, and performs at the Malthouse Theatre and elsewhere.

Dancehouse is a centre for research, training and performance in contemporary dance, and gives performances in its studios and elsewhere around the city.

The Australian Ballet Centre
Tel: 9669 2700
www.australianballet.com.au

Chunky Move
Tel: 9645 5188
www.chunkymove.com.au

Dancehouse
150 Princes Street, North Carlton
Tel: 9347 2860
www.dancehouse.com.au

Opera

The Victoria State Opera merged with the Sydney-based Australian Opera in the 1990s to form Opera Australia. Most performances are now in Sydney, but there are regular seasons in Melbourne's Arts Centre.

The local torch is now carried by Victorian Opera, rapidly establishing a name for itself with backing from the State Government, and performing throughout Victoria, as well as at various venues in the city.

Opera Australia
Tel: 9685 3777
www.opera-australia.org.au

Victorian Opera
Tel: 9001 6400
www.victorianopera.com.au

Cinema

You won't be short of options for film in Melbourne. There are plenty of theatres where quality art and independent films are shown, including the fabulous Astor Theatre, the Kino, Cinema Nova and the Australian Centre for the Moving Image (ACMI) at Federation Square. The Melbourne International Film Festival each winter is three weeks packed with the world's best and emerging film talent.

In the summer there are outdoor screenings in the Royal Botanic Gardens, on a rooftop of an office block and year-round at a couple of Drive-Ins.
www.melbournefilmfestival.com.au
www.stkildafilmfestival.com.au
www.caths.org.au/rivoli.htm
www.suntheatre.com.au
www.villagecinemas.com.au

Astor Theatre
1 Chapel Street, St Kilda
Tel: 9510 1414
www.astor-theatre.com
An Art Deco delight featuring cinema classics.

TICKETS

Tickets for theatre, sport, music and other events are often sold through agencies. Names and numbers are published in listings. Tickets can be booked by phone, online or in person. The two main ticket agencies are:

Ticketek
225 Exhibition Street; Crown Casino, Southbank; Rod Laver Arena, Batman Avenue; Virgin Music, Southern Cross Station
Tel: 132 849
www.ticketek.com.au

Ticketmaster
Athenaeum Theatre, 188 Collins Street; Etihad Stadium, Gate 2
Tel: 136 100
www.ticketmaster.com.au

Cinema Nova
380 Lygon Street, Carlton
Tel: 9347 5331 or 9349 5201
www.cinemanova.com.au
Melbourne's largest arthouse cinema complex. Also screens feeds from London's National Theatre and New York's Metropolitan Opera.
ACMI (Australian Centre for the Moving Image)
Federation Square
Tel: 8663 2583
www.acmi.net.au
Featuring rare, arthouse and cult films.
IMAX
Melbourne Museum, Rathdowne Street, Carlton
Tel: 9663 5454
www.imaxmelbourne.com.au
Documentaries, 3D films and often the latest mainstream films are featured in the massive IMAX format.
Hoyts Cinema Centre
Melbourne Central, corner of Swanston and Latrobe streets
Tel: 8662 3555
www.hoyts.com.au
Mainstream cinema.
Moonlight Cinema
Royal Botanic Gardens, Birdwood Avenue, South Yarra
Tel: 1300 551 908
www.moonlight.com.au
Open December to March. Bring a picnic and a blanket.
Rooftop Cinema
Level 6, Curtin House, 252 Swanston Street, Melbourne
Tel: 9663 3596
www.rooftopcinema.com.au
Open December to April. Relax in a deckchair and get distracted by the skyscrapers towering above.

NIGHTLIFE

Melbourne has a huge choice of nightclubs and bars offering cheap gigs. Just stroll along Brunswick Street, Fitzroy and take your pick. St Kilda still buzzes as it has for years, while newer hubs for an action-packed night out include Sydney Road, Brunswick, and High Street, Northcote – both to the north of the city centre.

Laneways in the CBD provide a mixed bag of bars, clubs and live-music venues. Many of these establishments are to be found behind anonymous doorways and attract punters through a mixture of word of mouth and discreet advertising. Most of the nightclubs in the "West End" King Street strip now exist as table-dancing and men's clubs.

For recommended bars, see the listings at the end of each Places chapter.

Gay-Friendly Bars

Candy Bar
162 Greville Street, Prahran
Tel: 9529 6566
Dance the night away here on Sundays.
DT's Hotel
164 Church Street, Richmond
Tel: 9428 5724
www.dtshotel.com.au
Cosy pub with drag shows, pool and regular barbecues.
Greyhound
1 Brighton Road, St Kilda
Tel: 9534 4189
www.ghhotel.com.au
Relaxed pub with drag shows, karaoke and live music.
The Opium Den
176 Hoddle Street, Collingwood
Tel: 9417 2696
Popular for its Drag Kings.
The Peel
Corner of Peel and Wellington streets, Collingwood
Tel: 9419 4762
www.thepeel.com.au
Sweaty dance club with a retro night on Sundays.
Xchange Hotel
119 Commercial Road, South Yarra
Tel: 9867 5144
www.xchange.com.au
Popular venue with video dance arena and drag shows five nights a week.

Live Music Venues

In Melbourne music is in the air you breathe. Whatever style or genre you prefer – including rock, alternative, electronica, hip-hop, funk, world, classical, jazz, blues, folk or fusion – you can find some of the best exponents in formal concert venues, unconventional spaces and more atmospheric pubs and bars.

At the classical end of the spectrum, the popular Melbourne Symphony Orchestra performs a packed season of concerts including huge arena specials. Chamber and choral music is hot, too, with a remarkable number of young players and composers creating work. Most, but not all, of these occur in the Central Arts Precinct.

Immersion in an authentic Melbourne nightspot means jumping on a tram, train or taxi to some of the key districts, mostly beyond the CBD. Here are some suggestions:

The Corner Hotel
57 Swan St, Richmond
Tel: 9427 9198
www.cornerhotel.com
The Corner is grungy, cosy and an easy place to be, with pool tables and a beer garden on the roof. The band room rocks to many top Australian and international bands.
The East Brunswick Club
280 Lygon Street, East Brunswick
Tel: 9387 9794
www.eastbrunswickclub.com
Friendly venue north of the city hosts local bands and roots-favouring international visitors.
The Esplanade Hotel
11 The Esplanade, St Kilda
Tel: 9534 0211
The "Espy" is one of Melbourne's quintessential music venues, with an ear-boggling history. Bands play every night. Try the legendary Gershwin Room, where SBS stages its weekly TV show, *RocKwiz*, or the front room.
Hi-Fi Bar
125 Swanston Street
Tel: 9654 7617

www.thehifi.com.au
Central venue offers close contact with big names. Stand-ups take over during the Comedy Festival.

The Night Cat
141 Johnston Street, Fitzroy
Tel: 9417 0090
www.thenightcat.com.au
This is definitely at the cool end of the choice spectrum, and has spawned a sister venue in the city (279 Flinders Lane). Big muso names drop in to listen to often danceable jazz, adding lustre to the retro ambience. If cool isn't working, head around to St David's Street and the **Rainbow Hotel**, for free live music every night, or **Bar Open**, an upstairs music venue in Brunswick Street itself.

The Northcote Social Club
301 High Street, Northcote
Tel: 9489 3917
www.northcotesocialclub.com
A cosy venue whose programming is eclectic, with folk, country, alternative, rock and various fusions. Really listening to fine artists is the thing here.

The Prince of Wales Hotel Bandroom
29 Fitzroy Street, St Kilda
Tel: 9536 1168
www.princebandroom.com.au
All kinds of international and local bands, rappers and DJs.

The Tote
71 Johnston Street, Collingwood
Tel: 9419 5320
www.thetotehotel.com
Archetypal sticky-carpet pub. Was a focal point in massive 2010 "save live music" campaign.

Other venues to check out include: **The Boite**, a more family-orientated world music café at 1 Mark Street, North Fitzroy (tel: 9417 3550); **Ding Dong Lounge** at 18 Market Lane in Chinatown (tel: 9662 1020; www.dingdonglounge.com.au) for alternative and indie rock; **Pony** at 68 Little Collins Street (tel: 9662 1026), which is more bohemian, with a mix of alternative music and special events;

the **Workers Club**, 51 Brunswick Street, Fitzroy (tel: 9415 8889) for DJs and quality live music; and **Revolver Upstairs** at 229 Chapel Street, Prahran (tel: 9521 5985; www.revolverupstairs.com.au) is a retro bar with an intimate space for live gigs. Also in Prahran, at 134 Greville Street, is **Boutique** (tel: 9525 2322; www.boutique.net.au), a lavish venue where the fashion-conscious come out to play.

Useful websites with information on these and other venues are:
www.spraci.com/directory/melbourne/venues
www.melbournebars.com.au
www.barfinder.com.au

Jazz

Both occasional jazz-lovers and real aficionados will find satisfaction in Melbourne.

Around May, the **Melbourne International Jazz Festival** delivers a remarkable line-up of local and international performers at a range of venues including Federation Square, Hamer Hall, Melbourne Town Hall and Bennetts Lane (www.melbournejazz.com).

Bennetts Lane Jazz Club (25 Bennetts Lane; tel: 9663 2856; www.bennettslane.com) is Melbourne's premier jazz venue, where sipping red wine and savouring high-calibre performances is the liturgy – tiny, cosy, relaxed, and open every night from 8.30pm, but worth arriving early to make sure of a seat.

Uptown Jazz Café at 177 Brunswick Street, Fitzroy (tel: 9416 4546; www.uptownjazzcafe.com), is the warmly regarded home to improvised music of all stripes.

The **Paris Cat** at 6 Goldie Place, off Little Bourke Street (tel: 9642 4711; www.pariscat.com.au), is cooler than cool, with a 1930s French jazz ambience. It is a featured venue during the annual Melbourne Fringe Festival in September.

For almost two decades, the **Wangaratta Festival of Jazz** has been a wonderfully laid-back, but high-quality, couple of days of jazz and blues in the regional town of Wangaratta, about three hours' drive northeast from Melbourne. It has evolved into a dense programme of about 100 events with nearly 400 artists (www.wangarattajazz.com).

Comedy

The Last Laugh was the birthplace of Melbourne's reputation as a comedy capital, and it is still going strong. The Melbourne International Comedy Festival offers three weeks of the best comedy in Australia and rivals

international festivals in Edinburgh and Montreal. Pick up the weekly street press (*Beat* and *Inpress*) for the latest listings. Useful websites are:
www.comedyfestival.com.au
www.melbournefringe.com.au
www.nica.com.au
www.circusoz.com

Last Laugh at the Comedy Club
Athenaeum Theatre, 188 Collins Street, Melbourne
Tel: 9650 6668
www.thecomedyclub.com.au
The Comic's Lounge
26 Errol Street,
North Melbourne
Tel: 9348 9488
www.thecomicslounge.com.au
Comedy is on the menu here seven nights a week.

Cabaret

You'll find cabaret, comedy and camp kitsch in equal measure at the Butterfly Club, housed in a Victorian shop in South Melbourne, open nightly except Mon–Tue.

The Famous Spiegeltent is a touring show of music, comedy and cabaret that plays a season in Melbourne most years, usually on the Arts Centre forecourt from October to December.
The Butterfly Club
204 Bank Street,
South Melbourne
Tel: 9690 2000
www.thebutterflyclub.com
Spiegeltent International
Tickets from Ticketmaster
Tel: 1300 136 166
www.spiegeltent.net

Gambling

Crown Casino, on the banks of the Yarra River, is Melbourne's most popular venue for gambling. Spanning two city blocks, it is the only casino in the state. There's the usual choice of traditional table games, plus what seem like miles and miles of poker machines (one-armed bandits). Designer shops, riverside restaurants, cafés and bars are also part of the complex, as well as a cinema and a five-star hotel.

Many pubs have a room where you can play electronic poker machines – the "pokies".

Crown Casino
8 Whiteman Street,
Southbank
Tel: 1800 818 088
www.crowncasino.com.au

Events and Festivals

A week rarely goes by in Melbourne without something being celebrated, and no other Australian city knows comedy like Melbourne's International Comedy Festival in March either. Sport is celebrated as eagerly as the arts, and there are highlights all year round. Spring is the busiest time of year, as footie fanatics from around the country descend on the city for the Australian Rules Football finals, while the Spring Racing Carnival brings the city to a halt on Melbourne Cup Day. *For more on festivals, see pages 146–7.*

Summer (Dec–Feb)

Boxing Day Test, 26 Dec
This cricket match at the MCG is a great sporting tradition.
Australian Open Tennis Championships, Jan
Tennis stars hit Melbourne for the first Grand Slam of the year.
Midsumma, Jan
Gay and lesbian cultural festival.
St Kilda Festival, Feb
Outdoor music and street party on festival day.
Chinese New Year, Feb
Chinatown comes alive with fireworks, lion dances and karaoke.
Melbourne Food and Wine Festival, Feb
The best Australian and international producers.

Autumn (Mar–May)

Australian Formula One Grand Prix, Mar
Albert Park roars with the excitement of track and off-track events.
Melbourne International Comedy Festival, late Mar
One of the world's biggest and best comedy festivals.
Melbourne International Flower and Garden Show, Apr
The best of Australian gardening is showcased in the World Heritage-listed Royal Exhibition Building and surrounding Carlton Gardens.

Winter (June–Aug)

Melbourne International Film Festival, July
Showcasing the best of world cinema.
Melbourne Design Festival, July
The Design Market at Federation Square is a highlight.
Melbourne Writers' Festival, Aug
Attracting more than 200 writers from around the world.

Spring (Sept–Nov)

Royal Melbourne Show, Sept
The countryside comes to town. Great for families.
Melbourne Fringe Festival, late Sept
Melbourne shows off its alternative side.
Melbourne International Arts Festival, Oct
The choicest morsels of world theatre, music, dance and opera.
Australian Motorcycle Grand Prix, Oct
Phillip Island provides a picturesque setting for this leg of the world championship.
Spring Racing Carnival, Nov
Australia's premier racing celebration, including the prestigious Melbourne Cup, "the race that stops the nation".

MELBOURNE FOR KIDS

There are plenty of attractions in Melbourne and its surrounds to keep both kids and parents happy.

Come face to face with some incredible Australian sea life in the 360-degree Oceanarium at the **Melbourne Aquarium** (corner King and Flinders streets; tel: 9923 5999). The **Melbourne Museum** (Carlton Gardens, Nicholson Street; tel: 131 102) features a children's gallery for three- to eight-year-olds, and the adjacent **IMAX theatre** offers plenty of family-friendly films. The forest gallery has more than 8,000 trees and plants from Victoria's native forests, and a 35-metre (115ft) -high roof to accommodate them all.

If you prefer to see a real-life forest, then just an hour east from the city centre you can travel by steam train, and in an open carriage, through beautiful forests and gullies on the historic **Puffing Billy Railway** (Old Monbulk Road, Belgrave; tel: 9757 0700).

Also about an hour's drive from the city, in the picturesque Yarra Valley, is **Healesville Sanctuary** (Badger Creek Road, Healesville; tel: 5957 2800), where you can get up close to Australia's native wildlife. It includes the Australian Wildlife Health Centre, where the sanctuary's vets have opened their doors for a behind-the-scenes look at the treatment of injured and orphaned animals.

A 90-minute drive from Melbourne takes you to the popular **Penguin Parade** on Phillip Island (Phillip Island Tourist Road, Cowes; tel: 5951 2800). Every evening at sunset, little penguins (the smallest penguins in the world) come out of the sea and waddle along the shore to their burrows.

Back in town, the **Collingwood Children's Farm** (end of St Heliers Street, Abbotsford; tel: 9417 5806) is a piece of the countryside in the middle of the city. Located on the banks of the Yarra River and open daily, it's a lovely setting and holds special monthly events that include Family Day (first Sunday) and farmers' markets (second Saturday).

And if all else fails, there's always Fairy Park at Anakie *(above, see page 204).*

SPORTS

To say that Melbourne is sport-obsessed is something of an understatement. This is the town that invented Australian Rules football, that hosts the country's favourite horse race and any number of international sporting events, the place where watching, playing or betting on sport is a major part of everyday life. *For more on Melbourne's sporting scene, see page 69.*

Spectator Sports

Australian Rules football – a mixture of rugby, soccer and Gaelic football – is at its best in Melbourne. Matches are held every Saturday, some Friday nights and Sundays during the March–September season. The finals pit the two top teams at the Melbourne Cricket Ground (MCG) before more than 100,000 fanatical supporters.

Another great passion is **horse racing**, held year-round on the metropolitan courses at Flemington, Caulfield, Moonee Valley and Sandown. Flemington is the home of the Melbourne Cup, an internationally famous racing event held on the first Tuesday in November.

December to February is the season for international **cricket** matches played at the Melbourne Cricket Ground, where the Boxing Day Test forms the year's highlight. If you're not up to the long slog of Test cricket, the short and sweet Twenty20 matches only take about three hours.

In January, the Australian Open Grand Slam **tennis** tournament is held on the banks of the Yarra at Melbourne Park.

Early March is the time for the Melbourne **Formula One Grand Prix** in Albert Park, while in October, bikers flock to Phillip Island for the Moto GP.

Soccer has blossomed since a national league was set up in 2005, followed by the national team's success at the 2006 World Cup. Founding "A" League member Melbourne Victory was joined by Melbourne Heart in 2010.

You can buy tickets at the gate for many sporting events, but you will need to book ahead for popular ones. Ticketek and Ticketmaster outlets sell tickets for a number of sporting events.

Melbourne Cricket Ground (MCG)
Brunton Avenue, Richmond
Tel: 9657 8888
www.mcg.org.au
This world-famous sporting ground and Australian shrine is close to the heart of any self-respecting sports fan. Home to the 1956 Olympics, the 'G hosts many major sporting events, including regular matches of Australian Rules football and international cricket. Tours available.

Flemington Racecourse
448 Epsom Road, Flemington
Tel: 1300-727 575
www.vrc.net.au
Melbourne's home of horse racing and host of the Spring Racing Carnival.

Melbourne and Olympic Parks
Batman Avenue
Tel: 9286 1600
www.mopt.com.au
Multiple venues host tennis, basketball and netball.

A distinctive new rectangular stadium, currently known as **AAMI Park**, opened in 2010. It can hold thirty thousand punters and hosts professional soccer and rugby.

Participant Sports

Golf

Melbourne harbours some of Australia's top courses in the famed "sandbelt" region in the southeastern suburbs. All "sandbelt" clubs are private, although golf tour operators such as Gimme Golf can organise access to exclusive courses, provided that players meet the clubs' strict requirements. Failing that, Melbourne has some of the nation's best public links. The Victorian Golf Association website has a comprehensive listing of clubs in the state.

Victorian Golf Association
15 Bardolph Street, Burwood
Tel: 9889 6731
www.golfvic.org.au

Huntingdale
Windsor Avenue, South Oakleigh
Tel: 9579 4622

Metropolitan
Golf Road, South Oakleigh
Tel: 9579 3122

Royal Melbourne
Cheltenham Road, Black Rock
Tel: 9598 6755

Yarra Bend
Yarra Bend Road, Fairfield
Tel: 9481 3729
Challenging public course.

Gimme Golf
Level 1, 1415 Toorak Road, Camberwell
Tel: 9809 1022
www.gimmegolf.com.au

Snow Sports

During a good season, an easy place to access the snow from Melbourne is Lake Mountain (www.lakemountainresort.com.au), a popular cross-country ski resort. There are also several toboggan runs here.

Further afield, Mount Buller (www.mtbuller.com.au), Mount Hotham (www.mthotham.com.au) and Falls Creek (www.fallscreek.com.au) are major downhill ski resorts with a variety of runs. The Victorian Snow Report has up-to-date information on snow, road and weather conditions (www.vicsnowreport.com.au).

Tennis

Melbourne Park, home of the Australian Open, has seven indoor courts and 22 outdoor courts available for public hire seven days a week, except in January.

Melbourne Park
Batman Avenue, Melbourne
Tel: 9286 1600
www.mopt.com.au

Watersports

Port Phillip Bay offers excellent sailing conditions, and yacht clubs are plentiful. Swimmers should head to the Melbourne Sports and Aquatic Centre (MSAC), the largest integrated sports complex of its type in Australia, on the edge of Albert Park Lake. Melbourne's Yarra River is great for canoeing and kayaking.

Melbourne Sports and Aquatic Centre
Aughtie Drive, Albert Park
Tel: 9926 1555
www.msac.com.au

Melbourne City Baths
Corner of Swanston and Victoria streets
Tel: 9663 5888
www.melbourne.vic.gov.au/melbournecitybaths
Pools, spas and saunas.

Fairfield Boathouse
Fairfield Park Drive, Fairfield
Tel: 9486 1501
www.fairfieldboathouse.com
Located on the Yarra River. Canoes, kayaks and rowing skiffs for hire.

The abundance of wind on Port Phillip Bay makes Melbourne a popular location for windsurfing and kite-boarding. Elwood and St Kilda are good spots.

Repeat Performance Sailboards
87 Ormond Road, Elwood
Tel: 9525 6475
www.rpstheboardstore.com
Equipment hire.

SHQ Boardsports
81 Beach Road, Sandringham
Tel: 9598 2867
www.shq.com.au
Learn windsurfing or kite-boarding here.

OUTDOOR ACTIVITIES

There are plenty of opportunities for outdoor activities both in the heart of the city and just a short drive out of Melbourne. *(For cycling see Transport on page 271.)*

Walking

Melbourne has an extensive system of trails that are shared by walkers and cyclists. The Capital City Trail loops around the city, taking in major attractions such as the Zoo and Southbank. With a total length of 29km (18 miles), you are better off tackling the entire trail on a bike; if you are on foot, snack on a bite-sized chunk.

Parks Victoria (www.parkweb.vic.gov.au) has a brochure, available in visitor information centres, called *Walking in Victoria's Parks* that highlights some excellent short and long-distance walks. One of the most popular hikes is the Great Ocean Walk, which stretches 91km (57 miles) from Apollo Bay to Glenample Homestead (near the Twelve Apostles). It can be broken down into shorter walks and takes in a lot of the coastal scenery that is missed by drivers doing the iconic Great Ocean Road.

Another destination that's rightfully popular with walkers is Wilsons Promontory National Park, the most southern tip of the Australian mainland.

Closer to Melbourne, there are some excellent short walks. You can hike among towering mountain-ash trees in the Dandenongs Ranges, while the Cumberland Walk in Yarra Ranges National Park leads you past beautiful waterfalls and to the tallest living tree in Victoria.

Beaches

Located on the shores of Port Phillip Bay, Melbourne's beaches have gentle waves and are packed in the summer months. St Kilda beach attracts the hordes in the summer and is a popular spot for promenading. Other popular beaches include South Melbourne, Middle Park, Brighton and Sandringham, which are all manned by lifeguards during the summer months (Nov–Mar).

Surfers will need to drive out of Melbourne to find some breaks. Torquay, about 95km (60 miles) southwest of Melbourne, is popular with day-trippers from the city and is home to the legendary Bells Beach, venue for the world-renowned Easter Surfing Classic.

GUIDES & TOURS

Popular tours include art and shopping tours in the city, golf tours, eco-tours and day trips to the Yarra Valley for wine tasting. *Neighbours* tours, which take visitors to see the real location of Ramsay Street and the studios for this long-running soap, are particularly popular with British travellers.

The Golden Mile self-guided walking tour takes in the city's historic sites of interest, while the Melbourne City Tourist Shuttle is a free hop-on, hop-off bus service that stops at key attractions across the city.

The Melbourne Visitor Centre at Federation Square can help you with information and the booking of all tours in Melbourne.

A–Z

AN ALPHABETICAL SUMMARY OF PRACTICAL INFORMATION

Admission Charges

Many attractions offer family tickets that can reduce the cost of entry considerably. Entry to Melbourne Aquarium, for example, offers generous savings on a family ticket.

Admission to Melbourne's public and private galleries is generally free, or a small fee. The National Gallery of Victoria is free, while the Melbourne Museum charges a token sum for adults and children are free. The major galleries may charge for major, temporary exhibitions.

The Smartvisit Card (www.seemelbournecard.com) gives the holder admission to more than 50 attractions in Melbourne as well as the surrounding regions. Attractions covered by the card include Melbourne Aquarium, Penguin Parade and Healesville Sanctuary. It comes in one-, two-, three- and seven-day versions, and can be purchased at the Melbourne Visitor Centre at Federation Square.

National Parks are generally free as well. During the peak summer period, popular spots such as Wilsons Promontory have a ballot system for camping and other accommodation that closes in July.

Budgeting for Your Trip

Australia has low inflation, and the basics – food, accommodation, admission charges – are still comparatively inexpensive. However, as a spin-off from the global financial crisis, the Australian dollar has become more expensive against other currencies, so prices for many international visitors have effectively gone up. A plate of noodles or pasta in an average Melbourne restaurant costs about A$15. A bottle of Australian wine from a bottle shop starts at about A$6, a 285ml glass of beer costs around A$3, and a cup of tea or coffee about the same.

Bus and coach travel is reasonable, and there are various saver tickets available if you are planning to travel on to regional Victoria or other states. Public transport in Melbourne is also inexpensive, with tickets starting at under A$4 and valid for two hours on all metro trains, trams and buses.

Hiring (renting) a small car

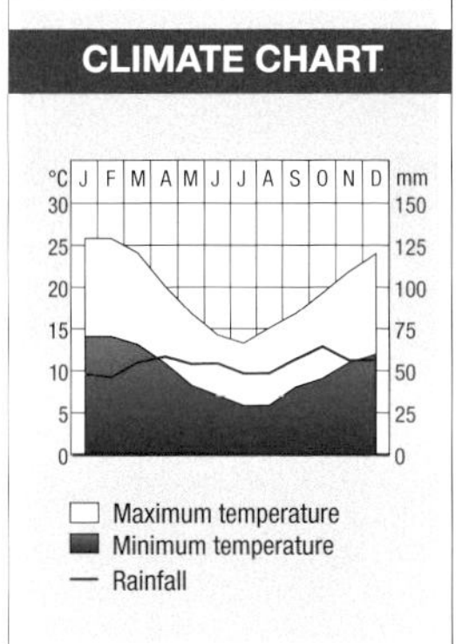

starts at A$35 per day. Petrol (gasoline) is more expensive than in the US, but cheaper than in most European countries.

A bed at a backpacker hostel is usually about A$20 a night, and a room in four- or five-star accommodation can start as low as A$200.

Climate

Melbourne has warm to hot summers. January and February are the hottest months, and the temperature can reach a sweltering 40°C (104°F) and beyond on some days. The summer average maximum is 25°C (77°C) and the average minimum 14°C (57°F).

In winter the average maximum temperature is 14°C (57°F) and the minimum 6°C (42°C), although wind chill can make it seem much cooler. Autumn and spring are generally mild, although early or long winters are not unusual.

What to wear: "Four seasons in one day" is a statement that locals regularly use to describe Melbourne's weather. Be ready for any conditions: a warm sweater may be necessary in the summer, and winter may call for heavy jackets, scarves and gloves. Bring wet-weather gear at any time of year and sunblock for the summer.

Dress is generally casual – shorts, a short-sleeved shirt or T-shirt and trainers or sandals are fine. Even fine-dining restaurants are generally smart rather than formal. Some restaurants and pubs draw the line at customers wearing tank tops, ripped jeans or flip-flops.

Crime and Safety

Australia is a relatively safe country. That said, you should use the same common sense and precautions as you would elsewhere regarding your possessions and personal security.

Issues surrounding prostitution, drugs and drunken behaviour occur as in all cities, but these are unlikely to affect travellers.

If an incident occurs, report it to the police or, for urgent attention, call the emergency services by dialling 000. Melbourne East Police Station is open 24 hours and is on Flinders Lane, between Swanston and Elizabeth streets.

Melbourne East Police Station
226 Flinders Lane
Tel: 9637 1100

Customs Regulations

Australia has extremely strict regulations about what can and cannot be brought into the country. Before disembarking from a plane, visitors are asked to fill in an Incoming Passenger Card. Australian customs officers check the information on the cards when passengers disembark, and may initiate a baggage search. There are heavy fines for false or inaccurate claims. It is always best to declare an item if in doubt.

Anyone over the age of 18 is allowed to bring into Australia A$900 worth of goods (not including alcohol, tobacco and, bizarrely, motor vehicle parts); 2,250ml (about 4 pints) of alcohol (wine, beer or spirits); 250 cigarettes, or 250 grams of cigars or tobacco products other than cigarettes. Members of the same family who are travelling together may combine their individual duty-/tax-free allowance.

Strict quarantine laws apply in Australia to protect the agricultural industries and native flora and fauna from introduced diseases. Animals, plants and their derivatives must be declared on their arrival. This may include items made from materials such as untreated wood, feathers or furs. The import or export of protected species, or products made from protected species, is a criminal offence. It is also illegal to export any species of native flora or fauna without a permit.

In addition, there are strict quarantine rules for produce when travelling between states in Australia.

Customs Information and Support Centre
Tel: 1300 363 263 (in Australia)
+61 2 6275 6666 (international)
www.customs.gov.au.

Disabled Travellers

Melbourne caters reasonably well for people with disabilities and mobility difficulty, but you would be wise to do some research before leaving home.

A good place to begin is the National Information Communications Awareness Network (NICAN), a national organisation that keeps an online database of facilities and services with access for the disabled, including accommodation and tourist sights.

City of Melbourne has set up the Melbourne Mobility Centre where numerous resources are available, such as equipment hire and recharging of scooter batteries. The council also publishes free mobility maps to the CBD and the sports precinct.

Easy Access Australia is a travel guide for people with a disability or mobility difficulty. It is available from good bookstores in Australia or can be purchased online at www.easyaccess australia.com.au. Access-able (www.access-able.com) is an online, international resource with travel information for mature travellers and travellers with disabilities.

NICAN
PO BOX 407, Curtain, ACT 2605
Tel: 1800 806 769
www.nican.com.au

Melbourne Mobility Centre
Level 1 Car Park,
Federation Square
Tel: 1800 735 266
www.melbournemobilitycentre.com.au

Electricity

The current is 240/250v, 50Hz, and Australia uses flat three-pin plugs. Most hotels have universal outlets for 110v shavers and small appliances. For larger appliances such as hairdryers, you will need a converter and a flat three-pin adaptor.

Embassies & Consulates

When travelling in Victoria contact:

British Consulate General
17th Floor, 90 Collins Street
Tel: 9652 1600
www.ukinaustralia.fco.gov.uk/en

Consulate of Canada
Level 27, 101 Collins Street, Melbourne (by appointment)
Tel: 9653 9674
www.canada.org.au

Embassy of Ireland
20 Arkana Street, Yarralumla, ACT
Tel: 02-6273 3022
www.embassyofireland.au.com
Visa and passport enquiries should be made to the embassy in Canberra.

United States Consulate General
553 St Kilda Road
Tel: 9526 5900
http://melbourne.usconsulate.gov

Overseas Missions

Canada
Australian High Commission, Suite 710, 50 O'Connor Street, Ottawa, Ontario
Tel: 613-236 0841
www.ahc-ottawa.org

Ireland
Australian Embassy, Fitzwilton House, Wilton Terrace, Dublin 2
Tel: 01-664 5300
www.ireland.embassy.gov.au

United Kingdom
Australian High Commission, Australia House, The Strand, London WC2B 4LA
Tel: 020-7379 4334
www.australia.org.uk

United States
Australian Embassy, 1601 Massachusetts Avenue, Washington DC 20036
Tel: 202-797 3000
www.usa.embassy.gov.au

EMERGENCY NUMBERS

For police, fire or ambulance simply call 000.

Gay & Lesbian Visitors

Melbourne has a thriving gay and lesbian scene. Clusters of the gay community exist around Commercial Road in Prahran, Smith Street in Collingwood, Brunswick Street in Fitzroy, High Street in Northcote and Sydney Road in Brunswick. Daylesford, a couple of hours' drive out of Melbourne, has one of the largest gay populations in regional Australia.

BnewS and the *Melbourne Community Voice (MCV)* are free publications you can find in cafés and bars, while JOY (94.9 FM) is Melbourne's radio station for the gay, lesbian, bisexual, transgender and intersex community.

Gay and Lesbian Tourism Australia promotes gay-owned or gay-friendly accommodation and tour operators via its website.

Alternative Lifestyle Organisation (ALSO) Foundation
Level 8, 225 Bourke Street
Tel: 9660 3900
www.also.org.au
For information on events and organisations serving the gay community.

The Gay and Lesbian Switchboard
Tel: 9663 2939
www.switchboard.org.au
Provides counselling and information services.

Gay and Lesbian Tourism Australia
Tel: 0422 632 690
www.galta.com.au

Health & Medical Care

Australia has excellent medical services. For medical attention outside working hours, go to the casualty department of a major hospital, or if the matter is less urgent, look for a medical practitioner in the Yellow Pages, or ask at your hotel for advice.

No vaccinations are required for entry to Australia. As in most countries, HIV and AIDS are a continuing problem despite efforts to control their spread. Heterosexual and homosexual visitors alike should use condoms if engaging in sexual activity.

For emergency medical assistance, tel: 000.

Pharmacies

Chemist shops are a great place to go for advice on minor ailments such as bites, scratches and stomach troubles. They also stock a wide range of useful products such as sunblock, nappies (diapers) and non-prescription drugs. If you have a prescription from your doctor, and you want to take it to a pharmacist in Australia, you will need to have it endorsed by a local medical practitioner.

Local Health Hazards

The biggest danger for travellers in Australia is the sun. Even on mild, cloudy days, it has the potential to burn. Wear a broad-brimmed hat and, if you are planning on being out in the sun for a while, a long-sleeved shirt made from a light fabric. It is recommended that you wear SPF30+ sunblock at all times, even under a hat. Avoid sunbathing between 11am and 3pm.

Care should be taken while swimming. Riptides resulting in dangerous conditions are fairly common, but not always obvious to those unfamiliar with the coastline. The best advice is to swim only at beaches that are patrolled by lifeguards, and to swim between the yellow and red flags. Never swim at night after a few drinks.

When doing outdoor activities in remote terrain, be aware that weather can change quickly and bring protective clothing for cold, wet and windy conditions.

Snakes will not attack unless directly provoked. As a prevention, wear covered shoes when walking in the bush. Snakes are also spotted regularly in some parks in Melbourne, particularly Yarra Bend Park, which has a lot of scrub and long grass. To be on the safe side, seek medical advice for any bite from snakes or spiders.

Internet Access

There are too many internet cafés or hotels with access to computers to list here. The Global Gossip organisation has 14 outlets in Melbourne alone. For those with their own laptops, Wi-fi hotspots are easy to find. Fed Square claims to be the biggest free Wi-fi site in Australia.

Left Luggage

There are few places where you can store luggage these days. Travellers Contact Point has short- and long-term luggage storage, and lockers are available at Southern Cross Station. Otherwise, your hotel may store bags for a few hours.

Travellers Contact Point
1st Floor,
361 Little Bourke Street
Tel: 9670 7252

Lost Property

The loss or theft of valuables should be reported to the police immediately, as most insurance policies insist on a police report. The police headquarters switchboard is staffed 24 hours a day, tel: 9247 6666.

For property lost on the major airlines or bus, coach and train services, try the following numbers:

Melbourne International Airport
Tel: 1800 687 374
Qantas Baggage Services
Tel: 8336 4100
Jetstar Baggage Services
Tel: 5282 6332 (Avalon airport)
Tel: 8836 5511 (Tullamarine Airport)
Virgin Blue
Tel: 9339 1750
Southern Cross Station Luggage Hall
Tel: 9619 2588
MetroTrains
Tel: 9619 2727
Yarra Trams
Tel: 1800 800 166

If you lose your traveller's cheques or want replacement cheques, contact the following:

American Express
Tel: 1800 688 022
Thomas Cook, MasterCard Traveller's Cheques
Tel: 1800 127 495
Interpayment Visa Traveller's Cheques
Tel: 1800 127 477

If you lose your credit card:

American Express
Tel: 1300 132 639
Diners Club
Tel: 1300 360 060
MasterCard
Tel: 1800 120 113 (for international visitors)
Visa
Tel: 1800 450 346

Maps

The Melbourne Visitor Centre has useful maps of Melbourne and regional areas, which often include information on supermarket opening times, the location of banks, ATMs, internet access and postal services. Ask for the *Melbourne Official Visitors Map*, which includes train and tram networks, but be warned that it can be difficult to get them to part with copies.

Media

Publications

To read some local news, pick up *The Age* or the *Sun-Herald*. For national news look for *The Australian* and the *Financial Review*, both thorough publications at the serious end of the spectrum, although the former can't hide its political leanings. There is a weekly Australian edition of *Time* magazine and *The Monthly* provides lively analysis. Most newsagents stock foreign newspapers.

Free street press includes *Beat* and *Inpress*, which are good for entertainment listings. You can usually pick these up at pubs, cafés and music stores. *MX*, a mixture of gossip, entertainment and news, is distributed free every weekday evening at train stations.

Radio and Television

The Australian Broadcasting Corporation (ABC) runs four national television channels as well as an extensive network of radio stations. ABC television offers excellent news and current affairs, as well as local and imported drama, comedy, sports and cultural programmes. Three commercial broadcasters, Ten, Nine and Seven, offer news, drama, soaps, game shows and travel shows. Channel 31 is Melbourne's community station. Hotels may provide access to cable television.

Of particular interest to overseas travellers is Australia's ethnic/multicultural broadcaster, SBS. The organisation's television channels offer many foreign-language films and documentaries, foreign news, international football, and Australia's best world news. SBS Radio (93.1 FM) has programmes in a variety of languages.

The local radio stations include Triple J (107.5 FM), providing alternative music, and

Classic FM (105.9 FM), which plays continuous classical music. Radio National (621 AM) has excellent national news and current affairs coverage. AM station ABC Melbourne on 774 is talk-based and features the peerless Jon Fain in the mornings. Community radio stations 3RRR (102.7) and 3PBS (106.7) are very popular in Melbourne, and feature anything from soul and reggae to programmes on architecture and gardening.

Money

The local currency is the Australian dollar (abbreviated as A$ or simply $), made up of 100 cents. Coins come in 5, 10, 20 and 50 cent units, and 1 and 2 dollars. Notes come in 5, 10, 20, 50 and 100 dollar bills. Single cents apply to many prices, and in these cases the amount will be rounded down or up to the nearest 5c. Carry smaller notes for tipping, taxi fares and payment in small shops and cafés.

There is no limit to the amount of foreign or Australian currency that you can bring into or out of the country, but cash amounts of more than A$10,000 (or its equivalent) must be declared to customs on arrival and departure.

Banks

The big four banks in Australia are the ANZ, Commonwealth, National and Westpac. Bendigo Bank is also big in Victoria. Trading hours are generally 9am–4pm Monday to Thursday, and 9am–5pm Friday. Some branches are open on Saturday mornings.

Credit Cards and ATMs

Carrying a recognised credit or debit card such as Visa, MasterCard, American Express or Diners Club is always a good idea when travelling. A debit card should provide access to EFTPOS (electronic funds transfer at point of sale), which is the easiest and often the cheapest way to exchange money – amounts are automatically debited from the selected account. Many Australian businesses are connected to EFTPOS.

Bank branches and Automatic Teller Machines (ATMs) are common throughout Melbourne.

Exchange

Foreign-exchange bureaux are located at Melbourne Airport and throughout the city. The Travelex branch at 261 Bourke Street (corner of Swanston Street) is open seven days a week.

Traveller's Cheques

All well-known traveller's cheques can be cashed at banks, hotels and similar establishments, and are as good as cash with many of the larger shops in major tourist areas. Smaller restaurants and shops may be reluctant to cash cheques, so you should also carry cards or cash.

Banks offer the best exchange rates on cheques in foreign currencies; most banks charge a fee for cashing cheques.

Opening Hours

Banks are generally open 9am–4pm Monday to Thursday, and 9am–5pm Friday. Some branches open Saturday mornings. Shops are open 9am–5pm (often later) Monday to Friday, and generally 10am–5pm at weekends. Thursdays and Fridays are late-night shopping in the CBD, with most stores keeping their doors open until 7pm or 9pm.

Postal Services

Post offices are generally open between 9am and 5pm Monday to Friday. There are a number of post offices in the CBD, including one at 250 Elizabeth Street and another at 45 Collins Street. There are also postal agencies in some newsagents.

Domestic Post

Posting a standard letter to anywhere in Australia costs 60 cents. The letter will reach a destination in the same city overnight, but may take up to a week if it is being sent to a far-flung part of the country. Keep in mind that postal deliveries are only made on weekdays.

Yellow Express Post bags and envelopes can be used to send parcels and letters overnight to other Australian capital cities. They represent very good value for money when compared with courier costs.

Overseas Post

The cost of overseas mail depends on the weight and size of the item. Postcards cost A$1.40 by airmail to the UK and the US. Standard overseas mail takes about a week to most destinations.

Express Post International (EPI) will reduce the delivery time to four or five working days for the UK and three to six working days for the US. It is priced according to weight and size. There is also an international courier service offered by Australia Post.

Post and EPI enquiries and information
Tel: 137 678
Express Courier International
Tel: 1800 007 678

Smoking

Smoking is banned in all enclosed workplaces in Victoria, which effectively rules out restaurants, bars and shopping centres. Covered train platforms and bus and tram spots are also included. Many venues have roof or courtyard refuges for smokers. There is also an increasing move towards banning smoking on beaches around the state, so look out for signs. This follows a vote for a ban by Port Phillip Council in November 2010, which affects many city beaches, including Port Melbourne and St Kilda. Other further-flung councils have adopted similar measures.

Student Travellers

Special rates are available for students across countless transactions during a stay in Melbourne. If in doubt, ask. A student union card from a reputable educational establishment is often enough, but there's no harm in investing in an International Student Identity Card or an International Youth Travel Card just to be sure.

Tax

A 10 percent Government Sales Tax is applied to virtually all purchases of goods and services in Australia. Most prices displayed in shops, hotels and restaurants already include GST so there are rarely last-minute surprises for the unwary.

Telecommunications

Telephones

Local calls in Australia are untimed, and cost on average 25c from private phones and 40c from public phones. Instead of making calls from hotel rooms, which can be double or triple the price, you should aim to use public phones. Having a phonecard will make this much easier. These are widely available from newsagents and other outlets displaying the Telstra logo. You can also send text messages (SMS) from a number of public phones.

Most interstate (STD) and international (ISD) calls can be made using phonecards. These calls are timed and can be expensive, but cheaper rates are available after 6pm and at weekends. Most overseas numbers can be dialled direct without the need for operator assistance.

You have to dial a regional code to call interstate. All regular numbers in Australia (other than toll-free or special numbers) are eight numbers long. The national code for Australia is 61 and the area code for Victoria is 03. If you are calling from overseas, drop the 0.

Numbers beginning with 1800 are toll-free. Numbers beginning with 13 are charged at a local rate, even if the call made is STD. Numbers beginning with 018, 04, 015, 019 are mobile-phone numbers.

Directory enquiries: 1223
Overseas assistance: 1225
Information on costs: 12552
International calls: dial 0011, followed by the national code of the country you are calling.

Mobile Phones

Most visitors will find that they can use their mobile (cellphone) without too much trouble. Contact your service provider before leaving home to find out what is involved.

You may find it easier to bring your own phone and buy a local SIM card kit and top it up with prepaid calls. There are reasonably cheap prepaid calls and mobile-phone deals from providers such as Virgin Mobile, Telstra, Optus, Three and Vodafone.

Internet-enabled handsets can save you a fortune by using Skype to make very cheap calls in free Wi-fi areas such as Fed Square.

Directories

The White Pages contain business and residential numbers in alphabetical order. Government numbers are also listed at the beginning of the book. Turn to the Yellow Pages directory if you need to find a particular service provider. It lists commercial operations under subject headings.

Faxes

There are many places from which you can fax documents, including hotels, video stores, newsagents, a variety of small businesses, and also post offices, where the rates are very reasonable.

Tipping

Tipping is not obligatory, but a small gratuity for good service is appreciated. It is not customary to tip taxi drivers or hairdressers, except perhaps by rounding bills up to the nearest dollar.

Restaurants do not usually include service charges, but it is becoming more common to tip waiters up to 10 percent of the bill for good service.

Toilets

Australians manage without euphemisms for "toilet". "Dunny" is slang that is rarely heard in the city, but "washroom", "restroom", "bathroom", "Ladies" and "Gents" are all understood. Some public toilets are restricted to daylight hours. If you get stuck, try the nearest pub or service station. Toilets are generally clean and have wheelchair access.

Public Holidays

New Year's Day 1 January
Australia Day 26 January
Labour Day 2nd Monday in March
Good Friday, Easter Saturday and Monday March/April
ANZAC Day 25 April
Queen's Birthday 2nd Monday in June
Melbourne Cup 1st Tuesday in November
Christmas Day 25 December
Boxing Day 26 December

Tourist Information

For pre-trip planning from overseas, a good starting point is Tourism Australia (www.australia.com). On its website you can get itinerary ideas and find a specialist Australian travel agent.

There is also the State Government-operated Tourism Victoria (www.tourismvictoria.com), which has excellent online resources. That's Melbourne, operated by the City of Melbourne, is another good source of information.

Accredited Visitor Information Centres are marked with the blue and yellow "i", and are usually open seven days a week. The thoroughly excellent Melbourne Visitor Information Centre is located at the northwest corner of Federation Square and is open 9am to 6pm daily. There is also a satellite operation in Bourke Street Mall. Red-jacketed volunteers can be found on the streets to help with enquiries.

Visit Victoria
www.visitvictoria.com
www.visitmelbourne.com
That's Melbourne
Tel: 9658 9658
www.thatsmelbourne.com.au
Melbourne Visitor Information Centre
Federation Square
Tel: 9658 9658
Australian Travel & Tourism Network
www.atn.com.au

Time Zone

Melbourne is on Eastern Australian Standard Time (EST), which is 10 hours ahead of Greenwich Mean Time, 15 hours ahead of New York and 18 hours ahead of California.

Daylight Saving operates from October to April: the clocks go forward 1 hour at the start of October, and back 1 hour at the start of April. With the seasons reversed from the northern hemisphere (where the clocks go back 1 hour in October and forward 1 hour at the end of March), Melbourne is 11 hours ahead of London (16 ahead of New York) in the Australian summer, but only 9 hours ahead during the Australian winter. The switch-over dates don't always correlate exactly.

Visas and Passports

Any visitor who is not an Australian citizen must have a passport valid for the entire period of their stay, and a visa that must be obtained before leaving home (except for New Zealand citizens, who are issued with a visa on arrival in Australia).

ETA Visas

The Electronic Transfer Authority (ETA) enables visitors to obtain a visa on the spot from their travel agent or airline office. The system is in place in over 30 countries including the UK and the US. ETA visas are generally valid for 12 months; single stays must not exceed three months, but return visits within the 12-month period are allowed. ETAs are issued free, or you can purchase one online for A$20 from www.eta.immi.gov.au.

Tourist Visas

These are available for continuous stays longer than three months, but must be obtained from an Australian visa office, such as an embassy or consulate. A fee of A$20 applies. Those travelling on tourist visas and ETAs are not permitted to work while in Australia. Travellers are asked on their application to prove that they have an adequate source of funding while in Australia (around A$1,000 a month).

Temporary Residence

Those seeking temporary residence must apply to an Australian visa office, and often must be sponsored by an appropriate organisation or employer. Study visas are available for people who undertake full-time registered courses. Working holiday visas are available to young people from some countries, including the UK, Ireland and Canada, who want to work as they travel.

Department of Immigration and Multicultural and Indigenous Affairs
Tel: 13 18 81 (in Australia) or the nearest mission outside Australia; www.immi.gov.au.

Weights & Measures

Australia uses the metric system of weights, measures and temperatures.
1 metre = approx 39 inches or 3.28 feet
1 kilometre = 1,093 yards or approx 0.6 mile
16 km = 10 miles
1 kilogram (kg) = approx 2.2lbs
1 litre = 1.75 pints
20°C = 68°F
30°C = 86°F

Every state in Australia has a different way of naming beer measurements. In Victoria, beer can be bought by the pot (285ml), pint (two pots) or jug. You can also buy beer in cans, stubbies (small glass bottles) or long-necks (750ml bottles).

FURTHER READING

Books are listed by author's name in alphabetical order

History

The Encyclopedia of Melbourne Edited by Andrew Brown-May and Shurlee Swain. With a happy irony, this astonishing doorstep of a book runs from Abattoirs to Zoo and captures every facet of the city in between.

The Melbourne Book: A History of Now by Maree Coote. Part-history, part-reflection, this book packs together interesting snippets on people, places and events that make up the city.

The Birth of Melbourne Edited by Tim Flannery. This fascinating anthology of extracts from journals, memoirs and newspaper reports traces the sometimes painful birth pangs of the settlement through to Federation at the beginning of the 20th century.

Architecture

Melbourne Architecture by Philip Goad (who wrote the Architecture chapter on page 77). A detailed analysis of the significant buildings in the centre and the suburbs, it takes a smooth chronological approach to the subject.

Walking Melbourne by Rohan Storey. National Trust-published guide to 250 of the buildings in the CBD. Reasonable detail and compact enough for a pocket.

Memoirs

Down Under by Bill Bryson. Covers Australia as a whole, including Melbourne and Victoria. The urbane, breezy style is deceptive – some serious research has gone into this entertaining travelogue.

In My Skin by Kate Holden. A tale of life on the streets as a junkie and hooker, set in St Kilda, but written with such verve and lucidity as to transcend the genre.

My Life As Me by Barry Humphreys. Hilarious, highly polished reminiscence of growing up in 1950s Melbourne, the genesis of his various characters and the path to a level of worldwide acclaim that saw Dame Edna Everage (not Humphreys, note) given the keys to her home city.

Unpolished Gem by Alice Pung. Leaving the Cambodia of Pol Pot as a child, Pung's assimilation to life in Footscray along with her extended family is the core of this revealing memoir.

Fiction

Shadowboxing by Tony Birch. Ten powerful, linked stories about a boy growing up in working-class Fitzroy in the 1960s.

Too Many Men by Lily Brett. One minute a domestic comedy, the next a surreal take on the Holocaust, it needs masterful control to pull it off. Brett achieves this with élan.

Illywhacker by Peter Carey. An expansive narrative by the 139-year-old self-confessed liar of the title takes us on a journey through history and the forging of the larrikin spirit that pervades the country. Funny and moving.

True History of the Kelly Gang by Peter Carey. The Kelly story in Ned's own words from "newly discovered" letters. A technical, if dry, tour de force.

The Art of the Engine Driver by Steven Carroll. Suburban Melbourne post-World War II is the setting for this measured look at how progress and change distort the lives of ordinary, struggling people. Low key but accomplished and beautifully written.

Man Bites Dog by Adam Ford. Facing the postman's traditional nemesis and dealing with other hazards in life after college, not least romantic ones, is the premise of this accomplished first novel, set in Melbourne.

Monkey Grip by Helen Garner. Captures with unremitting accuracy the tedium of life with self-obsessed hippies and junkies in 1970s Carlton.

Cocaine Blues by Kerry Greenwood. The first in an ongoing series of detective novels set in 1920s Melbourne featuring the feisty and sexy Phryne Fisher. Written with deft wit and a sardonic delight in her heroine's antics.

The Getting of Wisdom by Henry Handel Richardson. One of the classics of Australian literature, this coming-of-age novel set in late 19th-century Victoria plucks sizeable autobiographical chunks from the life of Ethel Lindesay (the author behind the pseudonym).

Power Without Glory by Frank Hardy. Lightly disguised story of corruption in business and political circles, this racy thriller is notorious for the libel case brought on behalf of the all-too-easily-identifiable protagonist.

Of a Boy by Sonya Hartnett. The story of nine-year-old Adrian, adrift in 1977 without family anchors and at a time when three other children have just disappeared. Heartbreaking but brilliant.

My Brother Jack by George Johnston. Strong enough to have inspired two television adaptations, this is a saga of two brothers living through 1920s and 30s depression-era Melbourne. Rich and complex.

Picnic at Hanging Rock by Joan Lindsay. Helped by Peter Weir's film version, this eerie story of schoolgirls disappearing in the picturesque Macedon Ranges is so convincing that many believe it to be based on real events.
Cricket Kings by William McInnes. The fabric of cricket underlies this novel set in Melbourne's western suburbs, and love for the game is as palpable as McInnes's love for his characters.
Seven Types of Ambiguity by Elliot Perlman. Barrister Perlman pitches into the legal world in this novel written from seven diferent perspectives, where a masterful storyteller is always in control of the threads. Recommended by the same author is ***Three Dollars***, a searing account of one man's descent into homelessness in the modern-day city.
On the Beach by Nevil Shute. Fifty years on, this novel still packs a punch. Melbourne is the last redoubt of humanity as the fallout from nuclear annihilation in the northern hemisphere heads remorselessly southwards.
The Broken Shore by Peter Temple. A sophisticated crime novel that reaches to the very heart of Australian society. It looks at small-town Victoria and the tricky interplay with the city, as well as the gnarled problem of white relations with Aboriginal people.
Everyman's Rules for Scientific Living by Carrie Tiffany. Set in the Mallee in northwest Victoria in the 1930s, Tiffany's novel tackles the conflict between the new world of scientific advance and an intractable land. Against this background a poignant love story plays out, but tragedy is never far away.
Loaded by Christos Tsiolkas. A story written with passion and quirky skill, *Loaded* unflinchingly sifts the problems of a gay Greek teenager coming to terms with both himself and a hostile city.
The Slap by Christos Tsiolkas. This time Tsiolkas skewers suburban Melbourne values in his bestselling, Man Booker prize-nominated novel.
Cafe Scheherazade by Arnold Zable. Taking as its starting point the (now closed) eponymous café in St Kilda's Acland Street, Zable weaves a testing tale of displacement and assimilation among the city's Jewish immigrants, and tracks his characters back to their disparate starting points.

Food

The Age Good Food Guide The bible for foodies in a city that is deadly serious about finding the best place to eat out. The definitive guide, published each August.
Cheap Eats Another annual *Age* publication, this time covering the best meals under A$30.
The Foodies Guide to Melbourne by Allan Campion and Michelle Curtis. Covers all the markets and specialist stores as well as cafés and restaurants – even cookery schools.

FEEDBACK

We do our best to ensure that the information in our books is as accurate and up-to-date as possible. However, some mistakes and omissions are inevitable and we are reliant on our readers to put us in the picture. We would welcome your feedback on any details related to your experiences using the book "on the road". The more details you can give us (particularly with regard to addresses, emails and telephone numbers), the better. We will acknowledge all contributions, and we'll offer an Insight Guide to the best letters received.

Please write to us at:
Insight Guides
PO Box 7910
London SE1 1WE
United Kingdom
Or send an email to:
insight@apaguide.co.uk

Other Insight Guides

Insight Guide: Australia is the complete guide to Oz, with features on food and drink, culture and the arts.

Insight City Guides cover ***Perth*** and ***Sydney*** in depth, while Regional Guides are available to ***New South Wales***, ***Tasmania*** and ***Queensland & the Great Barrier Reef***.

Insight Pocket Guides feature tailor-made itineraries and include a pull-out map. Titles include: ***Brisbane & the Gold Coast***, ***Cairns & the Great Barrier Reef*** and ***Perth***.

Insight Step by Step Guides contain a host of self-guided walks and tours produced by local writers. The series includes ***Sydney*** and ***Brisbane***, ***Cairns & the Great Barrier Reef***.

Insight Smart Guides are a new series with a unique A–Z approach. Titles include ***Perth*** and ***Sydney***.

Insight Fleximaps combine clear, detailed cartography with essential travel information. The laminated finish makes them durable and weatherproof. Titles include ***Brisbane & the Gold Coast***, ***Melbourne***, ***Perth*** *and* ***Sydney***.

MELBOURNE STREET ATLAS

The key map shows the area of Melbourne covered by the atlas section. An index of street names and places of interest shown on the maps can be found on the following pages. For each entry there is a page number and grid reference.

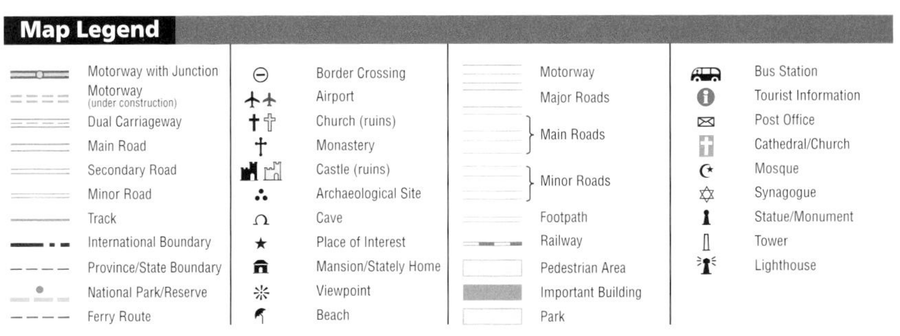

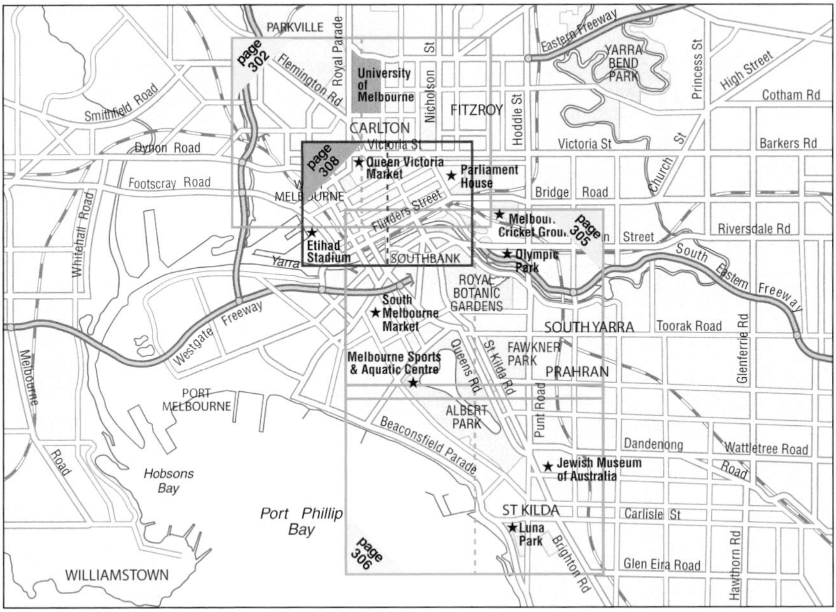

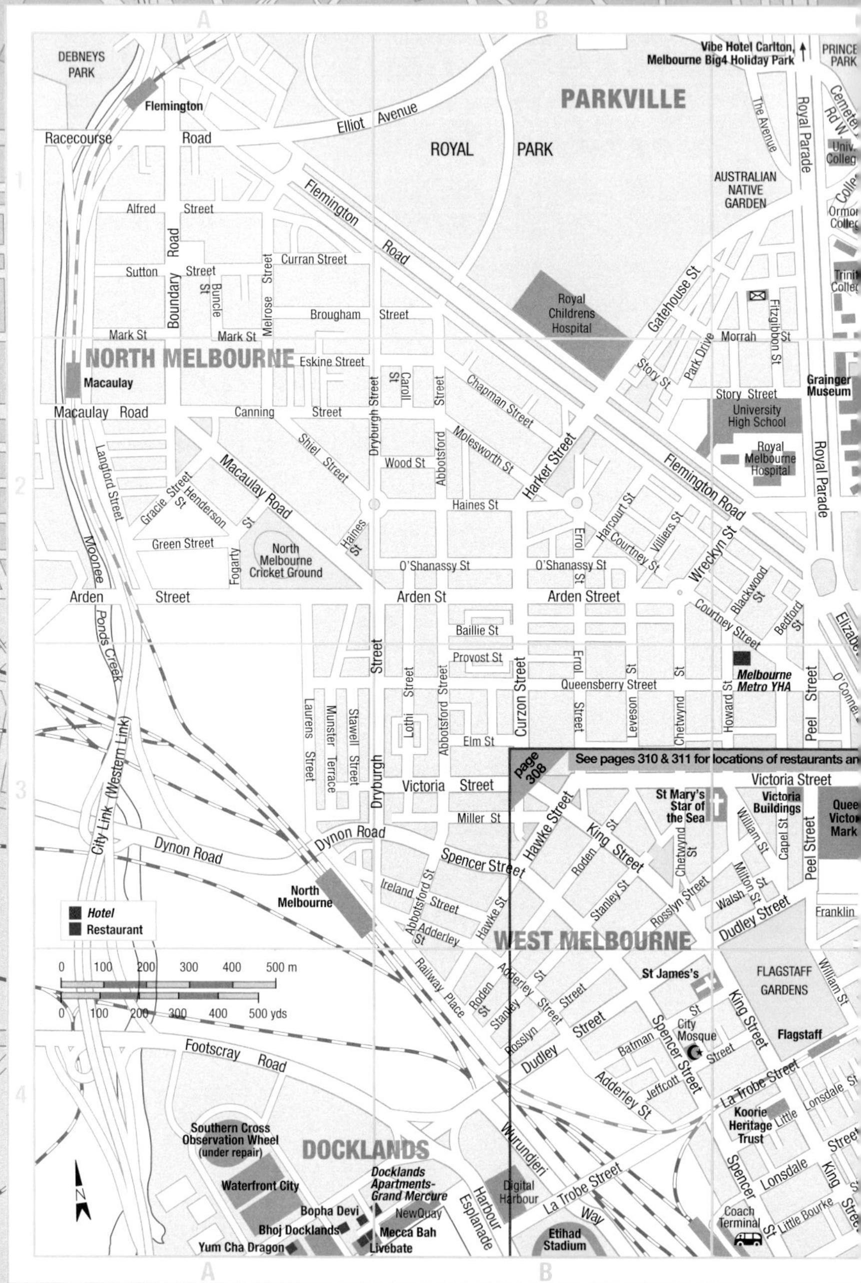
A
B
1
2
3
4
DEBNEYS PARK
Flemington
Racecourse Road
Elliot Avenue
PARKVILLE
ROYAL PARK
Vibe Hotel Carlton, Melbourne Big4 Holiday Park
The Avenue
Royal Parade
AUSTRALIAN NATIVE GARDEN
Flemington Road
Alfred Street
Curran Street
Sutton Street
Boundary Road
Buncle St
Melrose Street
Brougham Street
Royal Childrens Hospital
Gatehouse St
Fitzgibbon St
Mark St
Morrah St
NORTH MELBOURNE
Eskine Street
Park Drive
Story St
Macaulay
Caroll St
Street
Chapman Street
Story Street
Grainger Museum
Macaulay Road
Canning Street
Dryburgh Street
University High School
Shiel Street
Wood St
Abbotsford
Molesworth St
Harker Street
Royal Melbourne Hospital
Langford Street
Macaulay Road
Gracie Street
Henderson St
Haines St
Harcourt St
Villiers St
Errol St
Courtney St
Wreckyn St
Green Street
North Melbourne Cricket Ground
Fogarty St
Haines St
O'Shanassy St
Blackwood St
Moonee Ponds Creek
Arden Street
Arden St
Arden Street
Courtney Street
Bedford St
Baillie St
Provost St
Errol Street
Melbourne Metro YHA
Queensberry Street
Curzon Street
Leveson St
Chetwynd St
Howard St
Peel Street
City Link (Western Link)
Laurens Street
Munster Terrace
Stawell Street
Lothi Street
Abbotsford Street
Elm St
See pages 310 & 311 for locations of restaurants and
page 308
Victoria Street
Victoria Street
St Mary's Star of the Sea
Victoria Buildings
Miller St
Hawke Street
King Street
Roden St
William St
Capel St
Peel Street
Dynon Road
Dynon Road
Spencer Street
Chetwynd St
Milton St
North Melbourne
Ireland Street
Abbotsford St
Stanley St
Rosslyn Street
Walsh St
Dudley Street
Franklin
Hotel
Restaurant
Adderley St
Hawke St
WEST MELBOURNE
0 100 200 300 400 500 m
0 100 200 300 400 500 yds
Railway Place
Roden St
Adderley St
Stanley Street
St James's
FLAGSTAFF GARDENS
William St
King Street
Rosslyn Street
Dudley Street
Batman Street
City Mosque
Spencer Street
Flagstaff
Footscray Road
Adderley St
Jeffcott St
La Trobe Street
Lonsdale St
Koorie Heritage Trust
Little Lonsdale
Southern Cross Observation Wheel (under repair)
DOCKLANDS
Wurundjeri Way
Docklands Apartments-Grand Mercure
Waterfront City
Digital Harbour
La Trobe Street
Spencer St
Lonsdale
King Street
Bopha Devi
NewQuay
Harbour Esplanade
Coach Terminal
Little Bourke
Bhoj Docklands
Mecca Bah
Etihad Stadium
Yum Cha Dragon
Livebate
N

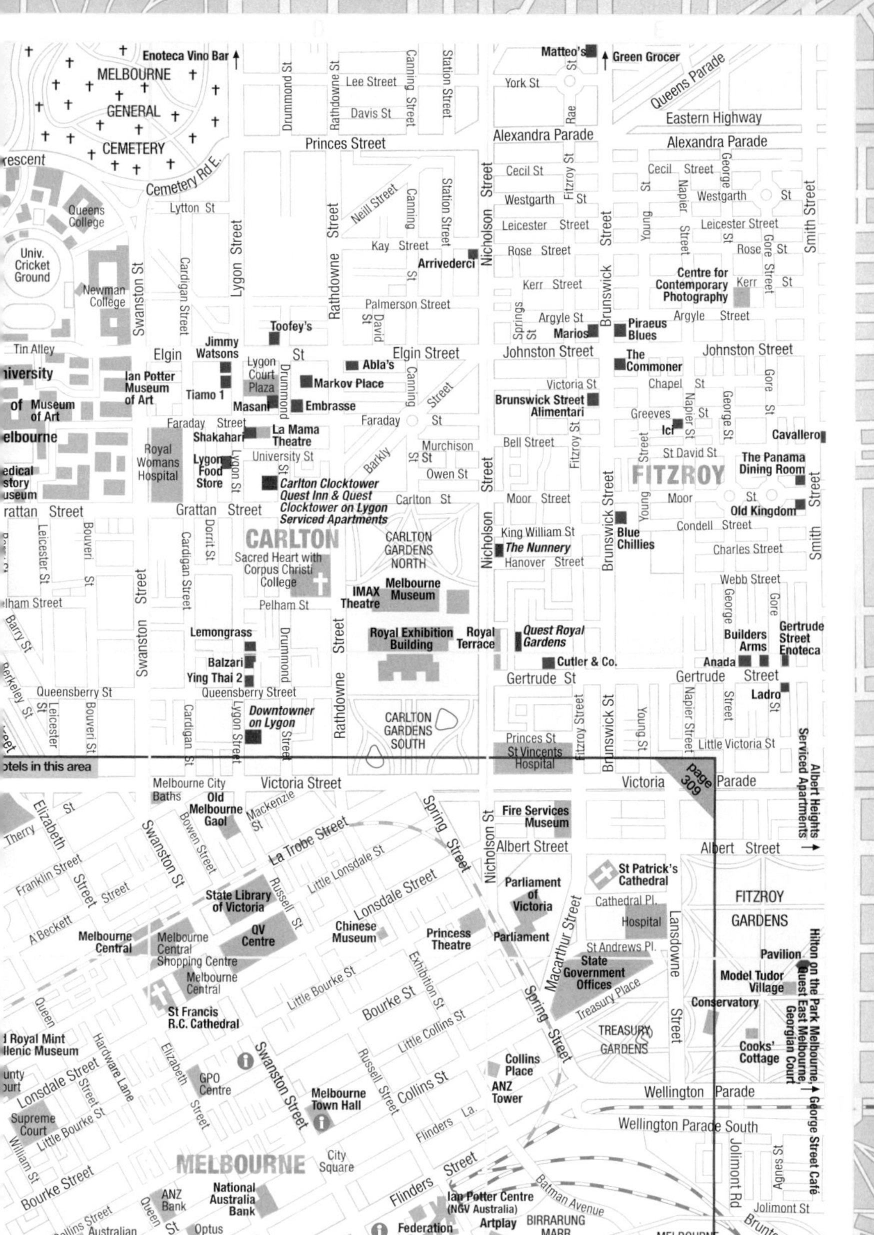

Enoteca Vino Bar
MELBOURNE GENERAL CEMETERY
Cemetery Rd E.
Queens College
Univ. Cricket Ground
Newman College
Tin Alley
University of Melbourne
Museum of Art
Ian Potter Museum of Art
Medical History Museum
Royal Womans Hospital
Jimmy Watsons
Tiamo 1
Lygon Court Plaza
Masani
Shakahari
Lygon Food Store
La Mama Theatre
Toofey's
Abla's
Markov Place
Embrasse
Carlton Clocktower Quest Inn & Quest Clocktower on Lygon Serviced Apartments
CARLTON
Sacred Heart with Corpus Christi College
CARLTON GARDENS NORTH
IMAX Theatre
Melbourne Museum
Lemongrass
Balzari
Ying Thai 2
Downtowner on Lygon
Royal Exhibition Building
Royal Terrace
CARLTON GARDENS SOUTH
Arrivederci
Matteo's
Green Grocer
Queens Parade
Eastern Highway
Alexandra Parade
Centre for Contemporary Photography
Marios
Piraeus Blues
The Commoner
Brunswick Street Alimentari
Ici
Cavallero
The Panama Dining Room
FITZROY
Old Kingdom
Blue Chillies
The Nunnery
Quest Royal Gardens
Cutler & Co.
Builders Arms
Anada
Gertrude Street Enoteca
Ladro
St Vincents Hospital
page 309
Albert Heights Serviced Apartments
Hotels in this area
Melbourne City Baths
Old Melbourne Gaol
Fire Services Museum
St Patrick's Cathedral
Parliament of Victoria
Parliament
Hospital
State Government Offices
FITZROY GARDENS
Pavilion
Model Tudor Village
Conservatory
Cooks' Cottage
TREASURY GARDENS
Hilton on the Park Melbourne, Quest East Melbourne, Georgian Court
George Street Café
State Library of Victoria
QV Centre
Chinese Museum
Princess Theatre
Melbourne Central
Melbourne Central Shopping Centre
St Francis R.C. Cathedral
Royal Mint Hellenic Museum
GPO Centre
Supreme Court
Melbourne Town Hall
Collins Place
ANZ Tower
MELBOURNE
City Square
ANZ Bank
National Australia Bank
Australian Club
Optus Centre
Flinders Street Station
Federation Square
Ian Potter Centre (NGV Australia)
Artplay
BIRRARUNG MARR
Federation Bells
MELBOURNE PARK
Wellington Parade
Wellington Parade South
Brunton Ave
Batman Avenue

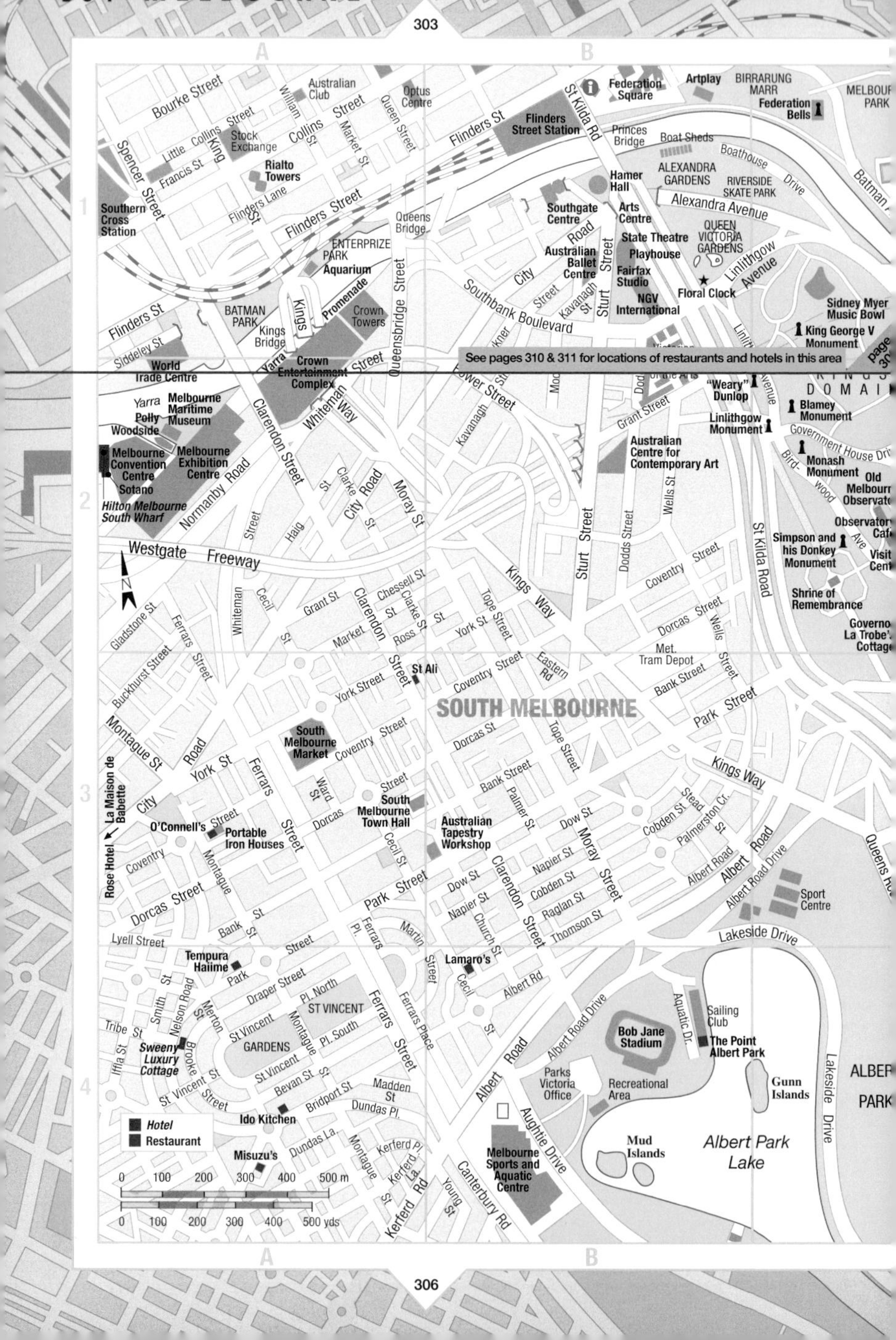

303

A B

1 2 3 4

Bourke Street
Australian Club
William St
King Street
Little Collins Street
Collins Street
Stock Exchange
Market St
Queen Street
Optus Centre
Spencer Street
Francis St
Rialto Towers
Flinders Lane
Southern Cross Station
Flinders Street
Flinders St
Flinders Street Station
St Kilda Rd
Federation Square
Artplay
BIRRARUNG MARR
Federation Bells
MELBOURNE PARK
Princes Bridge
Boat Sheds
Boathouse Drive
Batman Ave
Hamer Hall
ALEXANDRA GARDENS
RIVERSIDE SKATE PARK
Alexandra Avenue
Arts Centre
Southgate Centre
QUEEN VICTORIA GARDENS
State Theatre
Playhouse
Queens Bridge
ENTERPRIZE PARK
Aquarium
City Road
Australian Ballet Centre
Fairfax Studio
NGV International
Floral Clock
Linlithgow Avenue
Sidney Myer Music Bowl
King George V Monument
BATMAN PARK
Kings Way
Promenade
Crown Towers
Queensbridge Street
Southbank Boulevard
Kavanagh St
Sturt Street
Kings Bridge
Siddeley St
World Trade Centre
Yarra
Crown Entertainment Complex

See pages 310 & 311 for locations of restaurants and hotels in this area

page 30

KINGS DOMAIN
Whiteman Way
Power Street
"Weary" Dunlop
Yarra
Polly Woodside
Melbourne Maritime Museum
Clarendon Street
Kavanagh St
Grant Street
Linlithgow Monument
Blamey Monument
Government House Drive
Melbourne Convention Centre
Sotano
Melbourne Exhibition Centre
Normanby Road
Australian Centre for Contemporary Art
Birdwood
Monash Monument
Old Melbourne Observatory
Hilton Melbourne South Wharf
Clarke St
City Road
Moray St
Wells St
Sturt Street
Dodds Street
St Kilda Road
Observatory Cafe
Haig Street
Westgate Freeway
Simpson and his Donkey Monument
Ave
Visitor Centre
N
Whiteman Street
Cecil St
Grant St
Clarendon St
Chessell St
Clarke St
Tope Street
Kings Way
Coventry Street
Shrine of Remembrance
Gladstone St
Ferrars Street
Market St
Ross St
York St
Dorcas Street
Wells Street
Governor La Trobe's Cottage
Met. Tram Depot
Buckhurst Street
St Ali
York Street
Coventry Street
Eastern Rd
Bank Street
SOUTH MELBOURNE
Park Street
Montague St
South Melbourne Market
Coventry Street
Dorcas St
Tope Street
Kings Way
La Maison de Babette
City Road
York St
Ferrars Street
Ward St
South Melbourne Town Hall
Bank Street
Palmer St
Stead St
Palmerston Cr.
Queens Road
O'Connell's
Street
Portable Iron Houses
Dorcas
Australian Tapestry Workshop
Dow St
Moray Street
Cobden St
Albert Road
Rose Hotel
Coventry
Montague
Cecil St
Napier St
Clarendon Street
Albert Road Drive
Dorcas Street
Park Street
Dow St
Cobden St
Sport Centre
Napier St
Raglan St
Bank St
Church St
Thomson St
Lyell Street
Ferrars Pl.
Martin St
Lakeside Drive
Tempura Hajime
Park Street
Lamaro's
Cecil Street
Smith St
Nelson Road
Draper Street
Pl. North
Albert Rd
Aquatic Dr.
Sailing Club
Merton St
ST VINCENT
Ferrars Street
Ferrars Place
Bob Jane Stadium
Tribe St
St Vincent
Montague
Pl. South
Albert Road Drive
The Point Albert Park
Iffla St
Sweeny Luxury Cottage
Brooke
GARDENS
Albert Road
Parks Victoria Office
Recreational Area
Gunn Islands
Lakeside Drive
ALBERT PARK
St Vincent St
St Vincent
Bevan St
Madden St
Street
Bridport St
Dundas Pl.
Ido Kitchen
Dundas La.
Kerferd Pl.
Mud Islands
Albert Park Lake
Misuzu's
Montague St
Kerferd La.
Kerferd Rd
Young St
Canterbury Rd
Aughtie Drive
Melbourne Sports and Aquatic Centre

Hotel
Restaurant

0 100 200 300 400 500 m
0 100 200 300 400 500 yds

306

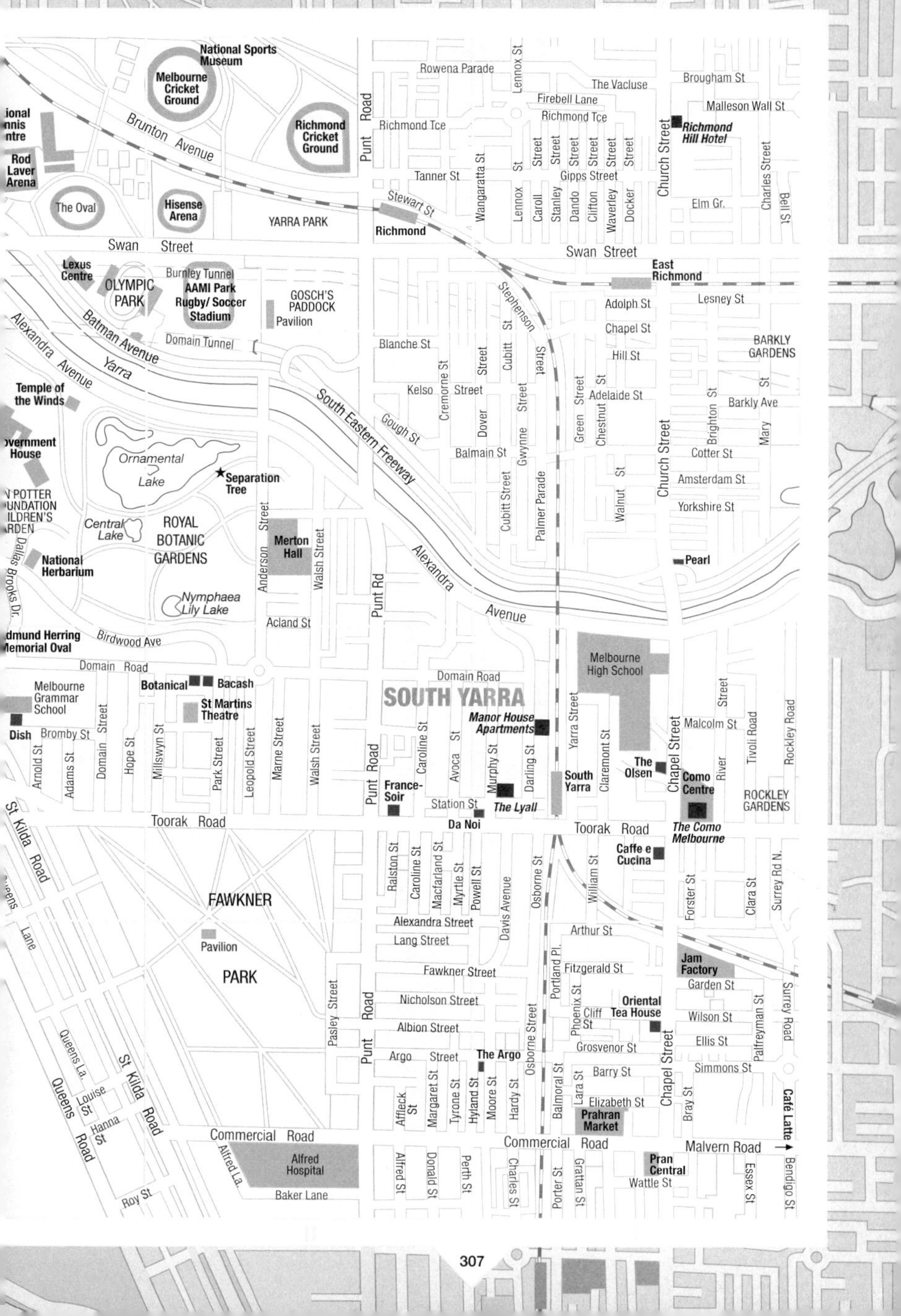
National Sports Museum
Melbourne Cricket Ground
Richmond Cricket Ground
Rod Laver Arena
Brunton Avenue
The Oval
Hisense Arena
YARRA PARK
Punt Road
Richmond Tce
Rowena Parade
Lennox St
The Vacluse
Firebell Lane
Richmond Tce
Brougham St
Malleson Wall St
Richmond Hill Hotel
Church Street
Tanner St
Wangaratta St
Gipps Street
Stewart St
Richmond
Lennox St
Caroll Street
Stanley Street
Dando Street
Clifton Street
Waverley Street
Docker Street
Elm Gr.
Charles Street
Bell St
Swan Street
Swan Street
East Richmond
Lexus Centre
OLYMPIC PARK
Burnley Tunnel
AAMI Park Rugby/ Soccer Stadium
GOSCH'S PADDOCK
Pavilion
Domain Tunnel
Batman Avenue
Alexandra Avenue
Yarra
Stephenson St
Adolph St
Lesney St
Chapel St
Hill St
BARKLY GARDENS
Blanche St
Cremorne St
Dover Street
Cubitt St
Street
Kelso Street
Gwynne Street
Green Street
Chestnut St
Adelaide St
Brighton St
Mary St
Barkly Ave
Temple of the Winds
South Eastern Freeway
Gough St
Balmain St
Cotter St
Government House
Ornamental Lake
Separation Tree
Cubitt Street
Palmer Parade
Walnut St
Church Street
Amsterdam St
Yorkshire St
Central Lake
ROYAL BOTANIC GARDENS
Anderson Street
Merton Hall
Walsh Street
Alexandra Avenue
Pearl
National Herbarium
Dallas Brooks Dr.
Nymphaea Lily Lake
Punt Rd
Acland St
Edmund Herring Memorial Oval
Birdwood Ave
Melbourne High School
Domain Road
Domain Road
Botanical
Bacash
Melbourne Grammar School
St Martins Theatre
SOUTH YARRA
Manor House Apartments
Yarra Street
Street
Malcolm St
Tivoli Road
Rockley Road
Dish
Bromby St
Domain Street
Arnold St
Adams St
Hope St
Millswyn St
Park Street
Leopold Street
Marne Street
Walsh Street
Punt Road
Caroline St
Avoca St
Murphy St
Darling St
Claremont St
The Olsen
Chapel Street
River
Como Centre
ROCKLEY GARDENS
France-Soir
Station St
The Lyall
South Yarra
The Como Melbourne
Da Noi
Toorak Road
Toorak Road
St Kilda Road
Caffe e Cucina
Ralston St
Caroline St
Macfarland St
Myrtle St
Powell St
Davis Avenue
Osborne St
William St
Forster St
Clara St
Surrey Rd N.
FAWKNER PARK
Pavilion
Alexandra Street
Lang Street
Arthur St
Lane
Fawkner Street
Portland Pl.
Fitzgerald St
Jam Factory
Garden St
Nicholson Street
Oriental Tea House
Phoenix St
Cliff St
Wilson St
Surrey Road
Pasley Street
Punt Road
Albion Street
Osborne Street
Ellis St
Palfreyman St
Argo Street
The Argo
Grosvenor St
Queens La.
Louise St
Hanna St
St Kilda Road
Queens Road
Affleck St
Margaret St
Tyrone St
Hyland St
Moore St
Hardy St
Balmoral St
Lara St
Barry St
Elizabeth St
Chapel Street
Simmons St
Bray St
Café Latte
Prahran Market
Commercial Road
Commercial Road
Malvern Road
Alfred La.
Alfred Hospital
Alfred St
Donald St
Perth St
Charles St
Porter St
Grattan St
Pran Central
Wattle St
Essex St
Bendigo St
Baker Lane
Roy St
307

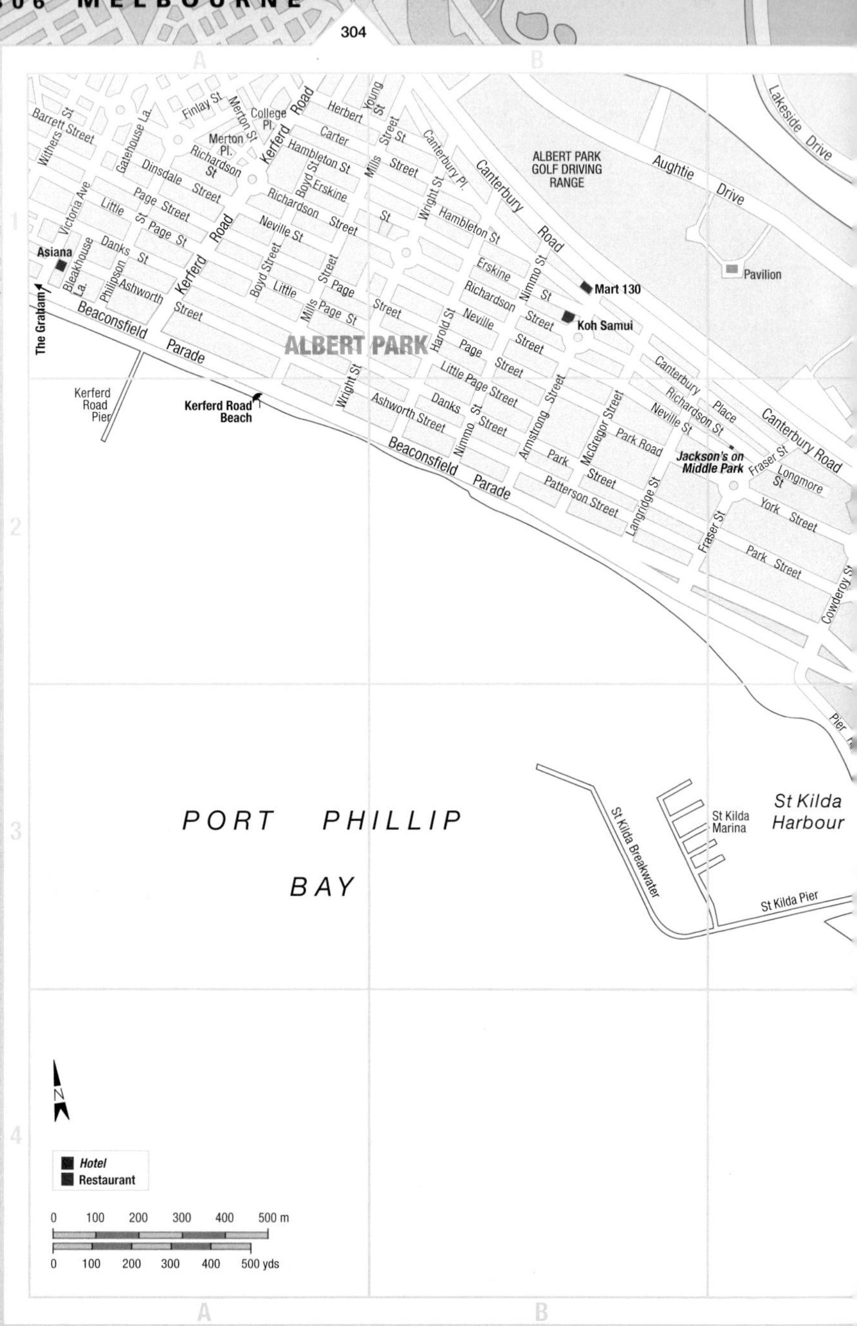

304

A B

1 2 3 4

Barrett Street
Withers St
Gatehouse La.
Finlay St
Merton St
College Pl.
Merton Pl.
Richardson St
Kerferd Road
Herbert
Young St
Carter
Hambleton St
Boyd St
Erskine
Mills Street
St
Canterbury Pl.
Canterbury Road
ALBERT PARK GOLF DRIVING RANGE
Aughtie Drive
Lakeside Drive
Dinsdale Street
Page Street
Victoria Ave
Little St Page St
Richardson Street
Neville St
Wright St
Hambleton St
Pavilion
Danks St
Asiana
Bleakhouse La.
Philipson
Ashworth
Kerferd Street
Boyd Street
Little
Page Street
Erskine
Nimmo St
Mart 130
Richardson Street
Koh Samui
The Graham
Beaconsfield Parade
Mills Page St
Street
Harold St
Neville Street
ALBERT PARK
Page Street
Canterbury Richardson St
Little Page Street
Armstrong Street
Wright St
Kerferd Road Pier
Kerferd Road Beach
Ashworth Street
Danks Street
Nimmo St
McGregor Street
Park Road
Neville St
Place
Canterbury Road
Jackson's on Middle Park
Fraser St
Longmore St
Beaconsfield Parade
Park Street
Patterson Street
Langridge St
Fraser St
York Street
Park Street
Cowderoy St
Pier
PORT PHILLIP BAY
St Kilda Breakwater
St Kilda Marina
St Kilda Harbour
St Kilda Pier

N

Hotel
Restaurant

0 100 200 300 400 500 m
0 100 200 300 400 500 yds

305

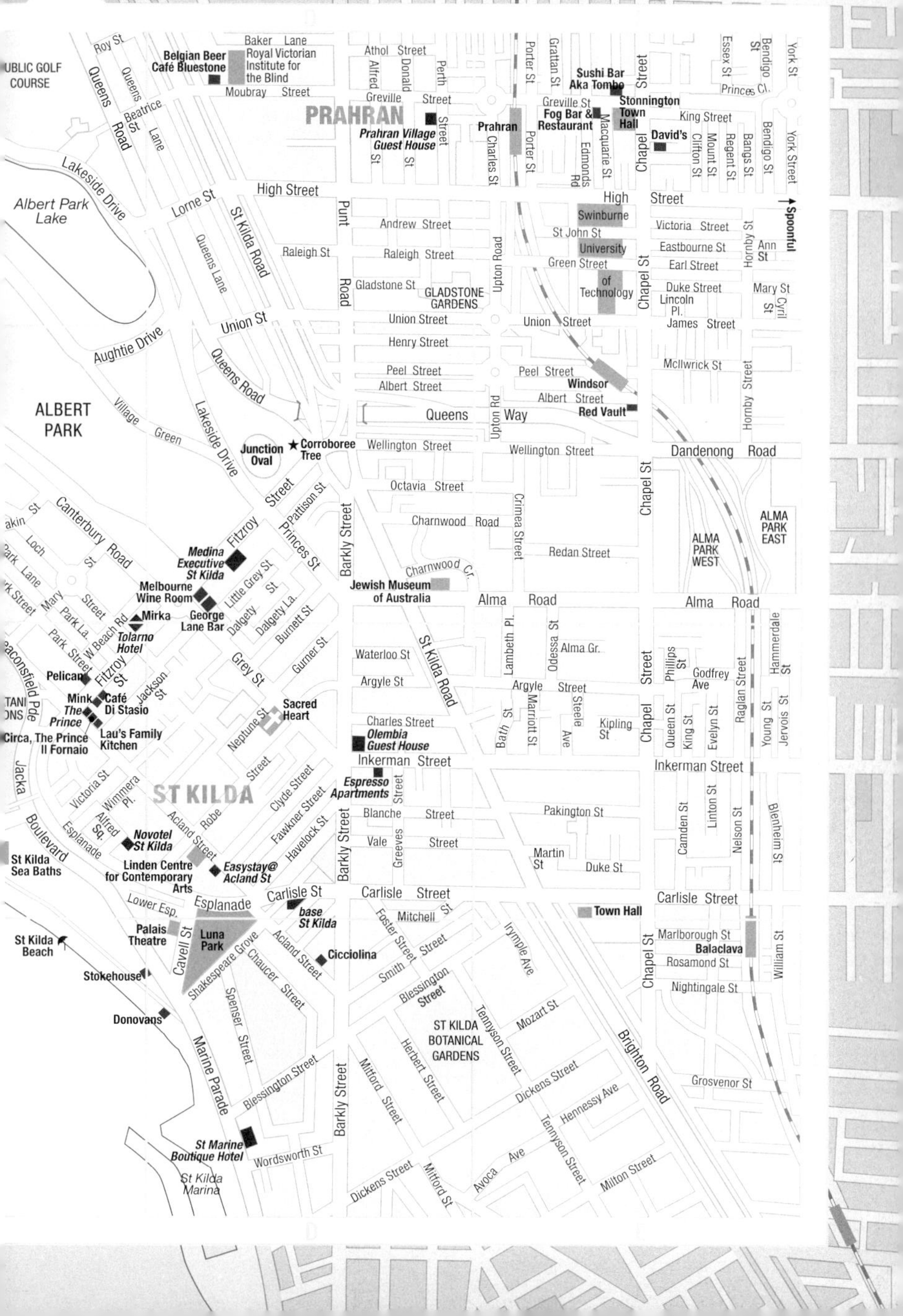

PRAHRAN

Belgian Beer Café Bluestone
Royal Victorian Institute for the Blind
Prahran Village Guest House
Prahran
Sushi Bar Aka Tombo
Stonnington Town Hall
Fog Bar & Restaurant
David's
Swinburne University of Technology
GLADSTONE GARDENS
Spoonful
Windsor
Red Vault
Albert Park Lake
ALBERT PARK
Junction Oval
Corroboree Tree
ALMA PARK WEST
ALMA PARK EAST
Jewish Museum of Australia
Medina Executive St Kilda
Melbourne Wine Room
George Lane Bar
Mirka
Tolarno Hotel
Pelican
Mink
Café Di Stasio
The Prince
Lau's Family Kitchen
Circa, The Prince
Il Fornaio
Sacred Heart
Olembia Guest House
Espresso Apartments

ST KILDA

Novotel St Kilda
Linden Centre for Contemporary Arts
Easystay@ Acland St
St Kilda Sea Baths
Palais Theatre
Luna Park
base St Kilda
Cicciolina
St Kilda Beach
Stokehouse
Donovans
Town Hall
Balaclava
ST KILDA BOTANICAL GARDENS
St Marine Boutique Hotel
St Kilda Marina

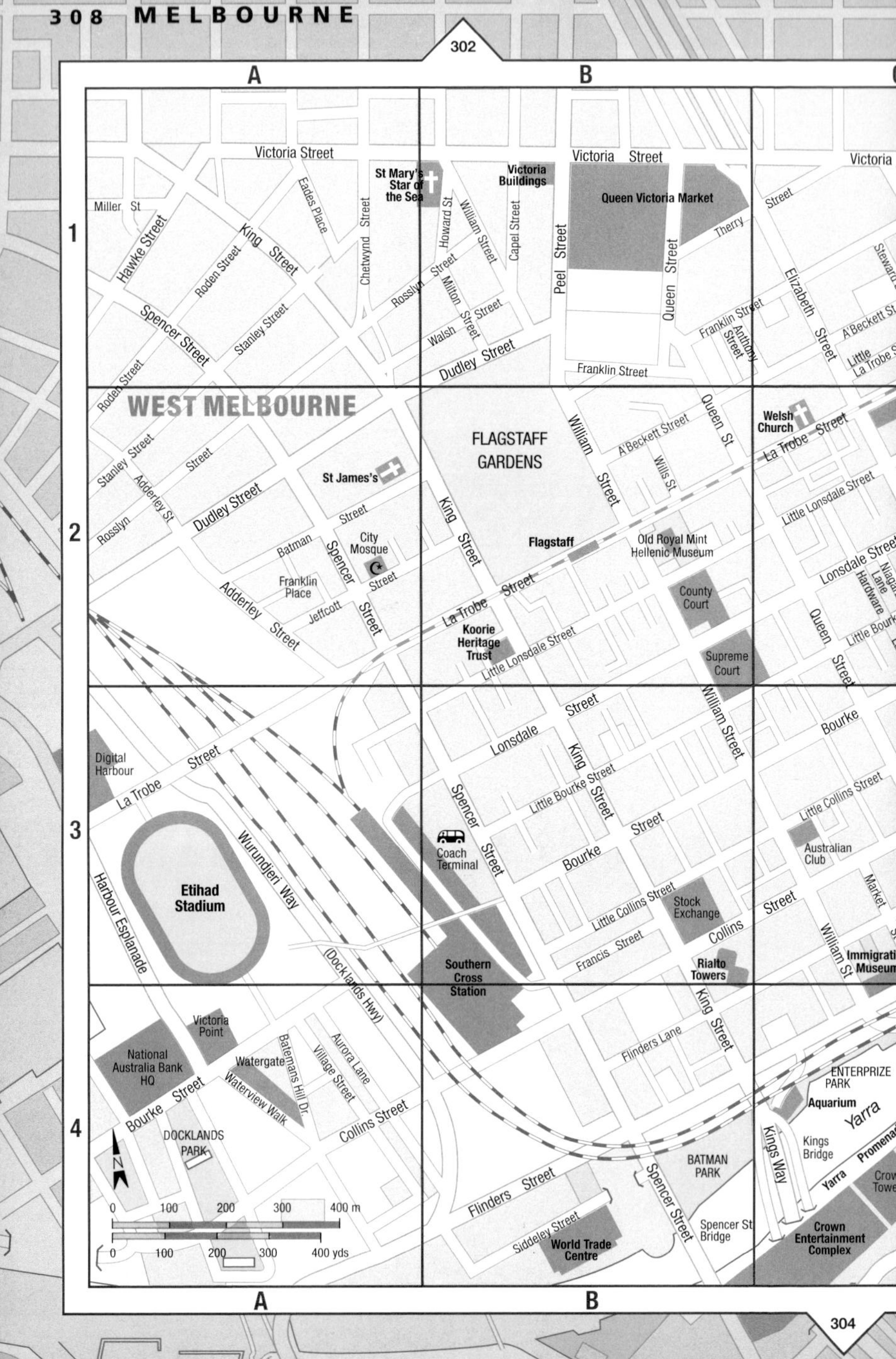
302
304
A
B
1
2
3
4
WEST MELBOURNE
FLAGSTAFF GARDENS
Victoria Street
St Mary's Star of the Sea
Victoria Buildings
Queen Victoria Market
Miller St
Hawke Street
King Street
Roden Street
Eades Place
Chetwynd Street
Howard St
William Street
Capel Street
Peel Street
Queen Street
Therry
Elizabeth Street
Steward
A'Beckett St
Little La Trobe St
Rosslyn Street
Milton Street
Walsh Street
Spencer Street
Stanley Street
Dudley Street
Franklin Street
Anthony Street
Welsh Church
La Trobe Street
Little Lonsdale Street
A'Beckett Street
Wills St
Queen St
St James's
City Mosque
Batman Street
Franklin Place
Jeffcott Street
Adderley St
Adderley Street
Rosslyn
Flagstaff
Old Royal Mint Hellenic Museum
County Court
Supreme Court
Koorie Heritage Trust
Lonsdale Street
Niagara Lane
Hardware Lane
Little Bourke
Digital Harbour
Bourke Street
Little Bourke Street
Little Collins Street
Coach Terminal
Australian Club
Etihad Stadium
Harbour Esplanade
Wurundjeri Way
(Docklands Hwy)
Stock Exchange
Collins Street
Francis Street
Market
William St
Immigration Museum
Rialto Towers
Southern Cross Station
Victoria Point
National Australia Bank HQ
Watergate
Waterview Walk
Batemans Hill Dr.
Village Street
Aurora Lane
Flinders Lane
ENTERPRIZE PARK
Aquarium
Yarra
Kings Way
Kings Bridge
Yarra Promenade
Crown Towers
DOCKLANDS PARK
BATMAN PARK
Flinders Street
Siddeley Street
World Trade Centre
Spencer St Bridge
Crown Entertainment Complex
N
0 100 200 300 400 m
0 100 200 300 400 yds

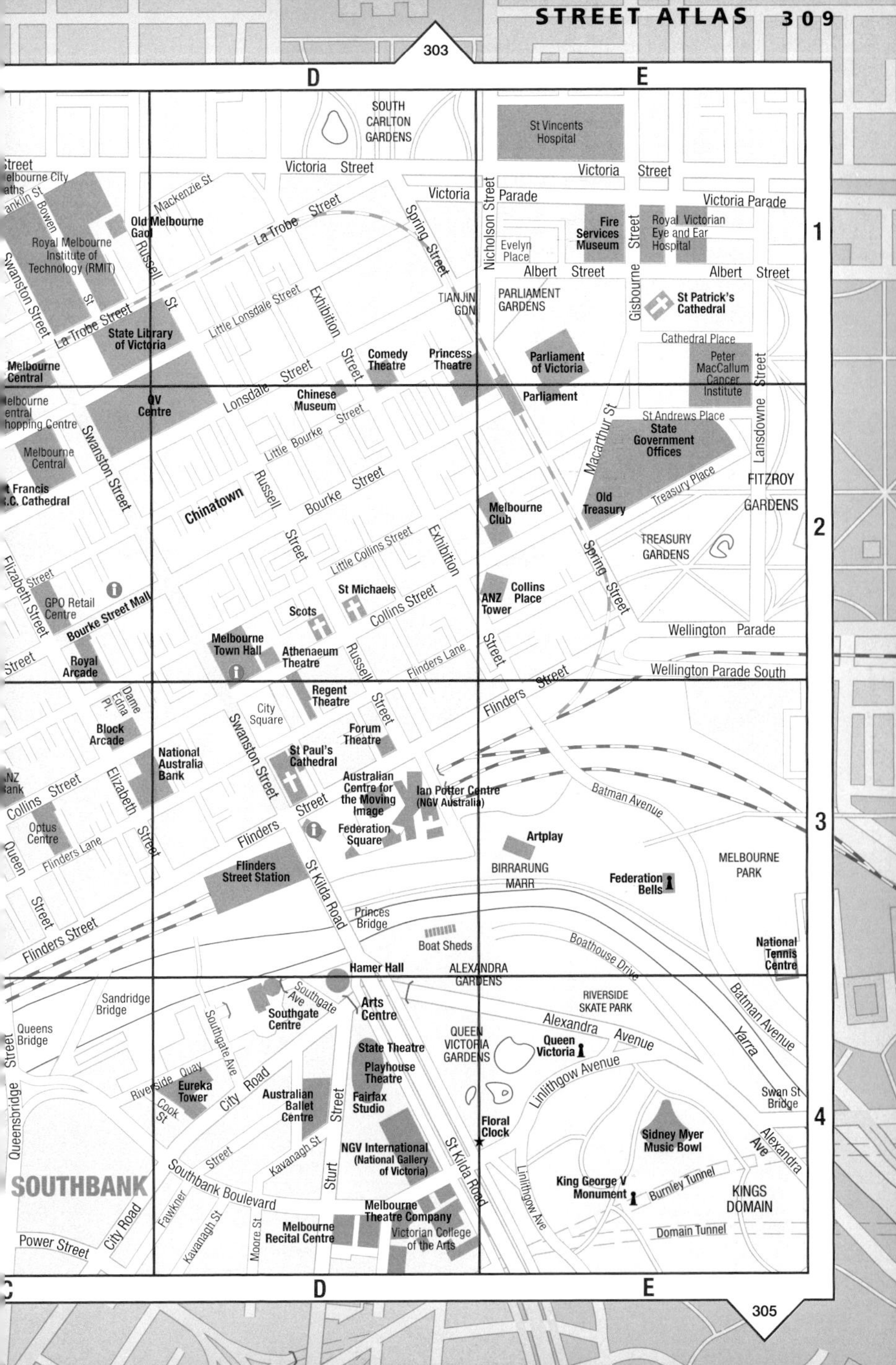
303
D
E
SOUTH CARLTON GARDENS
St Vincents Hospital
Victoria Street
Victoria Street
Victoria Parade
Victoria Parade
Nicholson Street
Mackenzie St
Old Melbourne Gaol
La Trobe Street
Spring Street
Fire Services Museum
Royal Victorian Eye and Ear Hospital
Evelyn Place
Gisbourne Street
Albert Street
Albert Street
Melbourne City Baths
Franklin St
Bowen
Royal Melbourne Institute of Technology (RMIT)
Russell
Swanston Street
St
TIANJIN GDN
PARLIAMENT GARDENS
St Patrick's Cathedral
Little Lonsdale Street
Exhibition
La Trobe Street
State Library of Victoria
Cathedral Place
Comedy Theatre
Princess Theatre
Parliament of Victoria
Peter MacCallum Cancer Institute
Melbourne Central
Street
Street
Lansdowne Street
QV Centre
Lonsdale
Chinese Museum
Parliament
Melbourne Central Shopping Centre
St Andrews Place
Little Bourke Street
Macarthur St
State Government Offices
Melbourne Central
Swanston Street
Russell
Bourke Street
Treasury Place
FITZROY GARDENS
St Francis R.C. Cathedral
Chinatown
Melbourne Club
Old Treasury
1
2
TREASURY GARDENS
Street
Little Collins Street
Exhibition
Spring Street
Elizabeth Street
Street
GPO Retail Centre
Bourke Street Mall
St Michaels
Scots
Collins Street
ANZ Tower
Collins Place
Wellington Parade
Melbourne Town Hall
Athenaeum Theatre
Russell
Flinders Lane
Street
Royal Arcade
Street
Wellington Parade South
Dame Edna Pl.
Regent Theatre
City Square
Street
Flinders Street
Block Arcade
Forum Theatre
National Australia Bank
Swanston Street
St Paul's Cathedral
ANZ Bank
Collins Street
Elizabeth
Australian Centre for the Moving Image
Ian Potter Centre (NGV Australia)
Batman Avenue
Street
3
Optus Centre
Federation Square
Artplay
Queen
Flinders Lane
Street
Flinders
MELBOURNE PARK
Flinders Street Station
St Kilda Road
BIRRARUNG MARR
Federation Bells
Street
Princes Bridge
Flinders Street
Boat Sheds
Boathouse Drive
National Tennis Centre
Hamer Hall
ALEXANDRA GARDENS
Sandridge Bridge
Southgate Ave
Arts Centre
RIVERSIDE SKATE PARK
Batman Avenue
Queens Bridge
Southgate Ave
Southgate Centre
Alexandra Avenue
QUEEN VICTORIA GARDENS
Queen Victoria
Street
State Theatre
Yarra
Playhouse Theatre
Linlithgow Avenue
Riverside Quay
Eureka Tower
City Road
Australian Ballet Centre
Street
Fairfax Studio
Swan St Bridge
Queensbridge
Cook St
Floral Clock
4
NGV International (National Gallery of Victoria)
St Kilda Road
Sidney Myer Music Bowl
Street
Kavanagh St
Alexandra Ave
SOUTHBANK
Southbank Boulevard
Sturt
Linlithgow Ave
King George V Monument
Burnley Tunnel
KINGS DOMAIN
Fawkner
Melbourne Theatre Company
Power Street
City Road
Kavanagh St
Moore St
Melbourne Recital Centre
Victorian College of the Arts
Domain Tunnel
C
D
E
305

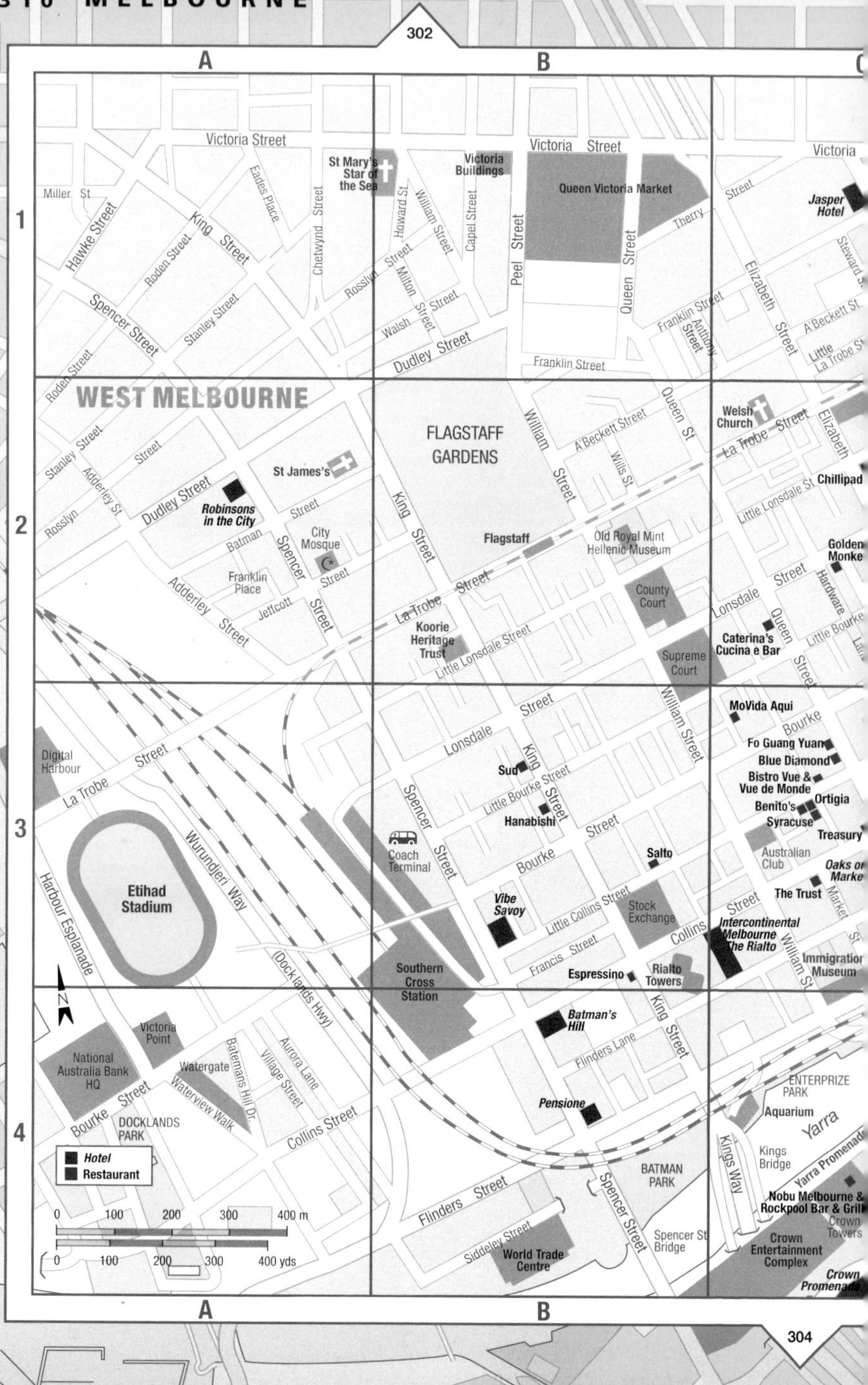

302

A B C

1 2 3 4

WEST MELBOURNE

Victoria Street
St Mary's Star of the Sea
Victoria Buildings
Queen Victoria Market
Jasper Hotel
Miller St
Hawke Street
King Street
Roden Street
Eades Place
Chetwynd Street
Howard St
William Street
Capel Street
Peel Street
Queen Street
Therry Street
Elizabeth Street
Steward St
Spencer Street
Stanley Street
Rosslyn Street
Milton Street
Walsh Street
Dudley Street
Franklin Street
Anthony Street
A'Beckett St
Little La Trobe St
Roden Street
FLAGSTAFF GARDENS
William Street
A'Beckett Street
Queen St
Welsh Church
La Trobe Street
Elizabeth
Stanley Street
Adderley St
Rosslyn
Dudley Street
Robinsons in the City
St James's
Street
City Mosque
Batman
Spencer Street
King Street
Wills St
Little Lonsdale St
Chillipad
Flagstaff
Old Royal Mint
Hellenic Museum
Golden Monkey
Franklin Place
Adderley Street
Jeffcott
County Court
Lonsdale Street
Hardware
Koorie Heritage Trust
Little Lonsdale Street
Queen Street
Little Bourke
Caterina's Cucina e Bar
Supreme Court
MoVida Aqui
Bourke
Fo Guang Yuan
Blue Diamond
Bistro Vue & Vue de Monde
Ortigia
Benito's
Syracuse
Treasury
Digital Harbour
La Trobe Street
Lonsdale Street
Sud
King Street
Little Bourke Street
Hanabishi
Etihad Stadium
Wurundjeri Way
Coach Terminal
Spencer Street
Bourke Street
Salto
Australian Club
Oaks on Market
The Trust
Market
Harbour Esplanade
Vibe Savoy
Little Collins Street
Stock Exchange
Collins Street
Intercontinental Melbourne The Rialto
William St
Immigration Museum
(Docklands Hwy)
Southern Cross Station
Francis Street
Espressino
Rialto Towers
Batman's Hill
King Street
N
Victoria Point
National Australia Bank HQ
Watergate
Batemans Hill Dr.
Village Street
Aurora Lane
Flinders Lane
Waterview Walk
Bourke Street
DOCKLANDS PARK
Collins Street
Pensione
ENTERPRIZE PARK
Aquarium
Yarra
Kings Way
Kings Bridge
Yarra Promenade
BATMAN PARK
Hotel
Restaurant
Flinders Street
Spencer Street
Nobu Melbourne & Rockpool Bar & Grill
Crown Towers
0 100 200 300 400 m
0 100 200 300 400 yds
Siddeley Street
World Trade Centre
Spencer St Bridge
Crown Entertainment Complex
Crown Promenade

A B

304